CRIMINOLOGY

CRIMINOLOGY

William B. Sanders
San Diego State University

ADDISON-WESLEY PUBLISHING COMPANY

Reading, Massachusetts • Menlo Park, California
London • Amsterdam • Don Mills, Ontario • Sydney

Library of Congress Cataloging in Publication Data

Sanders, William B., fl. 1974–
  Criminology.

  1. Crime and criminals—United States.   2. Criminals
justice, Administration of—United States.   I. Title.
HV6789.S26 1983   364′.973   82-11332
ISBN 0-201-07765-5

ISBN 0-201-07765-5
ABCDEFGHIJ-DO-89876543

Preface

THE STUDY OF CRIME has a rich and varied background. Today, we find many different approaches to the study of crime even within a single discipline. Additionally, there are many facets to criminal behavior patterns, and criminologists are, like other social scientists, really investigating many different forms of behavior. Further, there is a complex network to deal with criminal behavior, social controls in society in general, and more specifically the criminal justice system.

For anyone writing a text for university students, the principal question is how to organize everything so that a representative picture of criminology can be presented in a coherent manner. One approach is to emphasize a certain perspective or theoretical model and present it as general criminology. This method has merit in providing an integrated, coherent picture of crime and criminology, but usually the many other perspectives are ignored or presented in an unfavorable light. If the model presented corresponds with the views of the instructor, such a text is quite useful; but if the instructor wants to provide a general introduction with the many perspectives shown, then a single-view text is of little use. On the other end of the continuum is the eclectic text in which all viewpoints are presented along with a discussion of their relative merits and shortcomings. Such texts often call for a multiple-factor approach and try to tie incompatible theories together. While this second type of text does a better job in presenting all points of view, it often creates scholarly havoc by artificially uniting conflicting views and by suggesting that "just about anything can cause crime." That doesn't tell students very much they don't already know.

Faced with these two very different kinds of texts, I tried to find an approach that would preserve theoretical coherence while at the same time provide an examination of the many different theories. To do this without interjecting my own biases as to which theory is the most appropriate approach required a rethinking of how criminology can best be presented to undergraduates. First, I decided to treat each major sociological theory of crime as though it were my own preference. That is, I tried to present each theory as I thought the most dedicated advocate of that theory would. Then I evaluated each theory's strengths and weaknesses in terms of its ability to explain patterns of crime, the social-psychological aspects of criminals, and the societal reaction to crime. I made no attempt to tie all of the theories together, for not only would that misrepresent the actual work of criminologists, it would defeat the very concept of theory. Rather, theories are presented as reactions to one another. That is, most theories were developed either as an extension of an existing theory or to overcome the shortcomings of others.

A second major consideration was to present a wide spectrum of criminological studies of the different kinds of crime. This involved a problem in that studies of crime either state or imply certain theoretical assumptions. The purpose was to present studies of the patterns of crime with a more or less open theoretical perspective so that each pattern could be viewed equally from any one of several perspectives. Fortunately, there are enough statistical studies of crime based on F.B.I., victimization, and self-report surveys to discuss patterns in a theoretical independent manner. Many patterns could be interpreted by several theories. On the other hand, the kinds of crime data of this nature focused almost exclusively on "common crimes," and there is almost no data on crimes by the more affluent "white-collar" criminals. Again, even using data from studies with a definite theoretical angle, it was possible to present the material with more than a single interpretation as to what the data could mean. However, it was not my intention to examine every aspect of crime in terms of the many perspectives; that would have required a multivolume text. Rather, by presenting the major findings of the studies outside of a single theoretical context, it is possible to examine these findings with more than a single perspective. Obviously, this was not always feasible, and some theories get more attention than others in examining patterns, but that was usually due to the fact that certain theories are used more than others as a basis for research.

Related to the issue of presenting a wide view of the different kinds of crime is that of studying crime itself. In examining most theories and research on crime, it can be seen that the real emphasis is on "criminals" and not "crime." That is, while criminologists can tell us a great deal about the social background of the typical criminal, he/she tells us very little about the typical criminal situation. Fortunately, some studies are now available that give us added insight into the criminal situation, and wherever possible I included data from these studies. This was to provide a better understanding of not only the criminal but also the criminal act. To a large extent, in fact, the theme of the book is "criminal actors and criminal acts."

The final major area of criminology is the criminal justice system. Here again, the studies in this area reflect more than a single theoretical perspective, and it is in this area that criminological theory—not legal theory—is the most crucial. For years, criminologists have confused legal theory and issues with sociological ones. We are inundated with case law, criminal procedures, and similar concerns of legal theory. However, like the study of other institutions and organizations, we should be concerned with institutional patterns, bureaucratic organization, and organizational adaptations rather than constitutional issues. This is not to say that legal issues are unimportant, but rather that criminologists attempting to be legal scholars become so embroiled in case law and key decisions that they forget the social science issues involved. Therefore, rather than focusing on legal and administrative procedures, the emphasis is on the typical patterns of the criminal justice system and how these patterns relate to criminal procedures.

Style

In preparing this text, I attempted to write in expository English, introducing and using criminological concepts where appropriate. Throughout the book there are extensive examples to aid in understanding concepts, theories, and patterns of criminal behavior. This helps illustrate points and is interesting for students. Fortunately, the study of crime is full of such examples, and when it came to a choice between a dull and interesting example to illustrate a point, it seemed logical to choose the more interesting of the two. Also, many charts, diagrams, tables, cartoons, and photographs are used. This, I hope, is sufficient to communicate a body of introductory information to those who have never before studied criminology.

Level

To aid in effective communication, I did not exceed what I considered to be introductory criminology. That is, this book would not be appropriate for and was not meant to be used in a graduate-level or advanced course in criminology. Each of the major theories is discussed in terms of its general concepts and major studies. I avoided getting into minute arguments and fine, subtle points of each theory, for not only would such a discussion go beyond the introductory level, it would confuse the larger issues at stake. This does not mean the material was oversimplified; it was simply introduced.

Organization

The three-part organization of the book was done to delineate clearly the major areas of study in crime. Obviously, there is an interrelation among theory, patterns of crime, and the criminal justice system, and one rarely finds a criminologist who deals with any one area independently of the others. However, it is easier to understand each part separately, and as the student progresses through the book this becomes obvious. Therefore, while there are divisions, the book attempts to tie them all together by its overall organization.

Related to the book's organization into coherent, discrete parts are the end-of-chapter glossaries. This organization reflects the way in which criminology courses are organized and the way in which students study. If the entire book were assigned at one time, a glossary at the book's end would have sufficed. However, since in teaching criminology (and virtually every other college course) there are discrete segments, the glossaries were placed at the ends of chapters. Not only does this aid the student in understanding the chapter material and what concepts are related to certain areas, it also aids in preparation for exams covering a limited number of chapters. In the index, glossary terms are printed in bold type so that the chapter glossaries can be used as a general glossary.

Finally, each chapter begins with a set of guides of what is important to look for and ends with a set of questions to provide a self-test in understanding. This is in relation to the inevitable question students ask in preparing for examinations and completing their reading assigments: "What's important in the chapter?" The beginning of chapter guides answer this question, and the end of the chapter questions provide a check for the student to see if he/she understood the material.

Acknowledgments

ACKNOWLEDGMENTS ARE RARELY SUFFICIENT to reflect the help one receives on a book—especially a general text. Over the years I have come into contact with many who have steered me in one direction or another, and all of these people have helped. My criminological "godfather" was Donald R. Cressey, and as the years go by I find that his direction and instruction increase in value. Two long-time colleagues, Howard C. Daudistel and David F. Luckinbill were also a part of the criminological course I have taken, and their influence can be seen in this book. My introduction to European criminology was through Albert Hess during a summer sojourn at Kriminologies Instituut, Rijkuniversiteit Leiden, The Netherlands. Another colleague, Charles Frazier at the University of Florida, gave me the insight into control theory that has influenced much of my later thinking. During the writing of this text, George Bryjak of the University of San Diego provided me with excellent material on deterrence theory, for which I am most grateful.

I appreciate the patience and suggestions of the book's reviewers. It is never an easy task to tell an author how to improve a book, but these reviewers did. My thanks to Candace Kruitschnitt, University of Minnesota; Brian Walsh, J. Sargent Reynolds Community College; Clinton Terry, University of Florida; Gary Jensen, University of Arizona; Robert Delaire, CUNY, Bernard Baruch College; Robert Meier, Washington State University; Kenrick Thompson, Northern Michigan University; Joseph Scimecca, George Mason University; Russell Ward, SUNY, Albany; and Robert Hillegass. Where I took their advice, they deserve the credit, and where I ignored such advice, I will take the blame. Ron Hill, my editor at Addison-Wesley, did an excellent job in coordinating everything, and I have never seen anyone keep better track of the several processes that go into a book's production. Terry Lombardi took a real mess, dropped everything else she was doing, and typed the final draft of the manuscript under deadline. Finally, my family was very patient during the period I was working on the text, and I can see why authors with less patient families are valued customers of the divorce lawyers. My wife Eli and sons Billy and David, having gone through this process on nine other occasions, are becoming veterans at understanding and patience.

Contents

19 Dealing with Crime: Criminological Research and Public Policy   455

PHOTO CREDITS

CRIMINOLOGY

1

Explaining and Measuring Crime

What to Look For:

The contrasts between public images and scientific studies.

The elements of criminological study.

The difference between social and legal issues.

The process of explaining crime.

The methodological issues in the study of crime.

Introduction

THE PUBLIC TENDS to view crime in such stereotypes as the "Atlanta Child Killer," "Son of Sam" and the "Manson Family"—relatively rare mass murderers. Similarly, rape-murders are a common stereotype of killings, and at one time, the public viewed robbers as desperados shooting their way into and out of banks. Crimes of burglary are romanticized in terms of black-clad thieves scaling mansion walls to nimbly open the Dutchess' safe and steal her jewels.

However, the most common murders, robberies, and burglaries differ significantly from these stereotypes. Most murders are committed by relatives, friends, or acquaintances of the victim. Most robberies are almost wholly unplanned, with the victim most likely to be a small grocery or liquor store or an individual walking down the street. Most burglaries involve breaking into a house and making off with a television set or stereo rather than jewels. These crimes do not make the headlines or the evening news, but they do make up the bulk of common crimes and constitute what is considered the "crime problem."

In the same way that crimes are stereotyped in extremes, so too are criminals. Usually people think of tough-looking, scar-faced men with tatoos and constant sneers, Italians in pin-stripped double-breasted suits craddling machine guns, or punks wearing gang jackets and carrying switchblades. Rarely do we think of white Anglo-Saxon executives committing crimes in organizing illegal cartels, a computer programmer electronically transferring funds illegally to his own account, or our parents cheating on their income taxes. Similarly, we rarely think about our own actions as "criminal." However, if you have ever slugged somebody during an altercation after a football game (battery), or smoked some marijuana (illegal drug possession), walked out of a store without paying for a tube of lipstick (theft), or had sex with a willing 17-year-old (statutory rape), you have committed crimes. How do we ourselves fit the stereotype of other criminals in our own behavior? We tend to view crime as something *they*, the criminals, do, and not people like ourselves. They are different than we are, and *they* must be studied and understood so that *we* can do something about *them*. To be sure, what criminologists call "career criminals" are different from the average person in some ways, but it is certainly not just because they commit crime. Virtually everyone commits at least some minor crimes, and the study of crime is in many ways a study of ourselves. This is simply another way of saying that the study of crime is the study of human behavior, and to the extent that we can explain many of our own criminal actions, we can perhaps understand others'.

Therefore, rather than reading this book and asking only, "How could *they* do such a thing?" we should also ask, "Why did I commit the crimes I did?" In this way, we can test some of the explanations on human subjects we know very well—ourselves.

In this first chapter we will focus on 1) what criminologists study; and 2) the methods they use for that study. We will first examine the scope of the field of criminology and what criminologists hope to accomplish, and how the book is organized in terms of these issues. Secondly, we will discuss the methods employed by criminologists and the problems in gathering and interpreting crime data.

What Is Criminology?

In the broadest sense, **criminology** is the scientific study of crime. With this broad conception, the field could include everything from the laboratory examination of fingerprints and blood samples to the development of techniques for career counseling in prisons. However, the primary focus in criminology is to find explanations of criminal behavior through the use of the scientific method. Sutherland and Cressey include three major divisions in that study: 1) the sociology of criminal law; 2) the sociology and social psychology of criminal behavior; and 3) the sociology of punishment and correction.[1] Gibbons defines the field more specifically as including the study of lawmaking (legislative process); lawbreaking and reactions to crime (the criminal justice system); the origins of criminal laws (cultural belief systems and morality); the extent and distribution of crime (patterns of crime); the sociology of criminality (theory of criminal behavior); the social psychology of criminal acts and careers (tracing individual biographies in crime); and social reactions to crime (general popular attitudes toward crime and criminals).[2] In this book, we also want to include, specifically, the classification of crime and criminal situations in the list of what criminologists study. This would include a breakdown of types of crime by behavior classifications and an examination of the interactions that occur during the actual commission of crimes.

Defining the Field

As a field of study, criminology has taken a part of social life that we can divide up into three areas of inquiry. First, criminologists study how the laws that define criminal behavior come into being. This includes the historical development of criminal law and the societal structures, both institutions and organizations, that house the law-making aparatus, such as legislatures and election of officials. We must consider the cultural context of a society's law in the study of law-making. Oftentimes we refer to this area as the "sociology of law," and Chapter 2 examines the law-making aspects of criminology. Secondly, at the heart of criminology lies theory.

The development of sociological and social psycholocal (social context of individual behavior) theories of patterns of crime and criminal selves (identities) directs inquiry to the root causes of crime. Later in this chapter we will deal with the development of theory, but for here it should be pointed out that criminologists are attempting to explain the general patterns of crime and how individual actors get caught up in those patterns. In Chapters 3–7 we will examine various theories of criminal behavior. Included in the theoretical component of criminology is the study of the different forms of crime, for even though criminology seeks to develop general theories of all criminal law violations, it is important to recognize there are significant differences between crimes—such as rape and government officials taking bribes. Therefore, by classifying crime along socio-legal dimensions—social patterns and forms plus legal definitions—we can see that while all crimes have certain similarities, there are important differences as well. Part II of the book, Chapters 8–14, examines the different forms of crime. Finally, the third area of interest in criminology is the societal reaction to crime. For the most part, this concerns the criminal justice system, including the police, the courts and correctional system, and the application of the laws. This includes the study of arrests, how the courts handle defendants, and what correctional measures are taken. The final section of the book, Chapters 15–19, look at this component of the field of criminology.

The following table gives an outline of the field of criminology showing its various parts:

Table 1.1   The Field of Criminology

Law Making	Criminal Behavior	Criminal Justice
legal institutions	explanations of crime	law enforcement
decisions to make laws	crime classification	adjudication/ prosecution
laws and social values	criminal identities and patterns of crime	courts/corrections

Despite the clarity of the above diagram, the topics encompassing the field of criminology are not mutually exclusive. For example, in studying the patterns of crime, by definition, there has to be a criminal law to be violated, and there must be some kind of reaction by the criminal justice system to make it a "crime in reality" (as opposed to one simply "on the books"). Likewise, in developing explanations of crime it is necessary to understand the extent that societal values support a particular law and whether or not the law is enforced by the criminal justice system. Therefore, to fully understand the patterns of crime, one must also understand the law-making process as well as the institutions that apply the law. A good example of this interrelation is drug legislation. Before marijuana and cocaine violations became a popular middle-class activity, the laws regarding possession of marijuana were very strict and the penalties harsh. However, with an influx of middle-class drug involvement, the criminal justice system began to back off strict application of the drug laws, especially those involving possession. Later, many states changed their laws regarding possession of marijuana. Since both the application of the law and changes in the law affecting marijuana possession changes, to understand the patterns of drug use, it is necessary to understand the changes in law-making and its application by the criminal justice system.

Defining the Subject Matter

The subject matter of criminology has its roots in the criminal law. Criminal law is a formal rule created by the state, which specifies that certain behavior is prohibited and, subsequently, may be subject to punishment. In Chapter 2, we will discuss the full ramifications of this definition, but for now it is enough to distinguish it from other types of rule violations. General rule violations are referred to as "deviance," and the study of deviance includes a far broader area of study than does criminology. For example, certain bizarre behavior that is legal, such as the worship of Satan and even behavior categorized as "mental illness," is included in the study of deviance along with crime. However, criminology includes only issues that involve the creation, violation, or application of criminal law.

For example, during the Prohibition Era, the Volstead Act made the sale, transportation, and possession of alcoholic beverages a crime. Criminologists would only be interested in the behavior that was related to the criminal law, and not the behavior before the law was enacted or after it was repealed. For example, a man sitting down having a beer during Prohibition would be a relevant subject for criminologists, but if the same man were doing the same thing the next day after the repeal of the Volstead Act, he would not.

Social and Legal Issues in Law

While interests of criminologists and legal scholars overlap in many places, there are important differences in what each seeks to study and understand. Criminologists are primarily concerned with the social parameters of the criminal law—the social patterns of making and applying the law. There is a difference between examining the creation and application of laws as a criminologist and as a legal scholar. The criminologist is mostly concerned with the institutionalized ways in which laws are actually made or applied, while the legal scholar is interested in topics such as consistency of a law with the U.S. Constitution and with case decisions. For example, in looking at the way the law is applied, a criminologist would want to know about what factors affect discretion. Do the police act more harshly with lower-class suspects than with middle-class suspects? How do the routines of a prosecutor's office affect typical patterns of charging defendants? These are questions about social patterns. Legal scholars would want to know whether a law is consistent, in terms of legal logic, with the Constitution, or they may ask whether all of the elements of due process are observed when an arrest is made. Legal questions would also include, "Is this proposed piece of legislation consistent with the most recent Supreme Court decisions," or "Are the guidelines set down in the *Miranda* decision* appropriate to ensure due process?" To be sure, there are areas of overlap in the interests of legal scholars and criminologists, but that is only in cases where social patterns and legal logic happen to coincide, such as cases where certain social classes are denied rights of due process. It is important for the criminology student to understand that there are distinct sets of inquiries posed by the different disciplines, and findings and explanations from one may be very different from the other.

Developing Explanations of Crime Patterns and Criminal Behavior

In an evaluation of criminology over the past fifty years in the United States, Donald Cressey examined the state of the profession and lamented that criminologists seem to have gone off in all sorts of irrelevant directions.[3] If criminology has any hope of achieving its aim of producing systematic studies of the process of making laws, breaking laws, and reacting to the breaking of laws, as Cressey suggests, it is necessary to focus on valid information regarding this set of interactions.[4] To the extent that criminology merely wanders hither and yon, bumping into various unrelated studies of crime or responding to random political interests in crime, there is little chance of developing a useful body of knowledge. Criminology must develop coherent theory.

Explaining Patterns of Crime

The first thing any theory of crime must do is to adequately explain **patterns of crime**. That is, we must look at the way in which crimes typically occur, who typically commits them, and any other recurrent social patterns that can be observed.[5] To illustrate, let us consider one familiar pat-

---

*The *Miranda* decision was a Supreme Court decision requiring that criminal defendants be advised of their Constitutional rights. Some legal scholars are now questioning whether the decision went far enough in assuring due process.

tern. We can observe that of those arrested for the serious violent crimes such as homicide, assault, and robbery, 89.8 percent are male.[6] The pattern seems to suggest that males commit more serious violent crimes than females (although, since our figures are based on arrests, even this can be no more than an assumption). The point is that any theory claiming to account for criminal behavior would have to explain *why* men commit more serious violent crimes than women—that is, it would have to explain the pattern.

For example, consider the statement, "Poverty causes crime." Does that statement account for the observed pattern of male and female serious violent crime? No, of course it does not. If poverty were the main determinant of crime then we would expect far fewer crime differences between men and women, since men generally earn more than women, go further in their careers, and have greater opportunities. In fact, if there existed the simple relationship between poverty and crime, we would *predict* more female crime.

Obviously the pattern we have examined showing an overwhelming proportion of violent crime arrests attributed to men rather than women is simply *one* pattern involving only a few types of crime and a single variable (sex). There are a number of other patterns to be considered as well, such as age, region, ethnic background, social class, and occupation. Likewise, there are several other kinds of crimes, such as burglary, theft, and fraud. If we only used the findings that show men are far more likely to commit violent crimes than are women, we could say, "Being male causes crime." Such a statement is consistent with the pattern, but we know that only a small proportion of males are involved in violent crimes; therefore, such a statement would be inaccurate. In the same way, it is inaccurate to conclude that poverty causes crime, for even though there are certain types of crimes that are most likely to occur in the lower classes, such conclusions are based only on a single variable and most poor people are not criminals—just as most men are not violent felons! Therefore, before making a general statement or theory explaining crime, we must consider the several social patterns of crime and not just those that conveniently support our theory. The more social patterns of crime for which a theory can account, the better the theory.

Explaining Why Individuals Commit Crimes

Any general criminological theory must also connect its explanation to the individual. That is, having explained the general social patterns of crime, it must show how the individual can be influenced by that pattern. It is the link between the *individual* and the *social* or *social psychological* processes. For example, in examining any explanation of crime that linked sex roles with the likelihood of committing a crime, that explanation would have to explain why an individual male would be more likely to be involved in crime than a female. If, for instance, we said, "Males are more likely to engage in criminal violence than females," we would have to explain why a particular male was linked to that pattern of crime. We might say, "Males are more likely to be socialized to use violence as a means of conflict resolution than are females." By making such a statement we do two things. First, we account for the pattern of criminal violence, and secondly we explain how an individual could be linked to that pattern. Thus, the explanation shows why men are more likely to engage in criminal violence than women.

Now, while we make these general statements, it is important to remember that we are dealing with only the few who commit such crimes. In examining serious criminal violence such as murder, rape, robbery, or aggravated assault, we do not mean all men commit these crimes. Men certainly are not socialized to be murderers, rapists, or robbers! In effect, our theory is saying that given the patterns of male socialization in comparison to female socialization, men are *more likely* to be involved in serious violent crime. The fact that *most men are not so involved* must be considered as well, for it shows us that the dominant part of socialization (or some other variable) is against involvement in serious violent crime.

Thus, to a great extent, criminologists must not only explain why people commit crimes, but they must explain why most people, most of the time, *do not* commit crimes. What criminologists do, then, includes explaining social behavior in general and not just criminal behavior.

Explaining the Criminalization Process

The final goal of criminological explanations is accounting for the **criminalization process**.[7] In the most general sense this refers to the process where some behavior comes to be officially regarded as criminal. This involves both the making of criminal laws and the administration of those laws. For example, if a person is selling cocaine, and he or she is arrested, convicted, and punished for that behavior, both the act and person have been criminalized.

We might wonder what explaining the criminalization process has to de with explaining patterns of crime, for most see the primary goal of criminology as explaining why crimes are committed and not the reaction to crime or making laws. To begin with, in order to have patterns of crime, it is necessary to have laws defining certain behaviors as criminal. If the laws are directed at certain groups in society, then those groups are more likely to be involved in crime than others. For example, the vagrancy laws were developed in the interests of the wealthy merchants who sought to stem the tide of highway robbery and put pressure on people who were not employed to take jobs in the factories.[8] While it may be true that there

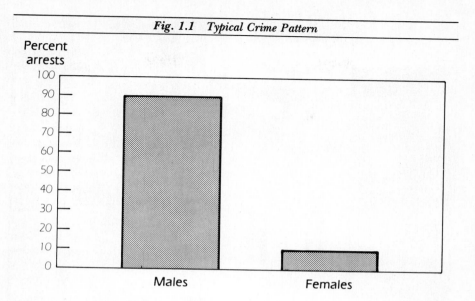

Fig. 1.1 Typical Crime Pattern

were a lot of "idle rich" whose behavior was no different from that of unemployed vagabonds, the vagrancy laws obviously were directed against the idle poor, not the idle rich. Therefore, in explaining the patterns of vagrancy, we have to realize that the law is directed at only certain segments of the population, who before the law was created were not considered criminals. By the same token, in examining violations of the Sherman Antitrust Act, a law aimed at controlling the conduct of corporate business practices, we are not going to find any poor people violating the law. Thus, in comparing vagrants with corporate criminals, the pattern cannot be understood unless we understand something about the creation of the law and the target population.

Likewise, in explaining crime, we have to understand the societal reaction. Creating laws certainly is going to lead to some patterns and not others, but laws are not always uniformly applied. An act has to be interpreted as an actual violation of the law for it to be treated and counted as such. For example, we looked at the arrests for serious violent crimes for men and women and found an overwhelmingly greater number of men arrested for such crimes. Included in the statistics was the crime of rape, defined in many states as being only committed by a *man*, and so by legal statute only men can commit rape, one of the serious violent crimes. However, aggravated assault can be committed by both men and women, yet are women arrested as often as men for aggravated assault? Even when all the legal elements of aggravated assault are present, if a woman

The Bedford-Stuyvesant section of Brooklyn is typical of an area where common crimes are extremely high and daily affect the lives of those in the community.

acts against a man, many times the act is not treated as a *real* instance of aggravated assault. For example, if a man insults a woman in a bar and she breaks a beer bottle over his head, all of the elements of an aggravated assault are present. However, what if the police do not take such an assault by a woman as seriously as if it were committed by a man? What

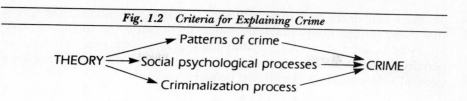

Fig. 1.2   Criteria for Explaining Crime

if they just tell the man to take care of his head and watch what he says to women in the future? Well, if the police typically treat violent acts by women as "not real crimes," then the pattern of arrests will be greatly affected by such a routine.

As can be seen by the above example, if routine practices of law enforcers are not as uniform as the laws assume them to be, then the known patterns of crime based on arrest records are a reflection of police practices and not just criminal behaviors. Therefore, any theory of crime is going to have to consider the effect of societal reactions, both in terms of how they affect patterns of crime and criminal identities. Fig. 1.2 summarizes the requirements of an adequate criminological theory.

The General Level of Analysis

It is important to understand that criminologists cannot explain everything about every possible crime. Rather by looking at several crimes, either over a long period of time, committed by certain groups, committed in certain areas, or in comparison between different groupings, it is possible to learn about the typical and general patterns of criminal behavior.

It is unlikely that criminological theory would prove very useful in tracking down criminals or even predicting if a certain person were going to commit a crime. That is not the goal of the theory, and if it were, it would be somewhat limited and of little value. By examining and explaining the larger trends of crime, we can see certain things that we cannot see in individuals, and thereby look for general causes. For example, if we go into the individualistic backgrounds of a rich man and a poor man who have been arrested for murder, we will learn of unique circumstances that led them to kill. We might learn that the rich man killed his mistress because he feared scandal, and the poor man killed his wife because he believed she was cheating on him. However, in neither case would we learn that the patterns of homicide show that criminal homicide is far more likely among the lower socioeconomic social strata. In looking at the individual case histories we see unique features, but in examining the larger pattern, we can determine causes of crime by *seeing what the crimes have in common*. To claim that every crime is unique is of little value, for in doing so, there can never be a general theory of crime. It would be like saying that every human body is unique, and so there can be no theory of physiology or biology. Therefore, criminology seeks to determine what causes certain patterns of crime to exist or change, and in so doing develops a general understanding of criminal behavior patterns.

Methodologies for the Study of Crime

In order to come to terms with the patterns of crime and criminal processes, it is necessary to have a methodology that can adequately research crime. Any flaws in our research methods can result in inaccurate pictures of crime, and if we are mistaken about crime trends, our theories and explanations of crime are bound to be incorrect. This section examines the strengths and weaknesses of various methods researchers have employed in the study of crime.

The Problem of Official Statistics

The most widely used source of data in crime studies has been crime statistics gathered by law enforcement agencies. These statistics are compilations of crimes reported to the police and recorded by them for various purposes, one of which is to have some kind of statistical profile of crime in the community. Individual law enforcement agencies then send their data on special standardized forms to the Federal Bureau of Investigation (FBI) for a national compilation of crime statistics. The annual report of these crime statistics is published in a widely circulated report called the **Uniform Crime Report**, or **UCR**. The FBI developed this uniform set of reporting procedures for law enforcement agencies in the hope that the *UCR* would be a standardized set of statistics that could detect changes and trends in crime. We could tell, for example, whether crime went up or down in a certain period; whether it was increasing in one part of the country and decreasing in another. We could even tell something about who was committing crimes, based on the sex, race, and age of the arrested individual.

However, even though the FBI's figures were a marked improvement over what preceded them, they are not an accurate reflection of crime. The following criticisms of the statistics show their weaknesses in representing an accurate picture of crime:[9]

1. *Not all crime is known in any given locality at a particular time.* Unless people report crimes, there is little chance the police will learn of them. For example, if a person were burglarized but did not report it to the police, it will be a crime that exists in society but is unknown for purposes of crime statistics. Fig. 1.3 shows the percent of crime victims who reported their victimization.

Fig. 1.3   Percent of Victimizations Reported to the Police, 1977

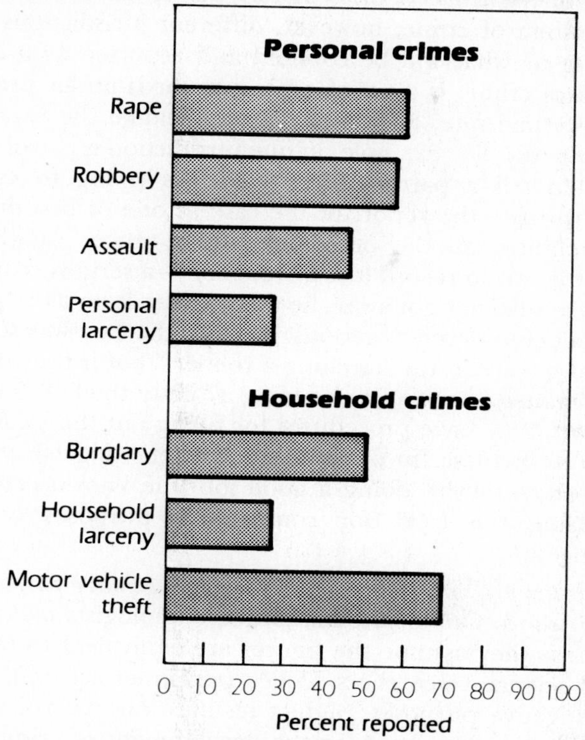

Source: *Criminal Victimization in the United States, 1977.* (Washington, D.C.: U.S. Department of Justice, 1979), p. 6.

As we can see from the above figure, only about a quarter of the larcenies, both personal and household, are reported, and so the *UCR* statistics miss roughly 75 percent of the larcenies occurring each year.

2. *Crime "indexes" do not maintain a constant ratio with the true crime rate.* Different crimes are reported to a greater or lesser extent, and we have no idea from official statistics what the ratio is. If we knew, for example, that 30 percent of all crimes were reported, then we could simply divide the *UCR* figures by .30 to arrive at the actual crime rate. However, we would have to use different figures for each crime, since some crimes such as auto theft have a high reporting rate (70 percent) while others have a relatively low rate such as that of household larceny (25 percent). Only by using other methods is it possible to learn of this ratio, however.

3. *There is a wide variation in conditions affecting published records of crime.*
The idea of the *Uniform Crime Report* was to have a standardized reporting system of crime; however, different jurisdictions have different criteria of what will be counted and reported as a crime and/or
what kind of crime. If a police administrator is under pressure to "reduce" the crime rate, he will sometimes change the reporting procedures to do this. For example, in one jurisdiction a patrol sergeant was
observed to tell a patrol officer who was trying to catch a purse
snatcher to write the report of the case in one of two different man-
ners depending on the outcome. If the officer caught the purse
snatcher, he was to record it as a "robbery"—a serious crime. However,
if the purse snatcher got away, he was to write it up as a "petty theft"—
a crime not considered as serious. Thus, if the case was solved, the police would get credit for "catching a robber," but if they did not, it was
simply a matter of not apprehending a "petty thief."[10] Similarly, other
jurisdictions may have procedures for filling out the *UCR* reports that
will tend to increase (in order to get higher budgets) or decrease (in
order to show they're doing a good job) the known crime rate. As a
result, using the *UCR* for comparative purposes can be highly
misleading.

4. *Crime statistics are compiled primarily for administrative purposes and not for
scientific research.* One of the mistakes criminologists make in using the
UCR data is they assume the figures are equivalent to those gathered
by social science researchers. Police personnel accumulate their data
for investigative purposes, budget justifications, patrol planning, and
similar objectives, and not for the development of criminological theory. Therefore, rather than being guided by scientific methodology,
they are guided by the practical considerations of running a police
department.

5. *Statistics on the variations in the recorded rates for some crimes are not routinely compiled.* Certain crimes are not a part of the FBI's crime index,
and so there are no figures available on them. For example, crimes
predominantly committed by the upper strata of society such as violations of the Sherman Antitrust Act, consumer fraud, and other white-
collar crimes do not appear in the annual figures of the *Uniform Crime
Report.* As a result, there tends to be a bias in attributing crimes almost
solely to the lower classes.

6. *The statistics on juvenile delinquency are inadequate because in America we
have no precise definition of delinquency.* Many of the crimes committed
are by juveniles, and special offenses that apply only to juveniles, such
as several juvenile status offenses (e.g., truancy), are not part of the

crime index. Because of the ill-defined notion of juvenile delinquency, the absence of most juvenile status offenses in the index, and the unknown participation of juveniles in the index crimes, the *UCR* statistics are of limited value in studying delinquency.

Before going on, it should be reiterated that the *Uniform Crime Report* is a genuine effort on the part of the Federal Bureau of Investigation to assess crime, and to determine patterns, types, and amounts of crime in the United States. However, it is important to understand the limitations of using such data in developing explanations of crime and deciding what is necessary to overcome these problems. To a large extent, the methods developed for obtaining crime statistics such as victimization surveys, were efforts to improve on the *UCR*, and were it not for the initial effort made by the FBI, it is unlikely that we would have the new methods.

The New Crime Statistics

Adolphe Jacques Quetelet, a French statistician, pointed out that most of the ratio of crime statistics to criminal behavior was unknown. That is, based on the number of known crimes, it was unknown how many crimes occurred but were never reported (ratio = known crimes to all crimes). He correctly noted,

> We are aware, then, how important it is to legitimate such a ratio, and we may be astonished that this has not been done before now.[11]

The importance of Quetelet's observation has been confirmed. Indeed it was one of our criticisms of the *Uniform Crime Report* data. Of greater interest is the fact that Quetelet's statement was made in 1842!

Beginning in the late 1960s, criminologists and the government began developing and employing methods that overcame many of the problems with the statistics based on police, court, and prison records. The instrument, called a **victimization survey**, is used by researchers to gather data from representative samples of various communities. In such a survey, a sample of a population is interviewed and asked about being the victim of different crimes, whether the crime was reported to the police, and other questions relating to victimization. The findings from these surveys have shown that there is indeed a good deal of "hidden crime," and the official statistics touch only the tip of the crime iceberg. Table 1.2 shows the percent of crimes reported to the police for different offenses.

The figures in Table 1.2 are a finer breakdown of what we saw in Fig. 1.3. Also, using victimization surveys, we can get a better idea of the reported crime ratio that Quetelet and others pointed out as a problem in official statistics. We have an estimate of what amount of unreported

crime there is for various offenses. For example, the official statistics figure for completed automobile theft is 88.6 percent of the total, but for
petty (less than $50) household larceny, official statistics represent only

Table 1.2   Percent of Victimizations Reported to the Police

Type of crime	Percent
All personal crimes	30.3
Crimes of violence	46.1
Rape	58.4
Robbery	55.5
Robbery with injury	66.1
From serious assault	75.3
From minor assault	54.7
Robbery without injury	49.6
Assault	43.5
Aggravated assault	51.5
With injury	61.1
Attempted assault with weapon	47.2
Simple assault	38.8
With injury	47.4
Attempted assault without weapon	35.8
Crimes of theft	24.8
Personal larceny with contact	37.2
Purse snatching	46.4
Pocket picking	33.3
Personal larceny without contact	24.5
All household crimes	37.7
Burglary	48.8
Forcible entry	72.5
Unlawful entry without force	39.1
Attempted forcible entry	31.6
Household larceny	25.4
Completed larceny[1]	25.3
Less than $50	14.4
$50 or more	47.4
Attempted larceny	26.4
Motor vehicle theft	68.4
Completed theft	88.6
Attempted theft	36.2

1. Includes data, not shown separately, on larcenies for which the value of loss was not ascertained.

Source: *Criminal Victimization in the United States, 1977.* (Washington, D.C.: U.S. Department of Justice, 1979), p. 65.

14.4 percent of all such crimes. Using these data from victimization surveys, we can make adjustments in the *Uniform Crime Report* findings to have a more accurate estimate of the actual amount of crime. This is done by simply dividing the number of reported crimes in the official statistics by the percentage that is reported to the police.

$$\frac{\text{Official Statistics Number}}{\text{Percent Reported to Police}} = \text{Adjusted Crime Figure}$$

For example:
The 1979 *Uniform Crime Report* showed there were 75,989 rapes in the United States. However, we know from victimization surveys that only 58.4 percent (or .584) were reported. Therefore, using our formula we divide 75,989 by .584 to arrive at our adjusted figure of 130,118.

Of course using the formula with official statistics will not always be correct, especially if we use the victimization ratio from one year and official statistics from another. In our example, the percent known to the police was based on victimization data collected in 1977 and compared with *UCR* statistics from 1979. However, since the *Uniform Crime Reports* are published more quickly than the victimization survey findings, it is often necessary to make estimates of report ratios from earlier surveys. The "Adjusted Crime Figure," then, is not the *real* amount of crime, but rather a closer approximation.

Since ratios of reported crimes change over the years, we must exercise caution in using ratios from one year to the next. In looking at the change in the percentage of rapes reported to the police, based on victimization surveys (Table 1.3), we see a steady increase in the percentages up to 1977, and then a sharp decrease in 1978.

There is a 10 percent increase in the reports of rapes from 1973 to 1977, but then a 10 percent drop from 1977 to 1978. This can either reflect a change in the reporting patterns of rape victims or a problem with the victimization survey. Rape victims could have actually increased their rate of reports from 1973 through 1977 and then decreased in 1978, or there may have been a change in the administration of the victimization survey during the periods of change.

In addition to report ratios differing over time, they also differ from place to place. For example, in San Diego, California, in 1973 victimization surveys found that 52 percent of the rapes were reported, but in Houston, Texas, only 34 percent were reported in the same period. This

Table 1.3 Changes in Reports of Rape	
Year	Percent of Rapes Reported to Police
1973	48.5
1974	51.8
1975	56.3
1977	58.4
1978	48.8
1979	50.5

Source: *Criminal Victimization in the United States, 1973, 1974, 1975, 1977, 1978, 1979.* (Washington, D.C.: U.S. Department of Justice).

difference might be attributed to the efforts San Diego has made in working with rape victims and the confidence women place in the police or some other aspects that are different between the two cities. When we compare San Diego's *overall* reporting rate of personal crimes with Houston's, however, we find that the difference is not as great. In San Diego, only 30 percent of all personal crimes were reported and 25 percent in Houston. Thus, while there is an 18 percent difference in rape reports, there is only a 5 percent difference in reporting of all personal crimes between the two cities.[12]

Limitations of Victimization Surveys

While there are many advantages of victimization surveys, there are some limitations as well. First of all, victimization surveys may run into the same problem as the *UCR*. Some people simply may not want to tell anyone about being victimized. Certain crimes, such as child molesting may be considered too sensitive to talk about, and other crimes may have been either forgotten or not mentioned because of fear of criminal retribution or for some other reason. For example, some business persons may not report a crime to the police because it will increase their insurance rates, and if they think a victimization survey is being used to determine insurance risks, they may intentionally underestimate their crime. The opposite kind of problem may also crop up in victimization surveys—that is, people will overestimate their victimization. For example, victimization surveys are designed to learn about crime in a certain year, and subjects often report crimes of other years to "help" or impress the interviewer. "Telescoping" occurs when an interview subject includes crime victimizations from outside the time period the research is examining. A final limitation to the victimization survey is in estimating *who* committed a crime.

In cases where the victim comes face to face with the offender, it is possible, in cases such as this purse snatching, to get relatively accurate information from the victim about the offender. However, in cases where the victim does not see the offender, as in most burglaries, information about offenders is more inferential.

With some crimes such as robbery, purse snatching, and aggravated assault—crimes where the victim and criminal come face to face—it is possible to learn something about the offender. However, with other crimes such as burglary, and most larcenies—where the victim does not see the offender—it is almost impossible to provide data as to the offender's age, sex, race, or other characteristics.

Self-Report Surveys

Self-report surveys are very much like victimization surveys, but instead of inquiring about victimization, the questions are about the interviewee's crimes.[13] In one survey, for example, 1,700 adults were asked to report whether they had committed any of a variety of offenses; anonymity was, of course, guaranteed. It was learned that 91 percent had been involved in a crime for which they could have gone to jail or prison.[14] Since the study was based on a random, representative sample of the population in the State of New York, we can assume that just about everyone except for 9 percent of the population could be considered a criminal!

Self-report surveys tell us more about the proportion of the population who break the law. Do people from certain social classes tend to break the law more than those from other classes? Are men more likely to be violent than women? Are non-minority groups less likely to be criminals than minority groups? According to the arrest data, the patterns indicate lower socioeconomic classes, men, and certain minority groups are more likely to commit crimes. However, self-report surveys indicate that just about everybody *admits* to having committed at least some serious crimes. How do we resolve these differences?

To begin with, even though the self-report surveys have found virtually everyone commits some crime, certain groups commit more crimes than others. For example, in examining self-reported delinquency, we find working- and middle-class youths have committed some crimes. However, when we compare the number of offenses we find lower-class youths have committed more than middle- or working-class juveniles. Similarly, in comparing blacks and whites, blacks have more offenses than whites. Table 1.4 shows these differences based on a self-report survey.

Also, in looking at the mean (average) number of self-reported delinquencies, we find higher rates for blacks and the lower class. For instance, the mean frequency of self-reported delinquency for whites was 46.79 and 79.20 for blacks, and so even though we can say that both black and white delinquencies are common, there appears to be a higher rate of delinquency for blacks.[15] Now, when we examine the arrest rates in the *Uniform Crime Report*, we find a higher proportion of blacks arrested than

Table 1.4   *Percentage of Respondents Reporting Specific Levels of Delinquency by Race and Class*

	Total Self-Reported Delinquency				
	Race		*Class*		
Number of Offenses Reported	White %	Black %	Lower %	Working %	Middle %
0–24	71.8	67.6	71.7	72.3	70.9
25–49	11.0	8.1	10.6	9.4	11.5
50–199	13.1	15.4	11.4	14.4	14.4
200+	4.1	9.8	6.3	3.9	3.2

Source: Delbert S. Elliott and Suzanne S. Ageton, "Reconciling Race and Class Differences in Self-Reported and Official Estimates of Delinquency," *American Sociological Review*, vol. 45 (February, 1980), p. 104.

whites. Of the total arrests for **index crimes**,* 65.3 percent were whites and 32.4 percent were blacks, while only about 12 percent of the population is black.

What self-report surveys tell us, assuming the probability of arrest is constant, is that the *frequency* of criminal involvement increases the chances of arrests.[17] This is important, for even though we know that police arrest patterns and policies can affect the arrest rates, and racial prejudice can lead to certain minorities being put in jail more than others, it is also clear that a greater likelihood of criminal involvement leads to higher arrest rates.[18] Therefore, while the *UCR* data does not reflect all crime rates and arrests, it is a fairly good barometer for several types of crimes and those committing them. However, it is only because of the victimization and self-report surveys that we can assess the value of the official statistics.

Limitations of Self-Report Surveys

Like victimization surveys, there are limitations to using self-report surveys. First of all, there is the problem of validity caused by deliberate falsification, inaccurate recall, "memory fade," and telescoping.[19] In other words, there are a lot of reasons that people may misrepresent their criminal involvement. However, in studies of such problems, it was found that they are minimal and the technique generally has acceptable validity and reliability.[20] The other two major problems with the technique have to do with proper construction of questions and representative samples. These last two problems are simply a matter of inadequate research methodologies and can be resolved by better questionnaire construction and more representative samples. However, since many self-report surveys have been poorly constructed, and the samples are unrepresentative, we must use caution when we employ them to describe patterns of criminal involvement.

Observations and Experiments

There are some kinds of information required to understand crime that cannot be readily quantified or that require *control* over variables in order to isolate significant variables related to crime. On the one hand, criminologists may want to find out about various processes and structures surrounding criminal activity, and data from self-report, victimization surveys, and official statistics tell them very little. On the other hand, with all

---

*Index crimes include murder and nonnegligent manslaughter, forcible rape, robbery, aggravated assault, burglary, larceny-theft, motor vehicle theft, and arson.[16]

of the possible relationships between crime and other variables, it is necessary to isolate and separate the ones to be studied, and as we saw in looking at all of the possible relationships between the variables in crime surveys and statistics, it would be very difficult to filter out the significant ones. To deal with these kinds of problems, criminologists use participant observation and field studies for understanding processes and structures, and experimental methods for isolating and controlling variables.

Observational Studies

In order to get into the whole lifestyle of groups that commit crime, to see crime from the "inside," criminologists use participant observation. This method involves living with some group and coming to understand their beliefs, values, habits, and way of life that are involved with crime. For example, in order to understand fencing (selling stolen goods), one researcher, Carl Klockars, befriended a professional fence, someone who made a living selling stolen goods.[21] The researcher was able to learn how the fence organized his illicit business, how the fence received and sold stolen property, and how he viewed the world so as to not see his activities as really being "bad." In another study by an anthropologist, the researcher lived in Chicago with a delinquent gang named the "Vice Lords." By observing their day-to-day behavior, he learned how their organization worked, how new members were recruited, and the social processes that led to ongoing battles with rival gangs.[22] In addition to looking at criminals, observational studies have been employed in studying the police,[23] courts,[24] prisons,[25] and various law-making processes.[26] Not only do these studies tell criminologists a great deal about crime and related social institutions in their own right, they also tell us how to interpret much of the quantitative data we gather.

Experiments

When criminologists want to see if the presence or absence of certain key variables will have an effect on crime or criminally related variables, they will sometimes use experiments. In its simplest form an experiment is a research design that compares two similar groups, exposing only one of the groups (experimental group) to the variable of interest—the experimental variable. By comparing the groups before and after the introduction of the experimental variable, criminological researchers are able to determine what effect, it any, the variable had.

Experimental studies have two basic forms. One, the laboratory experiment, creates a setting where equivalent conditions of "crime" are arranged, and the other, the field experiment, uses natural settings to test experimental variables. For example, in one study, a researcher arranged a laboratory situation where certain experimental subjects would be exposed to norm violations and negative group definitions of the person (stigma).[27] Negative comments generated in the experiment were assessed by the researcher to see how they affected the experimental group's self-image. This allowed the researcher to examine the effects of the stigma (negative comments directed toward the experimental subjects). In a field experiment, another researcher wanted to see if the police discriminated against automobile drivers having certain political views. To do this, the researcher gave a group of students with exemplary driving records "Black Panther" (a radical black political group of the 1960s and early 1970s) bumper stickers and learned very quickly that the group with the stickers began receiving traffic citations.[28] In both cases, by assuming that the label (the stigma experiment) and the bumper stickers (traffic citation experiment) were the only difference between the experimental and control groups, the researchers were able to focus on key variables and determine their effect in relation to some aspect of crime and criminological theory.

SUMMARY

In this first chapter, we have sought to clarify and map out what criminology is all about and what criminologists are attempting to do. The field includes how societies go about making laws, why people break laws, and the societal reaction to crime. All three of these concerns are interrelated, and to understand one aspect, we have to understand something about the others.

Important in the study of crime is the development of explanations of how laws are made, why certain patterns of crime emerge, and why society reacts the way it does. However, not just any explanation will do, and instead of merely looking at a few laws or crimes, we have to examine patterns. That is, we are concerned with dealing with the typical and not the exceptional, and our explanations have to take into account numerous variables and patterns, leaving the kinds of crimes and criminals that make the headlines to others.

In order to construct our explanations, we have to have adequate data about crime. Like any other social science, criminological theories are based on empirical data—data that can be measured or described through some form of observation. As we saw, however, there are advantages and disadvantages with the various sources of data and methods for gathering data. Therefore, rather than looking at a single source, we have to use many to employ all different kinds of data, checking one against the other. In addition, since some kinds of data do not tell us what we want to find out, it is necessary to employ one or another methodology or several at the same time. Certain patterns of crime can be understood using surveys, but when attempting to understand processes and structures in crime, we have to use observational studies. For focusing on key variables and testing their influence on crime or criminal justice processes, some criminologists employ experimental methods either in the laboratory or the field.

Whatever the method used by criminologists, however, the primary purpose is not merely to collect unrelated information about crime. Instead that information is organized around generating understanding and explanations about crime.

Glossary

Criminalization Process   The social process whereby certain acts and individuals are defined as being criminal.

Criminology   The systematic, empirical study of how societies make laws, why laws are broken, and what the societal reaction to breaking the law is. Central to criminology is the development and testing of theories of the patterns of law making, law breaking, and societal reaction.

Experiment   A research method used to determine the effect of one variable on another by controlling for all but a single variable of interest. The classic experiment employs two similar groups, exposing only one of them to the experimental variable and then comparing them after introduction of the experimental variable to assess its effect.

Index Crimes   Eight crimes used by the FBI as a measure of all crimes. They include murder and nonnegligent manslaughter, forcible rape, robbery, aggravated assault, burglary, larceny-theft, motor vehicle theft, and arson. The index has been criticized for focusing only on crimes typically committed by the poor and minorities, leaving out common crimes of the middle and upper classes such as income tax evasion, consumer fraud, corporate crimes, and crimes by the government.

Observational Study   A research method where an observer spends time with the research subjects making direct observations of their activities.

Patterns of Crime   Uniformities in criminal activities and occurrences of crime. Omits most idiosyncratic and sensational crimes and focuses on the typical and routine ways in which crimes occur. Most patterns are determined by examining large samples.

Self-Report Survery   A survey asking a random sample of the population about their involvement in criminal activity. Such surveys are employed to discover "hidden criminals" and to offset any effects of arrest patterns in determining which groups in society are most likely to be involved in various crimes.

Uniform Crime Report   Published under the title, *Crime in the United States*, this is a compilation of all crimes known to the police and forwarded to the Federal Bureau of Investigation. Despite the problems with the report, there have been efforts to improve the reporting procedures, and it is still used to some extent by criminologists for assessing various patterns relating to crime and the societal reaction to it.

Victimization Survey   A survey asking a random sample of the population about their being a victim of crime and their reporting it to the police. It has been widely used to discover "hidden crime" not reported to the police.

Questions

1. What is the purpose or goal of criminology? What are the general methods and underlying philosophy to meet these goals?

2. What are the major social and legal parameters that must be considered in the study of criminal law?

3. In criminological theory, what are the major criteria for assessing the validity of the theory?

4. What are the limitations in using official statistics and what can be done to overcome these limitations?

5. What are the main methods criminologists have developed to gather more valid and reliable information about crime?

Notes

1. Edwin H. Sutherland and Donald R. Cressey, *Criminology*, 10th ed. (Philadelphia: J.B. Lippincott, 1978), p. 3.

2. Don C. Gibbons, *The Criminological Enterprise: Theories and Perspectives*. (Englewood Cliffs, N.J.: Prentice-Hall, 1979), pp. 6–7.

3. Donald R. Cressey, "Fifty Years of Criminology," *Pacific Sociological Review* **22,** 4 (October, 1979): 457–480.

4. Cressey, 1979, 457.

5. Gibbons, 1979, 7–8.

6. Federal Bureau of Investigation, *Crime in the United States, 1979*. (Washington, D.C.: U.S. Government Printing Office, 1980), p. 199.

7. Clayton Hartjen, *Crime and Criminalization*. (New York: Praeger, 1974).

8. William J. Chambliss, "A Sociological Analysis of the Law of Vagrancy," *Social Problems* **12,** 1964: 67–77.

9. Donald R. Cressey, "The State of Criminal Statistics," *National Probation and Parole Association Journal* **3** (1957): 230–241; Donald J. Black, "Production of Crime Rates," *American Sociological Review* **35** (1970): 733–747.

10. Personal observation by the author while conducting research on police patrol, 1976.

11. Aldolphe Quetelet, *A Treatise on Man*. (Edinburgh: William and Robert Chambers, 1842).

12. *Criminal Victimization Surveys in San Diego*. (Washington, D.C.: U.S. Department of Justice, 1977); *Criminal Victimization Surveys in Houston*. (Washington, D.C.: U.S. Department of Justice, 1977).

13. Delbert S. Elliott and Suzanne S. Ageton, "Reconciling Race and Class Differences in Self-Reported and Official Estimates of Delinquency" *American Sociological Review* **45** (February 1980): 95–110.

14. President's Commission on Law Enforcement and Administration of Justice, *The Challenge of Crime in a Free Society*. (Washington, D.C.: U.S. Government Printing Office, 1967), p. 43.

15. Elliott and Ageton, 1980, 102.

16. Federal Bureau of Investigation, 1980, 200.

17. *Criminal Victimization in the United States, 1977*. (Washington, D.C.: U.S. Government Printing Office, 1979).

18. Donald J. Black and Albert J. Reiss, "Police Control of Juveniles," *American Sociological Review* **35** (February 1970): 63–67.

19. Elliott and Ageton, 1980, 96.

20. Several studies have argued in favor of the validity and reliability of self-report surveys, but for some unknown reason the focus has been on delinquency and not on adult criminality even though the method is as applicable to adults as it is juveniles. The following are some of the studies dealing with the validity and

reliability of these surveys: Ivan Nye and James Short, JR., "Scaling Delinquent Behavior," *American Sociological Review* **22** (1956): 326–331; David P. Farrington, "Self-Reports of Deviant Behavior: Predictive and Stable?" *Journal of Criminal Law and Criminology* **64** (1973): 99–110; Robert Hardt and Sandra Peterson-Hardt, "On Determining the Quality of the Delinquency Self-Report Method," *Journal of Research in Crime and Delinquency* **14** (1977): 247–261; Michael J. Hindelang, Travis Hirschi, and Joseph Weis, *Social Class, Sex, Race and the Discrepancy between Self-Reported and Official Delinquency*. (Washington, D.C.: Center for the Studies of Crime and Delinquency, 1978).

21. Carl Klockars, *The Professional Fence*. (New York: Free Press, 1974).

22. R. Lincoln Keiser, *The Vice Lords: Warriors of the Streets*. (New York: Holt, Rinehart and Winston, 1969, 1979).

23. Johnathan Rubinstein, *City Police* (New York: Ballantine, 1973; William B. Sanders, *Detective Work*. (New York: Free Press, 1977).

24. David Sudnow, "Normal Crimes: Sociological Features of the Penal Code in a Public Defender Office," *Social Problems* **12** (1965): 255–276.

25. John Irwin, *The Felon*. (Englewood Cliffs, NJ: Prentice-Hall, 1970)

26. William J. Chambliss and Robert B. Seidman, *Law, Order and Power*. (Reading, MA: Addison-Wesley, 1971).

27. Thomas Moriarty, "Role of Stigma in the Experience of Deviance," *Journal of Personality and Social Psychology* **29** (1974): 849–855.

28. F. K. Heussentamm, "Bumper Stickers and the Cops," *Trans-action* **8** (1971): 32–33.

2

Criminal Law and Criminology

What to Look For:

Differences between natural and man-made laws.

The elements of criminal laws and criminal acts.

Arguments as to the origins of criminal law.

The organizational/interpretive application of the law.

The relationship between the criminal law and crime.

Introduction

WHEN WE THINK ABOUT CRIME, especially the more violent and heinous ones, we rarely think in terms of **criminal law**. There is a feeling that the act is so bad that it is a "natural crime" against human nature and society. However, in some societies, what we would consider murder, even the worse kind, may not be a crime. For example, among the Comanche, a husband could kill his wife, and it was considered an absolute privilege-right.[1] It was not a matter of having a good reason, but rather it was the custom of the Comanche society. On the other hand, if a man killed another man in the same tribe, that was considered wrong, and the kin of the murdered man were expected to take revenge by putting the killer to death. Such a murder was not a crime; it was the responsibility of the victim's kin and not the group as a whole to do something about it.

Social rules of any sort, and crimes in particular, have to be understood in special contexts different from natural laws. Natural laws of biology, physics, and chemistry exist in all societies and under all kinds of social circumstances. Whenever a natural law is in force (which is all the time) any "transgression" of the law will result in an immediate reaction. For example, if you step off the roof of your house, the law of gravity will pull you to the ground, and we assume that if someone in Katmandu or Timbuktu steps off the roof of his house the same thing is going to happen, no matter what the societal rules are. On the other hand, we are very much aware of the fact that criminal laws are only in effect under certain circumstances. Not only do different societies have different laws, as we have just seen, but even different states have different laws. For example, in many states, the traffic laws allow a right-hand turn at a red light after first stopping. However, in other states, making such a turn at a red light is a legal violation, subject to some kind of punishment. Also, we understand certain circumstances where breaking the law is non-criminal, such as killing in war or assault in self-defense. What's more, unlike the ever-present natural laws, in order to be punished for violating a criminal law, you have to first get caught. (Try stepping off your roof and not get "caught" by the law of gravity.)

In comparison to natural laws, criminal laws are transitory. What is the law one year may be different the next. Or where no law existed at one time, new laws are passed. For example, in California, there is a law that prohibits smoking while standing in line, a law that was non-existent a few years ago. However, the biological and chemical laws determining what happens to people who smoke have always been the same.

30

This chapter will examine the relationship between criminal law and criminology. First, we will define criminal law to differentiate it from other kinds of social rules. Secondly, we will examine two major theories of how laws come into being and then discuss the implications of these theories for understanding society. Third, we will look at the ways in which the criminal law is typically made and applied in different contexts. Finally, we will see how the crime and the criminal law are interrelated and how such a relationship can help us understand patterns of criminal behavior.

What Is Crime?

We will begin by defining a criminal law, and by implication a crime, and then examine its components to see the unique features of criminal law.

A criminal law is a specific rule whose infraction is considered to be against the society as a collective and is uniformly sanctioned in the name of the state by the state.[2]

Any violation of a criminal law, in a formal sense, is a crime, but for a crime to be committed, the rule must have all of the features of a criminal law. We will examine each feature separately to see its implications and what it means.

Specificity

The first ideal feature of a criminal law is that it must be specific. It must state as precisely as possible, *exactly* what behavior is prohibited or demanded by the law. If a rule simply said, "Behave yourself," it would be considered too imprecise to be a law. Moreover, if a law does not include certain behaviors, as spelled out in the rule, any such actions that people might generally think "naturally" go along with the rule cannot be included as a violation of the law. For example, if a boy is sexually assaulted by a man, many people would consider the act to be a violation of the rape laws. However, in most states rape is defined as being an act against a woman.[3] In California, the rape law states, "rape is an act of sexual intercourse, accomplished *with a female* . . ." and so by definition boys cannot be raped.[4] Now, of course, there are other laws prohibiting such sexual assaults, such as the child molestation laws, but since the law *specifically* states that rape is only applicable in cases where females are victims, our example of a man sexually assaulting a boy would not be rape.

Politicality

When an action is considered to be against the group as a whole and redress is in the name of the group, we can point to the "politicality" of the offense. In discussing the Comanche rules regulating the killing of one man by another, we noted that the offense was seen to be against the victim and his kin and not the entire tribe or Comanche nation. As such, the violation was *not* a crime, for the action taken against the killer was not by or in the name of the entire group, but rather his kin. It lacked the element of politicality.

We can see the politicality of criminal laws in the manner our courts charge a defendant. For example, if a man named Smith robbed a man named Jones in Chicago, the case would be called *Illinois v. Smith*. Crimes are considered to be against the corporate body and not the individual.

A general distinction made between crimes and other kinds of offenses is between *public wrongs* and *private wrongs*. Crimes are considered public wrongs and *torts* are private wrongs. In our illustration of Smith robbing Jones, the act of robbery is defined as a public wrong in the law, and so it is a crime. However, since it is clear that Jones's being robbed is certainly a private wrong (against Jones specifically), the offense is also a tort. In a court of law, therefore, there could be two cases dealing with the same offense. On the one hand, the case referred to as *Illinois v. Smith* involves violation of the criminal law, and the case *Jones v. Smith* involves the tort violation. In the second case, Jones is taking Smith to civil court for the losses he personally suffered in the robbery. In the first case, Smith is being held accountable for his crime against the people of the State of Illinois. Our focus is only on the former case involving politicality, since it is the only one dealing with crime.

Uniformity

The third feature of a criminal law—in its ideal form at least—is that crimes and their accompanying punishment apply to everyone uniformly. This means that everyone, no matter what their social position, is subject to the same set of laws. There is nothing in a criminal law that sets down one criteria for one group and another for a different group. The laws do not say that blacks will go to jail and whites will be placed on probation. There is nothing in the laws that states the death penalty will be carried out only against the poor killer but not when the killer is wealthy. Everyone is supposed to be equal under the ideal of the criminal law.

In reality it may be the case that people with power get treated in one way and those without power are treated in another. However, that does not diminish the fact that the *ideal* of uniformity is a part of the criminal law. When President Ford pardoned Nixon for any crimes he may have committed, many Americans were upset, and some analysts even said the pardon was a major reason that Ford lost the election to Carter. The fact that the population was upset strongly suggests that there is a *social expectation* of uniformity in the same way there is an ideal of uniformity in criminal law.

The concept of "uniformity" holds that no one is above the law. In reality that is not always the case, but in the Watergate affair many powerful people were punished by the law.

Penal Sanction

A final feature of criminal law is a penal sanction. In this feature, we can see both the features of politicality and specificity. First, a penal sanction, a punishment of some kind, is to be administered by the state in the name of the state—not by or for the individual victim. Secondly, a specific punishment has to be tied to a specific law. A penal sanction cannot simply state, "You'll get in trouble for breaking this law," but rather, like the law itself, it must be precise. For example, the following punishments are linked to robbery:

[Punishment for robbery] Robbery is punishable by imprisonment in the state prison as follows:

1. Robbery in the first degree for not less than five years.
2. Robbery in the second degree for not less than one year.[5]

On the other hand, the crime of battery, using force or violence on someone (hitting someone in the nose is a good example), is considered less serious than robbery, and so the punishment is less.

[Punishment for battery] A battery is punishable by a fine not exceeding one thousand dollars ($1,000) or by imprisonment in the county jail not exceeding six months, or by both.[6]

The penal sanctions for both crimes, while specific, provide some leeway to be sure. However, compared to other kinds of laws, such as civil laws, the penal sanctions for crime are very specific. In civil law, such as in a law suit, there is no exact figure attached to any civil transgression. Although some states may have a maximum figure for damages, unlike criminal law, there is no punishment spelled out for a defendant losing a case in a civil trial. If no penal sanction is attached to a law, it is not a *criminal* law.

Criminal Law and Marxist Criminology

While we have provided a definition of criminal law based on what has been passed by a society's law-making body—whether democratic or dictatorial—there is another view of what properly constitutes criminal law and appropriate concerns for criminology. Marxist criminologists argue that to study only state-made law implicitly accepts the ruling class definitions of harm and wrongfulness. That is, if we study repressive laws aimed against the powerless, for example, we lend a certain legitimacy to those laws and the behavior they define as criminal. Therefore, crime has been redefined by the Marxists more broadly as actions that violate human rights. Included are such violations as war, environmental pollution, hazardous work conditions, extortionate profiteering, marketing of unsafe products by capitalists, imperialist racism, and sexism.[7] To be sure there are some criminal laws that prohibit these very violations suggested by the Marxists, and they certainly include violations of freedom in noncapitalists countries such as the Soviet Union and those under its control, such as Poland, Hungary, Czechoslavakia, and any other countries whose freedom has been curtailed by Soviet domination. Likewise, the racist policies of Japan, South Africa, and China come under the same criminal code in this broad conception of crime. Naturally, this leads to some problems where these violations exist in noncapitalist nations, but if the ideal of a socialist society is met, the Marxists firmly believe that these violations of human rights will diminish to the point of insignificance, for the laws will be built on a true consensus of the people, and not by the ruling elite found in capitalist societies.

The Criminal Act

As we have noted, a **criminal act** is simply a violation of the criminal law. However, there are specific features to the acts which are defined as criminal. We will discuss three basic parts of the criminal act, all of which are legal elements of the act. All must be present for the act to be considered a criminal act.

Criminal Intent

Criminal intent or **mens rea** refers to the deliberate intention to commit a crime.[8] This means that before a violation of the criminal law can be considered a criminal act, the person acting in violation of the law must have had in his mind the intention to carry out the behavior. For example, if a man were cleaning his gun in his garage using reasonable care, and it accidentally went off sending the bullet through the wall and into the kitchen where it struck and wounded his mother-in-law, the act would not be considered a crime. Obviously, it is a violation of the law to shoot someone, but if it is done accidentally, and the person is not acting recklessly or with negligence, it is not a criminal act, because it was not in the mind of the person who caused the violation to commit the act.

Sometimes there is a confusion between *intention* and *motivation* in discussing *mens rea*. Motivation refers to the reasons behind doing something, but intention refers to the desire only. For example, if a person broke into a pharmacy and took some medicine to save his child's life, we might agree that such an act was not really bad since the motivations were noble. However, since the man *intended* to break into the pharmacy and steal something, the act is just as criminal as if he had stolen the medication to get high or sell it to junkies. Under the law, only the *intent* to commit the act is relevant, but the motivations behind the intent are not.

However, in cases where an insane person commits a criminal act, the element of *mens rea* is lacking. If a person cannot differentiate right from wrong, he cannot control what he does. Therefore, he cannot have the intent because he lacks the necessary mental state to understand his actions.[9]

Criminal Conduct

A second element of a criminal act is the actual conduct of the prohibited act or **actus rea**. It is not enough to simply think about committing a criminal act, one must actually do it. For example, it is difficult to watch an armored car drive by without thinking about robbing it, even though we would never actually do it. Such daydreaming is not a criminal act; nor is thinking about any other crime.

Included in criminal conduct is the actual criminal harm. If, for example, a person shoots a gun at someone and misses, even though the shooter intended to kill and took action to kill, there has been no criminal harm in terms of homicide. Clearly, the act of *attempted murder* has occurred, but not the actual harm of murder (i.e., a dead victim.)

Connection of Intent and Act

The final element of criminal conduct is a connection between the intent to commit a crime and the actual crime itself. For instance, suppose two men were enemies, and one went and got a gun to shoot the other. On the way to shoot his enemy, the man with the gun accidentally ran over and killed his enemy. Since the intent of the man with the gun was *to shoot* his enemy, not to run over him with his automobile, there is no connection between the act and the intent.

This connection between intent and the act becomes complicated in some cases. For instance, a man with a knife was chasing another man. The fleeing man ran into the street and was struck and killed by a car.[10] Since the man with the knife caused the man to run into the street, he was held accountable for murder! The man with the knife must have seen the risk in trying to cut the victim with the knife. On the other hand, if the two men had been playing baseball, and one had batted the ball, causing the other to run out in the street to catch it, where he was run over and killed, there would be no connection between the intent to cause harm (for there was none) and the death of the man who ran to catch the ball (he could have been more careful because there was no immediate threat to cause him to run out in the street.)

For the most part, criminologists do not concern themselves with the nuances of the law and whether or not some of the finer elements are present or absent. Rather, criminologists assume that a crime exists if it is treated as such by those who deal with the intricacies of law. However, since criminology does deal with crime, and crime is a legal creation, it is necessary to know something about the rudiments we have discussed above. Understanding these basic features, we now focus on major criminological interests and leave the fine points of the law to legal scholars. The focus of criminology is on the actual patterns of how the law is used in society, the topic of the following section.

Origins of Criminal Law

When we look at crimes, we might well ask, "Why is that a crime?" or, alternatively, "Why isn't that a crime?" Certain acts we feel are intuitively wrong, and we have a gut feeling that they are evil. Such laws are referred to as **mala in se** and are seen to be prohibited because of what is considered to be innately wrong in the act. Crimes such as murder, rape, robbery, and arson are of this kind, and their origins in this country can be traced back to English Common Law,[11] or in the case of Louisiana, to the Napoleonic Code.[12] Other crimes, though, are not seen to be inherently bad, but they are wrong simply because the law says so. These are called **mala prohibita,** and they have many different sources and points of origin. Box 2.1 lists a number of unusual laws, all of which can be considered *mala prohibita,* since it is doubtful there is any kind of social consensus that the conduct prohibited is inherently evil.

Box 2.1   IT'S THE LAW!

The following are some interesting state and local laws in the United States:

- In Star, Mississippi, it is a punishable offense to ridicule public architecture.
- Wearing suspenders is illegal in Nogales, Arizona.
- Spitting against the wind is illegal in A Sault Sainte Marie, Michigan.
- In Natoma, Kansas it is illegal to practice knife-throwing at someone in a checkered or striped suit.
- In Oregon, it is illegal for a dead juror to serve on a jury.
- In Baltimore, Maryland, it is illegal to mistreat an oyster.
- In Indiana a mustache is illegal on anyone who "habitually kisses human beings."
- In Topeka, Kansas it is illegal to worry a squirrel.
- In Los Angeles you cannot use the U.S. Mail to complain about cockroaches in your hotel room.
- In Kentucky a wife must have her husband's permission to move the furniture in the house.
- A Minnesota law requires that men's and women's underwear not be hung on the same clothesline at the same time.
- It is unlawful to mistreat a rat in Denver, Colorado.
- Lexington, Kentucky law prohibits carrying ice cream cones in your pocket.

Source: Professor John Johnson, Arizona State University.

In looking over the laws in Box 2.1, we might ask, what prompted anyone to make such laws? How did they come about and who was responsible for them? Are the laws reflections of the general social values in the states and cities where they were made, or are they the creation of special interest groups or power cliques? Did something happen to cause people to enact the laws, as the Lindbergh kidnapping resulted in making kidnapping a capital offense, or were the laws the result of a certain logic or belief system? For criminologists, the question is an empirical one. The goal is to examine the social institutions and practices to see how the laws come about; not how laws are ideally supposed to be created, but rather how they actually are made. Roscoe Pound referred to this as the study of "law in action," and it is distinguished from what legal scholars do, in that the focus is on patterns of behavior rather than on legal precedence or what laws on the books say.

Explaining the Creation of Laws

The two major approaches to the study of legal origin are the **consensus approach** and **conflict approach**. Both of these approaches attempt to explain how the laws on the books have come into being, and each is primarily concerned with law creation in democratic capitalist societies. The consensus perspective holds that the laws are a reflection of the general will of the people, while the conflict perspective contends that the laws reflect class conflict and differences. Both perspectives recognize consensus *and* conflict, but treat these concepts in different ways.

Consensus Approach

The consensus approach to the study of the creation of criminal laws assumes that society is characterized, in general, by agreement on what is right and wrong. In other words, there is a general value consensus, and even though there may be some differences in particular areas, there is overall agreement. By studying basic societal values and institutions, it is possible to see how the laws reflect them.

Roscoe Pound's theory of law stresses *social interests,* arguing that the law serves the needs of society. As Pound puts it,

> For the purpose of understanding the law of today I am content to think of law as a social institution to satisfy social wants—the claims and demands involved in the existence of civilized society—by giving effect to as much as we may with the least sacrifice, so far as such wants may be satisfied or such claims given effect by an ordering of human conduct through politically organized society.[13]

In other words, Pound is saying that if a law exists, in some way it is for the good of society because it meets some kind of need.

Since it is fairly obvious that not everyone agrees on what laws are the best for society—simply by noting Congressional debates over a given law—it might appear that Pound was a bit optimistic. However, Pound was well aware of different interests in society and that not everyone agreed as to what laws should be on the books. In fact, Pound differentiated between 1) individual interests, 2) public interests, and 3) social interests.[14] Individual interests referred to what would immediately affect a particular individual, such as the state wanting to put a highway through a farmer's land. If the farmer wanted to have a law prohibiting the highway going through *his* land, then the interest would be an individual one. Public interests were more general, usually referring to a specific interest group. For example, if a group of farmers worked together to have laws forbidding highways going through farm land for *all farmers,* the interest would be a public one. Finally, social interests affect what is good for society as a whole. If the farmers claimed that putting highways through farm land was bad for *everyone* because it reduced the acreage on which to grow food for the survival of society, then the interest would be considered a social one.

Pound was aware that people often presented individual and public interests as social interests, and there were objective overlaps between the different types. However, he argued that the important interests were the *social* ones, for they were reflected in basic criminal law. Moreover, while there may have been different public interests in society, and certainly different individual ones, the social interests were essentially the same, since what benefitted society as a whole benefitted everyone in society.

While Pound described society as characterized by consensus and cooperation, he also noted a **pluralistic** power base. At first this may seem to be contradictory, but the pluralism viewed by Pound was in terms of checks and balances. No single public interest or institution reflecting a single interest was powerful enough to dominate the social interest. Whenever one interest group threatened to have laws beneficial to themselves at the expense of society (social interests) other groups with an equal amount of power would step in to balance the scales in favor of society as a whole. Thus, the laws that emerged served to resolve conflict and to reflect the social good.

Conflict Approach

The second approach to the study of the origins of criminal law begins with the opposite assumptions about society. Instead of assuming a basic consensus, it assumes that conflict is the basic condition of social life. Richard Quinney, one of the major conflict theorists, states that society is characterized by diversity, conflict, coercion, and change rather than by consensus and stability.[15] Like Pound, though, Quinney saw an understanding of the origins of law in terms of interests, but Quinney saw the laws to be a result of *specific* interests rather than *general* ones. For any law on the books, the conflict theorists would argue, it is there because a specific group was able to wield enough power to get it there. Laws, Quinney argues, did not simply emerge out of society for the good of society, but instead, represent the interests of the capitalist ruling class. For example, in the tax laws, there is something called an "oil depletion allowance," which gives oil companies a tax write-off. Now even though everyone with an oil well in his back yard can take advantage of the law, the law is far more beneficial to the oil companies who save billions of dollars in taxes. Furthermore, it was the oil companies, and not society as a whole, who worked to get the law passed, and so in order to understand how laws come into being, the conflict theorists argue, we must understand who worked to have the law passed and what their specific interest was in doing so.

" . . . and here's Judge Cramer with the
dissenting opinion."

Source: From *Wall Street Journal,* permission Cartoon Features Syndicate.

From the conflict perspective, laws may or may not serve a social need. If a law happens to satisfy a general social want, it is more or less accidental, and there is nothing in the conflict approach that implies that laws are serving anyone other than the specific interest that worked to have the laws enacted or deleted. Chances are, though, that the laws do not serve society as a whole but only certain groups.

In order to closely examine the conflict approach, we will examine some of the basic propositions articulated by Richard Quinney. Some will be consistent with the consensus approach, but most will not be.

> **Proposition 1:** *Law is the creation and interpretation of special rules in a politically organized society.*

This first proposition is not in basic disagreement with the consensus approach. It simply notes that laws are made and interpreted by certain people. The agents of creation can be kings, dictators, churches, presidents, parliaments, or whatever socially sanctioned person or bodies a society happens to have. The agents of interpretation include the courts, the police, and the citizenry. On a formal level, as well as an active one, the courts explain how the laws are to be properly understood, but at the same time, there is a good deal of interpretation of the law by the police and the citizenry. The simple interpretation of an act as criminal by a citizen (and reason to call the police) makes every citizen an interpreter of the law. Given the agents of creation and interpretation, Quinney points out that the law is dynamic and not static, as implied in much of the consensus approach.

> **Proposition 2:** *Politically organized society is based on an interest structure.*

The conflict approach begins to emerge with this second proposition. It points out that there is an interest structure, but at the same time does not say, as does the consensus approach, that there is an overall interest for everybody in society. Rather the conflict perspective points to various segments of society having different interests. The more homogeneous a society, the less varied the segments and the accompanying interests. In a heterogeneous society, such as the United States, there are several segments and different interests. Moreover, each institutional order has its own set of concerns, not necessarily harmonious. The political, economic, religious, kinship, and educational orders have different interests as well as segments that cross all of these institutional orders.

There are two kinds of interests in each order and segment—the *formal* interests and the *active* interests. Formal interests are those that are advantageous to segments but not necessarily known or recognized as such. For example, years before there was any recognition of the problem of air pollution to public health, it was in the interest of public health to control what was emitted into the air people breathe. Active interests, on the other hand, are those interests that are manifest in individuals and interest groups within segments. These are interests people *actively* attempt to have something done about. For example, over the issue of abortion, there are "pro-choice" and "anti-choice" groups who work to have the abortion laws either broadened or restricted. Although most groups involved in active interests claim their position is in the formal interest of a segment or society as a whole, the main issue is that they actively attempt to have the laws changed to reflect their own interests. For the conflict theorists, the active interests are the only relevant ones, for their behavior can be studied to determine how the laws actually come into being.

Proposition 3: *Interest structure of politically organized society is characterized by unequal distribution of power and by conflict.*

At first this third proposition appears to be in agreement with the consensus approach, in that it recognizes different powers. That is, it appears to be pluralistic. However, quite the opposite is the case. Pluralism implies a more or less equal distribution of power across the segments of society, each cancelling out domination by one segment. For the conflict theorists, the inequality of power suggests that *certain segments dominate over others*. Taking a Marxist view of the major segments in society, the conflict theorists see a wealthy **elite** making up one segment—those are the owners— and everybody else who works for the owners making up the other segment. The owners, or capitalists, and the workers, or proletariat, do not have equal power and are in conflict. Each has a different interest from the other because of their relative positions in the social structure.

Proposition 4: *Law is formulated and administered within the interest structure of a politically organized society.*

This final proposition of the conflict theorists brings out the total contrast of its position with that of the consensus theorists. What it means is that the laws support one interest at the expense of others. If one segment has more power than another, it is able to get the laws that are in its interest and *against the interests of other segments.* In the case of the capitalists and the proletariat, laws that are good for one are at the expense of the other. Therefore, rather than reflecting consensus in society, the laws reflect conflict. This is because whenever a law is passed, it represents one segment's ability to prevail over others.

In the more recent works by the conflict theorists, there has been an increasingly Marxist orientation. Rather than simply noting that in all societies there is an unequal distribution of power and conflict, the focus has been only on capitalist society. The conflict theorists have argued that since the capitalists, who make up a small elite minority, have the great majority of power, the law has been a tool to exploit and control the workers.

Evaluating the Consensus and Conflict Approaches

Both of the positions we have discussed have helped criminologists better understand the origins of the laws. They have focused the attention of researchers to the law in action—how it is actually made. In addition, the opposite poles represented in the two positions have encouraged researchers to go out and collect data about how laws come into being. So whether one side or the other better explains legal origins probably is not as important as the fact that each has stimulated research.

In order to evaluate these two positions, we will first summarize their main points in Box 2.2.

The strength of the consensus approach lies in the general use of the law. Taking the common criminal laws, such as burglary, robbery, murder, and rape, we can see that just about everybody uses these laws. They benefit both the poor and the rich. Moreover, an examination of victimization data reveals that the poor and minorities are the most likely to be in need of these laws and to use them for protection.[16] It is true that the origins of these laws can be found in the "propertied interests," but their use by the population as a whole suggests they enjoy a good deal of consensus. If the criminal laws were only for the benefit of the elite, the nonelite would not use them to the extent they do. Such thinking is labelled as "false consciousness" by the Marxists, but to a poor person who is mugged, burglarized, or assaulted, the laws seem to be warranted.

Another strength of the consensus approach is that there is clearly more than a single homogeneous power in society. For example, even

Box 2.2   THE ORIGINS OF LAW

	Consensus	Conflict
Society	stable consensus	diverse, changing, conflict, coercion
Interests	social, for general good	specific, only for certain segments
Power	pluralistic, balanced	elitist, unequal, in the hands of few
Purpose of law	meet social needs, resolve conflicts	meet needs of special interests, no overall social good intended
Result of law	serves to keep society harmonious	reflects social conflict and unequal distribution of power in social structure
Research	general, illustrative	specific, empirical

Source: Derived from Richard Quinney, *Crime and Justice in Society*. (Boston: Little, Brown, 1969), pp. 1–30.

though it is certainly true that the owners of the giant corporations have enormous power relative to their numbers, they are balanced by the power of labor unions and other organized groups. If the elite, whose power rests on their financial position, attempt to have laws that are good for them at the expense of the workers, the labor unions are powerful enough to stop them. By the same token, if the labor unions ignore the needs of business, not only can they be checked by the power of the owners, it will threaten the existence of the businesses and the jobs of the workers. Therefore, power in society, instead of being one-sided, is many-sided or pluralistic.

The major problem in the consensus approach is research. In part, this is because of the vague assumptions that have been made regarding how laws emerge from society into a general social good. Scholars working within a consensus framework have failed to specify the precise mechanisms of how a social need is identified and then made into a law. As a result, their explanations and "research" is *post facto*—that is, they take a law already on the books and simply say how it meets a social need. So instead of having a precise direction, their research is vague, general, and relatively unfocused.

Another problem with the consensus approach is in its inability to account for social change. If the laws are for meeting social needs, how are changes in the needs and the accompanying laws explained? They really are not, except for the allusion to new needs to be met by new laws. However, since there is no research to support this, it is weak empirically.

One of the most dramatic problems in the consensus approach can be seen in the prison population. There is a massive overrepresentation of poor and minorities in prison. If the laws were to benefit everyone equally, they would affect everyone equally in their application. However, since only a handful of the elite ever suffer criminal sanctions, there is evidence that the laws are weighted in their interests against the poor.

Related to the problem of overrepresentation of the poor in prison is that of the dearth of criminal laws affecting the elite. For example, if a poor person (or just about anyone else) is the victim of corporate fraud or consumer fraud, they cannot call the police and ask for the "White Collar Squad" to go and make a criminal arrest. This is because most of the laws regulating the elite are either "administrative laws" or nonexistent.

Turning to the conflict approach, we see almost the opposite set of strengths and weaknesses. The common and cross-class use of the criminal laws suggests a good deal of consensus as to the need for certain laws by everybody and not just the elite. Moreover, the various power groups whose interests are clearly at odds—such as certain labor and business segments—while in conflict as suggested by the conflict approach, are not in open war and are dependent on one another to survive. Also, there is not a wholly one-sided ability of one segment to predominate over the other at all times. The business elite have lost legal battles with workers' unions, and there are numerous laws meeting the needs of the workers.

The strength of the conflict approach lies in its ability to demonstrate empirically that interests are specific and beneficial to one segment over another. In several studies, conflict researchers have shown that laws do not emerge like steam from the ground, but rather they exist because certain groups work to have their own vested interests met.[17] As we saw in the example of Chambliss's study of the vagrancy laws, the business interests wanted cheap labor and had the power to have laws enacted to make idleness a crime.[18] However, power to have vested interests advanced need not come solely from business interests. Before the Drug Enforcement Administration, Federal drug control was in the hands of the Treasury Department's Bureau of Narcotics. When new laws were proposed to deal with marijuana in 1932, the Bureau saw it as an opportunity to increase its own power and budget, for the law would give them new responsibilities of enforcement. By providing self-serving information to the Congressional committees working on the law, the Bureau was able to get the law passed.[19] In 1931, the Bureau of Narcotics reported,

> This publicity tends to magnify the extent of the evil and lends color to an inference that there is an alarming spread of the improper use of the drug (marijuana), wheras the actual increase in such use may not have been inordinately large.[20]

However, during debate over the bill from 1932 until the Marijuana Tax Act was passed, the Bureau began referring to marijuana as a "lethal weed" and urged for vigorous enforcement of local and state cannabis laws.[21]

Furthermore, various professions work to have their interests furthered. One good example can be seen in the development of the sexual psychopath laws in the late 1930s. In this case the vested interests were the psychiatrists whose profession was just gaining respectability at the time in the United States. By characterizing sexual deviation as a lifetime ingrained problem, the psychiatrists were able to have sexual psychopath laws passed that would enable psychiatrists to confine those convicted of sexual deviation to institutions for an indefinite period, to be released only if judged "cured" by a psychiatrist. By fanning the flames of hysteria caused by sensational child murders and molestations, the psychiatrists were able to have these offenders redefined so that even first-time offenders could be locked up for life.[22] Without the power to defend themselves and with no group, other than a few psychiatrists who knew that it was virtually impossible to identify a true sexual psychopath, there was little opposition to the laws, and so those convicted for child molestations and other sexual deviations could be labelled as sexual psychopaths with little hope of ever leading a normal life again.

The research into the origins of the criminal law generally finds a specific interest being met, and since it is virtually impossible to argue that any single piece of legislation is either for or against the general social good independent of a larger social context, the most important kind of research is that which identifies the groups actually involved in lobbying for or against it. In this respect the radical theorists have done a much better job in that they can show the specific groups whose interests were met.

Overall, both the conflict and consensus approaches have strengths and weaknesses. The key to understanding the development of laws, though, lies in research. At this point, there have been studies showing support for both positions as well as flaws in each. Future research and the development of new approaches and models will further clarify exactly how laws come into being.

Application of the Law

One of the most interesting developments in the sociology of law has been in the area of how laws are actually applied. From a legalistic point of view, all that is important is that the laws be applied uniformly, the elements of a crime be present, and due process be employed. (In the last section of this book, we will more closely examine some of these issues.) However, the social reality of legal applications and the criminological interest in how the criminal laws are applied has to do with observable patterns of behavior. In order to understand some of the social patterns of interest, we will introduce some key concepts here that will be developed later in the book.

Organizational Concerns

Whatever the ideal application of the laws, they are administered within a bureaucratic framework of the court and police organizations. These organizations have policies, as do all organizations, about how to best get their work done. Besides the strictly legal considerations that the police and courts take into account, practical concerns must be met as well. For example, cases of spouse abuse (husband–wife assault and battery) rarely result in arrests. All of the legal elements may be present for assault, battery, or some other similar crime, but the prosecutors know that the key witness is such cases, the husband or wife, will not testify against his or her spouse; thus, there is no prosecutable case in most instances. Likewise, the police know that since the case will not be prosecuted, there is little point in making an arrest, and in cases of battery, they may not even have legal cause to make an arrest since they did not actually see the crime. As a result, the typical charge in such cases, if any, is "disturbing the peace" with no arrest or prosecution, only a warning to calm down.

Another organizational concern has to do with allocation of resources. In one town the police were cracking down on robberies, and so they allocated most of their force to working on catching robbers. At the same time this happened, they cut back on their traffic units, so they cited far fewer people for traffic violations. As a result, the traffic laws were not applied with their usual vigor.[23] Similarly, in prosecutor's offices, in order to minimize the number of cases going to court, rather than applying the law literally, prosecutors routinely reduce charges against defendants so they will enter a guilty plea, thereby avoiding a court trial and taxing the office's resources.

A third organizational concern found in legal applications involves other organizations and institutions. If, for example, a community demands vigorous enforcement of drug laws while wanting lenient enforcement of gambling laws, both the police and courts will reflect these concerns. The result will be allocation of resources, strict enforcement, and harsh punishment for drug violations and the opposite for gambling crimes.

Interaction and Interpretation

All events that are construed as being crimes must be interpreted by *some* observer to be "an actual instance of crime" and not something else. For example, if two men are hitting one another with their fists, the event can be many things. An observer may view the interaction as a "a fight" with

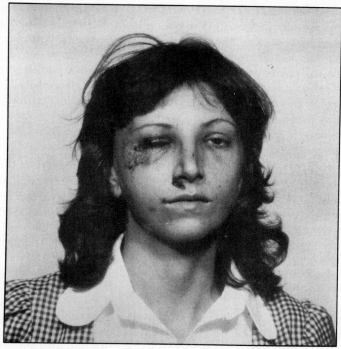

Assault victims are often related to their attacker, and because of the social norms governing relatives, very seldom do the victims in such cases cooperate in criminal prosecution.

both men committing the crime of battery; it may be seen as one man attacking another, with one committing battery and the other self-defense; or it might be seen as simply two men involved in "horse play," and not any kind of crime at all. Whatever the case, though, some kind of "interpretative work" is necessary in order for the act to be considered to be *real crime.*

The interpretations are based not just on legal criteria, however. In addition to assessing the event as an actual instance of a crime, those making decisions about how to apply the law in a given instance consider the social situation and the assumed character of the participants. For example, in a case of statutory rape (generally a man having consensual sex with an underaged girl) a 21-year-old man and a 16-year-old girl met at the beach and decided to have sex with one another. The girl's parents caught the man with their daughter and called the police who arrested the man. In deciding what to do with the case, the prosecutor decided that the girl was very "mature" and had engaged in sex on other occasions with other men, and the man was very "immature" and not a " dirty old man" seducing a young, innocent girl. Given this interpretation of "what *really* happened" or "the *true* nature of the circumstances," the prosecutor's office decided to drop the charges against the man. Thus, even though all of the legal elements of the crime were present, the event was interpreted to be something other than a breach in the implied intent of the law.[24]

Throughout this book we will be discussing crime and criminals, but it is important to understand that our discussion will deal with events and people who are in some way considered by others to have broken the law. This is not to say that people who break the law or who are considered criminals are merely the victims of someone's interpretive work. Rather, we hope to show *how* actions come to be a criminal reality in the context of social interaction and interpretations. For the sake of clarity and simplicity, however, we will not discuss every criminal event or person as "interpreted to be so," since that would be awkward and redundant. Instead, in talking about crimes and people who break the law, we will assume that some social understanding has been reached that defines the events and people in question to be criminal.

The Relationship between Crime and Morality

Throughout this chapter we have discussed what criminal law is, theories of how laws come into being, and how laws are applied. When the laws change, so too does what is considered to be criminal, and since criminology is the study of criminal behavior, we are restricted to those behaviors that are in violation of the law at the time the law is in force. Thus, while crime in the 1920s included the sale and transportation of alcoholic beverages when the Volstead Act was in force, such behaviors today are not interesting to criminologists except in studying crime in the 1920s.

There is oftentimes a confusion between morality and crime; that morality and crime are one and the same. This is not the case, and even though some criminologists have argued that sexism, racism, and war are crimes against humanity, and therefore are proper topics for criminology, criminology's correct topic is crime. Violations of civil rights laws and affirmative action laws are certainly relevant to criminology; they do involve racism and sexism; and criminologists do not argue that the only morality is what is defined in the criminal law. Rather, criminologists separate morality from crime, and by doing so can focus on what society defines—either through a general consensus of the populace or the narrow interests of an elite in the power structure—as crime.

Another important aspect of separating morality from crime is that it prevents confusion between norms in general and the special norms called "crime." The study of norm violations is generally called "deviance" and it encompasses a far broader range of topics than does criminology.

Furthermore, in certain instances breaking the law can be considered moral. For example, during the Vietnam War there were numerous demonstrations and protests by citizens who in some cases intentionally broke the law for what they considered to be moral reasons. They burned their draft cards, held illegal assemblies, and committed other crimes for a moral cause.

To study crime, then, is not necessarily a case of studying immorality. In fact, it can be quite the opposite. Therefore, for the time being, we will set aside morality as an issue in examining crime.

Having understood that the study of crime and morality are two different things, we are *now* in a position to ask the effect of morality on crime. For example, in Iran, when the Shah was overthrown and a Muslim theocracy took control, the Muslim morality had a great influence on what the laws were and how they were applied. Production and sale of alcohol, for example, were prohibited by law, reflecting the *Koran's* teachings that alcohol consumption was sinful. However, in bringing in morality to look at crime, we are treating morality simply as another variable, just like we might be interested in the variables of economic conditions, population, social class, or ethnic background. In order to treat morality as a variable though, we first had to separate it from the notion of crime.

SUMMARY

This chapter has been a brief look at some of the sociolegal aspects of criminal laws and their application. In later chapters we will elaborate on one aspect of the law or another as it relates to either the commission of crime, creation and changes in criminal laws, or the ways in which laws are actually applied. Our focus will be on the *law in action*, or how it is typically and routinely created and employed, and not on what it ideally is supposed to do.

However, it is important to understand the formal features of crimes and criminal acts: as we saw, crimes constitute a very special kind of rule violation and what may be a crime in one society may not be in another. Likewise, criminal acts have certain formal features to them that must exist before we can call an act a crime. The *use* of criminal laws to describe and define criminal acts is the primary interest of criminologists.

The creation of laws is another major interest of criminologists, and we saw how very different the concerns of criminologists were from legal scholars in examining the consensus and conflict approaches to explaining the origins of criminal laws. Legal scholars are concerned with the formal procedures and constitutional consistency of legal codes, while criminologists focus on explaining the social causes and processes. Similarly, in looking at the application of laws, we saw that the criminological concerns were with organizational and interactional matters instead of the formal legal issues of due process. This is not to say that criminologists are unaware of the formal processes, but rather, they are attempting to see how these processes operate in fact and not in legal theory.

Finally, in the last section of this chapter, we briefly explained the relationship between crime and criminal law as a summary statement of what criminologists are attempting to understand. We separated morality from crime, enabling us to look at morality as a separate variable instead of an inherent part of crime. This is important, for rather than being a moral crusade, criminology is a behavioral science that seeks to explain crime in its many dimensions. We do not mean to ignore morality as a social force in crime and the reaction to crime, but instead we simply wanted to put it in its proper place where it can be a tool for understanding instead of a hindrance.

Glossary

Actus Rea A Latin term referring to actually committing the criminal act, not just thinking about it.

Conflict Approach The perspective that focuses on the inherent conflict, segmentation, and unequal power in the social structure. Marxist version of this perspective emphasizes problems in capitalism.

Consensus Approach Perspective that stresses homogeneity of society and similarity of interests in laws. Linked to structural functionalism theory in sociology.

Criminal Act An actual behavior that intentionally violates the criminal law in circumstances where the actor can distinguish between right and wrong. Excludes such situations as war and self/other defense.

Criminal Law A specific rule whose infraction is considered to be against the society as a collective and is uniformly sanctioned in the name of the state by the state.

Elitism The position that power is centered in the hands of a few.

Mala in Se Criminal laws based on strong societal sentiments that an act is inherently evil and wrong. Most common law crimes are of this nature.

Mala Prohibita Criminal laws whose evil or wrongness is only in the fact that a law prohibits it. Most white collar crimes are treated and legislated in this manner.

Mens Rea This Latin term refers to criminal intent. It does not apply to motives or accidents.

Pluralism The position that power is in many different segments of society, and no single power group can prevail over all others combined.

Questions

1. What are the major features of criminal laws that differentiate them from other forms of laws and norms?

2. What is the major difference between "legality" and "morality" in assessing an act as criminal or not?

3. What are the major features of a criminal act? Why are *mens rea* and *actus rea* important elements of the criminal act?

4. What is the difference between criminal laws that are *mala in se* and *mala prohibita*?

5. In explaining the origins of criminal law, what are the differences between the "consensus approach" and "conflict approach?" What are the basic underlying assumptions of each?

Notes

1. Ernest Wallace and E A. Hoebel, *The Comanches: Lords of the South Plains*. (Norman, OK: 1952), pp. 3–16.

2. Howard C. Daudistel, William B. Sanders, and David F. Lukenbill, *Criminal Justice: Situations and Decisions* (New York: Holt, Rinehart and Winston, 1979), p. 5.

3. American Law Institute, *Model Penal Code* (Philadelphia: American Law Institute, 1962).

4. Elizabeth R. Gatov, ed., *Sex Code of California: A Compendium* (Sausalito, CA: Graphic Arts of Marin, Inc.), p. 156.

5. *California Penal Code*. (Sacramento, CA: Department of General Services, 1971), (abridged edition), p. 40.

6. *California Penal Code*, p. 44.

7. David F. Greenberg, ed., *Crime and Capitalism*. (Palo Alto, CA: Mayfield, 1981), pp. 4–5.

8. Allen Gammage and Charles Hemphill, Jr., *Basic Criminal Law*. (New York: McGraw-Hill, 1974), pp. 87–97.

9. Gammage and Hemphill, Jr., 1974, 138.

10. Gammage and Hemphill, Jr., 1974, 98.

11. Gammage and Hemphill, Jr., 1974, 101.

12. English "common law" was adopted as a whole and includes such crimes as murder, rape, and robbery. It was based upon and reflected the general consensus of the people in England when it was developed, and it is still a group of laws that enjoys general agreement, with the exception of some of the more archaic provisions in the original laws.

13. The Napoleonic Code is a similar set of laws as the English common laws.

14. Roscoe Pound, *An Introduction to the Philosophy of Law*. (New Haven, CT: Yale University Press, 1922), p. 98.

15. Roscoe Pound, "A Survey of Social Interests," *Harvard Law Review* **57** (October, 1943).

16. Richard Quinney, *Crime and Justice in Society*. (Boston: Little, Brown and Company, 1969), pp. 26–30.

17. See, for example, Sheila Balkan, Ronald J. Berger, and Janet Schmidt, *Crime and Deviance in America: A Critical Approach*. (Belmont, CA: Wadsworth, 1980); David F. Greenberg, *Crime and Capitalism*. (Palo Alto, CA: Mayfield, 1981).

18. See "The Hispanic Victim," National Crime Survey Report SD-NCS-16A, NCJ-67706 (Advance Report, June 1980) U.S. Department of Justice, Bureau of Justice Statistics, Washington, D.C. In the *Uniform Crime Report*.

19. Howard S. Becker, *The Outsiders*. (Glencoe, IL.: The Free Press, 1963), pp. 135–146.

20. U.S. Treasury Department, *Traffic in Opium and Other Dangerous Drugs for the Year Ended December 31, 1931*. (Washington, D.C.: U.S. Government Printing Office, 1932), p. 51.

21. Bureau of Narcotics, U.S. Treasury Department, *Traffic in Opium and Other Dangerous Drugs for the Year Ended December 31, 1935*. (Washington, D.C.: U.S. Government Printing Office, 1936), p. 30.

22. Edwin H. Sutherland, "The Diffusion of Sexual Psychopath Laws," *American Journal of Sociology* **56** (September 1950): 142–148.

23. This observation was made by the author while conducting research on police patrol, 1976.

24. Daudistel *et al.*, 1979, 21.

25. Daudistel *et al.*, 1979, 21–23.

3

Early Criminology

What to Look For:

The pre-classical conception of crime.

How the classical school was a first step
   in the scientific study of crime.

How the early criminal statisticians gathered data on crime.

The nature of biological determinism and
   how it differed from classical thought.

The different socialists' view of the causes of crime.

Introduction

IN ORDER TO UNDERSTAND contemporary criminology, we have to understand something about the paths criminologists have taken. Some of the paths have led to dead ends, others have been systematically developed, while others have stopped and then started up again. We will see that social beliefs and predominant philosophies (or even fads) have a marked effect on how people think. With social changes come changes in thinking about crime, some narrowing the perspective and some broadening it. Perhaps the most intriguing aspect of many of the early criminologists was their insight into patterns and causes of crime that we think are new ideas. As we will see, some very old ideas are considered fresh insights, some very good and some long ago disproven.

In a day and age of instant communication, computer assisted analysis of data, and a general acceptance of scientific procedures, it is easy to forget that the early criminologists had none of these tools and lacked the social support criminologists enjoy today. However, despite all of these comparative disadvantages, they did remarkable work in developing theory and gathering data to test their ideas. Some of the ideas may appear to be prejudiced and even preposterous today, but there were not the same guidelines and foundations we have today.

The Devil Made Me Do It: Some Early Notions of Crime

Before scholars began to scientifically study the causes of crime during the eighteenth and nineteenth centuries, understandings of crime were tied to whatever beliefs prevailed. Since many of the beliefs were linked to one type of religious dogma or another, most of the understandings of crime were in terms of these dogma. The most important feature of these beliefs was the inherent connection between the evil act and the evil actor. Evil spirits, devils, witches, and other supernatural sources were seen to be linked with criminal behavior. There was absolutely no conception that criminal behavior was connected to social values, economic conditions, or any number of other variables outside of the actor.[1] If one were possessed by the devil, the best thing to do was to rid the community of the evil, using torture to make sure the evil spirits felt the wrath of God (or gods). It did not really seem to matter whether a person accidentally "caught" the evil spirits like the flu or made a pact with the devil himself or herself, the spirits had to be tortured, boiled, roasted, or in some similar way dispatched.

While religious dogmas provided ways for dealing with evil and evil spirits, it was impossible to begin to think about crimes as being separate from the persons who committed them. Theories to explain criminal behavior were a long way off.

The determination of evil spirits followed the same ideology that created the spirits. As was common knowledge at the time, witches could fly and demons were impervious to fire. Therefore, in trials by fire and water, suspected witches were thrown in water to see if they could float. If they did, then it was a sign they were witches. Likewise, suspected demons were thrown into fire, and if they burned like normal folks, they were innocent.[2] (I know of no case where a suspected demon was thrown into a fire and danced happily around, and then with an evil grin came running after those assembled at the trial.) One can imagine the collective fright of judges and on-lookers were such an instance to occur, and the fact that it did not suggests that the "trials" were more a collective ritual to symbolize the community's reaffirmation of the norms than a true court to determine innocence or guilt. In Holland, rather than having innocent defendants burned to death or drowned, they employed "witches' scales" to find who was possessed by evil and who was not.[3] A suspected witch was put on the scales, and if she did not weigh over about 90 pounds, then it was a sure sign she was guilty. (Plumpness was an obvious virtue.)

Whether the application of the laws was as severe and certain as they appear to have been (especially given the large number of innocents who must have suffered) is open to question and research. However, the fact that the judicial practices even existed bears testimony to a belief system in which the evil actor and evil act were one and the same. Until that idea changed, there was little hope for the systematic study of crime.

Classical Conception of Crime

The **classical school** began not as a criminological tradition, but as a juridical one. The savagery and injustice of the treatment of suspected law breakers was seen as a negative force in society, and in order to change that system of dogmatic cruelty, a new conception of crime was needed.

The most important contribution of the classical school was to separate the criminal actor from the criminal act.[4] The classical thinkers pointed out that the evil of an act rested with community norms. That is, an act was considered evil because the community or state had enacted provisions that made it so. Therefore, rather than residing in some demon or supernatural being, the norms *defining* evil were in the community. Furthermore, people were not possessed by evil, but rather they were rational actors who weighed the costs and benefits of committing a crime. The costs were in terms of the punishment they would receive if caught, and the benefits were in terms of the gains from the crime.

Fig. 3.1 shows the different ideas about crime based on **pre-classical** and classical thought.

Fig. 3.1   Conceptions of Crime

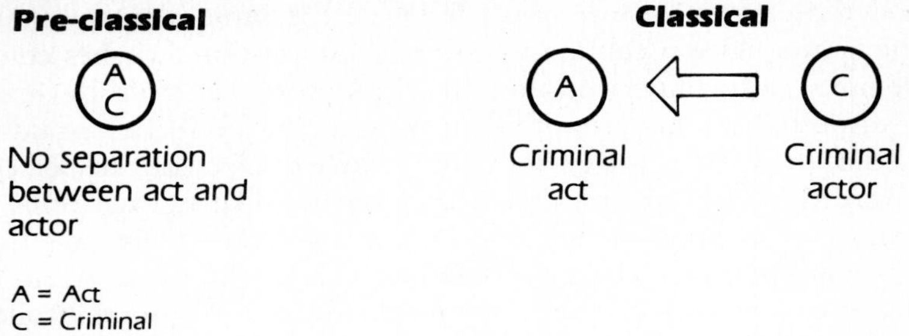

Pre-classical   **Classical**

No separation   Criminal   Criminal
between act and   act   actor
actor

A = Act
C = Criminal

The classical school enabled the scientific study of crime by providing something to study, namely the criminal actor. It was now possible to ask, "Why are certain people criminal and others not?" By the same token, now that the source of evil (not the cause) was in the community norms, it could also be asked, "Why are certain acts considered to be criminal?" Thus, not only was it possible to treat crime as a dependent variable (the variable that is caused by something) in terms of the events and forces surrounding the person who committed the crime, but it was also possible to examine crime as a dependent variable in terms of the community that made the norms.[5]

Classical Theorists

Two major theorists of the classical school were Cesare Becarria (1738–94) and Jeremy Bentham (1748–1832). Becarria, an Italian scholar, belonged to a group of reformers who sought to remedy judicial injustice. Becarria's treatise, articulating the problems with the Italian (and most of the European) system of justice, including prison conditions, became a model for modern legal systems. (See Box 3.1 for some of the insights Becarria brought to juridicial thinking.)

Box 3.1   OBSERVATIONS BY BECARRIA

On Interpreting Laws

There is nothing more dangerous than the common axiom, *the spirit of the laws is to be considered.* To adopt it is to give way to the torrent of opinions. This may seem a paradox to vulgar minds, which are more strongly affected by the smallest disorder before their eyes, than by the most pernicious though remote consequences produced by one false principle adopted by a nation.

On the Obscurity of Laws

If the power of interpreting laws be an evil, obscurity in them must be another, as the former is the consequence of the latter. This evil will be still greater if the laws be written in a language unknown to the people; who, being ignorant of the consequences of their own actions become necessarily dependent on a few, who are interpreters of the laws, which, instead of being public and general, are thus rendered private and particular. What must we think of mankind when we reflect that such is the established custom of the greatest part of our polished and enlightened Europe? Crimes will be less frequent in proportion as the code of laws is more universally read and understood; for there is no doubt but that the eloquence of the passions is greatly assisted by the ignorance and uncertainty of punishments.

On Torture

A very strange but necessary consequence of the use of torture is that the case of the innocent is worse than that of the guilty. With regard to the first, either he confesses the crime which he has not committed, and is condemned, or he is acquitted, and has suffered a punishment he did not deserve. On the contrary, the person who is really guilty has the most favourable side of the question; for if he supports the torture with firmness and resolution, he is acquitted, and has gained, having exchanged a greater punishment for a less.

On the Severity of Punishment

In proportion as punishments become more cruel, the minds of men, as a fluid rises to the same height with that which surrounds it, grow hardened and insensible; and the force of the passions still continuing in the space of a hundred years the *wheel* terrifies nor more than formerly the *prison*. That a punishment may produce the effect required, it is sufficient that the *evil* it occasions should exceed the *good* expected from the crime, including the calculation of the certainty of the punishment, and the privation of the expected advantage. All severity beyond this is superfluous, and therefore tyrannical.

On the Death Penalty

The death of a criminal is a terrible but momentary spectacle, and therefore a less efficacious method of deterring others than the continued example of a man deprived of his liberty, condemned, as a beast of burden, to repair, by his labour, the injury he has done to society. *If I commit such a crime,* says the spectator to himself, *I shall be reduced to that miserable condition for the rest of my life.* A much more powerful preventive than the fear of death which men always behold in distant obscurity.

Source: Cesare Becarria, *An Essay on Crimes and Punishments.* (Philadelphia: Philip H. Nicklin, 1819).

A more prolific contemporary of Becarria was British philosopher Jeremy Bentham. Bentham developed what he called a theory of **felicific calculus**. In his theory, Bentham reasoned that people were rational actors who calculated the costs and benefits of committing a crime. If the costs outweighed the benefits, people would choose not to commit crimes. Bentham assumed **free will** in the sense that people could either choose to commit a crime or not, but since this choice depended on evaluating the costs of committing a crime, the law could influence that choice. If the laws made chosing a particular crime more costly than not doing so, rational actors would typically choose not to commit crimes. Thus, even though Bentham, along with other classical theorists, believed in the concept of free will, the idea of law and its effect was very much deterministic, for it set up conditions that would affect rational choices.[6]

Even though Becarria and Bentham were not criminologists, their juridicial theories had a great deal of influence on later criminological theory. Direct descendants of the classical school included nineteenth century neoclassical criminology, which held identical assumptions as the classical school, and contemporary control theory. Neoclassical criminology extended classical thought by postulating that uniformity of penalties be mitigated for children and lunatics and that judges be given discretion in sentencing. Likewise, modern deterrence theory and certain aspects of control theory, to be discussed in Chapter 6, trace their origins to the works of Becarria and Bentham.

The Criminal Statisticians

One of the most ignored contributions to modern criminology is the work of the eighteenth-century statisticians who began collecting data pertaining to criminal behavior. They argued that in order to understand social behavior, it was necessary to make observations of aggregates, not individuals. Called **moral statistics,** the figures gathered and analyzed by these statisticians showed certain regularities and patterns in, among other things, crime. It was noted that certain regions had more crime than others, different age groups had different crime rates, and several other variables showed definite patterns. For example, Table 3.1 shows the different crime rates for men and women for the years 1826 to 1831. (Note how similar the ratios are to contemporary data of the same nature—namely the *Uniform Crime Report* statistics.)

In considering the crime ratios found between 1826 and 1831, it is clear that there are definite differences in crimes between men and women and those differences remain fairly constant over time. Given these differences, how would a classical theorist explain them? Are women more rational than men, since they are less likely than men to commit crimes? Or can we say that women are more rational in crimes against persons but

Table 3.1   Early Nineteenth Century Crime Statistics

Years	Crimes against Persons			Crimes against Property		
	Men	Women	Ratio	Men	Women	Ratio
1826	1,639	269	0.16	4,073	1,008	0.25
1827	1,637	274	0.17	4,020	998	0.25
1828	1,576	270	0.17	4,396	1,156	0.26
1929	1,552	239	0.15	4,379	1,203	0.27
Averages	1,601	263	0.16	4,217	1,091	0.26
1830	1,412	254	0.18	4,196	1,100	0.26
1831	1,813	233	0.13	4,567	993	0.22
Averages	1,612	243	0.15	4,381	1,046	0.24

Source: Adolphe Jacques Quetelet, *A Treatise on Man* (Edinburgh: William and Robert Chambers, 1842).

less so in property crimes? Surely we can think of reasons the classical theorists might give to explain the higher crime rate of men compared to women, but there is nothing in their logic or theoretical framework that would account for such differences. Likewise, modern theories we will explore will run into the same kind of problems explaining these kinds of patterns—ones that have persisted for over a century!

While the statisticians represented a great step forward in the methodology for studying crime and the profound influence such a method and its findings would have on criminological theory, they themselves really offered no theory. They pointed to different patterns that could be found by examining various ecological, geographical, and social factors, but the choice of what to examine was not directed by any guiding set of propositions. The observed patterns could certainly serve as the basis for theory. In the late nineteenth and early twentieth century, criminologists of the **ecological school,** especially those identified with the Chicago school, such as Thrasher,[7] whose study of delinquency was used as the basis for subcultural arguments, used these methods. However, the main reason that the criminal statisticians have been overlooked in the history of criminology rests on the fact that they did not develop explanations or theory.

Adolphe Jaques Quetelet (1796–1874)

In order to understand why the early statisticians did not develop theory in criminology, we have to understand their concerns and points of reference. Quetelet, whose works bore directly on patterns of crime in society, was originally drawn to the study of probability (statistics) through an interest in astronomy. By observing social behavior in much the same manner as astronomers and meteorologists observed the heavens and the weather, he believed he could discover patterns. However, it is equally important in the study of crime to explain these regularities.

Of course, once Quetelet found certain patterns of crime, he did begin to grapple with some kind of explanations, but by and large these accounts focused on the fact that there were regularities. The following is representative of Quetelet's most advanced level of theorizing:

> Supposing men to be placed in similar circumstances, I call the greater or less probability of committing crime, the *propensity to crime*. My object is more especially to investigate the influence of season, climate, sex and age, on this propensity.
>
>   I have said that the circumstances in which men are placed ought to be similar, that is to say equally favorable, both in the existence of objects likely to excite the propensity and in the facility of committing the crime. It is not enough that a man may merely have the intention to do evil, he must also have the opportunity and the means. Thus, the propensity to crime may be the same in France as in England, without, on that account, the *morality* of the nations being the same. I think this distinction is important.[8]

In and of themselves, Quetelet's observations and quasi-theoretical statements were of little significance. This is because there really was nothing to tie the disconnected observations together other than the fact that some of the dimensions examined by Quetelet seemed to show greater amounts of crime than others. The real significance of Quetelet's work lay in the implications for further theory and research. The fact that there were social regularities in criminal behavior showed that the causes of crime did not merely lie in random personality disorders *or* biological impairments.

Early Positivism

While the statisticians were organizing the study of crime around a methodology borrowed from the astronomers, other researchers of crime borrowed methods from medicine and biology to study crime. It was argued that if physical abnormalities were caused by some kind of disease or genetic disorder, so too could criminal behavior. After all, if the brain guided behavior, then a damaged or mutant brain could lead to criminal behavior.

The underlying philosophy of this approach is called **positivism,** and the early positivistic theories in criminology were biogenic ones. Positivism itself refers to the idea that all actions are caused by some prior event. The early criminologists, however, focused primarily on biological causes rather than the psychological and social causes in contemporary positivism.

Focus on the Criminal Actor

The classical and statistical schools of criminological research sought to find answers in the conditions surrounding criminal behavior, but the positivist looked directly at the actor himself. Even if it were true that under certain circumstances would those with a "propensity for crime" commit crime, the question still remained as to who had such a propensity. Further, it was clear that even under the most favorable conditions to commit crime only a small proportion of the population did so. Therefore, by studying the individual criminal actor, the positivists hoped to discover the true root cause of criminal behavior.

After thirteen years of abuse Francine Hughes murdered her husband by setting fire to his bedroom while he slept. Here she is shown looking back at her children before entering the courtroom. Deterministic theories would conclude that those years of abuse inexorably led to the killing. She was acquitted on the basis of temporary insanity.

Determinism and Crime

The central concept of the positivist school is that of **determinism**.[9] Following the other sciences, this idea applied to the study of crime holds that certain elements in the world inexorably cause people to commit crimes. In the same way that a virus will cause disease, wholly independent of the free will of the person who contracts the virus, there are causes of crime over which the individual has no control. The saying, "He's not bad, he's sick" is an application of such reasoning, and the idea of treatment instead of punishment is an outgrowth of this kind of biogenic deterministic logic. For the classical theorists, punishment would be effective since the rational actor could *choose* whether or not to commit a crime. For the biogenic positivists such social harshness was both barbaric and ineffectual, since the criminal had no choice in his actions. Only by treating the cause of the "illness" could crime be "cured."

The methodologies for studying the causes of crime were those of the clinical physiologist or physician. By careful measurement and observation of any biological impairments or abnormalities, it would be possible to discover the cause, and in time, effect a cure. Therefore, examination of body proportion, diseased tissues, and autopsies of criminals was the favored technique for the study of crime causation. In later positivistic studies, more sophisticated techniques were employed, and the use of drugs in the study and treatment of criminals was common.

Cesare Lombroso (1835–1909)

Often called "the father of modern criminology," Cesare Lombroso was an Italian physician whose interest in crime began in psychiatric institutions and post mortem examinations of expired criminals. In describing the beginning of Lombroso's work, Sylvester painted the following picture:

> On a cold, grey, November morning—so the story goes—a brigand named Vilella breathed his last in an asylum in Pavia. A young physician on the staff was assigned to the post mortem examination. As Lombroso later described it, he had laid open the skull and had begun to examine its contents when he discovered on that part of the occupant where a spine should be found in the normal individual a depression which he named the "median occipital fossa." This condition, he claimed, was correlated with hypertrophy of the vermis—an anomalous condition in man but often found in the lower apes, rodents, and birds.[10]

Upon observing this abnormity, Lombroso saw himself on the brink of a whole new understanding of crime. He wrote,

> This was not merely an idea but a revelation. At the sight of that skull, I seemed to see all of a sudden, lighted up as a vast plain under a flaming sky

the problem of the nature of the criminal—an atavistic being who produces in his person the ferocious instincts of primitive humanity and the inferior animals.[11]

In some respects, Lombroso's "insight" might be seen as regressive rather than progressive, setting back criminology considerably. After all, there was not a great deal of difference between the notion of **atavism**— regression to a lower form of species—and the pre-classical idea of inherent evil. Rather than the evil taking on the form of a demon, it simply took on the form of a mutation.

One important feature of Lombroso's hypothesis, like all good scientific theories, was that it could be readily tested. By making precise measurement of various body parts, a researcher should be able to distinguish between criminals and noncriminals. Lombroso made many such comparisons, but his statistical methodologies were quite weak, and what appeared to Lombroso as significant differences were not found to be by others. Perhaps the most famous test of Lombroso's theory was a study by Charles Goring published in a work entitled *The English Convict: A Statistical Study*. In a comparison of several different groups, Goring concluded that there were no significant differences between criminals and noncriminals based on Lombroso's body characteristics. For example, in comparing 1,000 Oxford students with 996 convicts, Fig. 3.2 shows Goring's findings; the measurement in millimeters, with the line representing the convicts and the bars the Oxford students. While they appear almost identical on the chart, there were slight differences, but none statistically significant.

Perhaps the most important contribution to modern criminology was Lombroso's approach to the study of crime. He stressed and employed careful measurement and observation, used control and experimental groups, and generally followed a program of empirical research. (In fact, the very methods espoused by Lombroso were used to disprove his theories by Goring and others.) Not all positivists took body constitution as the root cause of crime, and it is important not to confuse Lombroso's theory as a whole with positivism, but rather the fact that Lombroso employed empirical methods rather than argument without data was a major step in the development of a scientific approach to the study of crime. Furthermore, the idea of clinical treatment over punishment, in both its mild and severe forms, can largely be credited to Lombroso, for he argued not only that punishment and torture were inhumane, but they were also inappropriate methods to change behavior.

However, Lombroso's ideas developed beyond his original notion of atavism, and he differentiated between certain forms of abnormal behavior, such as epilepsy, and forms of insanity and criminality. In his later writings, he identified several other kinds of criminals who in no way were

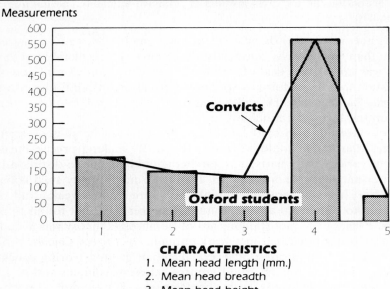

Fig. 3.2 Goring's Comparisons

CHARACTERISTICS
1. Mean head length (mm.)
2. Mean head breadth
3. Mean head height
4. Mean head circumference
5. Cephalic index

physiologically abnormal, including the "habitual criminal" whose socialization, not biology, was responsible for his criminal behavior pattern. The very idea of a criminal typology was largely credited to Lombroso.[12]

Enrico Ferri (1856–1929)

While the positivist criminologists can certainly trace their heritage back to Lombroso, Enrico Ferri was probably more responsible for the more general acceptance of positivist criminology. Ferri laid out the tenets of positivism and broadened it in depth and scope. In laying out the ideas of his approach to the study of crime, Ferri both addressed his critics and stated his intentions:

> *The Programme* The positive criminal school does not consist, as it seems convenient for many of its critics to feign to believe, only in the anthropological study of the criminal; it constitutes a complete renovation—a radical change of scientific method in the study of criminal social pathology and in the study of what is most effectual among the social and juridical remedies that social pathology presents. The science of crimes and punishment was formerly a doctrinal exposition of the syllogisms brought forth by the sole

force of logical phantasy. Our school has made of it a science of positive observations, which, based on anthropology, psychology, and criminal statistics
as well as on criminal law and studies relative to imprisonment, becomes the
synthetic science to which I myself gave the name "Criminal Sociology."[13]

The influence of Lombroso was clear in Ferri's statement, but we can also
see that Ferri expanded the horizons of criminological positivism and directly attacked the classical theorists. He characterized them as "armchair
theorists" in reference to their "syllogisms" based on "logical phantasy"
rather than empirical observations.

One of the most important of Ferri's contributions was in the treatment
of criminals. Interestingly, after his attacks on the classical theorists, he
still referred to punishments, but saw a "social responsibility" rather than
the "legal responsibility" of the classical criminologists. Instead of the
punishment to be a deterrent, it would serve as a substitute for indemnity
to society and be treatment-oriented so that offenders would be less likely
to repeat their crimes. As such, punishments were a form of social retribution in addition to treatments, two ideas that often conflict in actual
practice.

The Socialist School

The **socialist school** took its lead from the works of Marx and Engels.
They proposed that the economic conditions that gave rise to the very
wealthy and the very poor forced the poor to commit crime. To be sure,
their thinking was not exactly profound, and they understood Marx only
in the most naive and superficial manner, but they did introduce the notion that *entire classes,* created by the economic system, engaged in crime.[14]
An additional important contribution of the socialist school was the methodology they employed to test their theory. It was borrowed from the statisticians such as Quetelet. These contributions formed the basic elements
of modern criminology.

Fig. 3.3   Criminal Statisticians' and Positivists' View of Crime

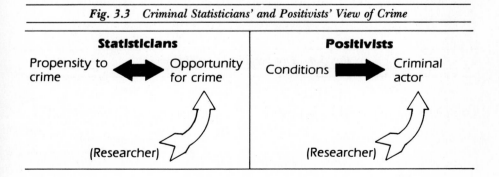

Willem Adriaan Bonger (1876–1940)

Of the early socialists, Willem Bonger stands out both as an intellectual theorist and sophisticated Marxist. Not satisfied with the simplistic notions of other socialists (such as the idea that poverty causes crime), Bonger sought to show how the conditions of capitalism led to conditions where crime was encouraged, and not just among the poor. Many of the ideas of the contemporary Marxist criminologists were first articulated by Bonger, and even though he is out of favor with many of the neo-Marxists, his contributions were considerable.

Bonger argued that crime was caused by egoism—self-interest above interest of the community and others. In societies characterized by altruism, the condition where people saw an act against society as an act against themselves, crime was lower. If certain social conditions led to higher degrees of egoism and lower degrees of altruism, then such societies would have higher rates of crime. Since capitalism emphasized competition and exploitation which led to egoistic adaptations, capitalistic societies as a whole would be more criminal.[15]

Using comparative and historical data, Bonger argued that biological differences as well as certain climatic factors (mainly the list created by the criminal statisticians) were insufficient to explain patterns of crime. First, he showed how social conditions and not biological ones determined whether or not a situation was criminal. He pointed out that the same biological processes should be at work in occasions defined as war as in occasions defined as murder: the act and biology being the same, but the social understandings being different. Next, Bonger, showed how societies living in very different climates but with basically the same altruistic social organization had similarly low crime rates. He argued that if climate really was a "contributing factor" to crime, then one would expect to see differences in crime rates in societies that were similar with respect to egoism and altruism.

Perhaps Bonger's most significant contribution to sociological criminology was linking the cause of crime directly to social conditions. Even

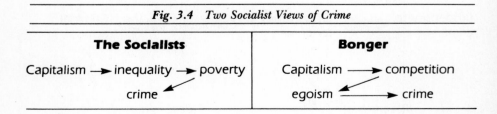

Fig. 3.4   Two Socialist Views of Crime

though the other socialist criminologists saw an indirect connection between the social organization under capitalism and crime, their main focus was on the situation of the poor—their economic, not social, state of affairs. Bonger, on the other hand, wholly bypassed the economic poverty as a cause, showing instead how the social organization produced either egoistic or altruistic adaptations leading to higher or lower levels of crime.

SUMMARY

Against popular superstitions about crime, the devil and behavior, the early criminologists began their work in a virtual vacuum of theory and data, and fighting ignorance, they made impressive gains. The classical school began by distinguishing between the criminal actor and the criminal act. The criminal act was defined by the community, and as such was not an inherent part of the criminal actor. This paved the way for the scientific study of crime, for it separated the actor from the act.

One of the first groups to make progress in the study of crime were the criminal statisticians who, gathering comparative data from official records, were able to show that crime varied depending on several geographical and social variables. While they did little in the way of developing a theoretical model, their methodological tools were extremely sophisticated for the time and are used with surprisingly little variation by some even today. Following the statisticians came the Italian positivist school led by Lombroso. Lombroso's methods in statistics were weak, but his insistence on using the empirical method over argument without data added support to the growing scientific approach to the study of crime. His followers, especially Enrico Ferri, further developed the argument for a rigorous scientific approach over theorizing without data.

The next major step in developing criminology came from the Marxists. Their contributions can be seen in both their theory and method. While admittedly using somewhat naive interpretations of Marx and Engels, they nevertheless introduced class variables to the study of crime and were able to show statistical relationships between social class and criminal convictions. A more sophisticated model was developed by Bonger to differentiate between capitalist societies and noncapitalist societies both with class differences but different patterns of crime.

While many of the early criminologists' theories and methods may appear crude and discredited today, it is important to remember the resources and knowledge they had available at the time. In the next several chapters we can see the influence of these early thinkers and begin to appreciate the foundation they laid.

Glossary

Atavism   A throwback to an earlier, more primitive, species; used by Lombroso to explain criminal man.

Classical School   School of thought that stressed juridicial reform as a primary goal, but contributed to criminology by providing a model of man that was rational, separating the criminal actor from the criminal act. (See *Felicific Calculus*.)

Determinism   Refers to a condition of cause and effect that eliminates free will or choice by the actor. (See positivism.)

Ecological School   Early criminal statisticians who sought to find patterns of crime in ecological variables were the founders of this school. They examined such variables as climate, weather, sex, age, and similar variables surrounding the individual.

Felicific Calculus   A Latin term used by Bentham to reference the idea that people rationally choose to pursue pleasure and avoid pain.

Free Will   The idea that even though influenced by a number of outside considerations, people ultimately choose their own actions. This idea was developed as a major concept in the classical school.

Moral Statistics   Term used by early criminal statisticians to describe crime data.

Positivism   Name given to idea that all actions are caused by some prior event. School of thought that emphasizes determinism in seeking explanations of crime.

Pre-Classical   This refers to the ideas and dogma preceding the classical school where supernatural forces were believed to be responsible for crime.

Socialist School   School of thought that emphasized economic conditions that create poverty as being the primary cause of crime.

Questions

1. What were the pre-classical notions of crime and evil? How did such a conception render the scientific study of crime virtually impossible?

2. What were the contributions of the "classical school" of criminology to the study of crime? How did this conception of the criminal act differ from pre-classical notions?

3. What were the contributions of the early criminal statisticians? How is their influence seen today?

4. How did the early positivist criminologists view crime causation? How did they differ from the classical school in terms of their basic assumptions about crime?

5. What contributions did the early socialist criminologists make to the study of crime? What methods and variables did they employ that are considered standard today? How did Bonger's theory alter the basic socialist framework for crime studies?

Notes

1. Edwin Sutherland and Donald R. Cressey, *Criminology*, 10th ed. (Philadelphia: Lippincott, 1978), p. 54.

2. Kai T. Erikson, *Wayward Puritans*. (New York: Wiley, 1966).

3. While in Holland in 1973, Professor Albert Hess, then at SUNY Brockport, showed the author these scales preserved in a Dutch town and explained their use.

4. Sawyer F. Sylvester, Jr., ed., *The Heritage of Moderm Criminology*. (Cambridge, MA: Schenkman, 1972), p. 3.

5. *Ibid.*

6. Jeremy Bentham, *An Introduction to the Principles of Morals and Legislation*. (London: Pickering, 1823); see also, Hermann Mannheim, *Pioneers in Criminology*. (Chicago: Quadrangle Books, 1960).

7. F. M. Thrasher, *The Gang*. (Chicago: Chicago University Press, 1936).

8. Adlophe Quetelet, *A Treatise on Man*. (Edinburgh: William and Robert Chambers, 1842).

9. David Matza, *Delinquency and Drift*. (New York: Wiley, 1964), pp. 5–13.

10. Sylvester, 1972, 63.

11. *Ibid.*

12. Sylvester, 1972, 63–65.

13. Enrico Ferri, *Criminal Sociology*. (Boston: Little, Brown, and Company, 1917).

14. For a general discussion of theories relating to the economic conditions of crime, see George B. Vold, *Theoretical Criminology*. (New York: Oxford University Press, 1958), pp. 159–182.

15. Willem Adriaan Bonger, *Criminality and Economic Conditions*. (Boston: Little, Brown and Company, 1916).

4

Individualistic Explanations of Crime

What to Look For:

Why certain theorists believed the violation
of the law was an illness.

The arguments for focusing on the individual
actor in the study of crime.

The findings of biogenic theorists and
how they were interpreted.

The similarities and differences between the psychoanalytic
and psychopathic theories of crime.

The methods used by the personality theorists and "mental
testers" and the different interpretations of their findings.

MUCH THEORY AND RESEARCH in criminology has focused on the individual criminal actor. The idea that criminals are "sick" instead of "bad" or "evil" typifies the kind of assumptions made by the individualistic theorists. The idea of replacing the concept of "evil" with that of "sickness" had wide appeal. It appeared to support a humanistic approach to the treatment of criminals, and it eschewed the use of torture and punishment as means of solving the crime problem. But at the same time there were a number of subtle implications in substituting "sickness" for "evil" that were far from humanistic and to some extent a throwback to pre-classical thought. For example, the classical theorists separated evil from the criminal actor and placed the source of the designation as evil in community norms (the rules and laws of the community) thereby enabling us to understand the changing notions of crime and criminal acts. However, by elevating the criminal act to an illness, the biogenic positivists suggested that criminal laws had the same status as natural laws—any violation or "abnormality" was due to some kind of disease, a naturally occurring phenomenon. This implies that all criminal laws, no matter how wacky or unjust they might be (as we saw in Box 2.1), were measures of what was "naturally correct." We can imagine how criticizing public architecture, which is against the law in Starr, Mississippi, could be conceived of as a sign of mental illness!

Observer: *"Boy, what an ugly courthouse."*
Police Officer: *"That's against the law, son, you must be sick."*

In this chapter, we will examine some of the major attempts to explain and measure criminal behavior in terms of individualistic dimensions. The focus of these approaches is on one of the following: 1) biological makeup; 2) psychiatric problems; or 3) psychological assessments of personality as measured by various tests. We will concentrate on the more modern explanations that are rooted in either the Italian positivist school of thought or psychiatric and psychological theory. To begin our examination, we will discuss the arguments that have been summoned for individualistic explanations of criminal behavior.

Focus on the Individual

An influential twentieth century individualistic writer was William Healy. His works stressed the necessity of studying the individual as the prime source of criminal and delinquent behavior. Working with juveniles in Chicago and Boston, Healy developed diagnostic and treatment tech-

72

niques to deal with what he saw as the root causes of delinquency in the personality. With a background in medicine, Healy understandably was attracted to psychiatric and psychoanalytic explanations, yet he was far more eclectic than the early biotypical Lombrosians.[1]

Healy's arguments for an individualistic study of crime reflected the general attitude held by others who saw the root cause to be found and cured within the individual. The following quote from the introduction to Healy's book on delinquency spells out this position:

> It is impossible to get away from the fact that no general theories of crime, sociological, psychological or biological, however well founded, are of much service when the concrete issue, namely the particular offense and the individual delinquent, is before those who have practically to deal with it. The understanding needed is just that craved by Solomon—the understanding of the one who has actually to deal with people, the one who formally is the therapeutist [sic]. It does not require prolonged observation of any treatment of the offender to realize what knowledge will prove of most worth in the procedure; one quickly perceives that it must be information concerning characteristic variations of physical and psychical equipment, concerning laws of mental mechanics, and the influence of the various forms of experience on various types of mankind. From this arises scientific and common-sense appreciation of the relation of antecedent to consequent in the life history of the individual offender whose actions and person are to be dealt with.[2]

Basically, the argument of the individualistic theorists as represented by Healy is that the only real progress in crime prevention and control is through the individual, since it is the individual who breaks the law. Thus, rather than finding general environmental or social patterns common to criminals and delinquents and changing those conditions in society, it is possible to focus on the specific problems of those who break the law and change the individuals themselves.

For example, Healy attributed the failure of England's Inebriate Acts to reduce drunkenness to the "fact" that many of the alcoholics were feebleminded, and the general measures taken to cure the problem did not take into account the individual's malady behind the drunkenness. Healy argued,

> In other words, many of the great army of topers are such because of their feeblemindedness, and it is that, and not the ingestion of alcohol, which must be fundamentally reckoned with.[3]

At the same time that Healy argued for a focus on the personality and similar individualistic characteristics, he, along with most other like-minded criminologists, recognized the importance of "other factors." These other influential factors included various social circumstances, such as family life, group norms (social environment), and any number of other factors that might be present in a criminal's life. Obviously, this kind of "theorizing," while opening up a wide range of possible sources to study, also gave rise to relatively unstructured and loose "causes" of crime and delinquency. To the extent that "anything" could be a cause, the theorists were left with no controlling variables to test and all explanations being essentially *post facto* (interpretations after the fact).

The final and most important element in the individualistic approach to the study of crime is the focus on treatment. Healy argued,

> Misconduct is only a branch of conduct in general; and nowhere can the relationship between conduct and mental life be perceived better than in studying the immediate causations of social misdoing. The robbery was preceded by the mental presentation, the plan; the assault followed upon the mental reaction of anger to the displeasing pictures which the spoken word brought up; the temptation was followed because the idea of immediate satisfaction was not counterbalanced just then by conscious representation of consequences. Thus, illustrations might be indefinitely multiplied of how a mental process immediately precedes conduct.
>
> Hence, it is clear *whatever* influences the individual towards offense must influence first the mind of the individual. It is only because the bad companion puts dynamically significant pictures into the mind, or because the physical activity becomes a sensation with representation in psychic life, or the environmental conditions produce low mental perceptions of one's duty towards others, that there is any inclination at all towards delinquency.[4]

This kind of argument represents the **reductionist** position. By reductionist, it is simply meant that while social conditions can be a primary cause of criminal behavior, they are not the root cause. The very fact that some people do and others do not commit crime given the same social background provides the individualistic theorists with a strong argument for turning to an individual's makeup instead of the larger social circumstances.

The problem with this approach, though, is the general acceptance of the laws and failure to recognize that definitions of crime differ not only from one society to the next, but change within the same society, and what may be an "illness" at one point in time will be "cured" simply by the fact that certain laws change. Similarly, since there clearly are general patterns of crime in certain areas of socioeconomic groupings, one is left with the conclusion that there is an "epidemic" of crime—the illness caught by a particular group or area. Since the "virus" has never been identified, they always find themselves slipping upwards to the social/economic/political level of explanation.

Beer being dumped into Lake Michigan, 1919. One problem with biogenic theories is the relativity of laws. During Prohibition liquor was illegal, but could we say that those who broke the liquor laws were biologically criminal? When liquor was legalized, did these people become biologically noncriminal?

Biogenic Theories

The **biogenic** theories, while having their roots in Lombrosian positivism, took several different directions. Some of the theories followed the general idea that certain physical types were more likely to commit crime than other types. One twentieth century advocate of the physical type school of criminality was Ernest A. Hooton. In his major work, *The American Criminal: An Anthropological Study,* Hooton concluded not only that certain physical types were characteristic of criminal populations, but also that offender types could be distinguished by their unique characteristics. After reexamining Goring's criticisms of Lombroso, Hooton decided that Goring's methodology was also faulty, and he set out to revive Lombroso's theory. Conducting a well-funded study, Hooton collected data on 17,076 criminals and noncriminals and concluded,

> Certain theoretical conclusions are, however, of no little importance. Criminals are organically inferior. Crime is the resultant of the impact of environment upon low grade human organisms. It follows that the elimination of crime can be effected only by the extirpation of the physically, mentally,

and morally unfit; or by their complete segregation in a socially aseptic environment.[5]

On a more specific level, Hooton found several characteristics he concluded were evidence of physical defects and typical of criminals. The following is a partial list of Hooton's findings:[6]

1. Tall, thin men tend to be murderers and robbers.
2. Tall, heavy men are killers and commit fraud and forgery.
3. Short, small men are thieves and burglars, but short, heavy men commit assault and sex crimes.
4. Men of mediocre physique commit a general variety of crimes.
5. Tattooing is more common among criminals than noncriminals.
6. Criminals are more likely to have the following characteristics:
   a. thin lips
   b. low and sloping foreheads
   c. thin necks
   d. sloping shoulders
   e. ear protrusion

Like Lombroso, Hooton's work was criticized on several points: 1) his sample of criminals was hardly representative since he used only a prison population, and we know that many criminals exist outside of penitentiaries; 2) his control group was not a random sample of noncriminals but rather a "convenience" sample of groups willing to be measured; 3) he disregarded many differences as great and even greater within the groups he measured; 4) he gathered no evidence that physical inferiority is inherited even though he claimed it to be true; and 5) he ignored the variety of criminal offenses his criminal group had committed in the past when describing specific criminal types, and all the differences found, other than skinny necks and the presence of smaller than average helixes, were subject to numerous interpretations and "corrections."[7] As a result of the overall lack of significance of Hooton's study, despite the large data base, there was little enthusiasm in the criminological community to resurrect Lombrosian theory.

However, others did continue to search for the causes of crime in heredity. Probably the most important are the works of Ernst Kretschmer and William H. Sheldon. The typologies set up by these two criminologists were more sophisticated than Hooton's, but they made essentially the same assumption that the host of crime was to be found in physical constitution. Kretschmer's major work based his findings on 4,414 cases, but he went about setting up his typologies without any statistical references to his data base![8] Included in his conclusions are that *athletic* types are more often involved in violent crimes and the *asthetic* are more likely to be petty thieves and con men. Like Hooton's work, though, the methodology was so poor that very few criminologists took Kretschmer's work seriously.

Sheldon's studies were more sophisticated than Kretschmer's. He assumed that the cause of crime originates in the human embryo and then develops into one of the three major types: 1) **endomorphic**, 2) **mesomorphic**; and 3) **ectomorphic**. The endomorphic is a "soft" type, extroverted and luxury-loving; the mesomorph type is an active, aggressive and dynamic person; and the ectomorphic is introverted, habitually tired and overly sensitive to noise and distractions.[9] Using a scale from 1 to 7, Sheldon used his typology to rank incarcerated delinquent youths as being predominately one of three types, but as Vold notes, his writing shows a certain lack of methodological objectivity. Consider the following example of one of Sheldon's conclusions:

> Thus, one of his cases, an extreme-mesomorph athlete, "a really healthy looking tomcat," whose excessive sexuality resulted in numerous cases of "trouble," is not judged delinquent at all, rather the opposite, because "he seemed to transmit a fairly good physical stock."[10]

The next major group of theorists who looked for constitutional inferiority to explain crime are those who examined IQ (intelligence quotient) scores. This group, including Healy, attempted to use mental tests to determine if criminals were of lower intelligence than noncriminals. This move is one from physical differences to mental ones, but there was still a belief that the mental differences were due to hereditary deficiencies. These researchers simply used "intelligence" tests instead of calipers for their measurements.

The mental testers began comparing prisoners' IQ scores with the average score (100) of the general population. The results, at first, revealed a relationship between low intelligence and criminality. For example, Goddard found that 70 percent of the prisoners were diagnosed as feebleminded—having slightly over 30 percent of IQ scores below 75.[11] However, based on IQ scores, World War I army draftees were feebleminded and almost half were borderline feebleminded with a mental age below 13.[12] This finding led to some questions as to what IQ scores were measuring and the validity of using the score of 75 as the upper limit of feeblemindedness. Further comparisons of prisoners and nonprisoners by Vold found no significant differences between the World War I draftees' scores and those of prisoners, and Murchison actually found that criminals scored higher on intelligence tests than did the draftee population.[13] As a result, the overall concept of feeblemindedness was dropped as an explanation of criminality. Further on in this chapter, we will see a modern revival of the use of IQ scores to explain delinquency. It is important to remember that the early mental testers believed intelligence and feeblemindedness to be a result of inherited biogenic factors.

Even though there has been little evidence that biogenic theories are appropriate for the general explanation of crime, these theories are still seen as possible contributing conditions to crime.

The most recent biogenic theories have focused on chromosome arrangement. A flurry of activity concerning biogenic causation of crime occurred when it was found that a number of male prison inmates had an extra Y chromosome. The normal pattern is XX for females and XY for males. The extra Y chromosome (**XYY**), it was argued, caused the men to be more violent and likely to commit crimes. The XYY males tended to be taller and less intelligent than the XY males, and this combination was seen to contribute to the tendency to employ violence as a means of conflict resolution.[14] For example, Richard Speck, the Chicago mass murderer was claimed (by his attorney) to have the XYY chromosome pattern (Speck did not). However, when researchers examined the criminal backgrounds of XYY prisoners, it was quickly found that they were more likely to have been convicted and imprisoned for property crimes. It was further found that the XYY group was less likely to be aggressive and violent among the inmate population.[15]

While only about 3 percent of all offenders have an extra Y chromosome, its presence has not been dismissed as a random oddity, and researchers are still trying to find a connection between this phenomenon and crime. One explanation suggested that given the lower intelligence and large body size of the XYY offenders, they are simply more likely to be caught for crimes than the smaller, more intelligent XY males. Thus, while not more likely to be engaged in crime, they are more likely to become prison inmates. So instead of being a cause of criminality, the extra Y chromosone only increases the chances of capture.[16]

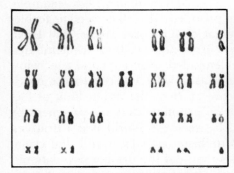 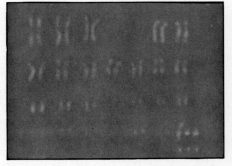

Modern biogenic theories hold that abnormal chromosome patterns cause crimes, such as the XYY chromosome pattern among males (right). However, not only does the chromosome theory run afoul of the same problems of other biogenic theories, it is supported by very weak evidence.

Overall, biogenic theories have not provided much hope for understanding crime. In part, this is due to the different directions and patterns of crime and the hypothesized connection between biology and crime. Since a physical disorder may make a person do any number of things, including criminal acts, it must be shown how a particular disease or biogenic abnormality leads to a specific criminal act. It was hypothesized, as we saw above, that an extra Y chromosome would lead to a greater violence, but the XYY inmates were found to be less violent. A more important problem in biogenic theory is in attempting to use a biological explanation for an essentially social phenomenon. Norms, organizations, value systems, and roles are social creations, and humans of the *same* biological makeup all have different content in their social institutions. Therefore, it would be very surprising to find that a biogenic source would explain all but a little crime.

As a final note on biogenic theories, it should be pointed out that these views equating biological deformity with moral deformity tend to develop stereotypes that are quite harmful. People with misshapen bodies due to birth defects, disease, accidents, and war face numerous obstacles in social life. Biogenic theories unintentionally heap further abuse on those with handicaps in supporting stereotypes that characterize these people as "madmen," "monsters," "fiends," and generally evil. The hunchback, bulging-eyed, drooling mouths and scarred sneer are seen to be "scary," for they fit the model that suggests something inside is as twisted as what can be seen outside. Britain's "Elephant Man," whose rare birth defect caused him to have immense head and body deformity was presented as a monstrous freak in a circus sideshow for years before being rescued by a physician who "discovered" that the man was not an idiot, feeble-minded, or even dull—a contention that had to be *proven* against the stereotype that such a body must house a sick or criminal mind. Biogenic theories tend to feed upon and gain support from these harmful stereotypes.

Psychogenic Theories

Psychogenic explanations of crime are more diverse than the biogenic. Besides having different disciplines, such as psychiatry and psychology, psychology itself is divided into two major disciplines—behavioral and clinical. Psychiatry has its roots in medicine, but **psychoanalytic theory** and practice focus on nonbiogenic problems residing in the human subconscious. Clinical psychology has various theories dealing with cognitive and behavioral problems in individuals that lead to criminal behavior. However, given the scope of this book, we will not examine every psychogenic theory but, instead, we will review four general categories under which specific theories of this type might be subsumed: 1) psychoanalytic;

2) psychopathic; 3) personality; and 4) behavior modification. Our discussion will concentrate on how these approaches tend to view criminal behavior.

Psychoanalytic Approach

The psychoanalytic school of thought has its roots in the work of Sigmund Freud, even though Freud never wrote about crime. According to Freudian theory, and the many variations of it, disorders occur in an individual when unresolved traumas and experiences exist in a person's mind.[17] Since most unresolved traumas occur during early childhood, before a person has developed an adequate ego to deal with the problems or even the ability to understand the problems, much of the Freudian approach examines a person's relationship with his or her parents. A common complex to be resolved is what Freud called the "Oedipal complex," in which a man wishes to seduce his mother and kill his father. Such thoughts lead to guilt feelings and subconscious torment manifested in bizarre, irrational behavior.

In some cases, the behavior caused by these subconscious problems is displayed in depression, compulsive spending, or some other legal but abnormal behavior. At other times, the problems are vented in the form of criminal behavior. In those instances where crime is the outlet of the internal turmoil, psychoanalysis, the recalling and resolution of distant traumas, is employed to resolve the problems and thereby put an end to the criminal behavior.

One of the major problems with psychoanalytic theory is in testing its validity.[18] No matter what behavior is manifest, as long as it violates a norm, it can be characterized as being caused by deep-seated, unconscious problems in the psyche. One cannot reach down and pluck out such a problem and measure it, nor even prove there is such a problem. Only by demonstrating that psychoanalytic treatment works in reducing criminal behavior is it possible to provide even indirect proof. However, since there is no consistent evidence that such treatment does work, and psychoanalysts insist in cases of failure that the theory is still correct but either the treatment was incomplete or incorrectly applied, we find very little evidence of its validity. Further, as we saw with the biogenic theories, there is no known link between a particular type of subconscious problem and a specific kind of crime, nor does the theory explain why people with similar problems vent their anxieties in a variety of different ways, only some of which are criminal. Finally, we must assume on faith that frustrations, anxieties, and other pent-up feelings are associated with subconscious problems and not more immediate problems. Looking at patterns of violent crime the evidence suggests that lower-class males are likely to engage in such crimes consistently over time. There would have to be some kind of evidence that lower class males suffer a unique common pattern of early childhood experiences not afflicting lower-class females and non-lower-class males to validate psychoanalytic theory attempting to explain violent crimes, but no such evidence is known to have been gathered or even to exist.

Psychopathic Theory

The concept of **psychopath** refers to a personality type that does not have normal moral constraints.[19] Sometimes called a **sociopath,** the psychopathic personality somehow does not develop what we call, in laymen's terms, a conscience. As a result, the psychopath is not controlled by guilt feelings or feelings of responsibility, obligation to obey the law, or other moral norms of society. In other words, a psychopath does pretty much what he or she pleases without any qualms or internal constraints.

As a concept, the idea of a psychopath (or sociopath) does focus on a particular area of interest: socialized internal self-control, but in terms of explaining *patterns* of crime, the concept of psychopath does little more than rename the criminal.[20] On the one hand, we know that patterns of crime are grouped in terms of various socioeconomic categories, with the lower classes committing one kind of crime and the upper classes another. Likewise, cross-cultural comparisons show that different rates and patterns of crime exist in different societies. Among delinquent gangs, for example, there is a very clear morality concerning loyalty to one's gang and territory, and much of the intergang violence results from an adherence to that morality and accompanying conscience rather than any lack of conscience.[21]

A further problem with the concept is that there is little consensus as to its exact meaning or cause. One examination of the psychiatric literature, for example, found 202 terms used more or less synonomously with psychopath and/or sociopath.[22] Such multiple definitions of a concept render it so vague that it could mean almost anything.

However, the idea that people break the law because of lack of internal control is an important one to consider. Many of the criminological theories we will examine focus on groups of people who for one reason or another do not feel internal constraints against breaking the law. By and large, though, criminological theories show how these internal controls are social psychological in nature and selective. For example, a businessman may have very strong moral constraints against robbery and burglary (especially those who have been victims), but at the same time not think twice about cheating on his income tax. Such common multiple standards regarding the law do not suggest a wholly warped personality, and it is a pretty good bet that the businessman has friends who do the same thing and provide social support for such illegal behavior. Thus, rather than being an antisocial crime, as suggested by the concept of sociopath, in-

Wealthy criminal fugitive Robert Vesco was involved in alleged business crimes, but many other financiers considered his actions "business as usual." Therefore, rather than a "personality" problem, Vesco simply may have been acting in accordance with business norms.

come tax evasion is a very social one, and the same can be said about other kinds of crimes as well.

Another problem with this theoretical construct lies in the evidence that criminals do have moral standards and are criminally active only in certain situations. First, as Matza has pointed out, delinquent activities only occur when they can be "neutralized" or made to conform with some moral standard.[23] For example, even the most criminally active persons have been found to believe that it is wrong to steal. However, their own thievery is "neutralized" (or rationalized) as being excusable. A thief might argue, for instance, that since he only steals from large department stores, the losses are negligible and the store is probably engaged in something illegal itself (such as consumer fraud). So while it is wrong to steal from just anyone, it is not "really criminal" to steal from the wealthy and powerful. Were a person devoid of moral scruples, it would be unnecessary to even come up with excuses, for there would be nothing to excuse. Furthermore, given the selective situations of crime, if a person were a psychopath, there would be no pattern of crime, but rather a random and constant stream of it. However, from examining patterns of criminal behavior, we find it to be fairly rational, selective and situational. As Erikson rightly noted, even the most criminally involved person spends only a fraction of his/her time engaged in crime.[24]

Personality Theories

Personality theories are more concerned with empirical evidence than either the psychoanalytic or psychopathic explanations of crime. While the psychiatric explanations are long on theory and short on empirically tested or testable propositions, the personality theories are just the opposite. They tend to have *post hoc* theory that is heavily operationalized from the instruments they employ to gather data. Using the **IQ** test, the **MMPI** test (Minnesota Multiphasic Personality Inventory), and other psychometric instruments, the personality theorists first attempted to find differences between those identified as criminals (usually employing inmate populations) and a control population.[25] Since many of these studies found a consistently lower mean IQ among criminals than noncriminals, there has always been an interest in the meaning of this relationship. (It should be noted that these later IQ studies did not necessarily imply an inherent biogenic problem leading to lower IQ's and crime. Our discussion of them here with the personality studies treats IQ as a facet of an individual's background, since both personality studies and IQ studies used psychometric measures; however, they are not the same thing.)

Since IQ tests purport to measure intelligence, it has been argued that low intelligence is related to crime. People who are not too bright, the argument implies, turn to crime in order to cope with life. Counter-arguments pointing out that IQ tests discriminate against minority groups and lower socioeconomic classes have attempted to show that IQ tests are culturally biased. That is, they are a measure of white middle-class intelligence, and not intelligence in general. However, in controlling for race, ethnic background, and class, intelligence, as measured by IQ tests, still showed an impressive inverse correlation to crime: those with lower IQs had higher crime rates.[26] (These tests were conducted by more sophisticated researchers than the earlier studies that found mixed results when comparing inmate populations with World War I draftees.) Thus, nonminorities from higher socioeconomic classes were more likely to commit crimes if they had lower IQ scores than minorities from lower socioeconomic classes with higher IQ scores. This relationship is less prominent when using self-report surveys instead of official records or inmate populations to measure criminal and delinquent involvement, but it still holds. The problem is in finding the nature of the relationship, understanding why this relationship emerges.

One answer has been that low intelligence causes crime, due to the effect of intelligence on the ability to compete effectively in legitimate pursuits. There have been other kinds of speculation as well. One explanation is that IQ tests measure one's accumulated knowledge as generated in educational institutions.[27] To the extent one is motivated to learn, he or she will score higher on IQ tests. The better the educational facilities, teaching programs, and related resources, the more a student will learn, excel in school, and do well on IQ tests. Thus, rather than being a measure of inherited intelligence, IQ scores measure the degree to which a person can accumulate institutional knowledge.

Aside from the findings of IQ tests showing what can be interpreted as being the degree to which an individual has been successfully socialized in the educational institutions, other tests have run afoul of some of the same problems that plagued the theories of psychopaths. First, in an examination of personality studies, Schuessler and Cressey found most of the studies to be flawed methodologically, and there was no single personality trait that differentiated criminals from noncriminals.[28] In cases where IQ tests were combined with personality measures, even if the IQ tests measured intelligence by some criterion, they did not distinguish between the personalities of those who had a high or low IQ. Secondly, in the studies differentiating between criminals and noncriminals, either using self-report surveys or official records, there is little that has been done on upperworld crime.[29] It may be true that robberies and burglaries along with other common crimes are committed by people with lower IQ scores, but as we will see in Chapters 11, 12, and 13, there are certain crimes that require more intelligence than other crimes, regardless of how one measures it. For example, those who commit "computer crimes" involving the transfer of funds from banks to their own accounts are dealing with extremely sophisticated computer programs and only those with markedly above average intelligence can even begin to understand the complexity involved in breaching that security. Likewise, the organization of illegal cartels, organized crime, and other highly profitable crime takes something more than someone who scores low on IQ tests. Finally, there are a good number of common criminals with uncommonly high IQ scores. For example, Gary Gilmore, who was executed in Utah in 1977 for homicides that occurred during two petty robberies he committed, was reported to have an IQ of 167.[30] By the same token, the majority of those with low IQ scores do not turn to crime. That is, low IQ scores do not cause crime, nor do high IQ scores prevent crime. The fact that IQ scores can vary from test to test and over time further suggests that IQs are not a function of some basic personality or innate intelligence but rather are from the social milieu that makes up education and learning.

Behavior Modification

The final individualistic theory we will examine is based on the behavioralist psychology of B. F. Skinner and his followers.[31] This approach to crime is one that examines only the overt behavior and the various stimuli that either encourage or discourage it. Behavioralism contends that such concepts as "self" and "personality" along with other theories that purport to know what goes on inside a person are of little value, since all that really matters is the observable behavior that can be measured. Thus, crime is studied in terms of what will and will not remove criminal behavior.

The basic model behind this theory is that human organisms avoid unpleasant stimuli and pursue pleasant stimuli. Behavior that is rewarded will be pursued while behavior resulting in pain will be avoided. By controlling the rewards and punishment, it is possible to change behavior in the desired direction. However, the behavioralists do not simply advocate punishment for criminal behavior. As Skinner notes,

> Punishment is designed to remove awkward, dangerous, or otherwise unwanted behavior from a repertoire on the assumption that a person who has been punished is less likely to behave in the same way again. Unfortunately, the matter is not that simple. Reward and punishment do not differ merely in the direction of the changes they induce . . . a man who has been imprisoned for violent assault is not necessarily less inclined toward violence. Punished behavior is likely to reappear after the punitive contingencies are withdrawn.[32]

There are several ways the behavioralists see that punishment will fail, and so unless there is a carefully planned program where "aversion therapy" is interwoven with rewards, it is not possible to remove criminal behavior patterns in individuals.

Even if we accept the premises of behavioralism, which many social scientists do not, there are numerous problems with the theory. Behaviorists are primarily interested in results—observable behavior. By ignoring everything but the actual behavior, it is believed that a better understanding of human behavior is possible. However, since there are so many elements that make up the stimuli of social life, from physical to cultural, its application seems to flounder on the ignored elements over which it has no control.

SUMMARY

This chapter has examined approaches to the study of crime that focus on the causes of individual criminality. The early approaches were refinements of Lombroso's biogenic theory, except rather than using the concept of "atavism," the modern biogenic theorists focused on different components of the human physiology—from heredity-based intelligence to chromosome arrangement. The greatest problem with this approach, in addition to its inability to isolate and prove any biogenic source of crime, was failure to account for the social and cultural relativity of crime and the changing nature of what was defined as crime. This problem is a considerable one given the relatively slow changes in human physiology by comparison to changes in the criminal law.

A second major approach to the study of individual criminality were psychopathic and personality theories. Besides having considerable difficulty in arriving at some kind of consensus as to the definitions of the various categories, there were conflicting findings and interpretations of the findings. The most promising recent findings showing a relationship between low IQ and crime have been subject to several different interpretations, including social control theories dealing with nonindividualistic criminal patterns. However, there has been very weak evidence linking either personality types or psychopathic categories and intelligence—except those that are defined by low intelligence.

A final major individualistic approach to crime is behavioral modification. Having its roots in experimental behavioralistic psychology, this approach has been adopted by many institutions for changing criminal and delinquent behavior. Like other individualistic theories dealing with crime, it ignores the large social and legal issues in favor of focusing directly on the behavior in question. However, in spite of its practical approach to criminal behavior, it has failed in most institutional applications for the very aspects it ignores—the social milieu of crime.

While many of the individualistic approaches to crime have been criticized in this chapter, there is an important need to consider these theoretical approaches. Not only is it possible to change criminal patterns by changing the individuals involved in them, but not all criminality can be explained by general patterns of crime. For the unique criminal, the individualistic theories promise the chance of dealing with criminal behavior outside the typical criminal pattern.

Glossary

Biogenic Explanations of crime that examine biological sources as the major cause.

Ectomorphic A biogenic category referring to a person who is introverted, habitually tired, and overly sensitive to noise.

Endomorphic A biogenic category referring to a person who is soft, extroverted, and loves luxuries.

IQ Test A test used to measure intelligence on the basis of an "intelligence quotient," comparing mental age with physical age.

Mesomorphic A biogenic category for an active, aggressive, and dynamic person.

MMPI Test A personality test, Minnesota Multiphasic Personality Inventory.

Personality Theory Theories of crime that look for the primary cause of crime in individualistic personality makeup.

Psychoanalytic Theory A form of theory and analysis that examines causes of crime in unresolved conflicts in the individual psyche.

Psychogenic General theories that attempt to explain crime in terms of psychological and psychiatric causes.

Psychopath A person who has not developed a "conscience"; (see also **Sociopath**).

Reductionist An approach to the study of crime that seeks to find causes by reducing the analysis to the lowest possible level.

Sociopath See **Psychopath**.

XYY Chromosomes A chromosome pattern found in some convicted male criminals. Normal chromosome patterns for males is XY, and the finding of the extra Y chromosome led some to suggest that it may be responsible for criminality.

Questions

1. What are the basic assumptions made by the "individualistic" theories of crime that are essentially different from the "social" theories?

2. What kinds of assumptions about the law and nature of humans are implicit in biogenic theories of crime?

3. How did the psychoanalytic theories see the crime problem to be solved?

4. What were the problems in defining criminal behavior in the psychopathic theories of crime?

5. What are the main methods used in personality theories to test their assumptions?

Notes

1. Sawyer Sylvester, Jr., *The Heritage of Modern Criminology*. (Cambridge, MA: Schenkman, 1972).

2. William Healy, *The Individual Delinquent*. (Boston: Little, Brown and Company, 1915), p. 1.

3. Healy, 1915, 3.

4. Healy, 1915, 6.

5. Ernest A. Hooton, *The American Criminal: An Anthropological Study*. (Cambridge: Harvard University Press, 1939), p. 309.

6. Ernest A. Hooton, *Crime and the Man.* (Cambridge: Harvard University Press, 1931), pp. 301–306; 376–378.

7. George B. Vold, *Theoretical Criminology.* (New York: Oxford University Press, 1958), pp. 63–65.

8. Vold, 1958, 68; see also Ernst Kretschmer, *Korperbau und Charakter.* 21/22 Auflage, Springer Verlag, Berlin, Gottinger and Heidelberg (1955).

9. William Sheldon, *Varieties of Delinquent Youth* (New York: Harper & Row, 1949).

10. Vold, 1958, 72–73.

11. H. H. Goddard, *Feeblemindedness: Its Causes and Consequences* (New York: Macmillan, 1914), p. 569.

12. L. D. Zeleny, "Feeblemindedness and Criminal Conduct," *American Journal of Sociology* **38** (January, 1933): 569.

13. Vold, p. 85; see also Carl Murchinson, *Criminal Intelligence* (Worcester, MA: Clark University Press, 1926).

14. W. H. Price and P. B. Whatmore, "Criminal Behavior and the XYY Male," *Nature* (February 1967): 388–395.

15. Theodore R. Sarbin and Jerremy E. Miller, "Demonism Revisited: The XYY Chromosomal Anomaly," *Issues in Criminology* **5** (1970): 195–205.

16. National Institute of Mental Health, *Report on the XYY Chromosomal Abnormality.* (Washington, D.C.: U.S. Government Printing Office, 1970).

17. See Sigmund Freud, *The Ego and the Id.* (London: Hogarth Press, 1970).

18. Don C. Gibbons, *Delinquent Behavior,* 2nd ed. (Englewood Cliffs, NJ: Prentice-Hall, 1976).

19. See Leonard P. Ullman and Leonard Krasner, *A Psychological Approach to Abnormal Behavior.* (Englewood Cliffs, NJ: Prentice-Hall, 1969).

20. W. Preu, "The Concept of Psychopathic Personality," in J. McHunt, ed., *Personality and the Behavior Disorders.* (New York: Ronald Press, 1944), Vol. 2., pp. 922–937.

21. See for example, R. Lincoln Keiser, *The Vice Lords: Warriors of the Streets.* (New York: Holt, Rinehart and Winston, 1969).

22. Hulsey Carson, "The Psychopath and the Psychopathic," *Journal of Criminal Psychopathology* **4** (1943): 522–527.

23. David Matza, *Delinquency and Drift.* (New York: Wiley, 1964), p. 67.

24. Kai Erickson, "Notes on the Sociology of Deviance," *Social Problems* **9** (Spring 1962): 307–314.

25. Vold, 1958, 78–88.

26. Travis Hirschi and Michael J. Hindelang, "Intelligence and Delinquency: A Revisionist Review," *American Sociological Review* **43** (August 1977): 571–587.

27. Ibid.

28. Karl F. Schuessler and Donald R. Cressey, "Personality Characteristics of Criminals," *American Journal of Sociology* **55** (1950): 476–484.

29. John Conklin, *Criminology.* (New York: Macmillan, 1981), p. 158.

30. Norman Mailer, *The Executioner's Song.* (New York: Warner, 1979).

31. B. F. Skinner, *Beyond Freedom and Dignity.* (New York: Knopf, 1971).

32. Skinner, 1971, 57–58.

5

Crime and the Social Structure

What to Look For:

The basic concepts of structuralism.

How Merton explained the role of social norms and cultural values in determining crime patterns.

How Cohen and Cloward and Ohlin developed subcultural explanations linked to the social structure.

The conception of social structure and crime held by neo-Marxist criminologists.

The limitations in structural explanations.

Introduction

THE MAJOR CRIMINOLOGICAL theories in sociology have, mainly, sought to explain variation in crime rates by examining the individual's place in the social structure. In order to fully appreciate how social structure plays a role in determining crime patterns, it is necessary first to review basic concepts and models of society. Also, some readers might be surprised to find a discussion of Marxist theory in this section since it is sometimes classified as a "radical" or "new" form of criminology. In certain respects this is true, but at the heart of Marxist theory is a core of structuralism, and it can be examined just like any other structural explanation of crime.

Overview of Structural Concepts

Probably the best way to think about structure in society is to compare it to engineering structures. Imagine a bridge across a river and the different designs that bridge might have. Keep in mind that we have a limited amount of materials to work with. In the same way, different societies present us with different structures. We can define **social structure** basically as the organization of a society's social relationships and group interactions. Thus, we have to examine institutions, roles, social classes, and distribution of wealth and power. Some societies are highly democratic in structure, in that power is distributed fairly evenly, while in other societies power is concentrated among a few. Likewise, some societies are open and mobile, while others are closed and immobile. These factors depend on the **social institutions**—a society's patterned ways of dealing with recurrent problems and life in general. For instance, despite efforts by the government to democratize social institutions, India still maintains a very strong caste system. Under the caste system, people are born into their station in life. If one is born at the bottom—an "untouchable"—that person is avoided by everyone except those in the same caste and few chances for upward mobility exist. Clearly, by a glance at a society that differs from our own we can see that social structures and the mobility they allow citizens vary tremendously.

Social Structure and Crime

Usually when we think of criminals, we see them as individuals who somehow went bad. Maybe we think they had an unhappy childhood or they are just plain mean, but we tend to rush some kind of individualistic explanation—in part because as Americans we have a highly developed sense of individualism. As we saw in Chapter 4, there are several theories that reflect this attitude. On a larger scale, though, when we look at patterns of crime, we find that there are certain trends. As we saw in previous chapters, there are a lot more men involved in violent crimes than women, but it is doubtful that men are more likely to have unhappy childhoods than are women. Likewise, when we compare societies, we find that some societies have more or less crime than others and that during different time periods, crime will increase or decrease. In other words, as we back away from the individual, patterns will often appear. Under one structure we find little crime, and under another we find a great deal.

Crime in Society: Individual in Society

The extent to which we understand that societies have a greater or lesser amount of crime helps us to begin to appreciate the idea that certain social forces generate crime. The question then becomes, "What forces generate high or low crime rates and particular types of crime?" For the structural theorist, the answer lies, not surprisingly, in the different social structures found in different societies. To visualize how structures work consider the typical organization diagrammed in Fig. 5.1.

On the bottom level there are several positions, and as we go up the ladder, these become fewer and fewer. If we randomly dropped people into the different positions, everyone would have an equal chance of getting each position.

However, people are not randomly dropped into positions, but rather they work their way into them in one manner or another—or at least that is what we like to believe. Let us suppose that a group of "clones" were all striving to be the president of our organization. All of the clones worked

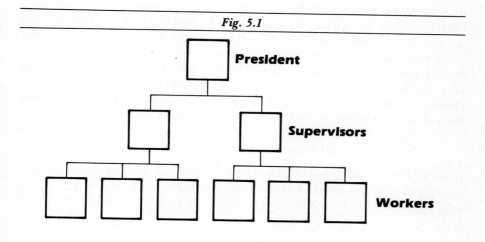

Fig. 5.1

President

Supervisors

Workers

Fig. 5.2

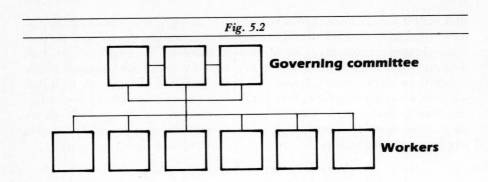

equally hard, had the same intelligence and were identical in every other way. Success will be defined in terms of reaching the top position. Now we cannot say that the clone who made it to the top was any smarter, harder working or industrious than the others since they were all exactly alike, but that is not the point. Rather, because of the structure in which the clones are operating, only one can reach the pinnacle.

Consider the different organizational structure illustrated in Fig. 5.2. In this organizational structure, many more can make it to the top and therefore the result of sending the clones into this organization will be different from the outcome in the typical organization we examined previously.

Looking at one's position in the structure as "winning" and "losing," we see far more "losers" in the first structure than in the second. Since we were using clones in our examples, we again can see that the difference between being a winner or loser is not the result of any personality characteristic, evil tendency or inferior genetic make-up. At this point we can begin to understand how social structure, regardless of the individuals in that structure, can determine what will happen to people. So far we have only scratched the surface of structural determinism, and in the theories we will be discussing we will substitute "criminals" for "losers" (in the sense that they are not winning in the legitimate structure), and examine overall societal opportunities to win or lose within a given system. However, the key idea to remember is that the theorists being discussed in this chapter examine the social forces surrounding the individual rather than the person himself or herself as the primary causal variable.

Social Structure and Anomie: Merton

Robert Merton's adapation of Durkheim's theory of **anomie** made a major contribution to the study of crime.[1] Merton began with the concept of anomie or "the state of normlessness." That is, people in society were uncertain what was expected of them and how they should behave. This was not an individual problem but rather a social one.

In American society, Merton saw anomie resulting from an overemphasis on *goals* at the expense of *means*. Since every society in an hypothetical state of "balance" has equal stress on the cultural goals and societal means to achieve those goals, whenever there is an emphasis on one at the expense of the other, there is an imbalance. In addition, the cultural goals in American society were such that they were ultimately unachieva-

The popular television series "Dallas" depicts those who have "won the game" in the pursuit of wealth. Both the characters of J. R. Ewing and his wife, Sue Ellen, are portrayed as ruthless in their pursuit of the goals with little emphasis on the means.

ble, and only a relatively small proportion of society could even appear to be truly successful.

To see how Merton viewed anomie, let's consider goals in American society. The dominant goal is financial wealth.[2] To be sure, there are other non-materialistic goals such as finding happiness in interpersonal relationships. Neverthelsss, financial success remains the most prominent goal. For instance, while a girl's parents may stress "love" in the choice of a husband, the first thing a prospective choice will be asked by her parents is what he does for a living and similar queries regarding his wealth. Even in raising a family, there is a great deal of stress placed on providing materialistic comforts.

Not only is there a great deal of emphasis on wealth, but there is also a vague conception of wealth. If we make a million dollars, we might be wealthy relative to where we were before, but we would then see that there are a lot of people with two or three million or more. There is no "stop sign" in society that says, "Okay, you've reached your monetary goal, you can stop." Thus, while we can look backwards and see progress relative to where we once were, if we look *ahead,* we cannot see ourselves any closer to an ultimate goal than when we began. This state of affairs in society is an anomic one.

Adaptations to Anomie

In Durkheim's study of anomie, he focused on a single adaptation—suicide—but Merton saw several different adaptations.[3] To examine the possible ways in which people could adjust to anomie, Merton separated the cultural goals and societal means of achieving these goals. The "goals" were those socially defined objectives people were to pursue and the "means" were the guidelines or rules they were to follow in their pursuit of the goals. By combining the logical combinations of accepting or rejecting goals and means, Merton developed the typology of adaptations shown in Table 5.1.

Table 5.1 Adaptations to Anomie		
	Goals	**Means**
Conformist	+	+
Innovator	+	−
Ritualist	−	+
Retreatist	−	−
Rebel	− (+)	− (+)

Conformist

The first adaptation to anomie, conformist, represents those individuals who accept the legitimate methods society provides for acquiring goals. For example, someone who went to college (an acceptable means) in order to obtain the education and degree necessary for a high-paying job (cultural goal) would be a conformist. A man or woman who became a business executive, doctor or lawyer after college would fit into the conformist mode, assuming they did not cheat or steal to obtain their position. For women, it would be an acceptable conformist adaptation to marry a conformist without striving directly for wealth herself, only indirectly through her husband.

Innovator

The second adaptation involves the pursuit of the goal while ignoring the means. The innovator is either denied access to legitimate means or is so obsessed with obtaining the goals that he or she uses illegitimate means to obtain the ends. This is an important adaptation to understand since illegitimate means represents criminal behavior. For example, a bank robber pursues an approved societal goal (money) but uses an illegitimate means (robbery).

For the most part Merton's innovators were seen to be the poor who were denied success through legitimate channels because of structural blockages. They started the race to success from far in the back, and by the time they neared the goals through legitimate channels, all of the positions were filled. However, there was still emphasis on success, and so illegitimate routes were taken. In this way, Merton explained the over-representation of the poor in the crime statistics.

Ritualist

A third adaptation appears to be wholly illogical in light of the fact that society is presumed to stress success over the ways in which that success is to be achieved. In a society where Vince Lombardi's pronouncement, "Winning isn't everything. It's the only thing!" is a cultural maxium, why would anyone want to reject the ends but embrace the means? That would be like playing the game by the rules but not trying to win!

There are different versions of the ritualist in society, but perhaps the most common and sensible is the one who is desperately trying to hold on to what he or she has. These are individuals who hold glamorless, dead-end jobs, but at the same time those jobs are sustaining and safe. While there is a great emphasis on success, there is an equal terror of total failure. Not only is there the financial deprivation of failure, there is also the social stigma attached to it. The old Puritan belief that failure represented being out of favor with God lingers in social evaluations, and total failure is akin to damnation.[4] Seeing the limited chances of achieving "real success," the ritualist finds a niche in society that guarantees security and perhaps modest advancement. Of course, the ritualist is not a criminal; that would be far too risky. By not taking any chances—legitimate or illegitimate—the ritualist avoids total failure.

Retreatist

The fourth adaptation discussed by Merton involves those who drop out of the game altogether. They do not pursue the culturally prescribed goals nor do they follow the rules. A skid row bum who spends his life drinking and involved in petty crime is a prime example of the retreatist. Retreatists are not interested in "making it," and they do not worry about "losing." They simply are not playing the same game.

One kind of retreatist is the "double loser." This person may have started out attempting to achieve goals through legitimate channels and failed. He then tried an illegitimate route, but failed there too, and finally gave up and dropped out. For example, one criminal record (or "rap sheet") seen by the author contained a single conviction for armed robbery ("innovation") and then a series of arrests for public drunkenness ("retreatism"). The money could not be obtained through either legitimate or illegitimate means, or even if it could it may not have been worth the cost, and so the goals along with the means are rejected.

Rebel

The final adaptation is one that is a difficult category to define, as Merton actually gave it little attention. The rebel is attempting to change society; that is, he or she rejects the conventional goal of society and, as well, the means of achieving that goal. Instead, they desire to pursue a new set of goals and means.

Structural Conditions and Adaptations

In order to see the important features of Merton's work, it is necessary to understand the relationship between the specific adaptations and the social structure. Examining these different adaptations to anomie, we alluded to some of the structural relationships inherent in this model. However, by seeing them all together, it is possible to get a better idea of how Merton's theory worked. Fig. 5.3 shows the adaptations in their structural context. The "Rebel" is not represented here since he/she builds a different structure.

Fig. 5.3 looks like an old-fashioned gas pump. If the bubble in the pump is taken to be the available number of "success" positions in society

Fig. 5.3

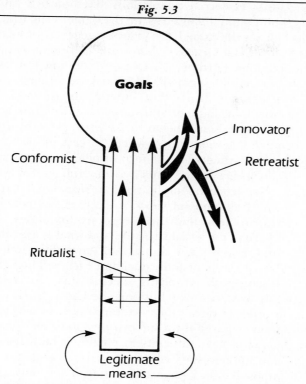

Source: Donald R. Cressey used a diagram similar to this in his course on sociological criminology at the University of California, Santa Barbara.

and the neck of the pump to be the parameters of the "legitimate means," we can see there is only so much room for a *conformist* adaptation. As the legitimate means become blocked, some participants leave the neck (and legitimate means) taking the *innovator's* route. Others, seeing the limited access to success goals, cling to what they have within the boundaries of the legitimate means, embracing them in a *ritualist* adaptation. Some who attempted the illegitimate means and failed, resort to a *retreatist* adaptation; they not only gave up on the means, but also on the goals. Finally, the *rebel*, who is not shown, rejects the entire structure and replaces it with an alternative one.

Structure and Criminal Subcultures: Albert Cohen

To some extent Merton's model of criminal and non-criminal adaptations to the social structure shows the adaptations of groups rather than individuals. It was the work of Albert Cohen that clearly showed how the social structure leads to **collective adaptations** taken on by a large number of individuals who found themselves in the same structural situation.[5] That is, while Merton developed the logical categories of adaptations to cultural goals and societal means, Cohen explained how such adaptations were group adaptations. Further, Cohen explained how the "tradition" of crime originates in certain segments of society beginning with criminal adaptations to a common frustrating situation in the social structure. Cohen showed how a delinquent subculture was fostered by the social structure, giving rise to criminal behavior patterns, patterns that were not randomly distributed in society, but "owned" by certain groups.[6]

Cohen argued that virtually any pattern of behavior is a form of problem-solving.[7] Problems are solved from a given "frame of reference," and more importantly for structural implications, a "situation." A frame of reference is made up of all kinds of views, prejudices and beliefs, affecting how one perceives problems and their solutions. Situations, though, determine where we are in the social structure and what is available for dealing with problems. Obviously, the situation of the wealthy individual is far different from that of the poor individual and each will be provided, as a result, with different problem-solving mechanisms. For example, if a wealthy man wants to start a new business, he has a variety of resources at his disposal in order to do so; the necessary financial backing, contacts, and the information required for a successful transaction. The poor man, on the other hand, will have difficulty in obtaining both the required financial means, and the necessary contacts to ensure a success. This is not to say that it is impossible for a poor man to start a new business and prosper in it, but it is simply more difficult, and compared to the rich man, it entails a greater chance of failure. This has nothing to do with either's frame of reference, personalities or intelligence—it is simply a matter of their different situations via the social structure.

In American society, the general solution to success is bound up in proverbs of "hard work, persistence, and prudent financial dealing" and a democratic ideology that "anyone who sticks with it"—no matter what their starting position—can ultimately make it. Examples of men and women of modest backgrounds who became millionaires are regularly paraded before us as evidence of what hard work can achieve. Colonel Sanders and his fried chicken empire were said to have been launched on his first welfare check, and a poor black reaped millions by marketing his "Famous Amos" chocolate chip cookies. However, a more common theme and experience among the lower class is not collective success, but rather collective failure. To the extent that the problem of failure is seen as a common one, then the solution to resolve the problem can be collective. The collective response is the beginning of a new subculture or collective manner of viewing and dealing with certain features of the world in a way different from the rest of society.

For Cohen, the subcultures did not emerge from nowhere and for no apparent reason. They occurred in certain parts of society as problem-solving mechanisms. Cohen stated,

> The crucial condition for the emergence of new cultural forms is the existence, *in effective interaction with one another, of a number of actors with similar problems of adjustment.*[8]

This idea suggests that crime is not evenly distributed in society, resulting from individualistic quirks and unfortunate family upbringing. Cohen saw the social milieu, not the family or individualistic happenstance, as the stage for criminality.

The key problem for the lower and working class youth was a status problem—the problem of achieving status in the eyes of one's fellows.[9] One solution to the status problem is the formation of a **delinquent subculture**. The subculture replaced status criteria which the youths could not meet with ones they could. If the youths who sought status could not meet the larger societal criteria by having cars, high grades in school and other success marks, they would create status symbols in the form of toughness and manliness that could be met by personal efforts well within the range of their abilities. Further, Cohen recognized that sex roles played an important part in the criteria. In the early 1950s, at the time Cohen was writing his theories, women had a different set of criteria for success in society; to be successful meant to be feminine in the passive, traditional sense.[10] Therefore, in his explanation of the structural elements that led to the formation of a delinquent subculture, Cohen allowed for the different rates of male and female delinquency, but for the most part, male-female differences were not emphasized in the theory.

We can summarize Cohen's position in the following propositions:

1. Criteria for success goals are communicated to all levels of society.
2. Structural conditions determine the likelihood of achieving success goals.
3. In attempting to achieve success goals, those in the lower social strata are more likely to experience failure.
4. The experience of failure is collective insofar as there is interaction between those with the same problem.
5. Solutions to the problem are delinquent or criminal to the extent that new criteria for success are in violation of the law.
6. Delinquent subcultures emerge as a result of collective delinquent solutions to problems of failure.
7. If the solutions can be achieved through conformity, then the delinquent solutions and their attending subcultures will not arise.

It is important to note that Cohen placed a good deal of emphasis on the fact that delinquent subcultures arise through structural conditions and predicted that if there was no structural necessity for delinquent subcultures, they would not develop; they can survive only so long as the structural disadvantages remain the same.

Opportunity Structures and Delinquent Subcultures: Cloward and Ohlin

Following the works of Merton and Cohen, Cloward and Ohlin attempted to explain how criminal subcultures developed.[11] Their work is distinguished by the fact that they not only show how delinquency is a collective adaptation, but also they explained how *different kinds of delinquent subcultures* developed based on the **opportunity structure** of the community. They saw the basis of delinquent subcultures as the inequitable opportunity structure for obtaining success goals. Those at the bottom of the structure had fewer economic opportunities to legitimately achieve success, and experiencing collective failure, turned to crime as a group solution.[12] Further, there were different criminal opportunities for those with limited access to legitimate success channels.

An important misconception of criminological theory pointed out by Cloward and Ohlin, echoing Cohen, was the idea that evil arose from evil and good from good. In much of the thinking by criminologists, there was the implicit assumption that something bad in society—an evil motive—led to criminal behavior.[13]

Differential Development of Subcultures

Perhaps the most important and unique contribution of Cloward and Ohlin was their explanation of how different forms of delinquent subcultures developed out of different community structures. For the two theorists, opportunity was a double-edged sword. On the one hand, there were greater or lesser opportunities to succeed legitimately in society, but there were also different opportunities to engage in criminal behavior.[14] While at first it may seem that criminal opportunities are limitless, upon closer examination, Cloward and Ohlin concluded that like legitimate opportunities, criminal ones were limited. Those with the least access to legitimate channels of achieving success goals and the most access to criminal ones were the most likely to engage in criminal behavior.

CRIMINAL SUBCULTURES   The first kind of subculture discussed by Cloward and Ohlin had its roots in an *organized* community structure characterized by relative *stability*. The idea that an organized and stable community structure would be the basis for any kind of criminality may seem strange since disorganization and instability are typically associated with

THE WALL STREET JOURNAL

"You can't plead not guilty by reason of
peer-group pressure."

Source: From *Wall Street Journal,* Permission—Cartoon Features Syndicate.

criminality. However, in such a community, the adult criminal element
can have stable and organized crime in the form of various rackets and
well developed systems of protection. In the poor slums, ghettos and bar-
rios, often the poverty is mistaken for disorganization and instability, but
on close examination we can find transgenerational ties, organization and
stability.

In situations where organized criminal activities are a part of a poor
community, the most visible evidence of success goals are "props" of the
various criminals. The racketeers, pimps, dope dealers and gamblers have
the expensive cars, clothes and jewelry. Further, the youths who enter
into the criminally organized enterprises may achieve more materialistic
success than those who either go off on their own in pursuit of criminal

careers or take employment in low paying jobs. Those who do take the legitimate route and are successful usually become *invisible* to the youth of the home community since they tend to move to other neighborhoods where their children will have greater legitimate opportunities and fewer illegitimate ones.

For the youth of the criminal subculture, then, there is a stable role model in the form of the successful adult criminal. Moreover, there are apprenticeship roles for youths who come into contact with the organized adult criminal activities through "fences" (buyers of stolen goods), positions as "runners" (in the numbers racket) and similar learning roles for the "good life" seen in criminal behavior systems. The juvenile gangs tend to fashion themselves along the lines of the adult criminal organizations with an emphasis on property crimes rather than gang violence. Thus, the juvenile groups are training units for the necessary skills of criminal organizations. It should be remembered, however, that socialization into criminal behavior patterns is in the direction of socially approved goals—accumulation of wealth—and not mindless criminal violence.[15]

CONFLICT SUBCULTURE   A very different kind of subculture develops in a disorganized, unstable, poor community. Without organization, the community is unable to provide both legitimate and illegitimate avenues to success. The poverty and instability combined generate a present-oriented perspective among the adults whose survival is measured in getting through one day at a time; there is no planning for their own or their children's future. Likewise, criminality is of a petty sort; it has a low probability of ever making any large amount of money and a high probability of eventually resulting in arrest. The unsophisticated con artist, petty thief, mugger, pickpocket and liquor store robber are examples of criminals found in the disorganized community. As individualistic and petty criminals, they offer little in the way of role models for success and virtually no process for systematically inducing the young into a stable and profitable organization.

Unlike the criminal subculture where cooperation is required for success in the adult rackets, in the conflict subculture, it is the individualistic attributes of toughness and personal achievement that are prized. Since there is no long range perspective of either legitimate or illegitimate means for achieving success goals, there are no perceived opportunities for achievement through either avenue. Being cut off from both the legal and criminal channels, the only dependable resource is one's own initiative. Demonstrating individualistic attributes of "worth" is in the manipulation of violence. Cloward and Ohlin state:

> The principal prerequisites for success are "guts" and the capacity to endure pain. One doesn't need "connections," "pull," or elaborate technical skills in order to achieve "rep." The essence of the warrior adjustment is an ex-

pressed feeling-state: "heart." The acquisition of status is not simply a consequence of skill in the use of violence or of physical strength but depends, rather, on one's willingness to risk injury or death in the search for "rep."[16]

The result of such a subculture is a high amount of violent crime, juvenile gang wars and continued instability. However, if opportunities, either legitimate or illegitimate, open up, Cloward and Ohlin hypothesized, the conflict subsides as success goals are pursued instead of fighting.

RETREATIST SUBCULTURE   The conflict subculture contained the seeds of its own destruction. Even in an anomic situation, the success goals of wealth were tangible and something to pursue, but the goals of individualistic toughness were narrow and seen even by the members of conflict subcultures as unproductive. Further, toughness was something that had to be continually reaffirmed, and the constant exposure to risk and danger took its toll.

On a more general level, even if we concede that there is enough status in the attainment of individualistic toughness to satisfy socially approved goal attainment (in the conflict subculture), there is a limit to the number of winners in that game. For one to achieve the goal of being the "baddest," someone else has to be the loser. In other words, to demonstrate toughness there must be someone weaker. Since Cloward and Ohlin were dealing with juvenile gangs as their main focal point, they saw collective defeat in the weaker gangs. Now, with both the legitimate and illegitimate channels of success blocked in the conflict subculture and the replacement goal of individual toughness blocked as well, the only way to turn was to retreatism. One form of retreatism, in this case, was drug use. Simply put, the boys who were "double losers" turned individually or collectively to drugs.[17]

At the time of Cloward's and Ohlin's work, drugs were primarily—in fact, almost exclusively—a lower class phenomenon. Further, research indicated that involvement in delinquency preceded drug use. In other words, instead of first becoming involved in drug use and then delinquency, the research indicated that youths were first involved in delinquency, and as a result of their delinquent associations became involved in drug use.[18] This sequence was consistent with that suggested by Cloward and Ohlin; after failing in illegitimate channels in delinquent activities, the double failures turned to drugs rather than first turning to drugs and then supporting the habit through crime.

Cloward and Ohlin rounded out the theoretical ideals begun by Merton and developed by Cohen. They were able to link the subcultural group adaptation to criminal behavior patterns through the opportunity structure in society. To the extent to which a behavior pattern was a group phenomenon, it could be seen as a subcultural pattern, passed on from one generation to the next, caught in the same structural situation. There is a clear link throughout their works between the subcultural and the social structure with the *structure* determining the *subculture*. But as we will see in the next section, the Marxist view of social structure and criminality takes not only a different view of the social structure itself, but also a different view of the relationship between crime and social structure.

Marxist Structuralism and Crime

Recently there has been a revival of Marxist criminology under the banner of "the new criminology," "radical criminology" and "critical criminology." Unlike their predecessors (e.g., Bonger, 1916), the new Marxists have redirected the focus of their explanations from those who break the criminal law to those who make the law in the context of a given social structure.[19] Thus, unlike Merton, Cohen, and Cloward and Ohlin, whose primary goal was to explain crime causation through an examination of criminal behavior patterns and the social structure, the Marxists shift the focus to an examination of the law itself to see how the structure determines what will be defined as criminal.

To understand the reason for the shift in focus from crime causation to crime "creation" in the form of law, it is necessary to examine the foundations of Marxist theory. First, the emphasis in Marxist thinking has always been on social stratification in terms of social class and power. In capitalist societies, the difference was dichotomized into the owners of the means of production and the workers—the two great classes of the **bourgeoisie** and **proletariat**. As capitalism developed, the working class (proletariat) would become larger and the owners of the means of production (bourgeoisie) smaller. Secondly, in the context of the capitalist system, Marxism saw a necessary conflict between the ruling and serving classes. Since the owners had a disproportionate amount of wealth and power, eventually the workers would want some kind of redistribution reflecting their numbers. Marx predicted that at some point in time the workers would band together and overthrow the capitalist system, but in the meantime the ruling capitalists would do everything possible to perpetuate their favored position in society.[20]

For the most part, communist revolutions did not follow the pattern predicted by Marx, but instead, capitalism was able to maintain itself despite the inequities of the system. To a large extent, the question addressed and answered by the new Marxist criminologists is how capitalism was able to sustain itself despite the fact that the bourgeoisie was relatively small and the proletariat relatively large. The answer to that question is that by controlling information (the mass media) the bourgeoisie manipulate the masses into a sense of "false consciousness," believing that the laws are a reflection of democratic institutions and are enforced in their own best interests.

The structuralism of Marx focused on the opposing classes created by capitalism. Since those with power made the criminal law, those without power were more likely to be defined as criminal.

Interest Structures and the Law

Marxist criminologists concentrate their examination of crime in the capitalist power structure. In part, they borrowed from non-Marxist scholars, such as Domhoff, who empirically demonstrated a concentration of wealth in the hands of a small elite in society.[21] By showing that a ruling elite did exist and exercised a disproportionate amount of power and influence, it was possible to argue that instead of a democratic (or pluralistic) power base in society, there existed a single one made up of members of the wealthy and privileged. Further, by controlling the major institutions, including the mass media, it was possible to present the façade of a democratic rule.

The next step was to develop and test propositions consistent with a refined version of Marxist theory stating the relationship between the power structure and making and applying the law. The purpose was to show that each social class had active vested interests that were incompatible and in conflict with one another due to their position relative to one another in the social structure. The elite's interest lay in maintaining the capitalist structure where they could continue to enjoy the privileges and powers of their inequitable wealth, while the interests of the non-elite, especially the lower and working classes, lay in redistributing power and wealth in a more democratic fashion. Given this situation, whatever one side gained was a loss to the other.

One of the most well known statements of the relationship between the capitalist social structure and the law came from Richard Quenney. It can be summarized in the following six propositions:

1. Crime is a legal definition of human conduct that is created by agents of the dominant class in a capitalist society.

2. Definitions of crime are compared to behavior that conflict with the class interests of the dominant economic class.

3. Definitions of crime are applied by the class that has the power to shape the enforcement and administration of criminal law.

4. Behavior patterns are structured in relation to definitions of crime, and within this context persons engage in actions that have relative probabilities of being defined as criminal.

5. Conceptions of crime are constructed and diffused in the course of communication.

6. The social reality of crime is constructed by the formulations and application of definitions of crime, the development of behavior patterns in relation to these definitions, and the construction of conceptions of crime.[22]

As these six propositions reveal, the emphasis is on the power to make and interpret laws rather than explain patterns of crime. However, there is an implicit explanation of the patterns of crime in the neo-Marxists' theories. Because the laws were hypothesized to be made by the elite and in the interest of the elite, there was a greater chance that the creation and application of the laws would be *against* the non-elite. Therefore, the poor would be disproportionately represented in criminal activity—not because they were blocked from attaining success goals as Merton argued but rather because those who had the power to define what was legal and illegal passed laws that discriminated against the non-elite. For example, the laws regulating corporations have relatively minor sanctions compared to the laws regulating common fraud, such as check fraud. A glance at the financial section of a local newspaper will show that there are fraud cases involving businesses, but rather than resulting in prison sentences for the guilty parties for illegally obtaining money, violations by the powerful are typically handled as misdemeanors. This occurs even though there are larger financial losses in business and corporate crime than in the crime typically committed by the poor. (In Chapter 14 we will closely examine crimes by the powerful.)

Evaluation and Research

To evaluate the theories discussed in this chapter we will look at some patterns of crime that these theories attempt to explain. It is important to remember that the theories deal with general patterns of crime, and so instead of taking individual case histories or some other inappropriate kind of data, we will examine the overall patterns and the structural theories' ability to account for them. Also, we will group Merton, Cohen, and Cloward and Ohlin into one category of structural theory and the Marxists into another.

One of the most persistent patterns found in studies of criminal behavior, based on both self-report studies and arrest rates, has been that men commit far more crime than do women. A general problem with structural theories of crime, and most explanations of crime, is their failure to address women's relative lack of criminal involvement. One work examining women and criminological theory pointed out that neither the Mertonian structural theories nor the Marxist ones really give much consideration to this phenomenon.[23] Cohen did note that there were different role expectations for men and women, and to some degree provided a reason why boys were more likely than girls to engage in delinquent pursuits. To the extent that sex roles are statuses or positions in society, we can see crime differences in terms of structural conditions. Since women's position traditionally has been inferior relative to men in terms of power to make the law and compete in financial circles, we would expect more not less crime by women according to structural theories.

Structural theory has also been criticized for failing to account for other groups in disadvantaged positions who commit little crime and for failing to recognize certain other groups that commit a good deal of crime. The elderly are often poor and disadvantaged, but they commit very little crime. Likewise, in the United States, Orientals, including Japanese, Chinese, Filipinos and Southeast Asians have relatively low crime rates compared to whites and blacks in the same economic position. On the other side of the coin, structural theories appear to fail to recognize hidden crime among the middle and upper classes. Self-report surveys have indicated that a good deal of crime is committed by the more affluent in society. Merton's structuralism ignores such crime or relegates it to a relatively insignificant or petty residual category, and Marxist theorists either argue that the laws against the rich are not enforced or that there are very few laws for the wealthy to break since they made them in first place.

Tests of these theories provide a mixture of findings, and hence, only partially resolve some of the questions we have raised. Spergel's research of different types of communities found evidence supporting Cloward's and Ohlin's contention that the various forms of delinquent subculture were determined by the structural organization of the communities.[24] He found that in the more organized communities, delinquent gangs concentrated more on property crimes than on intergang violence, while in the disorganized communities, there were far more incidents of gang fights and other nonutilitarian delinquency. However, that research was limited only to lower and working class communities. Further, while self-report surveys have found that crime and delinquency is not an exclusively lower and working class phenomenon, there is more delinquency and more serious delinquency in the lower classes of society.[25]

Research findings concerning the development of the law, while not unequivocal, do support the Marxist position that the laws, rather than being a general reflection of the common will, are largely created by powerful forces for their own interests. Becker's study of the Marijuana Tax Act traced the origins of the law to the Federal Bureau of Narcotics, which lobbied for the law to expand its power and funding. Sutherland's study of sexual psychopath law found that the psychiatrists and social workers furthered their interests in establishing the laws, and Chambliss's study of the vagrancy law, far from being the general social sentiment, was a way certain mercantile interests could use the law to guarantee a large and cheap labor pool.[26] Similar studies by Marxist and non-Marxist scholars found further evidence that the laws were not generally developed for the interest of society as a whole but rather reflected conflict between different classes and interest groups. Further, other than the common law that the United States adopted more or less as a whole from England, the laws tended to benefit the elite over the non-elite. Ironically, though, it is the common law kinds of crime—murder, rape, robbery, burglary—that have the most general consensus and are the most likely to result in harsh punishment; so while the Marxists can show the creation of laws to be largely in favor of the elite, those laws that are most identified with crime appear to reflect the general sentiment of society.

A final area of evaluation where both kinds of structuralism leave room for doubt is in comparing different societies. In comparing the social structure of the United States to other countries with similar structures, we find very different crime rates. For example, Canada has a much lower rate of violent crimes than the United States, but it is very similar structurally. True, the demographic make-up and cultural heritage is different, but since the argument is based on social structure, we should find more similarities than we do. Likewise, the Marxists fail dismally when it comes to comparing crime in one capitalist society with another. For example, in Clinard's cross cultural study of crime in urban areas, one of the cities he examined was Zurich, Switzerland, about as capitalistic a city as one could find. Compared to virtually any American city of the same size, Zurich had far less crime.[27] Unfortunately, there is very little reliable comparative data between modern capitalist and non-capitalist societies, and so it is almost impossible to say what effect a wholly socialistic socioeconomic system has on crime. From what studies of crime in the Soviet Union are available, crime was found to be concentrated largely among young males—a pattern not unlike most capitalist societies.[28]

SUMMARY

Structural theory took a bold step away from the essentially psychological explanations of crime by pointing to conditions in society that would inevitably lead to crime among a certain portion of society. This was not because the people were bad, evil or even sick, but rather because they were pursuing socially approved goals—albeit in unapproved ways. Since the structure allowed for only a limited number of successes through the legitimate channels and there were cultural pressures to succeed, crime was virtually inevitable.

However, since everyone who did not succeed did not turn to crime, it was necessary to show the different adaptations possible. Merton showed five possible ways of adapting to cultural values and social norms—some criminal and some not. Following Merton, Cohen showed how adaptations to the social structure could be collective as well as individual and lead to the development of criminal and delinquent subcultures. Once established, the delinquent subculture became the primary group adaptation to collective failure, passed on from one generation to the next. In further refinement of the same idea, Cloward and Ohlin showed that delinquent subcultural development could take on a number of different forms depending on the structure of the community; thus, instead of a single kind of criminal adaptation, there were several.

Following a different line of reasoning, the Marxists examined the social structure in terms of the distribution of wealth and power. They sought to explain how certain acts came to be defined, as crimes, and so instead of attempting to explain the patterns of crime, they examined the process of "crime creation." Hypothesizing that a conflict of interests existed in society between the elite and non-elite, they studied whose interests were being served by the criminal laws and concluded it was the interests of the elite. Thus, rather than the laws reflecting a social consensus, crimes were a reflection of class conflict and power struggles.

Both kinds of structural theory—Mertonian and Marxist—have strengths and weaknesses when evaluated in the light of research findings. Neither theory seems to have done a very good job in accounting for sex, age and ethnic differences in crime, but both theories can provide an explanation of the overrepresentation of crime among the poor. Likewise, neither theory is strong in explaining cross cultural data. The Marxists have been negligent in comparing capitalist and non-capitalist societies' crime rates, yet they remain adamant about the effect of capitalism on crime. More research and theory refinement is required, for while structural theories do explain some patterns of crime, they fail to explain a good deal.

Glossary

Anomie   A state of "normlessness" where it is unclear to social members what the norms and goals really are. This is a characteristic of society as a whole but manifested in individual members.

Bourgeoisie   In Marxist theory, the social class that owns the means of production. It is in direct conflict with the working class and, even though in the minority, has the bulk of the power. It uses this power to pass laws favorable to its own interests and against the interests of the workers.

Collective Adaptation   An adaptation to conditions in life by a group who experience the same condition.

Conflict Subculture   In Cloward and Ohlin's theory, a delinquent subculture characterized by violent conflict and individual toughness; found where there is weak community organization.

Conformist   An adaptation from Merton's theory where the individual accepts both the cultural values and societal goals.

Criminal Subculture   In Cloward and Ohlin's theory, a delinquent subculture found in communities where there are organized criminal activities, characterized by high rates of financial crimes.

Delinquent Subculture   The collective adaptation to the collective experience of failure in conventional society, described by Cohen.

Innovator   An adaptation from Merton's theory where the individual accepts the cultural goals but rejects the societal means. This is one of the major criminal adaptations.

Opportunity Structure   The relative individual and societal opportunities available to achieve cultural goals described in Cloward and Ohlin's theory.

Proletariat   In Marxist theory, one of the two great social classes. This class does not own the means of production but works for and is exploited by those who do, the bourgeoisie. According to Marxist theory, this class is more likely to break the law since the laws were designed to serve the interest of the bourgeoisie.

Rebel   An adaptation from Merton's theory that rejects both the social norms and cultural goals and favors an entirely different structure.

Retreatist   An adaptation from Merton's theory that rejects both the cultural values and the societal norms. Typical adaptations are alcohol and drug use.

Retreatist Subculture   A subculture that develops in a disorganized community, according to Cloward and Ohlin. It usually adapts by alcoholism or heavy drug use.

Ritualist   An adaptation from Merton's theory where the individual rejects the cultural goals yet accepts the means. This adaptation is found in low level functionaries who rarely commit crimes but religiously follow the rules.

Social Institutions   Organized, repetitive and habitual patterns of dealing with conditions and problems in society.

Social Structure   A society's organization of social relationships and group interactions. Structural concepts include social classes, roles and norms.

Questions

1. What is the relationship between social structure and crime? How does the makeup of social structure determine opportunities?

2. According to Merton, what are the adaptations to "anomie" and which of these adaptations are criminal?

3. How did Cohen explain the development of delinquent subcultures?

4. What were the various forms of group adaptations according to Cloward and Ohlin? What was the relationship between community structure and its subculture?

5. What are the main structural variables used by the neo-Marxists to explain crime? Why do the neo-Marxists focus on the creation and administration of the criminal law rather than criminal behavior itself?

Notes

1. Robert K. Merton, *Social Theory and Social Structure*. (New York: Free Press, 1957). Emile Durkheim, *Suicide: A Study of Sociology*. Trans. by J. A. Spaulding and George Simpson, ed. by George Simpson (New York: Free Press, 1951).

2. Merton, 1957.

3. Ibid.

4. Max Weber, *The Protestant Ethic and Spirit of Capitalism*. Trans. by Talcott Parsons (London: Allen & Ulwin, 1930).

5. Albert Cohen, *Delinquent Boys: The Culture of the Gang*. (New York: Free Press, 1955).

6. Donald R. Cressey, "Fifty Years of Criminology: From Sociological Theory to Political Control," *Pacific Sociological Review* **22** (October 1979): 462–463.

7. Cohen, 1955, 50–56.

8. Cohen, 1955, 59.

9. Cohen, 1955, 65.

10. Cohen, 1955, 137–147.

11. Richard A. Cloward and Lloyd E. Ohlin, *Delinquency and Opportunity: A Theory of Delinquent Gangs*. (New York: Free Press, 1960).

12. Cloward and Ohlin, 1960, 145.

13. Cloward and Ohlin, 1960, 38.

14. Cloward and Ohlin, 1960, 152–153.

15. Cloward and Ohlin, 1960, 161–171.

16. Cloward and Ohlin, 1960, 175.

17. Cloward and Ohlin, 1960, 184.

18. Cloward and Ohlin, 1960, 182. Solomon Korbin, *Drug Addiction Among Young Persons in Chicago*. (Illinois Institute for Juvenile Research, October, 1953). Harold Finestone, "Narcotics and Criminality," *Journal of Law and Contemporary Problems* **22** (Winter 1957): 69–85.

19. Ian Taylor, Paul Walton, and Jack Young, *The New Criminology: For a Social Theory of Deviance*. (New York: Harper & Row, 1973); Richard Quinney, *Critique of the Legal Order: Crime Control in Capitalist Society*. (Boston: Little, Brown, 1973); Austin Turk, *Criminality and the Legal Order*. (Chicago: Rand McNally, 1969).

20. Karl Marx, *Capital*, Vol. 1. Trans. by E. Aveling and H. Moore (Moscow: Foreign Languages Publishing House, 1965).

21. William Domhoff, *Who Rules America?*

22. Richard Quinney, *The Social Reality of Crime*. (Boston: Little, Brown, 1970).

23. Eileen Leonard, *Women and Crime: A Critique of Theoretical Criminology*. (New York: Longman, 1981).

24. Irving Spergel, *Racketville, Slumtown and Haulburg*. (Chicago: University of Chicago Press, 1964).

25. Delbert S. Elliott and Suzanne S. Ageton, "Reconciling Differences in Estimates of Delinquency," *American Sociological Review* **45** (February 1980): 95–110.

26. Howard Becker, "Becoming a Marijuana User," *American Journal of Sociology* **59** (November 1953): 235–242; Edwin Sutherland, "The Sexual Psychopath Laws," *Journal of Criminal Law and Criminology* **40** (January–February 1950): 543–554; William Chambliss, "A Sociological Analysis of the Law of Vagrancy," *Social Problems* **12** (1964): 67–77.

27. Marshall B. Clinard, *Cities with Little Crime: The Case of Switzerland*. (Cambridge: Cambridge University Press, 1978).

28. Louise Shelley, "The Geography of Soviet Criminality," *American Sociological Review* **45** (February 1980): 111–122.

6

Social Control and Criminal Acts

What to Look For:

The basic assumptions of control theory.

The sources of social control and how they operate.

Matza's criticism of positivism and the nature of "soft determinism" as seen in the concept of "drift."

The ways in which criminal acts are negated and neutralized.

Hirschi's social bonds and how they were more binding on adults as compared to juveniles.

The nature of deterrence theory in contrast to control theory.

Introduction

I N THIS CHAPTER we will examine theories emphasizing the external control surrounding social actors. Called *control theory,* this set of explanations of crime seeks to explain the presence or absence of crime by a society's ability to control unwanted criminal behavior. This feature sets it apart from most structural theory we examined; in the structural explanations, while the external social structure was very much a part of explaining crime, the internalized values of the individual were the driving forces that led people to crime. In control theory, though, the question is not so much why people commit crime—and thereby what inner force causes this—but rather, "What prevents people from committing crime?"

Control theory assumes that unless prevented from doing so, people will commit crime. To some extent, as suggested by Empey, this tenet can be seen as part of a Puritan heritage in that it poses some kind of "original sin."[1] That is to say the control theorists do not differentiate between "good folks" and "bad folks," but rather assume that everyone is basically capable of criminal behavior.

Another View of Durkheim

Like Merton's structural theory, the control theorists take Durkheim as their starting point.[2] However, the control theorists take a much more orthodox view of anomie than did Merton. Like Durkheim, the control theorists attempt to explain the conditions under which social norms will be strong or weak and how norms, as primary external control mechanisms, create conformity and reduce deviance. Where norms are strong and enjoy a high consensus, there will be less crime than in situations where they are weak and have minimal consensus. There are basic questions of social solidarity and organized social life.

Without social organization, there is chaos, massive deviance and nonconformity. This is because there is no normative system to control behavior. Since social organization—an ordered system of norms and roles—is taken to be a human construction, and not a natural condition, conformity, *not deviance* is the unnatural human condition.[3] As a result of this state of affairs, humans must work to generate law-abiding behavior; otherwise, humans will revert to their "natural" state of nonconformity and criminality. Thus, according to the control theorists' interpretation of Durkheim, since the natural state of humanity is essentially deviance, criminal behavior need not be explained in terms of special drives and motives such as subcultures or structural blockages. Thus, a failure in the social control mechanism explains criminal behavior.

In summarizing the control theorists' use of Durkheim, Frazier[4] cites the following passage:

> Man's characteristic privilege is that the bond he accepts is not physical but moral; that is social. He is governed not by a material environment brutally imposed on him, but by a conscience superior to his own, the superiority of which he feels. Because the greater, better part of his existence transcends the body, he escapes the body's yoke, but is subject to that of society.
>
> But when society is disturbed by some painful crises (e.g., economic depression) or by beneficient but abrupt transitions (e.g., economic prosperity), it is momentarily incapable of exercising this influence; thence come the sudden rises in the curve of suicides.[5]

The important feature of this interpretation of Durkheim, is that the control theorists claim to do more than simply explain lower class criminality, as do the structuralists. The control mechanisms affect all segments of society; and so not only can the theory be employed to explain lower class criminal behavior, but it also can be used to understand criminality in the higher social classes as well. Studies that have shown a good deal of "hidden criminality" in the middle and upper social strata lend support to this kind of general theory of crime. As we saw in the previous chapters, one of the criticisms of structural theory was its inability to do more than provide an explanation of lower class crime.

Sources of Social Control

As a starting point in modern control theory in criminology, we will look at the early works of Albert Reiss, Jr. and Ivan Nye. Both theorists were interested in the sources of **social control** and they attempted to specify what those controls were and how well they operated.

Reiss specified three sources of control that, in operation, generated conformity and prevented crime and delinquency.[6] First were *community and institutional* controls. These included the community-based control of the local population and prevalent institutions such as schools. Secondly, primary *group* control consisted of the family's control over its members— especially the children. The third sphere of control was *personal* controls, which consisted of internalization of institutional, community, and primary group norms. The family is seen as being the major source of this internalization process. Each of those control mechanisms is deemed to be effective insofar as it generates conformity to community standards.

At the same time that Reiss laid out these sources of control, he also stated the conditions of ineffective controls. There were four that resulted in nonconformity and criminal behavior: 1) when previously established controls have broken down; 2) where there is an absence of definite social rules among important reference groups; 3) when there is a conflict in

A major source of social control is one's primary group, namely the family. To the extent family ties are strong, the control of the family will also be strong. All members of the family pictured above are trained auctioneers.

social rules among important reference groups; or 4) when the individual has not internalized conventional control norms.[7] The first three areas of breakdown are external and consistent with the emphasis in control theory, but the fourth type of control breakdown, personal internalized norms, is apparently very much like subcultural. Taken on face value it seems to suggest that criminal values are part of the subculture to which one belongs. However, this is not what Reiss or the control theorists are saying. Rather, the very lack of personal control will lead to deviance and crime.

In another work attempting to delineate control mechanisms in society, Ivan Nye first pointed out two very different ways crime can be generated.[8] First, he said that crime can be "produced," in that certain motivations for committing crime may be learned in the process of socialization. Secondly, and more in line with the control theory perspective, he said that crime can occur in the "absence" of social control. Of the two crime generating mechanisms, Nye took the second to be far more common and important than the first.

Nye posits four mechanisms of social control that prevent crime and deviance.[9] First, there is *direct control* by external forces that restrict and punish crime. Being prosecuted for a crime and ultimately sent to prison is a good example of this type of control mechanism. Secondly, people develop a conscience that functions as an **internalized control**. This conscience is a personal morality that produces guilt if internalized norms are violated. Third, there are *indirect controls* in the identification with significant others such as parents and noncriminal friends. To avoid offending this group, a person would not commit crimes. Finally, there is control through the availability of *legitimate routes* to goal and need satisfaction. In contrast to Merton, Nye is saying that the availability of legitimate channels of goal achievement serves to control behavior, in that conformity is rewarded with the accomplishment of the goal.

These control mechanisms are similar to those discussed by Reiss, but Nye places more emphasis on the success of external controls. To Nye any internalized control is a measure of the success of external control—mainly the family. He takes social control as a constant process applied to members of society from an early age, a process that can change and break down over time. Therefore, if the external controls fail at some point, so also can the internalized ones. This clearly places a different emphasis than theories stressing early childhood development and socialization, in that Nye does not see such socialization carrying over to situations where the external controls fail.

The emphasis in Nye's work is on juveniles and the family. All of the controls emanated from the family, both in its direct control and the influence it had over a child's orientation to other control mechanisms. Therefore, while Nye recognized a complex network of social control, it emerged from the family's work with a child; the family provided the direction their child would take in relationship to the other controls in society. However, it is important to again emphasize that Nye's theory was not that of socialization. The controls were seen as an ongoing mechanism and not simply an early experience to be held all through adolescence and into adulthood. Thus, if the controls broke down, socialization probably would not be sufficient to prevent criminal or deviant behavior.

Soft Determinism, Drift, and Neutralization: David Matza

One of the most significant intellectual turns in control theory came in the work of David Matza's *Delinquency and Drift*. Matza's work was as much an attack on positivism as it was a reconceptualization of control theory. In order to understand this shift in theoretical perspective, we will break down our discussion into several parts.

Critique of Positivism

Matza began the development of his theory with a thoughtful criticism of positivism. Basically, positivism is a philosophical position in criminology that seeks the causes of crime in the motivational and behavioral systems

of criminals.[10] The legal system that generates and administers the laws
that define criminality are considered secondary or even irrelevant. Further, positivism is characterized by "scientific determinism," or the notion
that all behavior is determined by some force over which the individual
has no control.[11] Finally, positivism assumes that criminals are essentially
different from non-criminals. Criminals have one kind of motivational
system unlike that of noncriminals. The differences caused either by
genes or subcultural values explain why some people are criminals and
others are not.[12] According to Matza's interpretation of the other criminological theories, they are all positivistic.

First, Matza saw positivistic criminology as ignoring the criminal law
and its application. Laws differ among different societies and change
from time to time in both their content and application. Therefore, the
law itself had to have some significant influence on crimes and criminals.
No matter what a law breaker's motivational system, there had to be a law
defining the behavior as illegal: for example, regardless of the individual's
motivational system, those who sold liquor during Prohibition were criminals, yet today they are not. Second, Matza criticized what he called, positivism's **hard determinism**, since it left no room for individual choice or
cause of action.[13] Matza suggested replacing hard determinism with **soft
determinism**. It was true that people's actions were determined by forces
over which they had no say or control, but this did not mean that individual choice was irrelevant. The extent to which individuals took a course
of action in the face of off-setting deterministic circumstances suggested
that the cause was the social actor. Matza notes MacIver's statement:

> "Those who oppose determinism to 'free will' are apt to forget that human
> beings, as individuals and as groups, are themselves dynamic participants
> within the causal order."[14]

Thus, instead of ignoring "will" altogether in favor of wholly deterministic
forces, Matza suggests that *while considering* deterministic forces it is important to understand that the social actors themselves are aware of the
social forces and make choices in relation to them.

A final problem Matza saw in positivism was its differentiation between
the criminal and noncriminal. First, Matza pointed out that most people
at one time or another commit crimes, and so it would be difficult empirically to establish an essential difference between groups of criminals and
noncriminals. Secondly, and more importantly, Matza argued that if criminals were essentially different kinds of animals, we would expect far
more crime from them than they actually commit. That is, if they were
driven to commit crime by some force over which they had no control,
they would have to commit crime virtually all the time. However, since
criminals only commit crimes occasionally, the positivists have what Matza
calls "an embarrassment of riches"—they predict far more crime than ac-

tually takes place. Furthermore, since most criminality occurs during adolescence and early adulthood, and even the worst delinquents "grow out" of criminal behavior patterns, a good deal of criminality can be seen to vanish with maturational reform, a process ignored by most positivists. Therefore, rather than treating criminals and noncriminals as essentially different, Matza argues they should be viewed as basically the same.[15]

Subculture of Delinquency and Drift

Matza argued that the subcultural theorists had incorrectly formulated the concept of "delinquent subcultures." Citing data that showed only an insignificant proportion (2 percent) of juveniles in high crime areas approved of crimes, he argued that delinquents did not have delinquent values.[16] He further added that if a delinquent subculture did have such values, criminality among juveniles would not decline with maturation. After all, if subcultural values were the cause of crime and delinquency, there would be no reason for criminal values to be abandoned with age. If anything, crime would increase with age as members became fully socialized. Furthermore, Matza noted that subculture theory explained more crime and delinquency than in fact existed. As in the notion of the "born criminal" there is an "embarrassment of riches" in that subcultural theory simply expects more crime than is, in fact, observed.

Accordingly, Matza attempted to modify the idea of subculture. Clearly, there appeared to be a different crime rate or at least crime style among the working and lower class as compared to the middle and upper class, and Matza wanted to explain that difference. First, he modified the conception of subculture by defining it around the notion of "publicity"—the common knowledge in a community that certain youths were involved in delinquency. He called this the **subculture of delinquency** (as opposed to delinquent subculture) and described the values as basically conventional. That is, the values in a subculture of delinquency were essentially the same as the rest of society. However, within these subcultures there existed certain **subterranean traditions**.[17] These traditions or patterns of beliefs are the residue of a pluralistic society. While the dominant or conventional values and beliefs are proclaimed as the proper ones to uphold, the wide variety of traditions of a pluralistic society linger. Thus, deviant and conventional viewpoints exist side by side. Sometimes there is an obscured similarity between the two views, coming together in a **subterranean convergence** where conventional values are seen in terms of deviant interpretations. For instance, Native Americans used drugs as part of religious ceremonies, and the purpose of drugs, and later alcohol, was to achieve a "religious experience." Combined with the conventional pastime of "social drinking," the convergence between the subterranean and conventional led to a high rate of public drunkenness among Indians.

In a situation where actions against the conventional values are neutralized through deviant interpretations of those values, it is possible to maintain a sense of conventional behavior while grossly violating the law. Since subcultures of delinquency are alive with subterranean traditions, it is easier to negate the controls in conventional morality, allowing individuals to commit crimes. This idea led to Matza's core concept of **drift**. What occurs in crime and delinquency is a release from conventional morality—a state between the conventional and deviant called "drift."[18] In the state of drift, individuals are free to choose a delinquent or criminal course of action; social actors are *not* forced to commit crimes, but they may choose to do so.

In employing the concept of drift, Matza does several things. First, he shows how controls work to keep social behavior in line most of the time. The state of drift is situational and episodic—not a constant state as is anomie. Second, he explains why those in even the most criminal areas usually do not break the law; they may commit more crime, but they do not do it all the time or as much as is suggested by the other subcultural explanations. Third, Matza explains how conventional morality dominates all areas of society but is neutralized in drift situations. It is not the case that groups of people are either criminal or non-criminal in their beliefs, but rather there is an overlap and convergence between the two.

Neutralizing Controls

The specific ways in which conventional morality can be neutralized falls into two categories. First, there are deviant interpretations of legalistic defenses.[19] These negations combine the law with subterranean traditions to neutralize crime—that is, the exceptions to culpability in the law, such as self-defense and insanity are interpreted far beyond the legal parameters. Secondly, the techniques of **neutralization**, while similar to the legalistic "negations of offense," are more general rationalizations for breaches in conventionality.[20] Unlike the conventional use of self-defense that allows violence only for protection in the face of an immediate attack, the subterranean interpretation of the concept provides far more leeway. For example, if a gang boy from another neighborhood comes into one's own territory, it is "self-defense" to attack him; or if someone makes an insulting remark, it is "self-defense" to make a physical attack. The reasoning goes something like this: "If I allow someone to insult me or don't defend my territory, I will lose respect. Once I lose respect, there will be nothing to prevent them from attacking me, and so to protect myself, I have to take self-defending actions against all threats." In the context of a subculture of delinquency, this is not a breach of conventional morality, but rather a reaffirmation of it, for it does not embrace "criminal values," it simply interprets conventional ones.[21]

A second legalistic negation is *insanity*. Like the legal defense for breaking the law, insanity relieves the actor of responsibility; however, since

The insanity plea is often used to negate an offense. In the murder conviction of Jean Harris for killing diet book author D. Herman Tarnower, her attorney unsuccessfully argued she was "insane with jealousy" and could not distinguish right from wrong when she killed Tarnower. Here she is pictured leaving the County of Westchester Courthouse with one of her attorneys.

being "mentally ill" is unmanly, the insanity is argued to be temporary and part of acceptable masculine behavior. For example, being "crazy with anger" or "mad drunk" releases the individual from responsibility and implies that the person really does hold conventional values when not "insane."[22]

A third negation is through *accident*.[23] This negation is a form of excusing deviance by claiming lack of intent or *mens rea*. If there is no intent; then there can be no crime. However, unlike the conventional version of establishing intent, the subcultural version includes "recklessness" as a kind of accident. According to Matza, it is understood as follows:

> An act either is intended or not. Recklessness is a state of mind which either implies intent or it does not. Clearly, I am reckless. I do not deny that. I did not bother to foresee the consequences of my line of action. But how could I? I am reckless. It's not a crime to be reckless. It's like being a wild child.[24]

Again we can see a distorted reaffirmation of conventional values—in ef-

fect agreeing with the wrongness of the act but claiming no responsibility
for it.

The final legalistic negation of social control is *accident of circumstance.*
In law, the concept of "extenuating circumstances" probably comes closest
to this justification for criminal behavior. The reasoning argues that one's
life is guided by fate, and one cannot alter fate. Therefore, if fate is the
cause of all actions, then the subcultural criminal or delinquent cannot be
held responsible. The state of being that engenders this condition occurs
when the actor experiences himself or herself as *effect.* Where the actor is
the *cause,* he or she is responsible, but when the person sees himself or
herself as the effect or some other cause, there is no responsibility on the
part of the actor. When experiencing self as effect, the individual is in a
state of drift and is freed from the conventional bonds of social control.[25]
It should be pointed out that this state sounds very much like positivistic
determinism, but instead of being forced into delinquency, the actor in a
state of drift makes a choice. Furthermore, the state is a subjective experience of the actor and not an objective state.

Related to the negations of an offense, an earlier work by Sykes and
Matza, identified five *techniques of neutralization.* The first is *denial of respon-*
sibility. This justification for delinquency places the blame for deviance on
conditions over which the actor has no control, such as social class, neighborhood or associates. Even sociological and psychological theories can be
employed to show that the actor was not responsible for breaking the law.
For example, a Chicano gang member might blame his delinquency on
the "barrio culture," citing tradition as the cause of delinquent gang activities. A second technique of neutralization is the *denial of injury,* a claim
that the crime really is not harmful. Stealing from a department store, for
example, can be neutralized by arguing the establishment is wealthy, and
so it is not really injured by losses from shoplifting. Third, there can be a
denial of victim. This is similar to denying injury, but rather than minimizing the loss, it minimizes the victim. For instance, criminal behavior can
be neutralized by claiming the victim was a criminal himself. In one interview with a Mafia killer, when asked if he felt bad about the people he
had killed, the hit man said no because he never killed anyone but other
gangsters. In effect, he was saying that the people he shot were not "victims" but people who did the same thing as he did and were condemned
by conventional morality anyway. Fourth, by *condemning the condemners,*
the focus is shifted from the law breakers to the accusers. The police are
charged with taking bribes, businesses with consumer fraud, and politicians with favoritism in legislation. In effect, this neutralization labels the
officials and their institutions as hypocritical and one's own transgressions
as minor by comparison. Finally, Sykes and Matza found that delinquents
will *appeal to higher loyalties.* This technique of neutralization involves the
claim that in the hierarchy of conventional morality, the greater good is

maintained at the expense of violating a lower level morality. For example, gang violence is neutralized in the name of protecting one's neighborhood and the solidarity of the group. Appeals to protecting life and property are cited as higher loyalties and obligations than avoiding gang violence.[26]

Taken together, the various negations of offense and techniques of neutralization stand as evidence of conventional morality. This is because they stand as *exceptions* to conventional morality rather than as a rejection of it. If subcultural criminals and delinquents held opposing values, they would need no justification for breaking the law, but since they feel obliged to provide some kind of neutralizing account for crime and delinquency, there must be some commitment to the values of conventional society. At the same time, the neutralizing techniques explain how social control is diminished and allows for violations of the law. By freeing subcultural criminals and delinquents from the bonds of control, they enter drift, a state in which they may choose deviant actions.

We can summarize Matza's theory of drift in the following propositions:

1. The law will be followed as long as social control is in force.

2. In situations where controls are absent (drift) the social actors are freed to commit crime, but they are not forced to do so.

3. The conventional values are the dominant ones in subcultures of delinquency.

4. The violation of conventional values occurs when they have been neutralized and the actor chooses to deviate.

5. The major force in neutralizing conventional values is subterranean convergence.

Social Bonds: Travis Hirschi

Hirschi, like the other control theorists, was primarily concerned with the ties that kept people from breaking the law. Quite simply, to the extent that ties or bonds existed, people would be controlled. Again, we can see in the work of Travis Hirschi the "soft determinism" of Matza, in that he did not say that anyone was forced to break the law. Rather, as Hirschi stated:

> If a person does not care about the wishes and expectations of other people—that is, if he is insensitive to the opinion of others—then he is to that extent not bound by the norms. He is free to deviate.[27]

In this statement we can see that the focus of Hirschi's work is on the bonds that hold one to conventional society.

Hirschi discussed four bonds that made up the bulk of social control in society: 1) attachment, 2) commitment, 3) involvement, and 4) belief. Each one played a role in keeping people in line with conventional morality and controlling their behavior, and a person or group could be more or less controlled by each bond.

The first bond, **attachment**, refers to the links an individual has to others.[28] To the extent to which one has ties with others, he or she is more likely to consider their opinions and views. If the links are to those who hold conventional morality or appear to hold it, any deviation would be seen as going against the wishes and opinions of those considered significant and important. This idea is similar to Emile Durkheim's concept of "collective conscience"—commonly held sentiments—that comes through attachments to society.[29] Like Durkheim, Hirschi also argued that the greater the degree of attachment to others the more likely that person is to be bound by their norms.

Attachments were not only important between individuals, but also between a person and institutions. One of the most important institutions for social control, according to Hirschi, is the educational system. If attachments to school were strong, the controls implied in the school's authority were also strong. Conversely, if attachments were weak, then the school's control was weak. Further, attachments to school were based on the child's liking school and being successful there. While poor students were more likely to dislike school and become involved in delinquency, the relationship between school performance and delinquency is linked to more than just the performance itself as can be seen in Fig. 6.1.

First, juveniles with an academic *impairment,* regardless of cause, were more likely to have poor *performance* in school. As a result, they were more likely to *dislike* school and *reject* school authority. Since the school's control rested on its authority, the failing students were released from its control and committed delinquency.[30] Several studies have shown a relationship between poor school performance and delinquency, but the *nature* of that relationship has been a long standing point of debate. For example as we saw in Chapter 4, some researchers claimed the causes were "feeblemindedness" and other nonsocial sources. Hirschi, though, provided an explanation based on social control rather than earlier theories that looked to biogenic or psychogenic causes of delinquency linked to "stupidity."

A second bond described by Hirschi is **commitment**.[31] This link to society and its controls is based on the extent to which one is tied to social comforts through legitimate positions. Negatively, we can evaluate commitment by determining what a person has to lose by violating social

---

Fig. 6.1

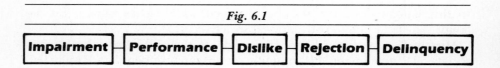

norms. For example, if a man with a secure, well-paying job is arrested for shoplifting, not only will he suffer criminal sanctions (which would probably be negligible), but he would also stand to lose his position in society. He might be fired from his job, lose his retirement benefits, respect of his friends and family, and the general social support he has built up over several years. On the other hand, a juvenile who is picked up for the same offense has much less at stake in society and has much less to lose since, in general, juveniles are less bonded to society than are adults. Hirschi uses the concept of commitment to explain why juveniles and young adults are more likely to break the law than older adults—those over twenty-five years of age.

A third bond is **involvement**. To the extent that one is engrossed in legitimate social activities, he or she can be said to have high involvement. When involved in conventional activities and routines, there simply is not the opportunity to deviate as there is when one is less involved. Again, Hirschi uses this social bond to explain why juveniles are more involved in breaking the law than are adults. Since they are not engrossed in a career, service organizations, and a whole range of other adult social involvements, they are not subject to the informal social control mechanisms of these groups.

Finally, Hirschi sees **beliefs** as a binding force in society. Like Matza, Hischi argues that conventional norms are the dominant beliefs in society, even in so-called delinquent and criminal subcultures. In other words, people from all parts of society have the same basic beliefs. However, the primary belief, that one should respect law and the authorities, can be strong or weak depending on attachments.

Beliefs for the control theorists in general, and Hirschi specifically, are not the same as internalized norms. Rather, they are understandings of what others, especially those to whom we are attached, expect of us. The concept of "beliefs" differs from the concept of internalized norms and socialization theories, for it keeps the major controls *external* to the individual. If one believes that it is important to obey the law, whether he happens to agree with the law or not, then he is controlled. In other words, a person might think a particular law is unfair, unjust, and unworthy but follows it nevertheless. However, as long as that person *believes* the law should be followed he or she will be under social control; therefore, it is unnecessary to internalize the values the laws express.

Like the other control theorists, Hirschi emphasizes external controls of society and minimizes internal ones. The basic assumption that people will break the law if not controlled is inherent in the theory. The bonds of attachment, commitment, involvement, and beliefs are all external to the individual, but the sentiments linked to attachments suggest some kind of internalization of society—not to norms but to others. However, if the bonds are somehow broken, social behavior will tend to deviate for there are no external controls to prevent it; thus, any internal sentiments are dependent on external sources. As a result, Hirschi argues that we must look to the social context outside the individual rather than to internal values and sentiments.

Containment Theory: Walter Reckless

Another control theory, called **containment theory**, was developed by Walter Reckless and associates.[32] This theory attempted to explain why so many people who were in a position to be socialized into criminality were not. It also was an effort to show how it was possible for people who were outside of external social control to be controlled by internal mechanisms. Generally, nuclear and primary groups were the main sources of external containment, and when an individual was outside their domain he or she was largely free of external constraints. As society became more heterogeneous, impersonal, and autonomous, the small groups played a decreasing role in containment, and the major source of control was internal containment. This shifted the emphasis of control from the external to the internal, for with so many individuals free of the primary groups and small personal organizations that provided the bulk of social control, it was reasoned that a good deal of containment had to come from within.[33]

Reckless delineated four components of internal containment: 1) favorable self-concept, 2) goal orientation, 3) frustration tolerance, and 4) norm retention. Each component had its own particular qualities, but all four were interrelated and a change in one could lead to a change in another. First, favorable self-concept is defined as having a view of self that was conforming and conventional. It is an identity that is likely not to engage in criminal activity since such behavior would be inconsistent with self-concept. Second, goal orientation referred to having goals and means that were consistent with societal values and the law. This idea is very similar to Merton's conformist—accepting both the goals and means. Third, frustration tolerance was the capacity to withstand the temptation to employ criminal means or goals in the face of failure or setbacks. Those who were able to find alternative legitimate routes to objectives and prevail over the pressures of others in adverse circumstances had high frustration tolerance and greater internal control. Finally, norm retention is the ability to maintain social norms in situations of alienation and anomie. When the external supports and pressures for abiding by conventional norms were not present, those with high norm retention were able to hold on to norms, thus obeying the law. *Norm erosion* occurs when the individual neutralizes or becomes wholly alienated from social norms and is freed to deviate.[34]

The inner containment system is more or less modeled after external control systems. It is a "self-management" mechanism grounded in internalization of conventional and conforming behavior.[35] Thus, we might think of the self as a microcosm of the external containment system—society within the individual.

Criminality is explained in this model by conceiving of the individual in terms of concentric circles with the innermost being organic and psychological and the outermost being society at large. In between are external containments provided by nuclear groups and internal containments of the self. Pressures to deviate come from both external and internal sources. On the outside, pressures include poverty, unemployment, inequality, and similar adverse living conditions. From the inside, feelings of inferiority, extreme hostility, compulsions, phobias, and similar psychological and even organic-based pressures can push the individual toward crime and delinquency. However, where there are strong internal and external containment systems, deviation is less likely since these pressures can be controlled.[36]

Evaluation and Research in Control Theory

A central tenet in **control theory** is the assumption that social behavior is not wholly deterministic. In Matza's words, we can better understand crime and delinquency in terms of "soft determinism" where the individual exercises some choice rather than the "hard determinism" of the positivists. All of the control theorists point out situations where the individual is "freed from control" where he or she "chooses" whether or not to deviate from conventional norms. In and of itself there may be philosophical arguments over hard and soft determinism, but the control theorists appear to contradict themselves in that they suggest control—when it is in effect—is highly deterministic, but in the absence of control, deviance is a matter of choice and not determined by external forces. In other words, the control theorists appear to employ "hard determinism" in discussing control but "soft determinism" to explain crime. If conformity is determined by control forces, then crime should be determined by criminal forces, or conversely, if deviance is a matter of choice, then so too should conformity. For example, if conventional external controls keep a person from committing a robbery, then if those same external controls were criminal, they should force criminal behavior.

On the other hand, the concept of "soft determinism" is useful in understanding the relative lack of crime in situations where we would expect it. Most of the highly deterministic theories demand more crime and delinquency than is in fact observed. "Drift" is a situational concept that describes deviance as episodic rather than constant. This concept describes the observed nature of crime and delinquency more accurately than concepts that suggest a person or group is wholly criminal all of the time.

Tests of control theory have confirmed many of its propositions, but to some extent the findings can be argued to be equivocal or subject to several interpretations. Research on school performance and delinquency has found relationships between poor scholarship and delinquent behavior.[37] Such findings have been employed to support control theorists' contentions that when students do poorly in school, they reject the school's authority and therefore are more likely to turn to delinquency. The same findings could be interpreted to support Merton's theory by saying that since legitimate means to success (education) are blocked, the juveniles turn to illegitimate means. However, somewhat more compelling research has been completed in the areas where values and commitments are concerned. In several studies, evidence has been found suggesting that delinquents and criminals generally hold conventional values but are less committed to positions in conventional society than are conformists.[38] Likewise, it was found that delinquents and criminals have fewer attachments than do others. Perhaps the most important finding of control

The relatively high arrest rate for juveniles has been attributed, in part, by failure to achieve success in school. This can be interpreted either as a breakdown in the control the institution exercises over the youth or a frustration reaction to reach success goals through legitimate channels.

theorists is the relative decrease in criminal behavior as juveniles move into adult statuses.[39] As people move from less controlled and committed statuses (juveniles) to more controlled and committed ones (adults), crime is greatly reduced. However, while such evidence exists for the more common crimes, there is evidence of massive white collar criminality by "respectable" adults that may offset this important observation. (See Chapter 14).

Deterrence Theory

Deterrence theory has its roots in the classical school and sees social control emanating from external sources in the same way as control theory. However, the main emphasis of deterrence theory is on formal social controls in the application of legal sanctions, even though more recent versions have begun to emphasize informal control and reciprocity in explaining patterns of crime. The philosophical basis of deterrence theory is in utilitarianism, a view of man as a "profit maximizer, a calculator of profit from estimates of gain and cost resulting from the projected act."[40] The criminological roots of deterrence theory can be traced directly to the works of Ceasare Becarria (see Chapter 3) and the classical school of criminology. Modern deterrence is a second revival of this approach after the neoclassical theorists of the nineteenth century.

The underlying utilitarian philosophy of deterrence theory calls for an examination of the possible rewards and punishments associated with a given line of action.[41] While most of the research and arguments in deterrence theory has focused on the effectiveness of possible punishments, including the perception of being caught, awareness of the sanction and its severity, some research and theory has been directed towards the pursued rewards. The basic argument, though, gives equal weight to both the reward and punishment and the actor's evaluation of each. Thus, "if the perceived rewards outweigh perceived costs, the act in question will be undertaken; if costs outweigh rewards, the act will be rejected."[42]

The central concept of the *rational actor* in deterrence theory hinges on perception. If an actor *perceives* a reward to be greater than the chance of being caught, the sanction being applied and the severity of the sanction, then the act is considered rational. This is true even though, unbeknown to the actor, the reward may be relatively small, the chances of apprehension and sanction application great, and punishment severe.[43] For example, if a man believed that the rewards for robbing a bank were far greater than chances of capture and application of a mild sanction, then there would be little deterrence for committing that act. Since bank robbers have a relatively high rate of arrest and comparatively severe sanctions are applied to them, the robber's perception can be said to be inaccurate. However, since the robber's perception of the situation was rational (i.e., he weighed the rewards against the punishment), the utilitarian principle of deterrence theory is maintained.

For the deterrence theorists, the main test comes in determining the actor's perception of rewards and punishments. The hypothesis is *not* that greater punishment will better deter crime, but rather that a perception of certainty of punishment combined with severity of punishment will result in deterrence. If a severe punishment is perceived as a certainty, the rational actor will avoid the punishable behavior. However, if there is a low perceived chance of being caught, even with a severe punishment there is relatively little deterrence. Likewise, if there is a perception of low severity, even though a perceived high probability of apprehension, deterrence is low.[44]

The two basic hypotheses in deterrence theory are: 1) additive and 2) interaction. The *additive* hypothesis sees a cumulative relationship between the certainty of apprehension and severity of criminal sanction. Both the perception of certainty and severity are weighed equally and added together. The interaction hypothesis, on the other hand, emphasizes the connection of certainty to severity so that the relationship between the two stands as a third variable. That is, the joint effect is greater than the effect of either one individually. This is because there is a perceived interaction between the two variables on the part of the actor evaluating possible behavior.

Two major trends have evolved in contemporary deterrence theory. First, the *ecological* approach sought to explain patterns of crime by examining aggregate data.[45] By determining the median number of months served for certain offenses by cohorts in given states, a measure of severity was established. Certainty of punishment was estimated by the number of reported crimes divided by the number of prison admissions.[46] Then, by comparing crime rates in states with different degrees of certainty and severity of punishment, it was possible to measure the effect of deterrence. Mixed findings resulted from these studies; but the deterrence researchers did conclude that, regardless of severity of punishment, the certainty of punishment appeared to reduce crime. The second approach is the *perceptual,* concentrating on the individual as a rational actor.[47] In this second group of studies the emphasis shifted from looking at aggregate data to individual cases to determine the extent to which the actor's perception of certainty and severity played a role in deterrence. To a large extent this shift in emphasis is due to the failure of the ecological studies in finding data to support deterrence hypothesis. Moreover, since the law enforcement and correctional records are of questionable quality for research purposes, even if validating data were found, it would be of marginal value. Therefore, in addition to looking at a different dimension of deterrence—the individual as a rational actor—the "perceptual" researchers employed such devices as self-report surveys instead of official records to determine crime involvement.[48] Findings from the perceptual research have been more promising than the ecological, but strong relationships in this area of research are difficult to establish because of the equivocal nature of perceptions.

Evaluation and Research in Deterrence Theory

As a theory of social control, deterrence theory is sometimes seen as nothing more than an "official rationale" for our current legal system. That is, rather than being a true criminological theory, it is in fact a justification for the continued reliance on punishment for social control. Donald Cressey characterized deterrence theory as:

> . . . a know-nothing criminology which assumes, sadly but correctly, that official terror will reduce the crime rates even if the terrorists have never heard of sociology or social psychology.[49]

Furthermore, the failure of the ecological research by deterrence theorists to confirm their propositions has not led to confidence in the overall theory, and while the supporters of deterrence theory rightly point to the fallibility of official statistics, there have not been any impressive ecological studies using other methods that overcome the shortcomings with the methods of the earlier research. The more recent work on deterrence in perceptual studies has gained lost ground by confirming the central hypothesis of deterrence; and there have been theoretical links between deterrence and exchange theory, providing a broader and more modern base for what is often considered archaic thinking in taking punishment as a central determinate in social control. However, as new theoretical changes have been made in deterrence theory, it is becoming less and less "deterrence theory" and more like control and exchange theory, since informal controls and reciprocity are emerging as key variables.

SUMMARY

This chapter has examined theories of crime that emphasize the external controls over social behavior. The control theories have stressed the various groups and institutions that surround and control individuals. Like Durkheim, the central concern has been one of group cohesion and conformity and the mechanisms that affect social control.

The basic assumption of control theory is the need to contain and control human behavior. If not controlled, individuals will deviate without requiring any special motivation to do so. Control, while basically an external force, can also be internalized under the right conditions, and so social control can be studied from both external and internal perspectives.

In contrast to control theory, deterrence theory focuses on institutional responses to criminality in the form of punishment. A direct descendant of the classical school of criminology, deterrence theory posits a rational model of a human being, weighing the costs and benefits of a crime. Crime will occur when the rewards of the crime are perceived as greater than the certainty and/or severity of the punishment. However, since there is a good deal of variation in perception, much contemporary deterrence theory has become an attempt to explain differential perception of the certainty and severity of punishment.

Glossary

Attachments   Links to others in conventional society. These links serve to increase social control.

Belief   The understanding of others' norms and values in control theory. In control theory, beliefs do not imply internalization of norms and values.

Commitment   The extent to which one is set into a course of action in social life. The greater the commitment, the greater the social control.

Containment Theory   Walter Reckless's version of control theory emphasizing both internal and external constraints to criminal behavior.

Deterrence Theory   A theory that emphasizes the effect of punishment as a deterrent to crime. This is generally not considered a control theory for it emphasizes the official controls and internalized values, norms, and perceptions.

Drift   The state between freedom and control where the individual chooses a course of action, either criminal or noncriminal. It is an episodic state and generally not a constant one.

Hard Determinism   A philosophic position generally associated with positivism. It holds that every human action is determined by a prior cause and rejects wholly the concept of free will.

Internalized Control   The social control individuals exercise over themselves.

Involvement   The engrossment that a person has in various pursuits. Control theory contends that the greater the involvement one has in legitimate societal activities, the greater the social control over activities.

Neutralization   The process of thought that construes a norm/law violation so that it is not wrong or evil in a given set of circumstances.

Social Bonds   The ties of an individual to society.

Social Control   The various ways that behavior is monitored and controlled by others in society.

Soft Determinism   A term used to characterize action that is partially determined by external forces and partially the result of will. As a philosophy it recognizes external forces to the individual and the individual's will to act.

Subculture of Delinquency   Matza's characterization of an area of high delinquency where there is public knowledge that delinquency is common. It is an alternative conception of a delinquent subculture and rejects the idea that "delinquent values" dominate.

Subterranean Convergence   The coming together of localized traditions with conventional values. This convergence often forms a neutralization for deviance.

Subterranean Traditions   These are values of various groups that are submerged but exist in various communities. They exist along with the dominant conventional values but are not expressed.

Questions

1. What basic assumptions do the control theorists hold about human nature? How are these assumptions essentially different from those of the structuralist theorists?

2. What are the different types of social controls according to Reiss and Nye, and Reckless?

3. How are the concepts of "hard" and "soft" determinism different? Explain Matza's concept of drift and show how it is an example of soft determinism.

4. What are the social bonds described by Hirschi and how can they be used to explain the difference between adult and juvenile criminality?

5. What is deterrence theory and how is it similar and different than control theory? What similarities are there between deterrence and classical theory?

Notes

1. LaMar T. Empey, *American Delinquency*. (Homewood, IL: Dorsey, 1978), pp. 228–229.

2. Charles Frazier, *Theoretical Approaches to Deviance*. (Columbus, OH: Charles Merrill, 1976), pp. 49–50.

3. Frazier, 1976, 54.

4. Ibid.

5. Emile Durkheim, *Suicide*. (New York: Free Press, 1951).

6. Albert J. Reiss, Jr., "Delinquency as the Failure of Personal and Social Controls," *American Sociological Review* 16 (1851): 196–207.

7. Reiss, 1851, 207.

8. Ivan Nye, *Family Relations and Delinquent Behavior*. (New York: Wiley, 1958).

9. Nye, 1958, 5.

10. David Matza, *Delinquency and Drift*. (New York: Wiley, 1964), p. 3.

11. Matza, 1964, 5.

12. Matza, 1964, 11.

13. Matza, 1964, 5–7.

14. R. M. McIver, *Social Causation*. (Boston: Ginn, 1942), p. 236.

15. Matza, 1964, p. 45.

16. Matza, 1964, 49.

17. Matza, 1964, 63–64.

18. Matza, 1964, 27–30.

19. Matza, 1964, 69–98.

20. Gresham Sykes and David Matza, "Techniques of Neutralization: A Theory of Delinquency," *American Sociological Review* 22 (December 1957): 664–670.

21. Matza, 1964, 75–81.

22. Matza, 1964, 81–85.

23. Matza, 1964, 85.

24. Matza, 1964, 86.

25. Matza, 1964, 87–89.

26. Sykes and Matza, 1957.

27. Travis Hirschi, *Causes of Delinquency*. (Berkeley: University of California Press, 1969), p. 18.

28. Hirschi, 1969, 18.

29. Frazier, 1976, 66.

30. Hirschi, 1969, 110–124.

31. Hirschi, 1969, 19.

32. Walter Reckless, *The Crime Problem*, 4th ed. (Englewood Cliffs, NJ: Prentice-Hall, 1967). See also, Simon Dinitz, Frank Scarpitti and Walter Reckless, "Delin-

quency Vulnerability: A Cross Group and Longitudinal Analysis," *American Sociological Review* **27** (August 1962).

33. Frazier, 1976, 62.

34. Reckless, 1967, 475–476.

35. Reckless, 1967, 476.

36. Reckless, 1967, 479–480.

37. See Travis Hirschi and Michael J. Hindelang, "Intelligence and Delinquency: A Revisionist Review," *American Sociological Review* (August 1977), pp. 571–586.; Kenneth Polk, "Urban Areas and Delinquency," *Social Problems* (Winter 1967): 320–325; Michael J. Hindelang, "Causes of Delinquency: A Partial Replication," *Social Problems* **21** (Spring 1973): 471–487.

38. See Matza, 1964; Sykes and Matza, 1957.

39. See Hirschi, 1969; Dinitz, et al., 1962.

40. M. Geerken and Grove, "Deterrence: Some Theoretical Considerations," Law and Society Review **9** (Spring 1975): 497–513.

41. George Bryjak, *Deterrence Theory and Anomie*. Unpublished Ph.D. dissertation (Norman, OK: University of Oaklahoma, 1980), p. 1.

42. Ibid.

43. Harold G. Grasmick and George J. Bryjak, "The Deterrent Effect of Perceived Severity of Punishment," *Social Forces* (December 1980).

44. Charles Tittle, "Sanction Fear and the Maintenance of Social Order," *Social Forces* **55** (March 1977): 579–596.

45. Jack Gibbs, "Crime, Punishment and Deterrence," *Southwest Social Science Journal* **48** (1968): 515–530; Charles Tittle, "Crime Rates and Legal Sanctions," *Social Problems* **16** (1969): 409–422.

46. Bryjak, 1980, 38–39.

47. Bryjak, 1980, 43–45.

48. See Grasmick and Bryjak, 1980; J. Teevan "Subjective Perceptions of Deterrence," *Journal of Research in Crime and Delinquency* **13** (July 1976): 155–164.

49. Donald R. Cressey, "Fifty Years of Criminology: From Sociological Theory to Political Control," *Pacific Sociological Review* **22** (October 1979): 457–480.

7

Interactionist Approaches to Crime

What to Look For:

The differences and similarities between the interactionist and control theorists in terms of level of analysis and primary concepts.

The nine propositions of differential association theory and what they imply about criminal behavior.

The basic assumptions in labeling theory and the role of the criminal justice system in criminal behavior patterns.

How the structural interactionists explain crime in terms of the concept of character.

The relative strengths and weaknesses of the interactionist theories.

Introduction

WITH A FOCUS on the actual occurrence of crime and delinquency in specific situations, the control theorists attempted to show how external control mechanisms either prevented crime or failed to do so. However, the control theorists, while taking a closer look at the connections between society and the individual, were never really able to explain why persons under the same control had different patterns of crime, or why different groups of law violators chose certain crimes over others. Furthermore, the control theorists had to assume that persons out of control would "naturally" turn to criminal means.

The interactionists, while having a similar level of analysis as the control theorists and similar assumptions about the nature of determinism (e.g., deterministic forces are "soft"), take more of a micro-social and social psychological view of crime. In the same way as Matza examined the episodic nature of crime, the interactionists are interested in the situations and interactions leading up to a criminal act; but they tend to pay more attention to the internal *self* as a primary variable than do control theorists. Furthermore, the social process of defining a situation as criminal is an important point of interest for interactionists, for unlike the control theorists, they do not assume that without control people would automatically turn to crime.

This chapter will examine the works of the "interactionists." For the most part, the criminological theories in this chapter have their philosophical and theoretical base in "symbolic interactionism," a sociological school of thought that focuses on the use of symbols in social interaction.[1] However, since the study of social interaction is examined by other theories that are not symbolic interactionism, we will use the more general term "interactionists" to refer to the level of analysis rather than a particular theory.

Beginning with differential association theory, we will examine three approaches to the study of crime in this chapter: 1) differential association, 2) labeling, and 3) structural interactionism. Each theory has in common the interactionists' level of analysis, but as we will see, each is very different.

The works of Sutherland,[2] Tannenbaum,[3] and Erving Goffman[4] as well as those who developed and expanded these theorists' works will be discussed. However, before getting into the different theories, we will first discuss the general areas of focus in these theories. We will look at: 1) associations, 2) the criminal justice system, and 3) interaction situations.

140

Associations

The primary socialization force consists of people with whom we associate. Generally, the primary groups of both the nuclear and extended family and the circle of friends we have in the neighborhood constitute those associates from whom we learn social norms and values. Our interaction is mediated through symbols we learn from and share with our associates—family, friends, fellow students, and the wider circle of people with whom we come into contact.[5]

The symbols we learn and use come to be our social reality. In general terms, we adopt a culture made up of symbols, and depending with whom we associate we have one version or another of culture. For example, if we are brought up in association with people in middle-class suburbs, we are likely to come into contact with symbols that assign value to education, long-range goals, and the promise of a stake in the "good life" provided to those who work hard. On the other hand, if we are raised in a slum, the symbols we come to know are more likely to assign value to immediate gratification, experience over education, and short-range goals. This is a simplification of a complex process, but the essential point is that we come to acquire our social reality in the process of social interaction—not by some vague or mysterious "laying on of culture" by society. Therefore, in order to understand the acquisition of a particular reality, we must understand the dynamics of social interaction and the associations in that interaction.

The Criminal Justice System

The criminal justice system is important to the interactionists in several ways. First, the system is the official **labeler** of those who are criminals—that is, of everyone who commits crimes, only certain people are arrested, and prosecuted, and thereby "made" official criminals. It is not so much the case of the criminal justice system labeling innocent citizens as it is the system *not* labeling those who have broken the law, and therefore the creation of selective criminal identities is of key interest to interactionists. Secondly, interactionists examine the interaction situations themselves. Included in the critical situations that determine the ultimate labeling of law breakers are encounters with the police, negotiations in the courtroom, and interaction between defense and prosecution. In Chapters 15 and 16 we will examine these situations in more detail, but it is important to understand something about them at this point so that we can appreciate certain arguments by the interactionists. Key elements in the criminal justice system, therefore, will be explained later in this chapter.

Interaction Situations

In addition to the situations where individuals are labeled criminal, interactionists are also interested in the situations where crimes occur. The familiar social axiom, "It depends on the situation," also applies to crime. On the one hand, interactionists study the "definition of the situation" or how the social actors perceive immediate events and courses of action.[6] On the other hand, there is an interest in situational structures themselves and how they lead to one kind of interaction or another.[7] As we will see, the interactionists attempt to show how certain crimes are dependent on particular situations.

Differential Association Theory

Since **differential association theory** was first introduced by Edwin Sutherland in the 1930s there have been some modifications and elaborations, especially by Donald R. Cressey. However, the principles of differential association remain very much the same as when Sutherland first introduced them. Beginning with the original nine propositions of the theory, we will discuss each and their implications in turn. It should be noted, however, that while differential association theory is very clear and apparently simple, it is full of very powerful and subtle insights that have withstood the test of time and research.

BOX 7.1   PROPOSITIONS

1. Criminal behavior is learned.
2. Criminal behavior is learned in interaction with other persons in a process of communication.
3. The principal part of the learning of criminal behavior occurs within intimate personal groups.
4. When criminal behavior is learned, the learning includes: a) techniques of committing the crime, which are sometimes very complicated, sometimes very simple; b) the specific direction of motives, drives, rationalizations, and attitudes.
5. The specific direction of motives and drives is learned from definitions of the legal codes as favorable or unfavorable.
6. A person becomes delinquent because of an excess of definitions favorable to violation of law over definitions unfavorable to violation of law.
7. Differential associations may vary in frequency, duration, priority, and intensity.
8. The process of learning criminal behavior by association with criminal

---

and anticriminal patterns involves all of the mechanisms that are involved in any other learning.

9. While criminal behavior is an expression of general needs and values, it is not explained by those general needs and values, since noncriminal behavior is an expression of the same needs and values.[8]

Learning Crime

The key principle of differential association is that crime is learned. This means that crime is not invented anew by people; it is not inherited through genes; and it does not come "out of the blue." Control theorists argued that everyone would turn to crime if they were not controlled, but they never were precise as to where the motivations for crime came from. Rather, they simply said that people were more or less naturally inclined toward crime unless somehow constrained. Sutherland, on the other hand, argued that, given observable criminal behavior patterns, it is unlikely that either: 1) there were a myriad of sources; and 2) each crime

THE WALL STREET JOURNAL

"We'll be right back with our program on sex, violence and crime, unless our sponsor decides to chicken out. . . ."

Source: From *Wall Street Journal*, Permission—Cartoon Features Syndicate.

was an independent invention. Therefore, crime was likely to be a learned behavior pattern.

The process of learning crime occurs in the course of communication, *primarily* within interpersonal groups. This simply means that learning occurs not only through verbal communication, but also in "conversation of gestures." The most important communication is in small interpersonal groups, especially primary groups such as the family and one's circle of friends. At first glance these statements do not appear to be very profound or controversial, but they imply, negatively, that people do *not* learn crime from reading the papers or watching television. For example, some people have argued that particular criminal acts occur because of the violence presented on television. However, according to differential association theory there is no patterned connection between mass media communication and crime. Isolated incidents of life reflecting something viewed on television are not a criminal behavior pattern. If media violence were the cause of real life violence then we would expect an even distribution of violence among all levels of society since they're exposed equally to media violence. Furthermore, when we consider the amount of crime and violence in best selling novels (far more than is ever allowed on television or in movies), we would expect a great deal more violent criminality among the middle and upper-middle classes who tend to buy and read such works. Thus, the proposition that crime is learned in small, intimate groups is far more important and laden with controversy than appears on the surface.

The fourth proposition deals with learning two very different but important aspects of crime: techniques and motives. Some techniques, such as how to steal an unlocked bicycle lying on the sidewalk, are so simple that little learning is involved. Other techniques are very complicated and require apprenticeships. For example, one safe-cracker (boxman) accompanied an experienced boxman for an entire year before he was allowed to crack his first safe.[9] Likewise, computer crimes involving the illegal transfer of funds from banks, confidence games, corporate fraud, and numerous other crimes can only be committed if the person has learned the techniques. With the simpler crimes, learning how to commit the crime may involve minimal instruction, but the techniques of escaping capture may be far greater. For instance, robbing a bank may involve nothing more than the techniques of holding a shotgun and talking in a loud, threatening voice; but the mechanisms for avoiding being filmed on the bank's camera, and using the stolen money require more than simple instructions.

A more important aspect of learning to commit crime has to do with learning the motives. In a critique of control theory, Cressey noted that even without social controls, it was necessary to specify how someone recognized the criminal potential in a situation.[10] That is, someone must learn how to define a situation as having criminal opportunities. For example, most women do not view men as prostitutes view them. Likewise, most men do not view people walking down the street as possible mugging victims.

The sociological understanding of motive is important here. Unlike the concept of **motive** that has inherent motives in people's make-up (e.g. needs, desires), the sociological concept of motive is one that is learned and becomes a part of our vocabulary of motives.[11] If we learn, for instance, that is it acceptable to steal from department stores but not acceptable to steal from a neighborhood "Mom and Pop" store, we have *learned* a motivation for department-store shoplifting. Likewise, if we learn that "everybody" does it (whatever "it" happens to be), we not only come to define the situation as possibly criminal, we may also have a motive or reason for committing the crime. Therefore, it is just as important to learn how to define a situation as criminal, as it is to learn the techniques for committing the crime.

The fifth and sixth propositions deal with definitions of the legal code as favorable or unfavorable and whether one comes to have an excess of definitions in one direction or the other. In a pluralistic society where different beliefs and ideologies abound, it is possible to learn both definitions that either favor following the law or breaking the law. One will be more likely to break laws if one learns that laws are worthless. Sometimes a person can learn that all laws are bad, but more often, one learns that only certain legal codes are wrong. For example, a person may learn from his or her friends that the marijuana laws are unfair and the drug is relatively harmless, but that same person would be horrified at the idea of robbing a liquor store or murdering someone for hire. Simply put, if the associations and the definitions of the legal code tend to favor following the law, then criminal behavior will be reduced. Put in a formula, the relationship would look like this:

$$\frac{\text{Definitions Favorable to Violating the Law}}{\text{Definitions Unfavorable to Violating the Law}}$$

$$\frac{\text{DFVL}}{\text{DUVL}}$$

If DFVL is greater than DUVL; then there will be criminal behavior, but if DUVL is greater than DFVL; then there will not be criminal behavior.

The seventh and eighth propositions state that associations have important qualitative differences, and learning crime is just like learning anything else. The qualitative differences of frequency, duration, priority, and intensity determine the strength and influence of an association.

- *Frequency.* The more often we associate with a person or group, the more likely we are to be influenced by their ideas. If we know a criminal, but we have infrequent associations with him or her, we are less likely to learn attitudes favorable to breaking the law than if the contacts are frequent.

- *Duration.* Time is an important element in how we treat the opinions and ideas of associates. Those whom we have only just met are less likely to have an influence on our beliefs and actions than long-time friends. If someone we have known a long time is involved in criminal behavior patterns, we are more likely to learn those patterns than from someone we have just met.

- *Priority.* Sutherland's use of "priority" refers to how early in life people are exposed to criminal or anticriminal behavior patterns. Definitions introduced early in life exert higher priority and more influence than definitions introduced later in life. Thus, if anticriminal behavior patterns are introduced early, they will have a more telling effect than criminal behavior patterns introduced later.

- *Intensity.* The stronger a relationship with an associate, the more influence they will have. People in love have intense associations while acquaintances have weaker ties. Those with whom we have intense relationships are more likely to mold how we view the world than people we simply "know."

Taken together, these variables determine the influence of learning and accepting definitions of the law that are favorable or unfavorable. Associations with the greatest influence are ones that we acquired early in life, have had for a long time, spend a lot of time with, and are personally close to. It is important that these variables are a part of differential association theory, for otherwise, we would predict that prison guards, criminal attorneys, judges, and others who have frequent associations with criminals would be likely to become criminal themselves. However, since the *quality* of these relationships is not intense and the relationships low priority in the lives of men and women working with criminals, they do not have the effect of "teaching" criminal behavior patterns.

Learning criminal behavior patterns has no special status in terms of learning in general. The same identical processes that go into learning anti-criminal behavior patterns also go into learning criminal behavior patterns. Thus, the same person can learn pro or anti-criminal beliefs without any special capacity for one or the other. No special "criminal teaching process" is required.

The final proposition in differential association theory is really a statement about general theorizing in criminology. The central idea behind the proposition is that we cannot explain criminal behavior by pointing to the ends or goals of crime since those same goals are pursued through legitimate channels. For example, if we explain prostitution by saying, "Prostitutes are in it for the money," we really do not explain anything about prostitution, since if a woman earned her living as an accountant we could also say, "She's in it for the money." Therefore, our explanation *for the money* does not differentiate legal from illegal pursuits. This is because we use general needs and goals as explanations.

What criminologists need to explain is why *criminal means* are employed to achieve goals. Thus, in explaining prostitution, or any other crime, we need to ask why a person turned to crime to achieve a goal. Therefore, rather than asking simply, "Why do prostitutes do what they do?" we would ask, "Why is prostitution used by some women to obtain money rather than some other means?"

Evaluation and Research of Differential Association

The reasoning behind differential association theory has been criticized on a number of different points. Nevertheless, the theory has been validated and re-validated over the years. The theory does, however, have its limitations and we cannot use it effectively if it is considered a means of explaining every aspect of criminal behavior. First of all, the theory has been criticized for not explaining the origin of criminal behavior patterns.[12] However, from Sutherland's perspective the primary problem of criminology is explaining how criminal and delinquent values come into existence, and the secondary problem is how such values diffuse to individuals.[13] Differential association theory relies on theories such as Cohen's, that do explain how criminal behavior patterns come into existence, and concentrates itself on how these patterns come to persist.

A second group of criticisms of differential association states that there are a number of different types of crimes and criminals that do not seem to learn crime.[14] For example, it has been said that rural criminals, white-collar criminals, impulsive murderers, and other apparent "loners" do not rely on learning criminal behavior. However, since very few of the claims of exception to differential association theory were tested by research, it is not at all certain that these criminals do not learn crime. For instance, in research on homicides by Luckenbill, there was clear evidence that in so-called "compulsive" homicides, the killers had learned that physical violence was the appropriate course of action in the situations where they committed murder.[15] However, in some kinds of crimes, such as embezzlement, there does not seem to be the same kind of learning process as suggested in Sutherland's theory.[16]

A third major criticism of differential association theory has been directed toward determining the ratio of learning criminal to anti-criminal behavior patterns. This criticism states that it is virtually impossible to tell whether there has been "an excess of definitions" favorable to crime. However, D. A. Andrews, in creative experiments using prisoners, probationers, and noncriminal volunteer subjects, found that it was possible to vary the definitions favorable to violating the law in structured situations.[17] In doing so, he was able to determine the effect of an excess of definitions that were either favorable or unfavorable to law violation. The findings clearly confirmed differential association theory's tenets.

The final criticism of differential association lead us more directly into the research. Besides direct empirical questions there have been questions of operationalizing the concepts. Many critics argued that it is virtually impossible to test any of the theory's propositions since the concepts are vague. These criticisms led to research that operationalized the various concepts so that they could be tested. For example, Akers and fellow researchers tested adolescent drinking and drug behavior and found strong support that differential association determined this pattern of delinquency.[18] Their research used behavioralistic conceptions of learning (e.g. reinforcement, stimuli, avoidance), arguing

> . . . the theory posits that the principal behavioral effects come from interaction in or under the influence of those *groups which control individuals' major sources of reinforcement and punishment and expose them to behavior models and normative definitions*.[19]

Thus, like many of the other criticisms of differential association theory, the problems have been largely a matter of operationalizing the concepts, but once that has been accomplished, the theory tends to be confirmed by research.

Labeling Theory

In Chapter 2 we discussed the problems in measuring crime and counting criminals. One of the findings of methods using self-report surveys has been that there are a lot more people committing delinquent and criminal acts than are ever arrested, convicted, or incarcerated. In fact, just about everybody has broken the criminal law at one time or another, and if given the maximum penal sanction, very few of the population would avoid spending time in prison.

The problem, then, is not necessarily why some people commit crimes and others do not, since just about everyone does, but rather why only certain people are labeled as criminals when so many have committed crimes. In other words, we ask, "Who gets labeled criminal and who does not and why?" This question is the essential query of labeling theory, and includes inquiry into the processes of labeling, the institutions and organizations responsible for labeling, the societal reaction to labeled individuals, and the management of a label by those identified as criminal.

The Labeling Process

When a person commits a crime, there is no automatic label attached to them identifying them as criminal. Instead a series of events has to occur before the person is even suspected of being a criminal. First, the act must be defined by someone as being a real crime. A criminal act might be defined as any number of things—an accident, a misplaced item, or simply overlooked altogether. Secondly, some kind of action must be taken regarding the act as a crime. Usually this involves calling the police, but significant action could be raising a fuss in the community identifying the crime and the culprit. Third, there has to be some consensus that the act is in fact an actual crime. Again, this usually involves the police treating the incident as an actual crime and taking steps to find the person who committed it. Fourth, a person has to be caught and identified as the culprit. This can involve a mistaken identity but usually it does not. Fifth, once a person has been caught and identified as the law breaker, he or she must be processed as a criminal. Usually, even when the police have caught and identified an offender, the person is let off with a warning. Sixth, once processed, the individual must be successfully labeled a criminal. If a person is given probation or a fine as punishment for a crime, and is not caught and processed in the future, it is unlikely that the person will be successfully labeled.

Even before someone is accused of breaking a law and labeled a criminal, there must be a law to be broken. Therefore, the labeling theorists also are interested in how the laws come into being. In Becker's words:

> . . . *social groups create deviance by making the rules whose infraction constitutes deviance,* and by applying those rules to particular people and labeling them as outsiders. From this point of view, deviance is *not* a quality of the act the person commits, but rather a consequence of the application by others of rules and sanctions to an "offender."[20]

This shifts the emphasis from how a person comes to commit a criminal act to how, in social interaction with others, he or she comes to be defined as a criminal—from the creation of the law to the actual labeling.

The process whereby one actually becomes separated from the rest of the community as being somehow different is described as a **degradation ceremony**.[21] Involved in this ceremony are eight steps summarized as follows:

1. The accused and the act must be defined as being extraordinary.
2. The accuser (witness) must be able to show that the perpetrator is of

a certain *type,* namely criminal, and that the act and motives cannot be better defined in any other way.

3. The denouncer must appear to be a public figure (e.g., a judge) to others and not a private figure against the accused.

4. The denunciation must be seen in the name of public values.

5. The denouncer cannot allow any implication of personal vendetta to enter into the denunciation.

6. The denouncer must act so as to be seen by others as a supporter of social values.

7. The denouncer has to be seen as detached from the person being denounced.

8. The person being denounced has to be set apart from the legitimate order—he must be defined as "not one of us."

Garfinkel argues that all of these elements of degradation must be present in the ceremony in order for it to be successful, and if they are not the labeling ritual will not succeed. For example, if the denouncer is seen to be involved in the degradation ceremony for personal gain or as an "outsider" to the witnesses himself, there is little chance the denouncement will be successful. Also, the target of the degradation may not only defend him/herself against the charges of the denouncer, he or she can put up a lively fight to define the situation so as to be seen as a "good person in bad circumstances." Various congressmen who were caught taking bribes in the "ABSCAM" investigation, and televised doing so, defended themselves even after conviction. They attempted to redefine their actions as being in line with social morality. For instance, one congressman said that he was attempting to get money for the district he represented and another claimed he was conducting an investigation into bribery himself! Apparently the electorate did not believe these alternative definitions of the congressmen's actions, for none were re-elected. Therefore, the degradation ceremonies conducted in the courts and House of Representatives were successful. (It should be noted that the denouncers had a good deal of evidence in the "ABSCAM" case, and the degradations were not "made up" merely to embarrass those denounced.)

The institutional labeling mechanism is the criminal justice system. In Chapters 15 through 18, we will examine the several contingencies that determine whether or not a person is labeled, but for now it is important to point out that the contingencies are determining variables.[22] For example, the availability of space in prison determines whether a person will be more or less likely to receive probation; city budgets for police departments determine the probability of being arrested; policies in the district attorney's office affect the chances of being charged with a crime and the

South Carolina Congressman John Jenrette was one of the officials photographed taking a bribe in the ABSCAM case. He, along with other congressmen who were caught in the same investigation, continued to deny his guilt and identity as a criminal. Here he is shown being consoled by his wife Rita (right) and daughter Elizabeth.

nature of the punishment for various offenses. All of these contingencies, and others as well, go to make up the labeling process.

The Looking-Glass Self

A central concept used in labeling theory is Cooley's **looking-glass self**.[23] This concept defines the social self as made up of what a person sees others seeing him/her to be. In other words, others are a mirror (looking-glass) to one's self. For example, if a person is treated as a kind, considerate person by others, that person is likely to see himself as such. On the other hand, if the same person is viewed by others as stupid, inconsiderate, and lazy, a self-image based on these characteristics is likely.

At first we may not see how strong others' definitions of our self is, but when we consider negative cases we can see clearly how the looking-glass self works. For example, people who make claims for themselves that others do not see or agree with are called "phonies" or "frauds." Since most people do not want to be seen as phonies, they can do one of two things: either back up their claims of self so that others will not call them phonies or drop their claims that cannot be confirmed. This adjustment alters behavior so that one's identity is in line with others' definitions of reality. In more extreme cases, we define insanity in terms of people making identity claims not recognized by others. If a man says he is Napoleon, we would probably think he was crazy—a schizophrenic with delusions of grandeur. The claims of self simply do not conform with our version of reality.

Stigma

A second key concept used in labeling theory is **stigma**.[24] Developed by Erving Goffman, stigma refers to any discrediting *mark*. It is the opposite of a status symbol. For the most part, stigmas are visible physical signs such as certain tattoos, missing appendages, or deformities. In some way, stigmas discredit the owners, and to the extent they are visible, the person is held in contempt (or pity) by those who view it.

There are criminal stigmas of varying degrees of visibility. Some stigmas, such as criminal records, are visible only under certain circumstances. For example, when applying for a job, a person may have to reveal a criminal past, either on an application form or in taking a lie detector test. Likewise, "holes" in one's resume can reveal criminal records. If a person was in prison for ten years, he will have such a "hole" to be either hidden by lying or revealed. Other criminal stigmas are visible in more subtle ways. For example, homemade prison tattoos or gang tattoos are stigmas of criminal pasts.

Taking the concepts of the looking-glass self and stigma together, we can begin to see how they are linked in forming a criminal identity. If a person has a criminal stigma, others see that person as a criminal and treat him accordingly. Since a person's identity is dependent on how other's see him, the person with a criminal stigma comes to see himself as a criminal. If the person makes claims to a noncriminal identity, others point to the stigma and argue, "If you are not a criminal, then why do you have a criminal record?" The retort, "I served my time," or "I paid my debt to society," is not taken to be evidence of reform or repayment.

Rather, it is confirmation that the person is indeed a criminal, for only criminals have to go to prison in the first place.

The rejection of the labeled criminal's claims to a noncriminal identity sets the person off from legitimate others. He is forced either into the company of those who share a similar label or off by himself. This fosters further criminality either because society's rejection gives him little opportunity in the legitimate social structure or because he is forced to associate with other labeled "criminals."

Edwin Lemert differentiates between "primary" and "secondary" deviance to explain the relationship between labeling and criminality.[25] Primary deviance is any kind of norm violation occurring before one is labeled and is not due to any specific cause. Since virtually everyone engages in some kind of primary deviance, it is not of prime interest. Secondary deviance, on the other hand, is the reaction to the societal reaction—an adjustment to the labeling itself. As we saw above, the criminal stigma leads to a criminal identity, which leads to "career criminality." This is what Lemert is referring to by "secondary deviation."

Lemert, however, does not argue that all primary deviance eventually leads to secondary deviance, but rather that there is a process involved in transforming an individual's identity from noncriminal to criminal. Degradation ceremonies constitute one example of the process of transformation, but even these ceremonies have only so much effect on a one-time basis. Thus, Lemert is not examining crime in terms of a single stimulus that leads to crime, but instead he sees a series of events that slowly transform one's identity from one state to another. At any time during the process, either because the societal reaction changes, or the actor abandons the deviant behavior, a person can return to a nondeviant identity. For example, at one time, virtually all marijuana smokers were in the same category as "drug addicts," and marijuana was smoked primarily by members of deviant subcultures; but as the drug became popular among the more respectable elements of society and penalties for possession were reduced, the societal reaction became less stigmatizing. As a result, a person whose only crime was marijuana use was able to move from a deviant to nondeviant identity. Likewise, a person who gives up crime can reclaim a nondeviant status. It is only when the behavior and societal reaction remain constant over a period of time that one comes to engage in secondary deviation.

Evaluation and Research of Labeling Theory

A common critique of labeling theory is that it has become a study of sociology of law rather than of why people commit crime.[26] To some extent such a criticism is quite valid, for there are a number of researchers identified with the labeling perspective whose primary goal has been to find out why certain laws are enacted and thereby define certain actions as criminal.[27] However, the study of secondary deviation has been directed toward how people become "career criminals" once they have been labeled. Therefore, the study of the labeling process is one of criminal causation as much as it is of the criminal justice system.

Similarly, critics have suggested that labeling theory ignores the fact that virtually everyone who is labeled a criminal *has* committed a crime, and if the crime were not committed they would not be labeled. Therefore, without a theory of the initial criminality (primary deviance), the labeling theorists simply avoid the important question of initial patterns of crime causation. However, this criticism is also weak in that the labeling theorists argue that self-report surveys show that virtually everyone commits crime, but only a few are labeled criminals and become career criminals. Since the labeling process differentiates criminals from noncriminals, in terms of social realities, the labeling process *is* the significant cause.

Perhaps the most interesting and strongest criticism of labeling theory is in the research. First, if secondary deviation is caused by criminal labels, those who have served time in prison are the most likely to have a strong stigma. However, as Glaser found in his study of prison and parole, only about a third of those who spend time in prison are reimprisoned for crime.[28] According to labeling theory, just about all people who spend time in prison should follow a criminal career; but according to Glaser, 95 percent of the men released from prison tried to go straight at first, and while many failed and returned to a life of crime, most did not.[29] Likewise, studies have shown that people do not passively accept labels; but instead they attempt to "de-label" themselves. For example, religious conversions, changing place of residence, and using financial and social power can successfully thwart attempts at labeling.[30] Thus, rather than being a wholly passive recipient of society's labels, people are far more active (and artful) at keeping themselves from being labeled. Similarly, certain people actually want to be identified as "tough" and actively seek criminal labels to enhance their identities.

Despite the various flaws in labeling theory, it is an important consideration in any discussion of crime. Cressey even noted that the criminal label can be a behavior pattern favorable to crime, and as such, an important element of differential association theory.[31] Moreover, given the amount of "hidden crime" in society, we are hard-pressed to explain crime as a whole without taking note of the social processes involved in designating certain people as "criminals." Finally, since crime is a social definition, the processes and institutions involved in defining what is and is not a crime—especially in a pluralistic, changing society—is of utmost importance in criminology.

Structural Interaction

The final explanation in criminology we will examine will be referred to as the **structural interaction** approach to crime and delinquency. Structural interactionism refers to the study of micro-institutions in social life that govern social interaction. We are familiar with the aphorism, "It depends on the situation," and the study of crime from this perspective emphasizes the little structures found in encounters when people come face to face with one another. This approach is a relatively new one in the study of crime, but it has a rich sociological tradition in the works of Emile Durkheim, Georg Simmel, Claude Levi-Strauss, and most recently and importantly, Erving Goffman.[32]

We can begin examining this approach by reconsidering the concept of the looking-glass self. Since people come to see themselves as others see them, what others see becomes important to the individual. In order to be seen in a favorable way, people can manipulate what others see. That is, they can present a "front" for others in interaction situations so that they will be seen, and see themselves, as socially good.[33] Most people, however, are aware that while day-to-day presentations of self are a good indication of who and what a person is, there are certain situations that are critical ones in telling us essential truths about ourselves and others. These are situations of "character tests" where a person's behavior is judged to be an indication of either strong or weak character.[34] Unlike the mundane everyday situations where we can fake or simulate identities, in situations of character tests, faking is not possible. The behavior required to establish character (or disestablish it) is in the act itself and not the telling. For example, it is one thing to claim to be brave in safe situations, but in situations fraught with danger, standing or running determine courage. Even if one is terrified but holds his ground or proceeds with a course of action that brings on the danger, courage is *demonstrated* to others. In such situations, one determines self, for it is only that person's actions that resolve the situation.

The situations that have the social and circumstantial ingredients are described by Goffman as "fateful."[35] On the one hand, such situations are problematic or chancy in that there is no certainty as to the outcome. On the other hand, they are consequential in that the results of the occasion will affect the person's life far beyond the bonds of the occasion where any action is taken.[36] For example, if a person bets his life savings at the gambling table the situation is fateful, for the throw of the dice is chancy and the outcome is consequential. Winning or losing will determine the individual's fate long after the dice have determined the outcome.

Besides the thrill of taking such life-determining chances, there is the satisfaction of determining one's fate. However, fateful situations are not always around when we need them. The various forms of character—courage, gameness, coolness—can only be demonstrated in problematic and consequential situations. Therefore, some people seek out fatefulness and take it on for its own sake. These situations Goffman describes as **action**.[37]

Among the young and those with much to gain and little to lose by way of establishing character, action is seen as a more inviting alternative to "being someone" than either the traditional grind of going to school or the scarce positions available in celebrity stardom such as professional sports. Various forms of interpersonal action are available.[38] In looking at delinquent gangs, for instance, Goffman cites one study showing how delinquent behavior and interpersonal action are connected:

> The quickened tempo of the testing of relationships on corners, in contrast with, for example, work groups, arises in part because leaders do not control important amounts of property, because there are few privileges or immunities they can bestow, and because there are no external institutional pressures that constrain members to accept the discipline of the gang.[39]

In this context, the community becomes the "field of action" and the pattern of delinquency is understood in terms of the "kicks" it provides. Noting Miller's observations of the lower class, the action, while not necessarily illegal, often is:

> Many of the most characteristic features of lower class life are related to the search for excitement or "thrill." Involved here are the highly prevalent use of alcohol by both sexes and the widespread use of gambling of all kinds— playing the numbers, betting on horse races, dice, cards. The quest for excitement finds what is perhaps its more vivid expression in the highly patterned practice of the recurrent "night on the town." . . . Fights between men involving women, gambling, and claims of physical prowess, in various combinations, are frequent consequences of a night of making the rounds. The explosive potential of this type of adventuring with sex and aggression, frequently leading to "trouble," is semi-explicitly sought by the individual. Since there is always a good likelihood that being out on the town will eventuate in fights, etc., the practice involves elements of sought risk and desired danger.[40]

The excitement, not the criminal gains, is the goal in such activity, and so the utility is in the action, which may be criminal. However, the question

Goffman is posing is *not*, "Why do people pursue action?"—that is a general goal pursued in legitimate fashions. Rather, Goffman is attempting to explain why certain forms of action that have a high probability of violating the law are pursued by the lower class, especially young lower-class males. The unique forms of action found in lower-class communities exist because of the limited access to legitimate forms of action and the traditions in these communities.

Character Contests

Another kind of interpersonal action that can lead to law violation is the "character contest." Describing such contests, Goffman notes:

> During occasions of this kind of action, not only will character be at stake, mutual fatefulness will prevail in this regard. Each person will be at least incidentally concerned with establishing evidence of strong character, and conditions will be such as to allow this only at the expense of the character of the other participants. The very field that the one uses to express char-

Gangs often come into conflict over "honor." Their identity with their gang is strong, and an offense to the honor of their gang is taken to be a personal affront to be avenged by violence. Southern California Chicano gangs often tattoo themselves with their gang affiliation.

acter may be the other's character expression. And at times the primary
properties at play may themselves be openly made a convenience, pointedly
serving merely as an occasion for doing battle by and for character.[41]

Such encounters put "honor" at stake, and when the utility of honor is
high, then the consequences of upholding it can be severe. In their study
of gang violence, Horowitz and Swartz describe gang violence as character
contests in that gang fights and assaults are caused by affronts to one
gang's honor and the "required" retaliation by the offended party.[42] Similarly, in a study of West Coast gang violence, it was found that even
disembodied insults to one's honor led to violence. Among the Mexican-
American gangs of Southern California, it is common practice to spray-
paint a gang's name (*placa*) along with its members' names on walls in the
gang's neighborhood or barrio. Character contests arise when a rival gang
crosses out a gang's *placa* or one of its members' names and puts its own
name in its place. The contest can be joined by doing the same thing to
the offending gang until one gang decides either to take direct violent action or accidentally runs into the offending rival. For example, the following incident occurred at a party celebrating a baptism:

> Members of the Sheridan gang were at the same party as members of the
> Monte Vista gang. Six months before the party, a Monte Vista member had
> X'ed out a Sheridan *placa* he found while serving time along with some
> Sheridan members in a youth detention camp. At the time of the original
> offense there had been a minor scuffle over the affront, and at the party the
> incident was recalled again. The Monte Vista boys were far out-numbered
> by the Sheridan members at the party, and after a short interlude at the
> party where all was forgotten and forgiven, the Sheridan boys jumped a
> Monte Vista boy, stabbing and beating him after he tried to run away from
> the party. Shortly thereafter, a second encounter led to a repeat of the first,
> and by the end of the party, two Monte Vista boys were in the hospital with
> stab wounds and a half-dozen Sheridan members were in police custody.[43]

Other character contests, besides the intricate ones of gangs, also lead to
crime. They can be anything from a drunken cowboy in the bar slurring
the man next to him to a new kid in school attempting to establish himself
by taking on all comers. The point is not so much to conquer others and
what is theirs as it is to make a statement about one's own character and
honor. If offenses only communicated something about the offender,
there would be no call for retaliation. But since in character contests the
offender must either stand up for himself or lose face there is a high potential for violence—since even verbal retaliation simply leads to escalating the probability of violence. Thus, when community or subcultural

standards put a high stake on personal honor and see violence as a legitimate means of redress, character contests come to be a source of violent crime.

Criminal Situations

Another area of interest in structural interactionism is the nature of the situations and occasions where crimes occur. In a concern similar to the control theorists, the question arises as to what kinds of situations does crime typically occur in and what is the nature of those situations? Both the research and theory in this area is sparse, but what there is suggests clear evidence that crimes are far more likely to occur only in certain situations.

On the most elementary level, we can characterize situations as relatively **loose** or **tight**. Loose occasions are those where the boundaries of appropriate behavior are vague and informal, such as parties, picnics, barroom gatherings, and "hanging out." Tight occasions, on the other hand, are formal, circumscribed, and clearly focused: such as work occasions, funerals, and formal receptions.[44] The structure of the situation defines the appropriate behavior while within the boundaries of that situation, and what is proper and improper "depends on the situation." The issue of defining the situation is only relevant in a general sense. For the most part the situation is defined beforehand, and those entering the situation can see what the situation is, and only occasionally is a definition problematic.[45] The variations in how to define a situation can differ according to class or subcultural traditions, and so a middle-class version of "a night on the town" is not the same as a lower-class definition of the same occasion; however, within a given context of a class or subculture, what the situation means is not generally a question to be resolved by renewed definitions as new participants enter the situation. However, regardless of class or culture, a "night on the town" would be loose and a "day at work" would be tight.

The expectations of this theory are that loose occasions would be more likely to generate criminal behavior than would tight ones. With less specific allocation of involvement, people are more likely to abandon self-control and intentionally or unwittingly break the law. Participation in one type of situation or the other will depend on social status and the overall social organization in which one type of situation or the other is found. Nevertheless, in a given social milieu, whether on a community or societal level, when the boundaries of an occasion are loosely defined and appropriate behavior for the situations broadly defined, crime is a more likely occurrence. This theory shares much with control theory in that control varies with the situation. However, the approach assumes a far livelier social actor and a greater role of self than does control theory.

Research and Evaluation: Structural Interaction

As with all newer approaches to the study of criminology, what we have called "structural interaction" has little research at this time, but what there is appears to be very promising for this perspective. However, the approach is limited to a certain extent and must be developed further for its full significance to be appreciated.

Perhaps the greatest limitation of this theory, like many others in criminology, is that it appears to account for only a certain spectrum of crimes, namely "common crimes" committed largely by the poor and juveniles. Elaborately organized corporate frauds, governmental bribes, and white collar crimes of various types appear to occur in something other than loose occasions. For example, bank embezzlement occurs at work, a tight occasion.[46] Likewise, organized price-fixing requires formal meetings to work out the details of how companies involved in the crime are going to split up profits.[47] However, since "tight" and "loose" occasions are relative to one another, it may be that upper-world crime is hatched in relatively loose occasions. From the ABSCAM videotapes, it was clear that the meetings in the hotel rooms where the bribes were passed to congressmen were relatively informal and loose. Further research into this aspect of upper-world and white collar crime requires investigation, and while it is clear that much of it does not occur in loose occasions, some of it does.

In evaluating the extent to which crime is done for the "action," including both the thrill and character-establishing features of such crime, Goffman was dealing primarily with delinquency. The extent to which big profits illegally gained in upper-world crime is seen as "action" may suggest that it is not just the juveniles who are looking for thrills. However, in comparing adult and juvenile criminality, there is clear evidence that juvenile crime tends to involve more risk-taking and less financial utility than adult crimes. Furthermore, establishing character is more problematic for juveniles and so it is more relevant to their delinquent activities. Therefore, rather than arguing that "action" accounts for all criminality, it is argued that it differentiates delinquency from adult criminality.

There is little actual research testing hypotheses dealing either with the structure of the situation or action. In Horowitz and Swartz's study of gangs, it was clear that much of the gang violence was due to "character contests," and other studies of gang behavior have found similar patterns in gang violence.[48] Likewise, other studies of crime and delinquency have found that the "thrills" and "kicks" involved in the activities have been an integral part of the crime.[49] In studies examining the structure of the situation where crimes occur, a study of homicide showed that the predominate occasion of murder was in loose occasions, and the same findings were found in a study of rape.[50] In a study of police mobilizations, it was found that 84.1 percent of the situations where police were called were loose as compared with only 15.9 percent which were tight.[51] Overall, though, there is a clear need for further research in this area as well as a further refinement of the concepts being employed, but given the findings so far, it is clear that the situational structures of crime have unique characteristics of interest to criminologists.

SUMMARY

Interactionists' theories have been identified with the social-psychological level of analysis, focusing on the individual. For the most part, this is an accurate depiction of the interactionists' work in the area of crime and deviance. Both labeling and differential association theories take as their key concepts elements in the development of self, and the structural interactions also pay close attention to the individual's self-concept. Thus, there is a strong element of individualistic explanation in these theories.

However, equally important in these theories are the often overlooked structural and subcultural elements. The structural interactionists treat social situations as micro-institutions and emphasize the important part played by the situation in allowing the opportunity for crime. Likewise, the labeling theorists point out the development of criminal and deviant subcultures emerging out of societal labels, and differential association theory points to criminal subcultures as the source of learning criminal behavior patterns. Therefore, while all of these theories recognize the importance of the individual level of analysis, they also recognize the social level.

In many respects the interactionists have bridged the gap between the structuralists on the one hand, and the individualists on the other. It has not been a synthesis or compromise between the different theories of the macro and micro levels, but instead, it is a level of analysis in its own right. As such, the interactionist approach to crime has provided a needed middle ground that allows the analyst to examine the multidimensional facets of crime.

Glossary

Action The willing entrance into a risky and consequential set of circumstances. Goffman uses this concept to explain the excitement some feel while committing crimes.

Degradation Ceremony The public labeling of an individual as deviant.

Differential Association Theory Sutherland's theory that crime is learned in association with others who are involved in criminal behavior patterns.

Label The social typing of an individual as belonging to a certain category. Criminal typings or tags are used to characterize certain individuals as "criminal."

Looking-Glass Self Charles Horton Cooley's conception of self. It suggests that people come to see themselves as others see them.

Loose Situations Circumstances where the norms of behavior are general and not clearly fixed.

Motive In sociological usage, a motive is a reason for doing something understood by others. Motives are treated as words in one's vocabulary that are learned from others.

Stigma A discrediting mark that is the opposite of a status symbol, visibly showing others that an individual has been involved in undesirable behavior.

Structural Interaction Refers to the study of micro-structures in interaction situations such as "situations" and "occasions."

Tight Situations Situations characterized by strict and clear rules with little flexibility.

Questions

1. What are the major conceptual variables in interactionist theories? What can concepts at this level of analysis tell us that is unavailable to theories on the macro-level of analysis?

2. What is involved in learning crime according to differential association theory, and why does learning violence from television viewing play such a little part?

3. How are the concepts of "looking-glass self" and stigma used in labeling theory?

4. How does Goffman explain the excitement and fun in delinquent acts?

5. What bearing does the social situation have on delinquency? What are the structural elements of social situations related to criminal acts?

Notes

1. Herbert Blumer, *Symbolic Interaction: Perspective and Method*. (Englewood Cliffs, NJ: Prentice-Hall, 1969).

2. Edwin Sutherland, *Principles of Criminology*. (Philadelphia: Lippincott, 1939).

3. Frank Tannenbaum, *Crime and the Community*. (New York: Ginn, 1938).

4. Erving Goffman, *Interaction Ritual*. (Garden City, NY: Doubleday, 1967).

5. George Herbert Mead, *Mind, Self, and Society*. (Chicago: University of Chicago Press, 1934).

6. Peter McHugh, *Defining the Situation*. (Indianapolis: Bobbs-Merrill, 1968).

7. Erving Goffman, *Frame Analysis*. (New York: Harper & Row, 1974).

8. Edwin Sutherland and Donald R. Cressey, *Criminology* (10th ed.) (Philadelphia: Lippincott, 1978), pp. 80–82.

9. Bill Chambliss, *Box Man*. (New York: Harper & Row, 1972).

10. Sutherland and Cressey, 1978, 80.

11. C. Wright Mills, "Situated Action and the Vocabulary of Motives," *American Sociological Review* **6** (December 1940): 904–913.

12. Sutherland and Cressey, 1978, 87.

13. Donald R. Cressey, "Fifty Years of Criminology," *Pacific Sociological Review* **22** (October 1979): 464.

14. Donald R. Cressey, "Epidemiology and Individual Conduct: A Case from Criminology," *Pacific Sociological Review* **3** (1960): 47–58.

15. David Luckenbill, "Criminal Homicide as a Situated Transaction," *Social Problems* **25** (December 1977): 176–186.

16. Donald R. Cressey, *Other People's Money*. (Belmont, CA: Wadsworth, 1971).

17. D. A. Andrews, "Some Experimental Investigation of the Principles of Differential Association Through Deliberate Manipulation of the Structure of Service Systems," *American Sociological Review* **45** (June 1980): 448–462.

18. Ronald Akers, Marvin Krohn, Lonn Lanza-Kaduce, and Marcia Radosevich, "Social Learning and Deviant Behavior: A Specific Test of a General Theory," *American Sociological Review* **44** (August 1979): 636–655.

19. Akers et al., 1979, 638.

20. Howard S. Becker, *Outsiders*. (New York: Free Press, 1963), p. 8.

21. Harold Garfinkel, "Conditions of a Successful Degradation Ceremony," *American Journal of Sociology* **61** (March 1956): 420–424.

22. Erving Goffman, *Asylums*. (Garden City, NY: Doubleday, 1961).

23. Charles Horton Cooley, *Human Nature and the Social Order*. (New York: Scribner's, 1902).

24. Erving Goffman, *Stigma*. (Indianapolis: Bobbs-Merrill, 1963).

25. Edwin Lemert, *Social Pathology*. (New York: McGraw-Hill, 1951).

26. Cressey, 1979, 465–466.

27. Becker, 1963; John Kitsuse "Societal Reactions to Deviant Behavior: Problems of Theory and Method," *Social Problems* **9**, 247–256.

28. Daniel Glaser, *The Effectiveness of a Prison and Parole System*. (Indianapolis: Bobbs-Merrill, 1969).

29. Glaser, 1969, 54.

30. Erving Goffman, *Stigma*. (Indianapolis: Bobbs-Merrill, 1963).

31. Cressey, 1979, 465.

32. The term "structural interactionism" is used here to describe Goffman's focus on the structure of social interaction. It is a descriptive term rather than a school of thought. See "Frame Analysis Reconsidered" by Norman Denzin and Charles Keller and "A Reply to Denzin and Keller" by Erving Goffman in *Contemporary Sociology* **10** (January 1981): 52–68.

33. Erving Goffman, *The Presentation of Self in Everyday Life*. (Garden City, NY: Doubleday, 1959).

34. Goffman, 1967, 149–270.

35. Goffman, 1967, 161–170.

36. Goffman, 1967, 161–170.

37. Goffman, 1967, 181–194.

38. Goffman, 1967, 212.

39. James Short and F. Strodbeck, *Group Process and Gang Delinquency*. (Chicago: University Press, 1965), p. 196.

40. Walter Miller, "Lower Class Culture as a Generating Milieu of Gang Delinquency," *Journal of Social Issues* **14** (1958): 11.

41. Goffman, 1967, 240.

42. Ruth Horowitz and Gary Swartz, "Honor, Normative Ambiguity and Gang Violence," *American Sociology Review* **39** (1974): 238–251.

43. Unpublished field notes by the author.

44. Erving Goffman, *Behavior in Public Places*. (New York: Free Press, 1963), pp. 198–215.

45. Goffman, 1974, 1.

46. Cressey, 1971, pp. 1–15.

47. Richard Austin Smith, "The Incredible Electrical Conspiracy," *Fortune* (April 1961): 132–180.

48. Horowitz and Swartz, 1974; Joan W. Moore, *Homeboys*. (Philadelphia: Temple University Press, 1978); William B. Sanders, "Forms of Gang Violence," Paper presented at American Sociological Association Annual Meeting, Toronto, Ontario (August 1981).

49. Harold Finestone, "Cats, Kicks and Color," *Social Problems* **5** (July 1957): 3–13; Carl Werthman, "The Function of Social Definitions in the Development of Delinquent Careers," *Task Force Report: Juvenile Delinquency and Youth Crime*. (Washington, D.C.: U.S. Government Printing Office, 1967); John Allen, *Assault with a Deadly Weapon*. (New York: McGraw-Hill, 1977).

50. Luckenbill, 1978; William B. Sanders, *Rape and Woman's Identity*. (Beverly Hills, CA: Sage, 1980).

51. William B. Sanders, "Police Occasions: A Study of Interaction Contexts," *Criminal Justice Review* **4** (Spring 1979): 1–13.

8

Common Crimes

What to Look For:

The elements of common crimes.

The groups that are most likely to be
involved in common crimes.

The most likely victims of common crimes.

Explanations as to why crimes by women are on the increase.

Changing patterns of crime.

The nature of armed robberies and use of lethal and
nonlethal weapons in interpersonal coercion.

The typical pattern of check forging in
comparison with other common crimes.

Introduction

HAVING EXAMINED several theories of crime, we will now turn to an examination of criminal behavior patterns. Our focus shifts now to determining the typical, patterned ways in which crimes occur. Using data from official statistics, victimization surveys, self-report surveys, and other criminological research, we move from the theoretical arena to the empirical.

Our shift in emphasis does not mean that we have left theory completely, but rather, we are now going to concentrate on the different kinds of crime and their patterns of occurrence. As we saw in the previous chapters, there are several different theories to explain these patterns; and while there will continue to be various discussions as to the theoretical import of the patterns, the main concern will be with describing the general features of crime. Understanding something about theory, the reader will be able to weigh the observed patterns of crime against what any of the different theories have had to say about them.

Research in criminology and even the compilation of crime statistics frequently requires that various types of criminal offenses be classified into rather broad and sometimes misleading categories. For example, crimes are distinguished along the lines of being property or nonproperty crimes. However, in making that kind of classification, we group white collar crimes together with shoplifting since they both involve the illegal appropriation of property. That would not tell us very much or be a useful typology since each of the two crimes involve different types and amounts of property taken and different roles in relation to the organization. For example, the typical white collar criminal works for the company from which he/she steals and the sums stolen tend to be in the thousands of dollars. By contrast, the typical shoplifter is usually a juvenile, who does not work for the company and typically only steals a few dollars at a time. One criminologist suggested crimes be classified as "ghetto," "white collar," or "organized," but while this classification is an improvement over the property/nonproperty distinction, it still is somewhat vague and even misleading.[1] Classifying crimes as to whether they belong to the FBI's "Index" provides one category, but it is not an index of all crimes. Gibbons refers to the index crimes as "garden variety" crimes, and he describes them as:

> . . . crimes of the underclass, but at the same time, these crimes, most of which are criminally unsophisticated, situationally induced, and regarded as "real crime" by citizens, are also engaged in by people from more comfortable social circumstances. What makes them garden-variety offenses is their ubiquity, crudity, and directness.[2]

168

This description is a good summation of what we treat as **common crimes**. They are the everyday kind of crime we read about in the newspaper, think about when discussing the "crime problem," and ponder how to correct. However, the term "common" does not suggest that the others we will be discussing in later chapters are rare; white collar and corporate crimes are very common.

For the most part we will be dealing with petty property crimes, where something of value is taken by stealth, force, or fraud. Typically, these crimes require a minimum of skill and little imagination. The crimes of stealth include theft and burglary, typified by shoplifting and residential break-ins. Robbery, on the other hand, involves the threat or use of force in taking another's property. Typically robberies include muggings and liquor store stickups. Finally, we will look at common frauds, from con-games to the illegal use of credit cards.

Common Criminals

In examining who commits common crimes, we will look at three characteristics: 1) age, 2) race, and 3) sex. These characteristics were chosen since they tend to show the greatest variability. Much of what we know about common criminals comes from arrest statistics. However, as we saw in Chapter 2, such figures can be a reflection of law enforcement practices; thus, we will also use figures from self-report surveys and victimization surveys to supplement the arrest data. In addition, we will use ethnographic and biographical materials to further our understanding of common crimes.

The Crimes of the Young

In looking at the arrest figures for index crimes we can see from Fig. 8.1 that such arrests overwhelmingly involve persons between the ages of thirteen and thirty, with the peak ages between sixteen and twenty-one.

These figures show that as people become older, they are less likely to be involved in index crimes, and the "over 65" age group is the least likely to commit such crimes.

Turning to the "common crimes," contained in the FBI index, Table 8.1 reveals what percentage of these crimes are committed by individuals under eighteen years of age and under twenty-five years of age.

We can clearly see that in 1979 the vast majority of the arrests for these crimes, with the exception of fraud, are of young people. While juveniles (under eighteen) are frequently arrested for burglaries, auto thefts, and larceny–thefts, they are rarely apprehended for fraud or forgery and counterfeiting cases. As Gibbons noted, most common crimes are crude and unsophisticated, and juveniles are responsible for the most simple of even these common crimes.

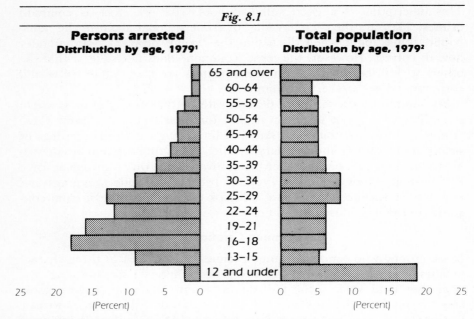

Fig. 8.1

Persons arrested
Distribution by age, 1979¹

Total population
Distribution by age, 1979²

¹Persons arrested is based on reports received representing 204,622,000 population.
²The total population is 220,099,000 for the U.S., based on Bureau of Census provisional estimates, July 1, 1979.

Source: *Uniform Crime Reports*, 1980.

	Table 8.1	
Offense	**Percent Committed by Age Group**	
	Under 18	Under 25
Robbery	31.5	74.4
Burglary	48.6	83.0
Larceny–theft	40.4	71.0
Auto theft	49.2	82.4
Forgery and counterfeiting	14.0	54.3
Fraud	3.4	35.8
Stolen property (buying, receiving, possessing)	33.1	71.4

Source: *Crime in the United States, 1979.* (Washington, D.C.: Federal Bureau of Investigation, 1980), p. 206.

However, to say that youths, both juveniles and young men and women, are too dull or unsophisticated to commit other than the most simple crimes may miss the point. In Chapter 7 it was noted that many crimes were committed mainly for the "kicks"—the thrills in taking chances and showing "character." The financial rewards are relatively small, and the risks are great for these kinds of crimes. So if we understand youthful involvement in them as something other than financial utilitarianism, we may better understand their nature. After all, while fraud requires some sophistication, it does not require a great deal, and it is far safer and more profitable than the other common crimes. Therefore, if these crimes were committed primarily for the financial rewards and done so while attempting to minimize being captured, we would expect far more juvenile involvement in them. An older thief explained this pattern as follows:

> Pete said that when he was a kid the guys used to go around from car to car and see if they could break into glove compartments. They did this mainly to see who was the best "stealer." Pete recalled that he was "busted" when he was fifteen years old for stealing hubcaps. Actually, he didn't get much money out of it. Much of it was a matter of who could steal the most hubcaps. Richie said that you couldn't help learning while you were doing these things . . . and when you got older you didn't rob for "kicks" but for money. That's what most of the guys who were in trouble did now.[3]

This follows the pattern suggested by Goffman in his theoretical concept of "action." It is something kids do largely for the fun of it. This does not make the crime any less serious, nor is it a statement to minimize the status of such crimes in criminological research. Rather, it suggests that the young take a romanticized view of their own involvement in common crimes, finding the danger and daring to be the main attraction and not the profits. Further, it suggests, as differential association theory argues, that a vocabulary of motives is learned that provides the rationale or definition for criminal acts as "exciting." However, as career law breakers become older, they learn, in adult company, that rather than being "play" crime should be primarily defined as "work" and be done in such a way to maximize profits and minimize risks. This pattern is similar to non-criminal development. Children play and adults work—the former being an end in itself and the latter a means to an end.

Race and Common Crimes

While a large proportion of common crimes are committed by juveniles of all ethnic backgrounds, there is an overrepresentation of certain minorities both as victims and offenders. As we will see, there is no Robin Hood ethic of robbing from the rich and giving to the poor, nor is there racism in stealing from another race not one's own. Typically, criminals are of the same race as their victims.

Table 8.2 shows the ethnic/racial breakdown of selected common crimes.

In comparing the arrests for common crimes, it is important to first understand something about the racial distribution of the American population. Blacks make up roughly 12 percent of the population, and Hispanics comprise roughly 7 percent; Orientals, Native-Americans, and other groups constitute the remaining percentage of the nonwhite population. (Hispanics were grouped with whites in the data presented in Table 8.2).

The most significant difference can be seen between blacks and whites in robbery arrests. While comprising only 12 percent of the population, blacks account for 62.5 percent of robberies. This is over 5 times what would be expected from the proportion of blacks in the population. In other common crimes, blacks commit roughly double their societal proportion. From sources other than arrest rates, it has been found that these figures do not reflect the criminal justice system's selective arrests of blacks, but in fact represent a higher proportion of these kinds of crimes by blacks.[4] Most theories suggest that a history of discrimination has in some way led to this pattern, but there is no consensus by sociologists or criminologists as to the exact reason.[5]

At the same time that blacks commit more common crimes, blacks are more likely to be the victims. Likewise, other minorities, with some exceptions, tend to be victimized more than whites. These findings suggest that most common crimes are committed against members of the same ethnic/racial groups as those who commit the crimes. Based on victimization surveys, the robbery rate for whites was 5.8 per 1,000 population, but 14.1 for blacks.[6] Other minorities had a robbery rate of 6.9—again higher than

Table 8.2 Race and Common Crimes			
Offense	White*	Black	Other
1. Robbery	35.0	62.42	2.4
2. Burglary	72.1	25.92	2.0
3. Larceny–theft	70.0	27.5	2.5
4. Auto theft	75.0	21.7	3.3
5. Forgery and counterfeiting	79.3	19.5	1.2
6. Fraud	70.6	27.9	1.5

*Includes Hispanics.

Source: *Uniform Crime Reports*, 1980, p. 201.

that of whites.[7] In studies separating Hispanics and whites, it was found that the Hispanics had a robbery rate of 8.7.[8] Likewise, the burglary rate for whites was 87.0 but 128.8 for blacks and 94.0 for others.[9] Hispanics' burglary rate was 100.9.[10] Only in household larcenies did whites, with a rate of 126.4, have a higher degree of victimization than blacks who had a rate of 114.2. Other minorities are more likely to be victims of household larceny with a rate of 135.0, and Hispanics had the highest rate of 140.5 per 1,000 population.[11] However, whites have the lowest victimization rate for auto theft at 18.5, compared to 26.8 for blacks, 27.6 for Hispanics, and 22.3 for others.[12]

With the exception of robberies, common crimes are disproportionately committed by minorities upon minorities even though the majority of crime in sheer numbers is committed by whites and Hispanics. Robberies are most likely to be committed by the poor against the poor, but otherwise there does not seem to be a general relationship between income of offender and victim; however, those in the higher income groups are more likely to have their cars stolen than the poorest income groups (and more likely to own cars!).[13]

Sex and Common Crimes

One of the best general predictors of crime—especially common crime—is sex. Males are arrested for the great majority of common crimes. Table 8.3 shows the arrest figures by sex for common crimes. As can be seen, women commit a minority of crimes even though they make up the majority of the population. Especially evident is the lack of female involvement in robberies, burglary, auto-theft, and the higher involvement in fraud. However, the 1979 figures represent an increase in female crime participation compared to the beginning of the decade. Table 8.4 compares the changes in arrests for men and women.

Table 8.3 Sex and Arrests for Common Crimes		
Offense	**Males**	**Females**
1. Robbery	92.6	7.4
2. Burglary	93.7	6.3
3. Larceny–theft	69.7	30.3
4. Auto theft	91.1	8.9
5. Forgery and counterfeiting	69.1	30.9
6. Fraud	59.6	40.4

Source: *Uniform Crime Reports*, 1980.

Table 8.4   Changes in Sex Ratios for Common Crimes, 1970–1979

Offense	Percent Change	
	Males	Females
1. Robbery	+ 36.0	+ 74.3
2. Burglary	+ 24.9	+ 71.6
3. Larceny–theft	+ 40.7	+ 61.9
4. Auto-theft	− 15.9	+ 54.0
5. Forgery and counterfeiting	+ 15.5	+ 62.4
6. Fraud	+ 64.5	+ 206.1

Source: Crime in the United States, 1979. (Washington, D.C.: Federal Bureau of Investigation, 1980), p. 191.

While there were increases in all categories except auto theft by males, in every category of common crime, females increased more—over 50 percent in every category and over 200 percent in fraud. It is important to keep in mind that males still commit the majority of common crimes. Table 8.5 shows that when we look at the percent changes of women arrested as a percent of total arrests, the changes are not as great.

Arrest rates for males have traditionally been higher than for females, and this difference has been attributed to sex role differences and sexism.[14] By comparison to their general representation in all offenses, women have been disproportionately overrepresented in crimes that reflect their sex role, such as prostitution.[15] Using Goffman's concept of "action" and "character" we can see that in their lack of participation in common crimes, women's status as being less than fully competent social participants is portrayed.[16] Compared to the stereotypic masculine sex role, women are not expected to be brave, gallant, or cool. Female hero-

Table 8.5   Female Arrests as a Percent of Total Arrests in Selected Crime Categories

Offense	1960	1973	Change
Robbery	5%	7%	+ 2%
Forgery	17	27	+ 10
Fraud	15	31	+ 16
Larceny	17	32	+ 15

Source: Crime in the United States, 1973, Uniform Crime Reports. (Washington, D.C.: Federal Bureau of Investigation, September, 1974), p. 126.

ines are occasionally pictured, but oftentimes in defense of the home or traditional female sex roles. Thus, with little character expectations—with nothing to "prove" and therefore without evidence of character—women are not as likely to be involved in the risky world of crime. From early in life, the sign on the treehouse reads, "No girls allowed," suggesting that even early adventures are for males only. This is not to recommend crime as a way of being someone of worth, but rather to the extent that "character" is defined in terms of manly attributes and crime is one means of

Lynette "Squeaky" Fromme first came to national attention for her involvement with the "Manson Family" murders and later for her attempted assassination of President Gerald Ford. However, she is not representative of women criminals, whose crimes tend to be nonviolent.

attaining those attributes, women will be underrepresented in both crime and character.[17]

The second question that has arisen concerning women and crime is the increase in female crime: If it has actually increased, we can ask what might be the cause of this increase. First, there is evidence that female crime has increased over a long period of time, not just the last decade. In an analysis of crime arrests since 1932, Rita Simon concluded that the proportion of female arrests for crime is greater now than in the last several decades; and if the rate of increase continues, by the decade of 2010, male and female crime will be equal.[18] The great bulk of the increase has been due to women's participation in property offenses, especially larceny.[19]

The women's liberation movement is one of the most commonly cited reasons for the noted upsurge in female criminality. Simon has suggested that greater economic independence and opportunities outside of the home have provided women with new opportunities for the commission of crime.[20] Likewise, in a cross-cultural comparison, Freda Adler argued that as women are given greater freedoms, they are more likely to be involved in crime.[21] However, arguments linking women's criminality with the women's movement, especially arguments that greater female participation in the labor market provides greater opportunity for crime, tend to be flawed in several ways according to Darrell Steffensmeier:

> First, even if increasing number of women went to work, crimes of employee theft and occupational fraud are unlikely to be reported and prosecuted, and therefore would not contribute to *official* arrest statistics, such as those for the Uniform Crime Reports. Second, the new occupational roles have not freed women from traditional domestic ones. Women have retained the roles of homemaker, child-rearer, nurse of the sick, and so on. The time and energy involved in these roles, along with the assumption of new economic roles, means it is unlikely that their opportunities for crime have undergone very much change. Third, work may lessen female temptations toward crime by assuring a steady income which enables them to satisfy material needs in a legal manner. Fourth, occupations vary in terms of criminal liability. Women are making *few* gains in traditional male occupations such as truck driver, dockworker, mechanic, and so on that are facilitative of criminal opportunities and the learning of crime skills. Fifth, to the extent that women have made inroads into traditional male occupations, they continue to have little access to the "old boy system" and the "male buddy network."[22]

In addition to Steffensmeier's points, it can be argued that were *opportunity* to commit crime a major force, then we would expect far more female involvement in daytime residential burglaries; as housewives, women have far more opportunities for such crimes than do males. In addition to having the time, women are also more likely to have information as to who is and is not at home and what valuables are available in households.

Steffensmeier sees two major factors contributing to the increase in female arrests—factors that also contribute to male arrests for the same crimes: 1) changes in *opportunities* for petty thefts/fraud and 2) changes in *social control* and law enforcement. He explains as follows:

> The greater reliance on self-service marketing and the purchasing of credit means that women, being the primary consumers, are faced with expanding opportunities for shoplifting, passing worthless checks, and so on. Increased opportunities for these kinds of thefts and frauds will have a greater effect on female than male crime because males are more likely to commit other kinds of larcenies and frauds. Similarly, the greater willingness of business officials to prosecute, the trend toward computerized records, and improvements in the detection of offenses such as shoplifting, bad checks, credit card fraud, and forged prescriptions would also tend to increase female, more than male, arrests for larceny, fraud, and forgery. An additional factor, but probably of lesser causal significance, is that poverty has become more and more of a female problem and may have pushed more women into petty thievery to support themselves and their families. In sum, the most crucial point, perhaps, is that trends in female criminality, as is true of male crime, appear linked to broader economic, legal, technological, and law enforcement changes than to specific changes in sex roles.[23]

Steffensmeier's argument, while providing an alternative explanation to that of the "liberated woman," still is somewhat weak. Not only does it rely on a "multiple factor" approach that really does not lend itself to any kind of theoretical development, but also it assumes certain patterns that may not reflect typical female property crimes. As we saw above in discussing age and property crimes, most such crimes are committed by juveniles or young adults. Therefore, it appears that what we are dealing with is not so much poor mothers supporting their families but rather teenaged girls shoplifting cosmetics or clothes. Since larceny–theft—and not fraud—make up the bulk of the common crimes committed not only by females but also by males, we are probably seeing a different set of learned criminality and action-seeking by juvenile girls. Girls still are socialized into the "shopping role," but they are learning increasingly how certain petty crimes are "fun," just as boys have learned for years. To some extent this may represent a change in sex role equality in that boys are teaching girls the same patterns of crime they have always learned—representing a partial increase in cross-gender communication and *respect* for young women by young men.

Turning to common crimes women are involved in, we find that certain kinds of shoplifting are very much female dominated. In one study of department store shoplifting, females were found to be far more involved

Table 8.6 Sex, Age, and Shoplifting			
Age	Female	Male	Total
17 and Under	62%	8%	70%
18 and Over	24	6	30
Total	86	14	100

Source: Steve Bounton, San Diego State University, 1977. Data from department stores represent a greater proportion of female clients, but it was found that even taking into account the relative proportion of males and females entering the store under study, a disproportionate number of shoplifters were female.

than men. Table 8.6 shows the breakdown in shoplifting by sex and age. These findings are consistent with the "shopping role" that women are socialized into. Like most other common crimes, shoplifting among women is largely a juvenile activity, and the majority of the adult shoplifting is by women under twenty-five. However, self-report surveys show that boys are more likely than girls to have engaged in shoplifting, even though a relatively high proportion of girls do shoplift compared with other juvenile female crimes.[24]

Characteristics of Common Crimes

While a great deal of research has been done on criminals, relatively little has been done by criminologists on crime itself. The belief has been that if we understand why people commit crime, there is little reason to concern ourselves with the nature of the crime itself. However, this conceptualization has led to erroneous conclusions about not only crime but also criminals. This is because certain motives are attributed to law violators on the basis of *untested* assumptions about criminal acts themselves. Upon closer examination of the crime and the criminal in the situation of offense, we find many features of crime to be unlike stereotypical assumptions. Therefore, the examination of crime characteristics, instead of being a sideshow to mainstream criminology, should be seen as a basic part of understanding and explaining criminal behavior patterns.

In order to understand what is involved in the various forms of common crime, we will focus on studies that examine what actually takes place in criminal situations. We will see many overlaps in the different kinds of offenses as well as the unique characteristics of each offense.

Larceny–Theft

The following definition of **larceny–theft** is used by the FBI to characterize this kind of common crime:

Larceny–theft is the unlawful taking, carrying, leading, or riding away of property from the possession or constructive possession of another. It includes crimes such as shoplifting, pocket-picking, purse-snatching, thefts from motor vehicles, thefts of motor vehicle parts and accessories, bicycle thefts, etc., in which no use of force, violence, or fraud occurs. . . . This crime category does not include embezzlement, "con" games, forgery, and worthless checks.[25]

This offense makes up the majority of all index crimes (54 percent) and the majority of property offenses (60 percent).[26] In other words, larceny–theft is the most likely of the common crimes to be committed and the one most likely to result in victimization. In 1979, there were reports of 6,577,518 larceny–thefts, but this represents only a fraction of all such offenses.[27] A 1975 victimization survey showed that personal larceny was reported in only 26 percent of the cases in which it occurred; thus, the great majority of such crimes—74 percent—were not even reported to the police. Therefore, tripling or quadrupling the FBI figures will give us a more accurate view of the crime's occurrence.[28] In other words, there were probably 19,732,743 cases of larceny–theft in 1979 or a rate of 8,965 per 100,000 population—roughly 9 percent of the country.

Not all larceny–thefts are alike nor are all of them following the same trends. First, as to the different kinds of offenses that are involved, Fig. 8.2 shows a breakdown of larceny–thefts into types.

A quick review of Fig. 8.2 reveals that there are several different forms of larceny–theft, and the largest single category is made up of miscellaneous forms. However, thefts involving motor vehicles (not including the thefts of cars themselves) make up the single largest categories—17 percent for thefts from motor vehicles and 19 percent of motor vehicle accessories or a combined 36 percent from both.

Fig. 8.3 shows the trends in larceny offenses between 1975 and 1979. The trends in the different larceny–thefts are based on reported crimes, but do reflect actual trends. For instance, pocket-picking is less reported (26.9 percent) than is purse snatching (48.7 percent).[29] However, the trends show that pocket-picking is up and purse snatching is down, and since the former offense is less likely to be reported than the latter, the actual pocket-picking increase is much greater. Other offenses, though, may show an increase in the willingness to report crimes or policies that encourage full recording of crime. For example, many stores that did not report all shoplifting at one time may have changed their policies and started to report such offenses. Thus, the 10 percent increase in shoplifting occurring between 1974 and 1979 may simply reflect an increase in reports to the police.

It is difficult to characterize the "typical" theft or thief. As we saw, there are several different kinds of thefts from snatching a purse to hopping on

Fig. 8.2   Larceny Analysis 1979

Larceny–Theft

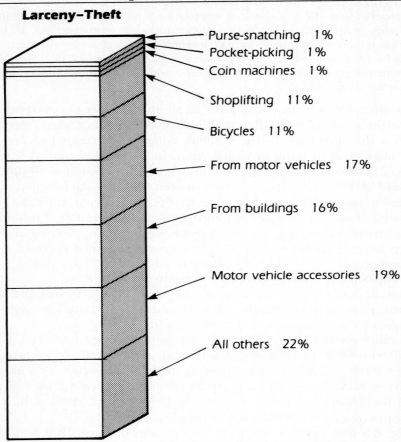

Purse-snatching   1%
Pocket-picking   1%
Coin machines   1%

Shoplifting   11%

Bicycles   11%

From motor vehicles   17%

From buildings   16%

Motor vehicle accessories   19%

All others   22%

Percentages do not add to 100% due to rounding.

Source: *Crime in the United States, 1979.* (Washington, D.C.: Federal Bureau of Investigation, 1980), p. 29.

a bicycle and riding off. Likewise, self-report surveys show that most people have committed some kind of theft at one time or another in their lives, and the "professional" thief, whether pickpocket or car stripper, usually has little in common with the "common thief." The following examples taken from field notes on a study of criminal investigations illustrate the wide variety of such offenses:[30]

Nine boxes of copper wire were taken from a construction site of a residential home. The construction manager complained that people in the neighborhood often help themselves to anything found around construction of new homes, including building materials, tools, and anything else not locked up.

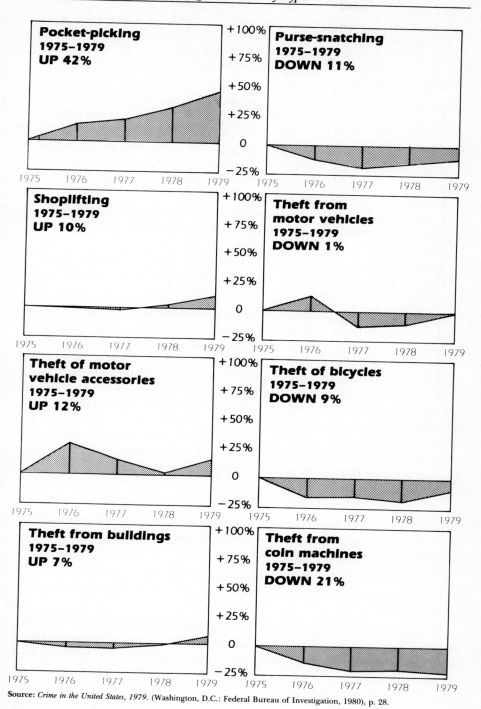

Fig. 8.3   Larceny Types

Pocket-picking
1975–1979
UP 42%

Purse-snatching
1975–1979
DOWN 11%

Shoplifting
1975–1979
UP 10%

**Theft from
motor vehicles**
1975–1979
DOWN 1%

**Theft of motor
vehicle accessories**
1975–1979
UP 12%

Theft of bicycles
1975–1979
DOWN 9%

Theft from buildings
1975–1979
UP 7%

**Theft from
coin machines**
1975–1979
DOWN 21%

Source: *Crime in the United States, 1979.* (Washington, D.C.: Federal Bureau of Investigation, 1980), p. 28.

181

Someone had neatly removed the left rear fender of a woman's car—a Volkswagen "beetle." The woman had no idea who wanted just her fender and nothing else, but the detective investigating the case said that car strippers sometimes will steal car parts "on order," and someone probably ordered a fender like the one on her car.

Two men filled their arms and jackets with meat in a supermarket and ran out the front door. Before anyone could stop them, they had disappeared with over $100 worth of meat.

An electric grinder used in a machine shop was stolen. The shop manager suspected one of the employees had simply placed the tool outside the fence, and then picked it up later after work. He said that a caliper, electric pencil sharpener, and some pads had also been taken.

A woman walking through a hotel arcade in the evening had her purse snatched by a young man who simply ran by her and grabbed her purse and fled.

Several college students had their bicycles stolen from outside their dormitory. All of the bicycles had been locked, but the chains and/or locks had been cut with bolt cutters.

All of the above cases illustrate the wide variety of these crimes. Every kind of larceny, from theft by suburbanites stealing building materials to bicycle theft rings making off with a dormitory's supply of bicycles are typical. The difficulty in analyzing these offenses then is in their ubiquity and diversity. To concentrate on the "professional" theft and thief, while a legitimate concern for a subtype of larceny–theft, only includes a minority of characters involved and a special type of offense. In order to understand the full scope of these crimes, it is necessary to understand the more mundane kind of theft and the actors involved. Unfortunately, there is little information on this. Since half the common crimes are some kind of larceny–theft, it is an area in need of massive research.

Burglary

Like larceny–theft, **burglaries** involve taking property from others; however, it is defined differently and has different socio-legal characteristics. The FBI uses the following definition:

> . . . [defines] burglary as the unlawful entry of a structure to commit a felony or theft. The use of force to gain entry is not required to classify an offense as burglary.

The typical sense of a burglary is some kind of breaking and entering to steal, but technically, it can include shoplifting, since a person enters a building to commit a theft. However, since shoplifting is usually treated as larceny–theft, except in cases of repeated offenses, it will be excluded from the analysis of burglary.

The major difference between burglaries and larceny–thefts can be seen in arrests of males and females. While women accounted for 30 percent of larceny–theft arrests, they made up only 6 percent of the burglary arrests. However, there are no significant differences in the arrests by age or race for the offense. About half the arrests for burglaries are juveniles, and the vast majority are under twenty-five. About two-thirds are white and one-third black.[31] Roughly the same holds true for larceny–theft.

It is most interesting that the main difference between the two offenses is the sex variable. Why are women far more likely to engage in larceny–theft than burglary? As we pointed out above, women have far more opportunity to commit daytime residential burglaries than do men, but it is clear that men commit most of these crimes. The technical requirements for breaking into a house or commercial building are not any different for men and women, and while men may be more likely to have skills for committing burglaries, there is no doubt that women could master them easily if they wanted to.

To understand the difference, we will have to return to the "shopping" or "consumer" role of women and the kinds of things women steal—personal items such as cosmetics and clothes. In stores, women are better able to find their exact taste and size in clothes, and burglarizing stores is more difficult than private homes. Since the shopping role is a normal and expected one for women, they are less noticeable in it, and they are more adept at the shopping role than men.

The trends in burglaries went up and down during the decade of the 1970s. (See Fig. 8.4).

Overall, the trend in nighttime burglaries has been down since the mid-1970s, and the daytime, up. For residential burglaries, this makes sense because people are less likely to be home during the day. However, it is difficult to explain the increase in nighttime commercial burglaries, since most businesses are closed at night and no one is around. We do know, based on victimization surveys, though, that there is a higher victimization and reporting rate in commercial burglaries than in residential burglaries. Commercial burglaries occur at a rate of 229 per 1,000 and are reported 80 percent of the time, while residential burglaries occur at a rate of 92 per 1,000 and are reported only 19 percent of the time.[32] The differences in rates probably reflect the quality of the burglary target and the size of the losses. While burglarizing a commercial structure, the burglar is more likely either to find the exact merchandise he wants, such as jewelry or furs, or money. While in household burglaries, money is less likely to be around in any great amount, and what can be turned into cash or be of use to the burglar is more uncertain.

From the few ethnographic studies on burglars available, we know something about their work. It is interesting to note that burglars develop preferences and specialties. One safe cracker or "boxman" only burglar-

Fig. 8.4

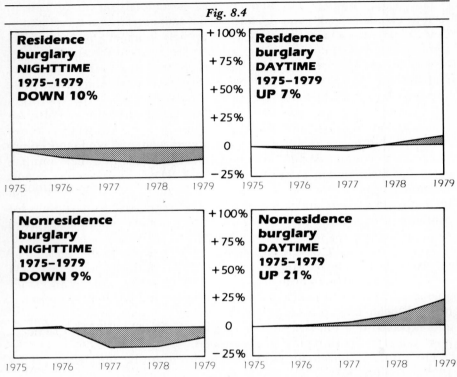

Burglaries of unknown time of occurrence are not included.

Source: *Crime in the United States, 1979.* (Washington, D.C.: Federal Bureau of Investigation, 1980).

ized safes in supermarkets, and his brother burglarized residential homes at night. For the boxman, going into a home was seen as dangerous and unnecessarily risky as the following excerpt illustrates:

I went with him one time to this house where he thought there was a safe. It was a big house in the Hollywood district. It belonged to somebody in the movie industry. There was a big patio right beside the house. It was an enormous big place. A big police dog was there which was supposed to be on patrol. My brother could charm these dogs. He could make friends with any of them. By the time we got this dog straightened around we climbed over the fence into the yard. This dog was following us around. I am walking on the white tile and I walked right into the swimming pool. I didn't even see it until I walked into it. That terminated that night because I was just like a drowned rat. We had to get in the car and go home. My brother was very unhappy that I was so stupid as to walk into the swimming pool. Supermarkets don't have swimming pools. As I say, to each his own. That field is not for me. I never cared for it and I never want anything to do with it. Especially the way he operates. He gets in his car and drives around until he finds a house where the lights are all out. On the same night he will knock off this house. Well we don't do it that way. We usually case a place for a couple or three days at least. Sometimes a lot more than that. But he does it one way and we do it another. He can't understand this laying on a joint for several days before we knock it over. By the same token I can't understand him knocking one over the same night he discovers that there is nobody home. He gets such a small percentage for what he gets in the way of jewelry and stuff like that. He has got some paintings that were real expensive paintings. When he peddled them he never got anything for them. Maybe a few dollars for them. And I know that the paintings cost thousands of dollars, because I recognized the names of painters that were on them. If he gets two percent for jewelry he is doing pretty good.[33]

Burglars of a "professional" bent specialize but they make up a minority of all who commit the crime.

Robbery

The third common crime involving theft of other people's property is **robbery**. Many consider robbery a crime of violence rather than a property crime because of the use of violence or its threat. The FBI defines robbery as follows:

Robbery is the taking or attempting to take anything of value from the care, custody, or control of a person or persons by force or threat of force or violence and/or by putting the victim in fear.

Like the other forms of common crimes we have discussed, robbery is of many different types. Table 8.7 breaks down the different kinds of robbery. However, victimization surveys show that only 55.5 percent of the robberies are reported to the police.[34] Also, people receiving injuries are

Table 8.7 Types of Robbery	
Type	**Percent**
1. Street/Highway	49.4
2. Commercial House	14.4
3. Gas or Service Station	3.8
4. Convenience Store	7.2
5. Residence	10.7
6. Bank	1.7
7. Miscellaneous	12.9

Source: *Uniform Crime Reports*, 1980, p. 16.

more likely to report that they have been robbed than those who have
not; thus, there is probably an overrepresentation of robberies with injuries in police data. Likewise, commercial robberies are more likely to be
reported than personal or household robberies. Fully 90.2 percent of
commercial robberies were reported to the police; suggesting that personal and household robberies may tend to be underrepresented in the
figures of total robberies.[35] A problem may exist, however, in both the police data and victimization data on commercial robberies. Accidentally,
evidence was discovered that several commercial robberies are either totally faked or involve the collusion of employees. The discovery occurred
when crime analysts were attempting to photograph robberies in various
frequently robbed businesses. They installed cameras in a number of
these businesses and waited for them to be robbed. Since the cameras
were concealed, only the employees and owners knew of their existence,
but once they were installed, no robberies occurred. Therefore, it was suspected that either the employees or owners were in collusion with robbers
or they were fabricating robberies altogether and stealing the money
themselves.[36] (Owners of businesses would "steal" from themselves to
avoid paying taxes on the money "stolen.") Since some of the businesses
were robbed as frequently as once a week before the installation of the
cameras, it is unlikely that the robbers simply stopped on their own ac-
cord. Likewise, it is unlikely that if a robbery were reported to the police,
in a victimization survey, the business would not include the "robbery" in
filling out the victimization questionnaire. Therefore, with the exception
of banks, where cameras record actual robberies, there may be a very high
over-reporting of commercial robberies in both the FBI and victimization
survey data.

In looking at the trends in robbery reported to the police between 1975
and 1979, we can see different trends depending on the type of robbery.
Fig. 8.5 shows these trends.

Keeping in mind that a number of reports of robberies of commercial
houses, convenience stores, and gas stations are known to be fabricated,
the trend has been mixed. The most significant change has been the increase in bank robberies, up 51 percent from 1975. Since banks probably
have the best documentation of robberies—often having cameras to record their occurrence—the trend is not a matter of changes in reports.
However, banks account for less than 2 percent of all robberies. Even
though they are the most profitable target with an average loss of $3,613
per robbery, they are also the most risky because of sophisticated security
devices.[37]

Almost half of the crimes reported as robberies are "street robberies,"
with an average loss of $355 per incident.[38] Unfortunately, "street robber-
ies" include everything from strongarm robberies where a mugger attacks
someone on the sidewalk to "highway robberies" in which an entire truck-

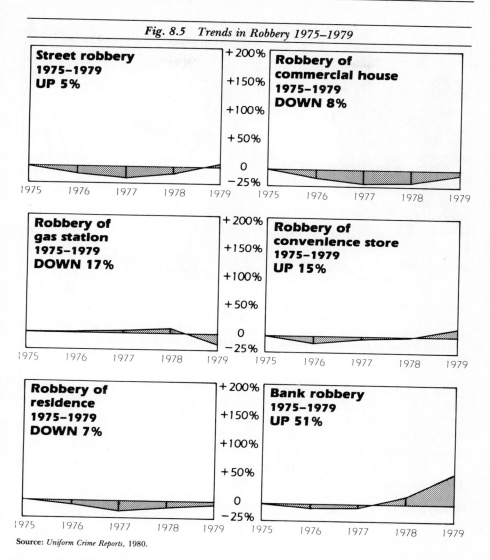

Fig. 8.5   Trends in Robbery 1975–1979

Source: *Uniform Crime Reports*, 1980.

load of goods will be taken. The average loss of $355 is divided between robberies of truckloads worth thousands and sidewalk muggings worth only a few dollars. In sheer volume, however, the muggings make up the vast majority of the street robbery figures.

Muggings

Robberies that involve attacking someone on the street and taking their values, mostly money, are not only the most common but they are also the offenses which are most likely to involve victim injury. About a third

While robbery involves violent means, it is essentially a crime to obtain property. However, since weapons are used in this type of offense, there is a greater likelihood of the actual use of violence than in other property crimes, such as theft and burglary. Here, a robbery suspect lies on the ground beside his bullet-ridden car after being apprehended by police.

(35.6 percent) of all robberies involved injury to the victim, and most of these were due to **muggings**.[39] This is because muggers often use weapons such as clubs, tire irons, or strongarm tactics. In an analysis of weapons and injuries in robberies, Luckenbill found that in using guns or knives, robbers were less likely to have to "demonstrate" to their victims that they were willing to use the weapon.[40] The following two excerpts from interviews with convicted robbers illustrate this point:

Money don't mean nothing when you're looking down a gun. When a person comes in on you and he's got a gun and he wants your money, you'll give up the money. . . . The money's not as important as your life. When he's got a gun, your life's in his hands.

In strongarms you have to put him out of commission for a few minutes. When you haven't got a gun or a knife, you can't tell him to do anything. He'll tell you to go to hell, or he'll turn on you. So all you can do is knock him out.[41]

According to Luckenbill's analysis, the main objective of the robber is to control the situation by interpersonal coercion. The robber will not use actual force to the extent to which he has control, from his perspective. Ironically, then, the more obviously lethal the weapon (e.g., a knife or gun), the less likely it will have to be employed.

Many of the victims of street robberies are other criminals themselves, especially in the illegal drug trade. Drug addicts make up a large proportion of the street muggers, and their victims often include some of the lower-level dealers. In explaining his own robberies, one drug-addict robber explained "doing bad" as having to rob in order to obtain drugs or money for drugs.

Later I got in debt kind of bad with Sam and this other dude, Chuck. Sam refused to give me any more drugs until I paid the money. Of course, that meant the word would be out, so I'd do bad. Then you say like "I'll rob a lot." But robbing people, the way we was doing it, we considered that as doing bad too, because we had to rob sometimes three or four people a day, depending on the amount of money and quality of drugs they had. See, if you can't find nobody big or get a lot of drugs or have a lot of money, you go where you know all the drug addicts hang out. There's always going to be four or five little dealers around there. We'd line them up, push them behind the bushes somewhere, and make them give it all up—right on the street.[42]

Of course, the addict-robber is not partial to robbing drug dealers— anyone believed to have money is a fair target. In recounting how he first became involved in muggings, another addict-robber explained:

I was sick, and I needed some dope. . . . I was with Ronnie, and mugging was his thing. This was in 1968, and we were in this building in the projects. . . . Ronnie knew what he was doing—I didn't know my way at all. We were in a lobby, and we saw this dude about as old as my father. We followed him into the elevator. . . . The dude knew what we were up to, and he tried to fight his way out of the elevator. Ronnie hit him in the jaw twice. He tried to grab the elevator door. Ronnie closed the door on his hands. He took his money—it was about twelve dollars—and we got out at the next stop and ran down the stairs. . . . It was late at night, 9:30 or so, and we went and found a connection and copped. We had only gotten twelve dollars, but bags at that time were six dollars, so we got off okay.[43]

It should be noted that in the description of how he became involved in muggings, the robber explained he learned this behavioral repertoire from a friend. This explanation is consistent with differential association theory, and even though there appears to be no great skill in such crimes to be learned, many muggers believe that it takes a special skill. One former mugger explained, in discussing a street robber friend still involved in muggings:

He has the eye; he knows where the money is. I would go to mug a dude, and he would have two dollars in his pocket. Jones goes after a dude and comes up with a hundred. He has really got the eye. He can make good money.[44]

Business Robberies

If a robbery is planned, we assume some sophistication and organization. Muggings appear to be only minimally planned and executed. However, the expectation of business robberies, including commercial houses, convenience stores, and banks, is that they are better planned, more rational and profitable than muggings.

Even at a cursory glance we can see that business robberies are not a great deal more sophisticated than muggings. To begin with, business robberies such as bank robberies requiring the greatest amount of planning and highest profits are the rarest. Convenience stores keep little available money on hand, but constitute the single most specific target robbed. Similarly, gas stations and liquor stores are favorite targets even though both kinds of stores typically take measures to minimize the amount of available cash on hand. In studies of the process of robbery, it was found that the majority of "planning" consisted of little more than building up courage to commit the crime.[45] Oftentimes robbers will choose a target simply by driving around until they see what appears to be a relatively safe and lucrative mark. Robbers often do not know how much money is in the store, where the exits are, or how to get the money that is there. The following describes a typical robbery and the lack of planning:

> *The robber went downtown looking for a place to rob. He walked around for a while until he saw a sporting goods store that he thought looked promising. After walking past it a few times to make sure no other customers were there, he went in and pulled a gun on the store's owner. After announcing that he intended to rob the store, customers began coming in. He felt obliged to rob them also, but soon the store began filling up with more customers; so the robber finally closed the door and turned the "closed" sign outward. After robbing everyone, he told the store's owner that he needed him to help him make his getaway since he did not have a car himself. Leaving the store with the owner, the robber told the customers he had a partner outside who would shoot them if anyone left before a half hour. Then he instructed the owner to drive him to a spot and let him out and then drive off without looking back. The owner did as he was told, and the robber then checked into a nearby motel to hide out. After what he felt was a safe period of time, the robber called a cab to come and pick him up at the motel, but as soon as the robber walked out the door, the police were waiting for him and made an arrest. Eventually the robber was convicted of robbery and kidnapping.[46]*

Not only was the robbery poorly planned in terms of maximizing gains and minimizing risks, it was poorly planned legally. Because he did not provide his own means of escape, the robber was convicted of two felonies—robbery and kidnapping—instead of just robbery.

Control and Violence in Robberies

If robbery has the potential for violence, it becomes more than a property crime. As we saw above in discussing muggings, weapons or strongarm tactics are means to gain property, but robbery can result in violence. Over the past several years, roughly 10 percent of all murders have occurred in robberies.⁴⁷ However, the primary use of weapons in robberies is to coerce the victim into giving the robber what he wants, and it is not a device to hurt the victim.

In his analysis of robbery and violence, Luckenbill found that depending on the kind of role the target (victim) was cast in and weapon employed, violence was more or less likely to occur. As we saw above, nonlethal weapons (i.e., weapons other than guns or knives) were more likely to be employed than lethal weapons, to demonstrate to the target the willingness to use such a weapon. If the robber required the assistance or participation of the victim to get the money in a robbery, he was less likely to use strong violence. Victim participation is required in opening safes or providing some similar aid to the robber. The following responses were given to the question as to why the robber did not take the money himself rather than making the victim do it:

Offender #1   *If you don't know where all the money is, then you need them (targets). You haven't got the time to look around for the money, so you tell them to give you everything.*

Offender #3   *Well, I didn't know where the money was, and besides, I didn't know how to open the cash registers.*

Offender #7   *He's really important. He knows how to open the safe and he can open the registers. It's funny. You got to have him, but you can't let him think you need him. . . . You want to make him think that you would just as soon kill him as do anything else, you know, that you don't need him. But you really do. If he won't open the safe, you're dead. You might as well leave.*⁴⁸

In muggings, there is little need for victim assistance, and so the robber can use incapacitating force, increasing the likelihood of harm. However, in business robberies, victim assistance is more often required. Therefore, the robber has to use intimidation that does not incapacitate the victim. Using lethal weapons, other warnings (verbal threats), or prodding force (poking or slapping) usually suffice. The following responses by convicted robbers illustrate how they employ force in situations where victims resist a robbery:

Warnings

Offender #2   *I remember this one woman. She said she wasn't going to give me the money. She probably figured I wouldn't do anything about it. You know, like I was scared to kill her or something. So I told her what I would tell everyone else. I said, "Lady, I spent five years in prison and I killed two men last week. If you don't give me the money, I'll kill you too." She got kind of scared, you know, and sure enough, you know, she hands over the money.*

Offender #15   *They wouldn't move. They just stood there, kind of looking at us like we were kidding them or something. So I told them that they'd better give us the* *money or I'd shoot them. And I shot it at the wall, you know, to show them it was loaded.*

Prodding Force

Offender #7   *I wouldn't kill anybody. Sometimes I'd hit them. You know, like this one guy was stalling around, saying he didn't know the combination to the safe. So I smacked him on the side of the head and said, "Open it." So he suddenly remembers the combinations. I guess he figured I'd waste him if he kept stalling me.*

Offender #8   *At first, he tried to get away from me. I just let him have it. I hit him. (Question: Why not shoot him?) If you hit him, it'll get the job done. All I wanted to do is make him realize I meant what I was doing, that I'd kill him if he tried anything else.*[49]

The overall orientation of the robber appears to be a fairly rational one in the context of obtaining money. Coercive force is employed in the context of: 1) the kind of weapon employed and 2) the role of the victim (target). Table 8.8 shows the nature of this interactive relationship:

Table 8.8 Weapons, Coercive Force, and Role of Robbery Victims				
	Role of Victim			
	Acquiescent		*Participatory*	
Level of Force	Type of Coercive Resource			
	L	N/L	L	N/L
Incapacitating	0	32	0	0
Prodding	1	0	17	4
Warning	4	0	45	3
Total	5	32	62	7

L = lethal N/L = nonlethal

Source: David Luckenbill, "Patterns of Force in Interpersonal Coercion," (Chicago: University of Illinois, 1979).

As can be seen, the extent to which a victim is in a participatory role and the robber uses a lethal weapon, actual violence is less likely to be employed. However, in cases where a nonlethal weapon is used and the victim is not needed, violence is likely to be used.

We noted that 10 percent of the homicides occurred in robberies, but of the reported robberies, killings occurred in less than one half of one percent of the cases (.46 percent). In other words, it would be a highly atypical robbery—less than 1 in 200—that would result in death to the victim. However, deaths do occur—both to the robber and victim. It is unknown, however, to what extent victim deaths are caused by the victim's resistance or if they are simply murdered after a robbery. There is evidence that some victims are killed for resisting a robbery, but there is also evidence that victims are killed who do not resist robberies. In Chapter 10 we will examine homicide in robberies, but here it should be noted that while murder in robberies does account for 10 percent of the murders, relatively few robberies result in the death of the victim.

Fraud and Forgery

Fraud comes in many different shapes and forms—from passing worthless checks to elaborate confidence games. In Chapter 13, we will discuss some of the more elaborate frauds of professional criminals. Here we will look at fraud as a relatively simply "common" crime. Likewise, **forgery** (along with counterfeiting) ranges from the simple to the elaborate, and here we will look at the simple forms.

The general definitions of these offenses used by the FBI are as follows:

Fraud Fraudulent conversion and obtaining money or property by false pretenses. Included are larceny by bailee and bad checks except for forgeries and counterfeiting.

Forgery and counterfeiting Making, altering, uttering, or possessing, with intent to defraud, anything false which is made to appear true.[50]

In the context of common crimes, fraud and forgery are mainly writing bad checks and the illegal use of credit cards. A "bad check" as we will be using the term here can be an intentional cashing of a check against an account with insufficient funds, cashing a check on another's bank account, or passing a forged check.

Bad Checks

Check forgers and bad check writers fall into two distinct categories. One category of cases represents a wide variety of contexts in which bogus check passing was 1) interspersed with periods of stable employment and family life, 2) simply an aspect of alcoholism or gambling, and 3) one of a series of criminal offenses having little or no consistency.[51] By contrast, people who write bad checks as a regular criminal pursuit fall into a unique category. They are not quite "professionals" in that they do not participate in a criminal behavior system nor do they see what they do as a regular business. However, they are "systematic." Lemert described the systematic behavior as follows:

1. They thought of themselves as check men.
2. They had worked out or regularly employed a special technique of passing checks.

3. They had more or less organized their lives around the exigencies or imperatives of living by means of fraudulent checks.[52]

The interesting aspect of systematic check forgers, according to Lemert, includes the amount of time they spend in prison, their motives, and their life styles. First, the systematic check forger spent more time in prison than out. They were out of prison only a few months to a year or two and then were caught and sent back. They would get out of prison, go on a bogus check-cashing spree, living it up along the way, become nervous and tense, and then either make a stupid mistake and get caught, or simply give themselves up. Secondly, they worked alone and did not appear to be motivated by the financial rewards—which were considerable. As one check man explained:

Nine out of ten check men are lone wolves. Those men who work in gangs are not real check men. They do it for the money; we do it for something else. It gives us something we need. Maybe we're crazy. . . .[53]

Third, the life style of the systematic check forger is mobile and alone. The professional thief and burglar, whom we will discuss in Chapter 13, is also fairly mobile, but the check forger is a loner. He cashes fraudulent checks in one town or city; then he moves on before his crimes are focused on him. However, he moves alone, while the professional thief moves either with other thieves or will be in the company of other thieves in the next place he goes. Check forgers avoid all associations with other check forgers and criminals altogether. Furthermore, while in prison, systematic check forgers do not get into the "life" of other criminals, including their world view and culture. They tend to be loners, use no special argot—either that of check forgers or the prison slang—and do not view themselves as criminals. In fact their view of themselves is amorphous or what Lemert calls a "pseudonymity."[54] This is due to constant use of false names and playing new roles for fabricated identities.

Since the time of Lemert's study, there seems to have been some significant changes in those involved in bogus checks. In Lemert's sample, taken from the 1950s, 10 percent were women. More recent figures show, however, that women's involvement in this type of crime is increasing. In 1979, 40.4 percent of the fraud arrests and 30.9 percent of the forgery and counterfeiting arrests were women.[55] As we saw with shoplifting, the "shopper" or consumer role of women may place them in a position to commit these crimes. However, since women were in essentially the same roles at the time of Lemert's study, this explanation is only a partial one. Further research on women in common crimes of this kind is necessary before we can say with certainty why women are involved to the extent they appear to be.

SUMMARY

In this chapter we have looked at only a small part of the entire picture of crime, but the crimes we examined are the ones people are most likely to identify as "typical" or "real" crimes. To a great extent, there is an over-representation of the young, males, and minorities as both victims and perpetrators of these common crimes, but as we saw women are increasingly involved in these offenses. The motives appear to be mixed—the young commit the crimes as much for the excitement as for the payoffs, and even some of the older criminals, such as the systematic check forgers, appear to engage in crime for something other than the property stolen.

There are several different kinds of common crimes and different patterns for the types and subtypes. Larceny–theft can be anything from children shoplifting to car theft rings; burglaries vary from residential break-ins to bank burglary; and street robberies can be simple muggings to hi-jackings. The bulk of these offenses, however, tend to be occasional offenses by noncareer criminals, usually juveniles, and involve small losses. On the other hand, fraud and forgery have been found to involve older offenders, fewer minorities, and more women. Also, while juvenile crimes tend to done in groups for kicks, check forgers are typically older loners.

The most interesting trend in common crimes is the increase in women's involvement. Initial explanations suggested that the women's movement and increasing employment opportunities for women led to the increase in crime; but given the patterns of female crime, this does not appear to be true. There may be more equality in crime as women become more equal, but the reasons behind this trend are unclear and, as in the past, constitute a needed area of research in criminology.

Glossary

Burglary   The criminal act of breaking into a dwelling with the intent to steal something.

Common Crimes   Those crimes that make up the bulk of criminal statistics and viewed in the public mind as "real crime." As used in this book, it is a characterization of common property crimes.

Forgery   The illegal making of documents to defraud others.

Fraud   Misrepresentations of oneself to others in order to make illegal gains.

Muggings   The slang term used to characterize strong-armed robberies.

Robbery   Using force or threat of force to take another's property.

Theft   Taking another's property illegally, but not by force of breaking and entering.

Questions

1. What is the relationship between age and common crimes? What different styles of crime exist between juveniles and adults?

2. What roles do such variables as race and sex play in explaining common crimes? What are the various explanations of the increase in women's involvement in crime?

3. In looking at larceny–theft and burglary, we find far greater female involvement in the former than in the latter. What explanations have been offered to explain this trend?

4. What kinds of robberies are the most typical? What kinds of coercive force and victim roles lead to the most violence in robberies?

5. What are the unique characteristics of check forgers according to Lemert's study? What changes in the sex-ratio have occurred since Lemert's study of forgery?

Notes

1. David M. Gordon, "Class and the Economics of Crime," *Review of Radical Political Economics* **3** (Summer 1971): 51–75.

2. Don C. Gibbons, *The Criminological Enterprise.* (Englewood Cliffs, NJ: Prentice-Hall, 1976), 197–198.

3. Irving Spergle, *Racketville, Slumtown and Haulburg.* (Chicago: University of Chicago Press, 1964), p. 51.

4. Ibid.

5. Ibid.

6. *Criminal Victimization in the United States, 1975.* (Washington, D.C.: U.S. Department of Justice, 1977), p. 21.

7. Ibid.

8. "The Hispanic Victim: National Crime Survey Report," (Washington, DC: U.S. Department of Justice, Advance Report, June 1980): 2.

9. *Criminal Victimization, 1975,* 1977, 21.

10. "Hispanic Victim," 1980, 2.

11. *Criminal Victimization, 1975,* 1977, 21.

12. Ibid.

13. Ibid.

14. Freda Adler, "The Interaction Between Woman's Emancipation and Female Criminality," *International Journal of Criminology and Penology* **5** (1977): 101–112; Lee H. Bowker, *Women and Crime in America.* New York: Macmillan, 1981).

15. Karen Rosenblum, "Female Deviance and the Female Sex Role: A Preliminary Investigation," *British Journal of Sociology* **26** (1975): 169–185.

16. Erving Goffman, *Interaction Ritual.* (New York: Doubleday, 1967); Erving Goffman, *Gender Advertisements.* (New York: Harper & Row, 1979).

17. William B. Sanders, *Rape and Woman's Identity.* (Beverly Hills, CA: Sage, 1980).

18. Rita Simon, "American Women and Crime," *Annals of the American Academy of Political and Social Sciences* **423** (January 1975): 31–46.

19. Ibid.

20. Ibid.

21. Adler, 1977.

22. Darrell Steffensmeier, "Patterns of Female Property Crime 1960–1978: A Postscript," in Lee H. Bowker, *Women and Crime in America.* (New York: Macmillan, 1981), pp. 59–65.

23. Steffensmeier, 1981, 63.

24. Max J. Mobley and Richard M. Swanson, *Indiana Youth Survey Final Report,* **2.** (Carbondale, IL: Center for the Study of Crime, Delinquency, and Corrections, Southern Illinois University at Carbondale, nd): D29.

25. *Crime in the United States, 1979.* (Washington, DC: Federal Bureau of Investigation, 1980), p. 26.

26. *Crime in the United States, 1979,* 1980, 27.

27. *Crime in the United States, 1979,* 1980, 26.

28. *Criminal Victimization, 1975,* 1977, 73.

29. Ibid.

30. Unpublished field notes of author's from study of criminal investigations, 1973.

31. *Crime in the United States, 1979,* 1980, 25.

32. *Criminal Victimization, 1975,* 1977, 13–14.

33. William Chambliss, *Boxman.* (New York: Harper & Row, 1972), pp. 94–95.

34. *Criminal Victimization in the United States, 1977.* (Washington, DC: U.S. Department of Justice, 1979), p. 65.

35. *Criminal Victimization in the United States, 1975,* 1977, 73.

36. George Sullivan, "Organized Crime," paper presented at the Western Society of Criminology Eighth Annual Conference, February 27, 1981, San Diego, CA.

37. *Crime in the United States, 1979,* 1980, 16.

38. *Crime in the United States, 1979,* 1980, 36.

39. *Criminal Victimization in the United States, 1977,* 1979, 55.

40. David Luckenbill, "Patterns of Force in Interpersonal Coercion," (Chicago: University of Illinois, Chicago Circle, February 13, 1979) mimeographed.

41. Luckenbill, 1979, 8–9.

42. John Allen, *Assault with a Deadly Weapon.* (New York: McGraw-Hill, 1977), p. 175.

43. James Willwerth, *Jones: Portrait of a Mugger.* (Greenwich, CT: Fawcett, 1974), 18–19.

44. Willwerth, 1974, 42.

45. Howard Daudistel, "The Disorganized Criminal," paper presented at the Western Society of Criminology Eighth Annual Conference, February 27, 1981, San Diego, CA.

46. This description is based on a letter sent to the author by a convicted robber in Florida, 1977.

47. *Crime in the United States, 1979,* 1980, 12.

48. Luckenbill, 1979, 15.

49. Luckenbill, 1979, 11–12.

50. *Crime in the United States, 1979,* 1980, 321.

51. Edwin Lemert, "The Behavior of the Systematic Check Forger," *Social Problems* **1** (Fall 1958): 141–148.

52. Lemert, 1958, 142.

53. Lemert, 1958, 143.

54. Edwin Lemert, *Social Problems and Social Control.* (Englewood Cliffs, NJ: Prentice-Hall, 1967).

55. *Crime in the United States, 1979,* 1980, 199.

9

Consensual Crimes

What to Look For:

The nature of consensual crimes and the
problems in researching such crime.

The arguments relating to victims in consensual crimes.

The concepts of "criminal tariffs," addict subcultures, and
the relationship between consensual and nonconsensual
crimes.

The ways in which the meanings of drugs,
including alcohol, change.

How situations affect the use of alcohol and drugs.

The nature of prostitution in legal and illegal contexts and
the process of becoming a prostitute.

How the gambling laws benefit organized crime.

Introduction

THIS CHAPTER EXAMINES those crimes that involve consensual behavior in breaking the law. Often called "crimes without victims" or "victimless crimes," consensual crimes include such offenses as the use of illegal drugs, prostitution, and gambling. During the commission of these crimes, there is no target or victim as such. Rather, those who take drugs consent to do so—they are not forced. Likewise, in prostitution, there is the consent of the customer and the prostitute to have sex as part of a financial transaction. Also in gambling, if a person loses money, it is not because someone was pointing a gun at him, but rather because he willingly entered a situation where money was being bet, and he was unlucky and lost.

Criminologists who study these kinds of crimes have a unique problem in research. In looking at crimes with victims, it is possible to use police reports and victimization surveys to get some idea of the patterns. However, it is impossible to have reports of crimes by victims or victimization surveys for crimes without victims! Therefore, we must rely on either data from arrests or self-report surveys. The arrest data tells us something about patterns in consensual crimes, but since police departments will vary greatly in their policies toward the enforcement of these crimes, arrest data tells us more about enforcement policy and community pressures on the police than they do about the crimes themselves. Self-report surveys, on the other hand, have given us very reliable information on people's involvement in consensual crimes, but they have tended to concentrate on juvenile drug use and ignored sex and gambling offenses. Also, unlike victimization surveys, they are not as available. Fortunately, though, self-report surveys are becoming more standardized and soon may be as available as victimization data.[1] Additionally, a number of excellent ethnographic studies have examined various forms of consensual crimes, and these studies give us the most depth and insight into the social structure and lives of offenders.

Crimes of Morality

To begin our examination of consensual crimes, we will look at "morality crimes" or crimes against the "public morals." Of course, most crimes are against public morality: if we did not think it immoral to rob, rape, and kill such acts probably would not be against the law. However, when we deal with crimes involving consenting adults (or juveniles for that matter), we tend to think of illegal behavior in terms of immorality since there is no direct victim to the offense—only immoral participants.

In examining the background to consensual crimes and how they became illegal, it is necessary to focus on certain aspects of legal development. Becker referred to those who took up a moral crusade against some form of behavior as **moral entrepreneurs**.[2] On the one hand, a moral entrepreneur might be seen as a "meddling busybody," who makes it his or her business to tell other people how to live. Such an individual might hold him/herself in high moral regard, leading a holy crusade against sin. Groups such as the "Moral Majority," a highly organized political–religious conglomerate, lobby for stricter laws regarding abortion, homosexuality, and similar "acts against morality." One leader of the organization in early 1981 went so far as to suggest the death penalty for homosexuals—a suggestion that was retracted but illustrative of the moral self-righteousness of the group. By contrast, it also should be noted that moral entrepreneurs often have a very strong humanitarian thread:

> The crusader is not only interested in seeing to it that other people do what he thinks right, he believes that if they do what is right it will be good for them. Or he may feel that his reform will prevent certain kinds of exploitation of one person by another. Prohibitionists felt that they were not simply forcing their morals on others, but attempting to provide the conditions for a better way of life for people prevented by drink from realizing a truly good life. Abolitionists were not simply trying to prevent slave owners from doing the wrong thing; they were trying to help slaves achieve a better life.[3]

Likewise, the reformers who were central to the development of unique legal statutes for juveniles and a separate adjudicatory system for youthful offenders were also responsible for the passage of various child-labor laws, which prevented the exploitation of children. The "child-savers," while responsible for certain repressive laws against juveniles, believed that the laws were good for the children and society at large.[4] Truancy laws, for example, made children go to school to learn enough to get a decent job and achieve social mobility. So while the moral entrepreneurs are certainly meddlers, they are not without their own kind of compassion and humanitarian motives.

However, another view of the reformers contends that rather than being interested simply in a moral code or humanitarian reform, moral entrepreneurs were in a power struggle, using morality and humanitarianism as nothing more than a smoke screen for vested interests. For example, in the early years, the Treasury Department's Bureau of Narcotics' anti-marijuana stance—rather than being an effort to save the citizenry from drug addiction—was more an effort to expand its power and increase its budget. To be sure, those in the Bureau of Narcotics may have believed marijuana to be harmful, but their campaign began at a time when the Bureau was set up to deal with the provisions of the Harrison

Act—a law prohibiting the use of opiate drugs for all but medical purposes—and not during a period of high incidence of usage. In fact, in
1931 the Treasury Department noted in a report:

> A great deal of public interest has been aroused by newspaper articles ap-
> pearing from time to time on the evils of the abuse of marihuana, or Indian
> hemp, and more attention has been focused on specific cases reported on
> the abuse of the drug than would otherwise have been the case. This pub-
> licity tends to magnify the extent of the evil and lends color to an inference
> that there is an alarming spread of the improper use of the drug, whereas
> the actual increase in such use may not have been inordinately large.[5]

Thus, given the Treasury Department's own assessment of the problem,
the campaign against marijuana by the Federal Bureau of Narcotics was
as much an effort to construct a "national menace" as it was to fight it. Of
course, the greater the menace, the greater the budget for the battle—
after all, why would Congress want to fund an agency with a goal to com-
bat a problem whose scope "may not have been inordinately large"?

The "morality" behind consensual crimes ranges from fanatical beliefs,
to humanitarian concerns, to cynical manipulation. Most people believe
their own causes to be "humanitarian" and good for society, while the opposition is either fanatical or motivated by power or money, manipulating
the masses. However, one thing is certain, without the power to influence
Congress, crimes against "morals" would not be passed.

Crimes Without Victims

Edwin Schur did more to advance the concept of "crimes without victims"
than any other analyst. Schur defines the concept as, " . . . the willing exchange, among adults, of strongly demanded but legally proscribed goods
or services."[6] This is essentially the same definition we have been using to
describe **consensual crimes** with a single crucial difference: in our definition there is no implied presence or absence of a victim. Thus, the issue
is over whether or not there are victims in the various **victimless crimes**.

It would be pointless to argue about "moral victims" and debate
whether one will go to hell because of breaking the law. Not only does
such a concept rest upon a single moral standard in a society characterized by dissension and heterogeneity, but it would be virtually impossible
to prove or disprove even with a single moral standard. Rather, the question is whether or not there are "victims" in consensual crimes as measured by losses to society or specific members of society, the consensual
criminal included.

It is fairly easy to argue that a heroin addict who robs in order to obtain
money to buy heroin is victimizing someone in order to support his habit.
The victim in this case is a "robbery victim," but since the robbery was

caused by the need to buy heroin, we can also say that the person is a "heroin victim." We will refer to such cases as involving **secondary victims**. However, while we can blame the heroin for the robbery, we must consider the use of heroin in the context of a society where it is illegal. Whenever goods and services are made illegal, the price goes up. This is due to the "criminal tariff" added to the cost of the goods or service.[7] Because of the extra risks involved and artificial scarcity, dealers in illegal goods and services can charge more. For example, while an ounce of coffee from Colombia costs less than 40 cents, marijuana from the same country costs $40 an ounce (or more), and cocaine from Colombia costs over $1,000 an ounce. The difference in price is because of the relative difficulty in producing and transporting the illicit drugs due to the laws forbidding their use. On the other hand, if the drugs were legal, their price would drop drastically since the criminal tariff would be removed. Furthermore, with the legalization of the heroin, addicts would be better able to hold legitimate jobs instead of turning to crime, since the same stigma would not be attached to them and there would not be an overwhelming need to obtain large sums of money to buy heroin. In a study of physician addicts, it was learned that they were able to function as addicts without turning to crime to support their habit.[8] This is not to say that heroin does not impair one's functions, for it clearly does—just as does the overuse of liquor, coffee, or cigarettes. However, heroin is far more addictive than other narcotics, and continued use requires higher doses to have an effect—sometimes only to offset withdrawal symptoms. However, regardless of heroin's addictive qualities, there is no inherent connection between its use and crime. Rather, the crime is related to the social context into which heroin users are forced. Included in that context are: 1) artificially high prices due to criminal tariffs, 2) criminal stigmas, and 3) addict subcultures, teaching and supporting criminal means for obtaining money to buy drugs.[9]

Given the current social context of heroin use, we can understand the relationship that *does* exist between heroin addiction and victim crime. Erich Goode summarized it as follows:

1. Men and women who eventually become addicted do not necessarily commit crimes prior to addiction. There is nothing magical in the attraction to heroin that dictates that the eventual user be of a criminal disposition. The pre–1900 addict, as we saw, was no more criminal than the rest of the population, either before or after becoming addicted. All early studies of the addiction–crime link have shown it to be weak, demonstrating extremely *low* pre-addiction arrest rates. Even generalizations made after the criminalization of heroin have to be made with caution, for the addiction–crime link is far from uniform, and is heavily dependent on age, race, location, circumstances of use, etc.

2. However, it is also true that most men and women today who eventually become addicted do commit crimes proportionally in excess of their numbers in the population before becoming involved with narcotics. To a degree, it *is* the "criminal who becomes addicted." The majority of the studies on the pre-addiction crime rates of eventual addicts show that addicts usually have a strikingly higher crime rate than the rest of the population.

3. It is equally clear that addiction sharply increases the frequency and diversity of crimes committed, the seriousness of them, and the addict's likelihood of arrest. If men and women who become addicts are not strangers to crime, still the onset of addiction is marked by an expansion of criminal activity. In one study, two researchers found that the arrest rate of their sample of addicts increased from 10 percent before addiction to 80 percent afterward; property crimes increased from 4 to 70 percent. Robbery increased 61 percent, shoplifting 77 percent, burglary 56 percent, and pickpocketing 75 percent. There seems to be no doubt whatsoever that addiction per se is a, possibly *the*, major factor in escalating the crime rate among addicts.[10]

Given the overall sociolegal context of heroin addiction in the United States, it is clear that there are secondary victims.

While it is possible to make an argument that heroin addiction is related to crimes with victims, the same cannot be said for other consensual crimes. Marijuana smoking, various illegal sexual activities, and gambling are not related to crime, per se. It is true that organized crime has infiltrated gambling, but they have also infiltrated vending machine distribution, garbage collection, various labor unions, and other legitimate businesses, but there has never been a claimed relationship between, say, garbage collection and crime. As for gambling leading to crime because of losses, if we consider that about 75 percent of all new businesses fail in the first few years, virtually any business enterprise is a form of gambling. This is especially true in the stock market, most notably in commodity trading. Thus, while some consensual crimes may include victims, most do not.

The Criminal as Victim?

A final consideration is whether the victim is the person who commits the crime. Aside from moral or religious issues, can we say that the harm done to the violator makes the criminal a victim? By making certain activities illegal, does society protect people from victimizing themselves? In cases of illegal drugs, there is clear evidence that amphetamines, heroin, and other drugs have an adverse effect on the user. However, so too do alcohol and cigarettes, and while not everyone who uses "legal drugs" becomes a victim of them, neither does everyone who uses illegal drugs. Likewise, while prostitutes may spread venereal disease, so too can the disease be spread in legal ways by sexually active males and females. As for losing gamblers being the victims of gambling, people lose (or gain) billions everyday in the legal trade of gold, silver, stocks, bonds, and other business transactions, and while they may win or lose, we consider them to be victims of bad luck or judgment, not the existence of the market.

Drugs

When we think of drugs, we tend to classify them into two major categories: 1) good and 2) bad. This distinction is based on the societal understanding we have developed about how drugs are properly used. In medical usage, drugs have been defined as "wonder drugs" and "miracle drugs," combating such diseases as polio, infection, and other maladies. On the other hand, drugs have been used for recreational purposes—to get high. The former is the "good" use and the latter, "bad." Between the good and bad drugs and uses of drugs, there is a gray area where drugs are seen to be used "improperly" or "unwisely." For example, certain tranquilizing drugs have been prescribed by physicians to patients who become almost wholly dependent on them. Such usage, while not recreational, is not exactly medical either.

Other distinctions in drugs and their usage centers around their legality and traditional uses in society. Alcohol, tobacco, and caffeine are not generally considered "drugs," but all of them are, in fact, drugs. In a report by the National Commission on Marihuana and Drug Abuse, the greatest drug problem in America was identified as alcohol abuse.[11] Likewise, Goode points out, *"The typical drug addict is an alcoholic, not a street junkie."*[12] However, the sociolegal distinctions between "dope" and "alcohol" are such that we treat and understand "junkies" in one way and "alcoholics" in another. Also, drug usage depends on the situation of use. In some Muslim sects, hashish is used as a sacrament, as is peyote in among certain Indian religions in the Southwest United States and Northern Mexico. Their use is comparable to the use of wine as a sacrament in many Christian churches.

In American society the "official" definitions of drugs are medical ones—descriptions of the physiological effects of drugs—but such definitions do little to tell us why they are used. Therefore, in this section, we will concentrate on how drugs are defined and used both legally and socially. That is, we will discuss drugs as a social phenomenon, not a medical one, for even though there are distinct effects of drugs that can be understood medically, especially pathological effects, there are other effects, ones that are socially defined and must be understood as such.

Beliefs, Facts, Fabrications, and Constructions

In understanding the use of drugs, W. I. Thomas's dictum, "If a situation if defined as real, it is real in its consequences," is a most applicable one.[13] If people believe, for example, that marijuana is a "killer weed," they are less likely to use it than if they see its use as "harmless and fun." Such definitions do not change the pharmacological makeup of the drug, but they can affect how and if the drug is used at all. Gang members believe that smoking marijuana will "get them up" for a gang fight and similarly during the late 1960s hippies believed that marijuana made them more loving and peaceful. These two very different definitions of the drug's effects *in fact* led to behaviors consistent with the definitions. Gang members "become" more bold and tougher, and the hippies "became" more loving and peaceful. These opposite behaviors were believed to be "caused" by the effects of marijuana. Likewise, people under the "influence" of alcohol exhibit behavior from barroom brawlers to loving romantics. Both love affairs and fights have been attributed to, "I had too much to drink." Therefore, rather than explaining the behaviors in terms of the effects of the drugs, we are dealing with the *effects of the users' definitions of the drug.*

Changing Meanings of Drugs

Ever since the mid-1960s when the hippies and their followers began proselytizing the use of certain illegal drugs, there has been an articulate counter-definition to the effects of drugs. Before the advent of the hippies, there were a few researchers who questioned the official version of the effects of drugs, most notably Lindesmith.[14] However, these researchers were not advocating drug use, and their arguments were confined largely to academic journals with limited exposure.

When the hippies emerged in their colorful garb, with their exotic lifestyle and transcendental philosophy, they were a natural "media event." At the same time, many of the various hippie spokesmen such as Timothy Leary, a professor at Harvard University, were articulate and well educated. This group clearly was not a bunch of slum-dwelling, ignorant junkies who were trying to "hook" the youth on expensive habit-forming drugs, but rather they were middle- and upper-middle class, articulate, and clearly not suffering from "killer weed" or any of the nonsense that had been fabricated by the government. In a very short period of time, drug use increased rapidly, especially the use of marijuana among college- and high school-aged persons.[15]

The Drug Culture

One prevalent explanation of the drug phenomenon that began in the mid-1960s was that of a "drug culture."[16] The concept was almost identical to that of a "criminal subculture," focusing on drugs rather than crime in general. The hippies were taken to be the generators and core of the culture, and as the culture spread, the use of drugs along with the beliefs of the hippies would permeate various parts of society, especially the young. Drug use, it was believed, was caused because people took on the **drug culture**.

To some extent, American society as a whole already was a "drug culture," since there was a widespread belief in the benefit of "good drugs"—ones that were legal. By the mid-1960s, the population had been exposed to a steady stream of commercials and advertisements advocating drug use to do everything from curing colds to making women better mothers. One researcher described Americans' belief in drugs as the "pain–pill–pleasure" sequence.[17] If a person counters a problem (pain), by taking drugs (pill), the problem would be solved (pleasure). However, the concept of a "drug culture" did not include the widespread legal use of drugs. It only focused on the illegal use by hippies.

As an explanation of what occurred in the transmission of drug use, the concept of a drug culture only had limited use. With the diffussion of drugs, there was not a comparable spread of the hippie philosophy or "ethic."[18] Rather, various groups who began using drugs maintained their own lifestyles and simply replaced some other drug, usually alcohol, with an illegal drug, mostly marijuana.[19] Current trends in drug use clearly show that while the hippies are only a vague memory, recreational use of marijuana and—among the wealthier—cocaine is still prevalent among college- and high school-aged persons. Thus, while the hippies may have first brought illicit drug use to the attention of the middle-class and provided the initial impetus for it, the idea of a drug culture as causing or maintaining a behavior pattern that involved using drugs simply does not explain the patterns of use. Such an explanation would be comparable to saying that an "alcohol culture" exists that accounts for the various styles and situations of alcohol consumption.

Alcohol Abuse

In discussions of "drug abuse," we rarely consider the abuse of alcohol. However, alcohol is a drug in the pharmacological sense, and its use is relevant to the study of crime. For example, it has been estimated that in the United States, between 50 and 60 percent of the murders involved alcoholic intoxication at the time of the homicide.[20] Likewise, in studies of sexual assault and child molestation, the findings have shown that between 40 and 65 percent occurred when the attacker was drunk.[21] However, like other drugs, we cannot say that alcohol causes these crimes: of all the individuals consuming alcohol, only a small percentage are subsequently involved in these kinds of offenses. Moreover, since alcohol is legally obtained, except among underaged users, its use does not constitute a consensual crime. Therefore, we will concentrate on those situations of use where alcohol is illegal—drunk driving and public intoxication.

Drunk Driving

As a consensual crime, drunk driving is a somewhat unusual offense to classify, but since it is both illegal and consensual, it is important to consider in this chapter. However, since there are often very clear victims of drunk drivers who in no way consented to the offense, it is not quite the same as other consensual crimes where victimization is equivocal. For example, if a drunk climbs into his/her car and is killed in an accident involving no one but him/herself, all the parties (all one) consented to the behavior that brought on the accident. However, if the drunk runs into someone else who is sober and in no way consented to the offender's drunkenness, the crime obviously is not consensual. Nevertheless, since the focus will be on *drunk* driving, an offense all by itself, it must be considered consensual.

In 1979, the highest single category for arrests, not including traffic citations, in the United States was for driving under the influence.[22] A total of 1,231,665 people were arrested for a total rate of 601.9 per 100,000 population. A number of those arrested were also charged with negligent manslaughter, since about half of all traffic fatalities involve alcohol. One of the most interesting patterns in drunk driving arrests is the increase of such arrests among the under-18 age group. From 1970 to 1979 there was an increase of almost 250 percent in the intoxicated driving arrests for persons under 18, while the rate change for those over 18 increased 62.3 percent.[23] However, even with the dramatic increase in arrests for under-18 drivers, they accounted for only about 2.5 percent of the intoxicated driving arrests, the remaining 97.5 percent being over 18 years of age. Similarly, women made up only about 10 percent of the arrests, but in the decade of the 1970s there was a 124 percent increase in their arrests compared to a 60 percent increase for men.

Drunk driving behavior comes under two very different categories: 1) chronic and 2) situational. The **chronic drunk drivers** represent those who have a serious drinking problem—literally alcohol addiction. They will have too much to drink on a regular basis and then drive. A typical type of chronic drunk driver is a working man or woman whose occupation involves entertaining business contacts at luncheons or other social–business occasions where drinking alcohol is seen as a means of enhancing the contact. Salespersons are oftentimes in this kind of position. Also, after work, groups will go to their favorite bar on a regular basis and drink enough to become intoxicated and then drive home. The chronic character of this kind of drinking lies in its routine, and not necessarily in the personality of the drinkers. Much has been written about "alcoholic personalities," but very little about "alcoholic roles" or "alcoholic routines." Nevertheless, since certain roles and routines demand drinking as a part of the position or standard pattern of behavior, it is an important dimension of the chronic drunk driver.

The **situational drunk driver** can be just about anyone at one time or another, and there are probably very few people who have not been in situations where they have driven home drunk after drinking as part of an occasion. Typical situations for such drinking include parties, dates, picnics, and other festivities where alcohol is a part of the event. New Year's Eve is probably the best-known occasion where people are expected to go to parties and drink late into the night and then go home. These drinkers differ from the chronic drinkers in that they are less likely to be in occasions where drinking is expected behavior, but the "cause" is the same—the social demands of the occasion to engage in drinking and then return home by car.

It may appear ironic that those who are problem drinkers—especially those who drink alone and without requiring a special occasion to do so— are probably less responsible for drunk driving than chronic or situational drinkers. This is because problem drinkers will wait until they are home to begin drinking, both because they may want to hide their alcoholism, and they can drink more and less expensively than in a bar.

Public Drunkenness

From the beginning of the decade of the 1970s to the end, there was a 46 percent *decrease* in arrests for public drunkenness.[24] The decline in the arrest rates reflects the changing laws regulating "being drunk in a public place." In Wiseman's study of skid row alcoholics conducted in the late 1960s, it was found that arrests of homeless men on public drunkenness charges became so routine that certain characters known to the police were picked up as "drunks" whether they had been drinking or not. In fact, when the jail required trustees with certain skills, they would ask the police to go pick them up so that they could have their talents put to work free! However many states changed their laws so that instead of being put in jail for public drunkenness, public drunks were taken to detoxification centers where they were put into nonsecure detention until they sobered up. The net result of the laws, as can be seen in the decline in arrests for drunkenness, was that fewer public drunks were picked up altogether.

However, the concept of a "public drunk" was virtually synonymous with "poor public drunks." In the city where Wiseman's study was conducted, numerous conventions were held, and conventioneers were commonly found walking to and from their hotels to convention centers in a state of public intoxication; however, they were rarely arrested on charges of public drunkenness. On those occasions when they were arrested, they were released on a low bail, usually $25, and if they did not appear in court, they were fined the amount of their bail, and the case was done with.[25] Therefore, when public drunkenness arrests are considered, before and after the changes in the laws, those who came under the attention of the laws were virtually always skid row men whose major crime was their poverty, not their intoxication.

The decrease in arrests for public drunkenness and increase in drunk driving arrests reflects an overall change in social priorities concerning the use of alcohol. The shift indicates greater concern with the deadly consequences of drunk driving than public displays of poor derelicts staggering around intoxicated. At the same time, the new trend in arrests will mean that a greater proportion of middle- and upper-class persons will come into the official statistics on crime.

Marijuana

In looking at the trends in drug abuse arrests from 1975 to 1979, there is an overall *decrease* of 11.2 percent.[26] Among juveniles, the decrease in arrests is the greatest: 21.4 percent. For the most part, the decrease represents changes in the marijuana laws and not any changes in the patterns of smoking marijuana. In the mid-1970s several states changed the laws regulating simple possession of marijuana. Overall, the effect of the laws has been to **decriminalize** possession of small quantities of marijuana to fines averaging $25.[27] By 1979, ten states—Alaska, California, Colorado, Maine, Minnesota, Mississippi, New York, North Carolina, Ohio, and Oregon—had passed such legislation.

Before the new laws, however, there was a sharp increase in marijuana arrests. Between 1965 and 1970, marijuana arrests increased by 1,000 percent, from 18,000 in 1965 to 188,000 in 1970.[28] By 1974, 445,000 people had been arrested on marijuana charges, and then there was an uneven decline into the 1980s. The new laws and declining arrests reflected changing attitudes toward marijuana in America. By 1977, more people believed that alcohol was more dangerous than marijuana, and a sizable proportion of the population had at least experimented with the drug.[29]

However, neither the laws nor law enforcement efforts changed in regard to selling or smuggling marijuana. In 1981, a major land, sea, and air operation intercepted several boatloads of marijuana coming into the United States from South America. It was estimated that close to a billion dollars worth of marijuana was seized in that operation. The result of the continued efforts to arrest the dealers has been to maintain the "criminal tariff" on the drug, and prices for an ounce of marijuana have increased to an average of about $40, up from $10 in the early 1970s. This has, in turn, led to an increase in home-grown marijuana both for personal use and sale. In certain counties of Northern California the main cash crop has become marijuana, and a number of companies have made millions selling indoor devices for the rapid (and potent) cultivation of marijuana. By decriminalizing the use of marijuana while maintaining and even increasing efforts to stop its transport and sale, the laws have created a lucrative market for the underworld. The price is kept artificially high by the criminal tariff, and by decriminalizing its use, there is a greater potential market.

The overall changes are explained by Goode as being the result of the kind of people who were using marijuana.[30] In the late 1930s when the original anti-marijuana laws were drafted, the users were both disorganized and disreputable. By the 1970s marijuana users tended to be the better educated and more affluent, with a positive correlation between the amount of education and proportion of the population who had tried it. They were also better organized to change legislation to decriminalize its use, and that is exactly what they did. As Goode notes:

> In this case, it isn't so much what the objective features of a marijuana user's behavior are, how much harm such behavior inflicts on society, or what science and medicine say are the effects of use. Rather, it seems to be the status, the image, the respectability of the user. Marijuana use has recently exited from the ranks of deviant and criminal behavior because of the characteristics of the individuals who engage in it, not because of the nature of the activity itself. Again, with regard to marijuana use, it seems to be the case that it matters far less what you do than who you are. Many activities are criminalized mainly because the participants are disreputable in the eyes of the majority or in the eyes of the most powerful members of society. And only secondarily—and often not at all—because the behavior in question is objectively harmful and damaging. Clearly the rationalistic view that laws are passed and enforced simply because the behavior that is outlawed is dangerous to society must be sharply challenged.[31]

While Goode's point is well taken, especially his challenging the idea that laws are drafted to protect society, it does not seem to be true that the respectability of the users alone can explain changes in the laws. In the following section we will look at cocaine use. Traditionally a "rich man's" drug, its use has not been decriminalized, even though celebrities (when arrested) contribute to its enhanced image.

Cocaine

Cocaine has a somewhat illustrious history compared to other drugs. Sigmund Freud at one time believed it to be a cure-all for various forms of depression, and for several years recommended its use. Likewise, numerous celebrities have been known to use it, and it is still considered chic among certain segments of the world of fashion, film, and the arts. Even Sherlock Holmes was a one-time user of the drug. However, while pen-

In Bolivia, where coca leaves are sold openly, there is no legal or social stigma attached to their use. Cocaine is made from coca leaves and is smuggled in a multimillion dollar business into the United States from Bolivia and other South American countries.

alties have changed over time in degree of severity, legalization of cocaine has never enjoyed the same widespread support as legalization of marijuana.

At first incorrectly classified as a narcotic by the Federal Bureau of Narcotics, cocaine is actually a stimulant.[32] It falls into the same category as amphetamines and is not physically addictive, but has a marked effect on the central nervous system. In describing its effects, one user said:

I was quivering like a joker in the hot seat at the first jolt. I tried to open my talc-dry mouth. I couldn't. I was paralyzed. I could feel a hot ball of puke racing up from my careening guts. I saw the green stinking puke rope arch into the black mouth of the waste basket. . . .
I felt like the top of my skull had been crushed in. It was like I had been blown apart and all that was left were my eyes. Then tiny prickly feet of ecstasy started dancing through me. I heard melodious bells tolling softly inside my skull.
I looked down at my hands and thighs. A thrill shot through me. Surely they were the most beautiful in the Universe. I felt a superman's surge of power.[33]

Cocaine's popularity among wealthier drug users may in part be explained by its traditionally high cost. Unlike marijuana, which has either been grown in the United States or in nearby Mexico, cocaine has always been imported, and the *tradition* of the high cost was maintained. Since heroin has also been an imported drug, but relatively lower in cost than cocaine, the import costs alone cannot explain its popularity among the wealthier drug users. Likewise, at one time, cocaine was seen to be a Negro-drug, responsible for blacks raping white women in the South.[34] Rather, like other traditions in patterns of crime, cocaine, once established as the rich user's drug in the 1920s and 1930s, was simply passed on from one generation to the next. Thus in addition to a criminal tariff, its high cost was maintained by what we might call a "snob factor" built into its price.[35] This same principle works with "designer fashions," clothes of average quality, but which sell for high prices.

One possible physiological effect of cocaine, along with other amphetamines, is the tendency toward violence and paranoia with continued use. By and large, however, because of the drug's cost and limited use, most people do not get to the point where they experience these adverse effects. Though if the drug were less expensive and more often used, the possibility of irritability, hyperexcitability, anxiety, and paranoia would be far greater.[36]

Heroin

Of all the illegal drugs, the one most identified with criminal behavior is heroin. Largely this image is due to the number of addicts or "junkies" who are identified as being muggers, burglars, and thiefs. However, as we pointed out previously in this chapter, the addict's lifestyle, including property crimes, is not due to the drug itself, but rather to the context of heroin use in society. In other words, there is nothing in heroin that leads people to steal, and if given an unlimited supply of the drug, most addicts would be content to expend as little effort as possible and simply enjoy being in a heroin stupor.

Like cocaine, heroin, an opium derivative, began as a medicine. Before the Pure Food and Drug Act of 1906, morphine, another opium derivative, was commonly used in home remedies—the elixirs of "medicine show" fame. During the American Civil War, a number of addicts were created when battlefield casualties were routinely given doses of morphine to soothe the pain of wounds.[37] Between the time of its large-scale introduction as a painkiller and its prohibition, opium-based drugs were commonly used. As Goode notes:

An addict then was viewed quite differently from the way an addict now is. Medical addiction at the turn of the century was not considered deviant. The public didn't approve of addiction, but it was considered an unfortunate affliction rather than a manifestation of immorality and depravity. The addict was considered sick and to be pitied rather than scorned. And the addict of 1900, unlike the addict today, was able to live a more or less normal life and carry out ordinary, everyday functions: he could work, take care of a family, attend school. There was no isolation or stigmatization of the addict before the turn of the century.[38]

To be sure, there were morphine addicts during the late 19th and early 20th centuries; however, as Goode further points out:

> There were for them no group norms or attitudes, no feelings of group loyalty, no sense of identity, no special argot, no ideology or lore surrounding the use of or experiences with narcotics, and no rejection of the nonaddict world: *There was no addict subculture.*[39]

In other words, while the addicts around the turn of the century were heavily involved with morphine, unlike today's heroin users, the drug was not their entire world, with all else being secondary.

Getting and Getting into Drugs

Given the existence of an **addict subculture** and an established drug-using behavior pattern in society among a sizable proportion of the population, it is not too difficult to see how people come to discover drugs. For the most part, when people associate with others who use drugs, they will simply learn from others how to use and enjoy them. Such an explanation may appear to be an oversimplification of the process, but from all accounts of drug use, differential association theory appears to be the best way to explain the introduction and use of drugs. It is *not* the case that users are introduced and seduced into drug use by greedy "pushers," except in rare instances or where the drug dealer happens to be a friend of the person introduced. From Becker's pioneering work on marijuana in the late 1950s and throughout the 1960s and 1970s, the pattern of friends introducing one another to marijuana has been a consistent finding.[40] Moreover, the same pattern has held for other drugs as well. For example, one addict explains how his uncle introduced him to heroin:

> *One day my uncle comes around and he's using heroin, but none of us know it at the time. He came over to see my mother, but she was downtown. So, he throws this $3 bag of dogie on the kitchen table and says, "Try some." I say, "Eddie, I ain't about to put any of that shit in my arm." He acts real surprised. "Hey, Manny, I'm not talking about shooting. I mean, you can snort it and get drove into the next country."*[41]

After trying the heroin by inhaling it through his nose, at his uncle's suggestion, the novice user becomes violently sick. Later, however:

> *So I snort again and hey, it's really something else. I mean, it's like the shit really hit the fan . . . you can't describe it. All the colors of Times Square tumble right over*

your forehead and explode in your eyeballs like a million, jillion shooting stars. And then, each one of them goddamn stars novas in a cascade of brilliant Technicolor.[42]

Shortly after using heroin by inhaling it, the novice user's uncle comes by again.

Then my uncle comes over one day with an outfit. And he says, "You wanna try fixing it?" "Hey, man, I don't know. I'm scared of needles." I'm still thinking that you can get hooked with needles, and that there ain't the danger to just snortin' the stuff. "Well, look," my uncle says, "you can go halfway and skinpop it."[43]

After learning that it is unnecessary to inject heroin in his veins to inject it with a needle, the novice shoots the heroin in his skin (skinpop). Finding this way of taking heroin leads to a quick effect, he learns that by injecting it directly into a vein (mainlining), one can have the fullest effect of the drug. Thus, beginning with a suggestion of a relative to try inhaling heroin, the novice user quickly learns that mainlining heroin is the best way to use it and is eventually addicted.

The learning process in drug use not only involves the mechanics of injecting, smoking, or inhaling it, but also the ways of thinking about it, especially at first. Most people who are heroin addicts are well aware of the life of a junkie and disapprove of it, but nevertheless, they get into it themselves. A more recent heroin fad among the upper-class user begins with the *belief* that by inhaling the smoke of burning heroin ("riding the dragon") one can enjoy its effects without becoming addicted. Of course, taking heroin in this manner is just as addictive as snorting it or even mainlining, but since the learned belief is otherwise, it is possible for people to "unlearn" what they "thought" they knew in the past and "discover" the "truth" about heroin.

Sex Offenses

Another consensual crime involves all kinds of sexual behavior ranging from prostitution to homosexuality. In recent years, the laws regulating various sexual offenses have been redefined either on the books or in the application of the law. Most states have either removed or do not enforce anti-fornication laws, but some such laws and enforcement do exist. However, there are considerable efforts and resources applied to other offenses regulating sexual conduct. In 1979, almost 90,000 arrests were made for prostitution and commercialized vice, and there was a 63 percent increase in such arrests between 1970 and 1979.[44] In addition, there were another 62,633 arrests for sexual offenses other than rape in 1979.[45] Many of the sexual offenses involved victims, such as child molestation, but others did not and were consensual crimes. In this section, we will look at some of these sexual offenses, concentrating on prostitution.

Prostitution

Prostitution is defined differently in different states, but in general it can be defined as " . . . the pursuit of sex as a vocation or occupation . . . with sufficient lack of discrimination, emotional indifference to the partner, and inconstancy so that there is no one-to-one relationship, even for a short period."[46] This definition excludes "kept women," mistresses or boys who are in the "favor" of older homosexuals. The two key concepts in distinguishing prostitution in the law are 1) it is having sex for hire; and 2) it is indiscriminate. That is, any man or woman who sells his or her sexual favors to anyone who comes up with the money is involved in prostitution.

In many countries, such as Holland and West Germany, for example, prostitution is legal. Also, in several counties in the state of Nevada, prostitution is legal as well.[47] However, in every other state in the United States, prostitution is against the law. In those places where prostitution is legal, including Nevada, it is controlled and regulated. Brothels are licensed, and regular medical checks are required to control the spread of venereal disease. Furthermore, the prostitutes and customers are protected by the law since any financial arrangement is legally binding; therefore, if either is beaten, robbed, or in some other way illegally treated, there is legal recourse. Where prostitution is *illegal* it is not controlled, and there is no practical legal recourse for either prostitutes or customers who believe they have been mistreated or defrauded. Finally, in those places where prostitution is legal, it can be taxed and is a source of revenue for the state. Since illegal prostitutes bring in between $7 and $9 billion annually, there is a considerable amount of money to be taxed.[48]

Prostitution, however, is restricted in most places because of religiously grounded moral beliefs. Usually such beliefs will be accompanied by some "practical" reasons for outlawing prostitution, such as its possible threat to the family and, ironically, the spread of venereal disease. It is also argued that legalized prostitution will encourage other immorality among prostitutes such as drug use, theft, robbery, and any number of other illegal activities. However, the opposite may be true. Where prostitutes and customers are protected by the law, it is far more difficult to blackmail, rob, or steal since the customer or prostitute can go to the police. MacNamara and Sagarin point out that in brothels that rely on return customers, there is far more protection against such offenses by prostitutes, and customers can be better controlled as well.[49] Likewise, as far as rape is concerned, in the counties in Nevada where prostitution is legal, the incident of reported rape is low, and it was found in a study in Australia that when prostitution was made illegal, incidents of rape increased.[50]

TYPES OF PROSTITUTES. Prostitution is not a monolithic occupation, but rather there are several different types and roles, stratified from top to bottom. MacNamara and Sagarin identify seven types:

1. Streetwalker
2. Bar girl
3. Hotel prostitute
4. Store prostitute
5. Convention prostitute
6. Call girl
7. Brothel prostitute[51]

The most familiar image of the prostitute is the streetwalker. How-ever, streetwalkers are at the bottom of the prostitute stratification system and are the most vulnerable to arrest and abuse.

The streetwalker is on the bottom echelon and the call girl at the top. The brothel prostitute is relatively rare, but common in Nevada where it is legal. Streetwalkers usually work for pimps who take most of their money, while the other types, although not wholly independent, usually have some kind of arrangement with others. For example, bar and hotel prostitutes typically have an understanding with bartenders or hotel managers to ply their trade in the places of business for a fee. Also, symbiotic relationships exist between bellhops, cabdrivers, and other service personnel who will steer a customer to a prostitute; and they too are paid. Store prostitutes, on the other hand, work out of a "massage parlor," and while they receive a token salary from the business, most of their income is derived from "tips" their customers give them. At the very top, the call girl develops a wealthy clientele, and she usually does not have to pay pimps, madams, or others to steer her customers. They are usually referred to her by her other clients.

Overall, the economics of prostitution are not as rich for the prostitute as the overall figures suggest. Gail Sheehy estimated there were between 200,000 and 250,000 prostitutes in the United States in 1973, and with profits at 10 times that of the Justice Department's annual budget, one would expect the prostitutes to be fairly well off.[52] However, in Winick and Kinsie's study, it was found that only about 5 percent of the prostitutes they interviewed had any money left by 30 years of age.[53] The majority of the money earned goes to pimps, lawyers, and others involved indirectly in prostitution. The pimps are especially greedy with the lowest paid of all prostitutes, the streetwalkers. Girls who earn from $200 to $250 a night get to keep only about 5 percent, the rest going to the pimp.[54] Other than offering some protection to his girls, the pimp does very little—or as one prostitute noted: "He doesn't do *nothing*. But the way he does nothing is *beautiful*."

And as Sheehy comments:

> That description, coming from a starry-eyed beginner in the stable of a Times Square pimp, hit the nail on the head. She sees it as a source of pride. It is her earning power that allows her "sweet man" to drive around town in glorified idleness.[55]

However, prostitution has declined over the years as there is a decreasing demand for prostitutes. A double standard still exists concerning sex, but it is nowhere as rigid as it once was, and premarital sex—as well as sex in general—has become far more open and accepted. Freda Adler, using data from the American Social Health Association, shows that prostitution as an organized business is not what it used to be.[56] The following figures are based on a scale from 100 to 0, with "100" being evidence of flagrant commercialized prostitution and "0" being the opposite:

Years	Average National Score
1920–1929	99
1930–1938	92
1940–1946	49
1947–1949	74
1950–1959	35
1967–	37

These figures suggest that even though prostitution may be a 9 billion dollar business, it simply is not the business it used to be.

Becoming a Prostitute

Given the relative decline in prostitution, the economic exploitation of prostitutes, and the general social condemnation of prostitutes, why do women get into the profession or "life"? Like many of the other forms of crimes we have discussed, most prostitutes learn the necessary motivations, techniques, and role requirements from friends or acquaintances.[57] The general pattern identified by Davis's research shows three stages:

Stage 1: Drift from promiscuity to first act of prosituation

Stage 2: Transitional deviance

Stage 3: Professionalization[58]

The first stage begins in early adolescence, where a girl who is sexually active becomes labelled as "loose" or promiscuous and is ostracized to others who have similar labels. In this new context, sexual experimentation and experience is encouraged, being seen very much as an adventure rather than a fall from grace. Opportunities for being paid for having sex are greater, since there is a higher probability that an associate will introduce the girl to a client. One such girl interviewed by the author explained, "A friend of mine needed an extra girl for these guys who were going to pay us to 'party' with them. I could use the money, and so I did it."[59]

The second stage occurs when the girl redefines herself from a "fun loving" adventuress who engages in sex for excitement to one who is in it as a business. This is a period marked by ambivalence and vacillation. As she comes to redefine herself in this stage, she also begins learning the skills and values of a prostitute.

The final stage occurs when the girl completely redefines herself as a "professional" for whom sex is a business and not an adventure. Her orientation is not toward excitement, newness, or romance, but rather a financial arrangement between herself and the customer. At this point she has entered a criminal career.

It should be noted that not all girls follow this pattern. Many girls will use prostitution as a means of working their way through college or to set up a business. Others will continue to see prostitution as exciting and adventuresome and never develop either a self-concept or lifestyle of a professional.[60]

Other Sex Offenses

The variety of laws that states have regulating sexual conduct other than prostitution vary greatly, but most have some laws banning sex with minors, various "unnatural" sex acts, such as sodomy, incest, and homosexual relations. Many states have revised their laws regulating homosexuality, and it is not pursued to the extent it once was by the criminal justice system. However, one pattern of homosexual activity has been the focus of and concern of the criminal justice system. This is homosexual relations between boys and older men. In the homosexual argot, the young boys are referred to as **chickens** and the men that pursue them, **chicken hawks**. One pattern of this relationship is a strictly business one, where the boys will have sex with the men for money, but do not see themselves or their activities as homosexual.[62] The boys simply see the arrangement as a means of getting money, dropping all homosexual encounters as they grow up. Another arrangement between the "chickens" and "chicken hawks" is where the younger boy is "kept" by the man for purposes of sex, giving the child toys and other treats. For the most part, these offenses are seen as a form of child molestation.

In non-homosexual encounters between adults and minors, either the statutory rape laws or child molestation laws are the most commonly applied. The application and even the content of the laws protect young girls from men. The U.S. Supreme Court upheld a California law defining statutory rape as a male (adult or minor) having six with a minor girl, but *not* a woman having sex with a minor boy. In about 20 percent of the cases of child molestation, there is some violence, but for the most part there is neither violence or coercion by the adult.[63] However, since minors by law are under the age of legal consent, technically they are crime victims. Therefore, it is problematic whether these offenses are "consensual crimes" or not. To the extent there is violence or coercion these offenses clearly are not consensual. However, since many children, especially the very young, have no idea of what is happening to them, it is difficult to call even cases where no violence or coercion is employed, "consensual" in the form being used in this chapter.

Gambling

Gambling falls into an unusual category of consensual crime due to its multifaceted character. In Chapter 13 we will discuss gambling as a major source of funds for organized crime, but not all gambling is run by or for the profit of organized criminals. Also, there is a good deal of legal organized gambling when we consider horse and dog racing, legal casinos in Nevada and Atlantic City, and various forms of lottery, bingo, and other games of chance that involve risking money to win money. Finally, there are "friendly" or "social" occasions of gambling consisting of a group of friends who play poker or shoot dice together.[64]

The laws regulating gambling vary from state to state in both content and application, but California's is representative of most.

> Every person who deals, plays, or carries on, opens, or causes to be opened, or who conducts . . . any game of (chance) . . . for money, checks, credit, or other representative of value, and every person who plays or bets at or against any of said prohibited games, is guilty of a misdemeanor. . . . [65]

Included in that definition is everything from slot machines to the "friendly" games of poker, and while there is not the same enforcement concern for games among friends as there is gambling run by organized syndicates, they are all illegal. However, there seems to be a lessening concern by law enforcement over gambling as well as changes in public

Gambling is not always a crime. In New York, for example, the off-track betting (OTB) offices have largely replaced the illegal bookie joints with the profits going to the state rather than organized crime.

attitude towards it. Between 1970 and 1979, there was a decrease in gambling arrests by 41.3 percent.[66] In part, this chance was caused by the legalization of "bookmaking" or "off-track betting" in such states as New York and the legalization of casino gambling in Atlantic City. It is also possible that by concentrating on those behind organized crime's gambling, fewer gamblers and more gambling profiteers were the target of arrests. Likewise, with the legalization of lotteries in several states, the "numbers" racket—a form of illegal lottery—is both less active and less prosecuted than previously.

Probably the most common form of illegal gambling is the "friendly" kind involving otherwise law-abiding citizens who put money into the office football pool, play poker on Saturday nights, or shoot dice in alleyways with their friends. Criminologists have no idea of the extent to which people involve themselves in such games of chance, and they rarely show up in the arrest figures. In fact, many people who are involved in these friendly games of chance do not even realize they are against the law, and if they do, they believe the law "really didn't mean" to prohibit the kind of gambling they do. They have, in other words, their own "techniques of neutralization" for breaking the law.

SUMMARY

This chapter has examined "consensual" crimes—crimes where all directly involved consent to the violation. For the most part these crimes are seen as being "against morality" instead of against our fellow men and women, and as such they tend to be the most controversial. However, in the context of their violation, there can be victims—"secondary victims"—who suffer because someone, such as a heroin addict or gambler short of funds, sees no alternative but to steal from a victim. Whether the legalization of offenses leading to secondary victimization would solve the problem is a point of contention, for while drugs such as heroin are illegal, alcohol is not, and a high proportion of certain victim crimes are committed by people intoxicated on alcohol. When the issue is the "general good of society," it is unclear whether the general good is better met by legalized control or simply prohibition.

Of the consensual crimes discussed, drunkenness is the offense for which people are most likely arrested, followed by drug arrests. Therefore, the laws regarding public drunkenness and possession and sales of drugs are those most likely to affect people's lives. However, the poor and powerless suffer the fate of the law's application disproportionately, for conventioneers staggering around in public or physician drug addicts rarely are arrested or prosecuted under the laws. To a great extent, then, while one's position in society may demand greater or lesser involvement in drinking (or drugs), the status of that position will determine the extent to which the laws will be applied to them. Therefore, the businessman whose routine calls for frequent drinking with clients may drink as much as a skid row derelict, but his chances of ever seeing the inside of a jail cell are comparatively remote.

Of the sex offenses, prostitution is the most common one involving intervention by official social control agencies, but like the application of the alcohol and drug laws, those on the bottom—the streetwalkers—are the most likely to suffer the law's consequences.

Finally, gambling, which is a strange mixture of legal and illegal kinds, appears to be only selectively applied. The friendly poker games and office football pool, while possibly involving billions of illegally gambled money, rarely invoke the interest of law enforcement; while an illegal crap game in an alley or garage is likely to. However, with the changes in the laws in several states, both the arrest rates and law enforcement interest in common gambling appear to be on the wane.

Glossary

Addict Subculture   The universe and world view of drug addicts developed through social condemnation and outlawing of the drugs they use.

Chickens/Chicken Hawks   Terms in homosexual argot to refer to young boys and the men who pay them for having sex.

Chronic Drunk Driver   Any person whose daily round of affairs includes moderate to heavy drinking and driving.

Consensual Crimes   Illegal acts in which all parties consent to participate.

Decriminalization   Taking away the criminal penalties for various crimes. This usually is associated with consensual crimes since there are no unwilling victims.

Drug Culture   A belief system supporting the use of drugs and an accompanying lifestyle.

Moral Entrepreneurs   People who actively become involved in urging legislation to support various moral and/or humanitarian laws.

Primary Victims   People who are directly victimized by crime, such as a robbery victim.

Secondary Victims   People who are indirectly hurt by crime, such as relatives of heroin addicts. Also refers to primary victims whose victimization was caused by consensual crime, such as robbery victim who was robbed by junkie who needed money to support habit.

Situational Drunk Driver   Person who drinks and drives only on special occasions, such as at a party.

Victimless Crimes   Crimes where there are no direct or primary victims. (See also **Consensual Crimes.**)

Questions

1. What are "moral entrepreneurs" and what effect do they have on consensual crimes?

2. What are "secondary victims" in "victimless crimes?" What is the relationship between crime victims and the legal context of consensual crimes?

3. What is a "criminal tariff?" What effect does the tariff have on the costs and consequences of consensual crimes?

4. What occurred in the mid-1960s that led to a rapid increase in middle-class drug use among the young?

5. Compare consensual crimes involving drugs, alcohol, sex, and gambling.

Notes

1. Delbert S. Elliott and Suzanne S. Ageton, "Reconciling Race and Class Differences in Self-Reported and Official Estimates of Delinquency," *American Sociological Review* **45** (February 1980): 95–100.

2. Howard Becker, *Outsiders.* (New York: Free Press, 1963), pp. 147–163.

3. Becker, 1963, 148.

4. Anthony Platt, *The Child-Savers: The Invention of Delinquency.* (Chicago: University of Chicago Press, 1969).

5. Quoted in Becker, 1963 from U.S. Treasury Department, *Traffic in Opium*

and Other Dangerous Drugs for the Year Ended December 31, 1931. (Washington, D.C.: U.S. Government Printing Office, 1932), p. 51.

6. Edwin Schur, *Crimes without Victims.* (Englewood Cliffs, NJ: Prentice-Hall, 1965).

7. Herbert Packer, *The Limits of Criminal Sanction.* (Stanford: Stanford University Press, 1968).

8. Charles Winick, "The Physician Narcotic Addict," *Social Problems* (Fall 1961): 174–186.

9. Eric Goode, "Drugs and Crime," pp. 227–272 in A. Blumberg, *Current Perspectives on Criminal Behavior.* (New York: Knopf, 1981).

10. Goode, 1981, 255–256.

11. National Commission on Marihuana and Drug Abuse, *Marihuana: A Signal of Misunderstanding.* The Technical Papers of the National Commission on Marihuana and Drug Abuse. (Washington, D.C.: U.S. Government Printing Office, 1972).

12. Goode, 1981, 248.

13. W. I. Thomas, *The Unadjusted Girl.* (Boston: Little, Brown, 1923).

14. Alfred R. Lindesmith, "Federal Law and Drug Addiction," *Social Problems* (Summer 1959): 48–57.

15. See, for example, James F. Short and Ivan Nye, "Extent of Unrecorded Juvenile Delinquency: Tentative Conclusions," *Journal of Criminal Law, Criminology and Police Science* **49**, 4 (1958) and W. B. Sanders, "Marijuana Use in Two Midwestern High Schools, 1970," in *Juvenile Delinquency.* (New York: Prager, 1976), p. 18. See also Daniel Yankelovich, *The New Morality.* (New York: McGraw-Hill, 1974).

16. The idea of a drug culture seemed to have more popular support in the mass media than anywhere else. See Thomas Wallace, "Culture and Social Being," Unpublished Masters thesis, University of California, Santa Barbara, 1972.

17. Arthur Berger, "Drug Advertising and the 'Pain, Pill, Pleasure' Model," *Journal of Drug Issues* **4** (Summer 1974): 208–212.

18. Sherri Cavan, "The Hippie Ethic and Spirit of Drug Use," in Jack Douglas, ed., *Observations of Deviance.* (New York: Random House, 1970).

19. Joseph Weis, "Styles of Middle-Class Adolescent Drug Use," *Pacific Sociological Review* **17** (July 1974): 251–286.

20. Goode, 1981, 248.

21. Ibid.

22. Federal Bureau of Investigation, *Crime in the United States, 1979.* (Washington, D.C.: U.S. Government Printing Office, 1980), p. 188.

23. FBI, 1980, 190.

24. J. Wiseman, *Stations of the Lost.* (Englewood Cliffs, NJ: Prentice-Hall, 1970).

25. These observations were made by the author while assisting Professor Wiseman in study of drunks in court. See reference 24.

26. FBI, 1980, 192.

27. Goode, 1981, 232.

28. Ibid.

29. "Poll Finds Turnabout on Softer Pot Law," *New York Post,* July 5, 1977.

30. Goode, 1981, 233–234.

31. Ibid.

32. Richard Lingerman, *Drugs from A to Z,* 2nd ed. (New York: McGraw-Hill, 1974), p. 47.

33. "Iceberg Slim," *Pimp: The Story of My Life.* (Los Angeles: Holloway House, 1967).

34. Richard Ashley, *Cocaine: Its History, Uses and Effects.* (New York: St. Martin's Press, 1975).

35. Lester Grinspoon and Janes Bakalar, *Cocaine: A Drug and Its Social Evolution.* (New York: Basic Books, 1976).

36. Goode, 1981, 243.

37. Goode, 1981, 251–252.

38. Goode, 1981, 252–253.

39. Goode, 1981, 253.

40. Becker, 1963; Wallace, 1972.

41. Richard Rettig, Manuel Torres, and Gerald Garrett, *Manny: A Criminal-Addict's Story.* (Boston: Houghton Mifflin, 1977), p. 33.

42. Ibid.

43. Rettig et al., 1977, 34–35.

44. Federal Bureau of Investigation, 1980, 90.

45. FBI, 1980, 189.

46. Donal E. J. MacNamara and Edward Sagarin, *Sex Crime and the Law,* (New York: Free Press, 1977), p. 99.

47. Richard Symanski, "Prostitution in Nevada," *Annals of the Association of American Geographers* **64** (1974): 357–377.

48. Gail Sheehy, "The Economics of Prostitution: Who Pays? Who Profits?" *Ms.* (June 1973): 58.

49. MacNamara and Sagarin, 1977, 112.

50. R. N. Barber, "Prostitution and the Increasing Number of Convictions for Rape in Queensland," *Australian and New Zealand Journal of Criminology* (September 1969): 169–174.

51. MacNamara and Sagarin, 1977.

52. Sheehy, 1973.

53. Charles Winick and Paul Kinsie, *The Lively Commerce.* (New York: Quadrangle, 1971).

54. Sheehy, 1973.

55. Ibid.

56. Freda Adler, *Sisters in Crime.* (New York: McGraw-Hill, 1975).

57. James H. Bryan, "Apprenticeships in Prostitution," *Social Problems* **12** (Winter 1965): 287–297.

58. Nannette J. Davis, "The Prostitute: Developing a Deviant Identity," in James M. Henslin, ed., *Studies in the Sociology of Sex.* (Englewood Cliffs, NJ: Prentice-Hall, 1971).

59. From an interview by the author with a college student who had tried prostitution a few times, but had no ambitions to become a "pro."

60. Gale Miller, *Odd Jobs: The World of Deviant Work.* (Englewood Cliffs, NJ: Prentice-Hall, 1978), p. 135.

61. MacNamara and Sagarin, 1977, 84–88.

62. Albert Reiss, Jr. "The Social Integration of Queers and Peers," *Social Problems* (Fall 1961): 102–120.

63. MacNamara and Sagarin, 1977, 76.

64. Louis Zurcher, Jr., "The Friendly Poker Game: A Study of an Ephemeral Role," *Social Forces* (December 1970): 173–186.

65. Penal Code of California. Section 330, "Gaming." (Sacramento: California Department of General Services, 1971).

66. Federal Bureau of Investigation, 1980, 190.

10

Assault and Murder

What to Look For:

The historical aspects of violence in American society and comparative types of violence in the United States and other countries.

Those most likely to commit and be victims of homicides and assaults.

The concept of "subculture of violence" and how it explains rates of violent crime in America.

The kinds of situations in which violent crimes are most likely to occur.

The social process and interaction sequences in homicides.

Differences in impersonal and personal forms of violence.

Introduction

VIOLENCE IN THE UNITED STATES has held a peculiar fascination for criminologists and the average citizen alike. Images of violence thread their way through American history from the early settlers in savage battles with Native Americans to an assassination attempt against President Reagan on television. As one of the few modern nations with virtually no controls over the ownership and distribution of guns, the United States is probably the most armed (or overarmed) society in the history of mankind. During the Vietnam War, more Americans were murdered at home than were killed in the war in Southeast Asia.

In this chapter we will examine two forms of violence—assaults and murder. Rape, another violent crime, will be treated as a separate topic in Chapter 11, due to its unique characteristics; and, robbery, as we saw in Chapter 8, is largely a property crime. Similarly, we have separated assault and murder from other common crimes in general because of the circumstances under which these crimes occur. We will deal with homicides and assaults that occur in the course of common crimes, but as we will see, assaults and murders usually do not occur in the course of a common crime. For the most part we will not be making sharp differentiations between assaults and homicides as a social encounter. Obviously, there is a good deal of difference between a victim living and dying, but the situations themselves are virtually identical for analytical purposes. We will treat most homicides as assaults where the victim died, and assaults as homicide attempts where the victim lived. This is not to trivialize homicide or expand the importance of assaults. Rather, it is a reflection of what characterizes these two forms of violence. Intent, from a legalistic point of view, matters little if a victim lives or dies. So if a killer only intended to "beat him up" or "teach him a lesson" in an assault, and the victim dies, we cannot say that the incident was "really" an assault. Likewise, if the attacker wanted "to murder" the victim, but the victim lived, we cannot insist the assault was really a "murder." Therefore, rather than trying to formulate a definition of these two events around legalistic terms or intentions, we will treat assaults and homicides as "violent assaults"—some resulting in death and some not. In looking at crime data, however, we will differentiate between murder and aggravated assaults since the data have been arranged in those categories.

To examine these two forms of violence, we will first take a look at a brief history of violence in the United States. Then we will examine the demographics and social situations of those involved in homicides and assaults. Finally, we will examine the social processes involved in homicides.

Violence in America

In looking at violence in American history, it is all too tempting to stereotype the American as a gun-toting, shoot-first-ask-questions-later character who loves violence. To be sure, Americans have had their share of violence, but to put things into perspective, consider the following observation by Stringfellow Barr:

> I used to swear that Americans were peculiarly addicted to violence. But fourteen years ago I was shaken by an Indian professor named Dar, with whom I was dining in Delhi.
>
> "Mr. Barr," asked Mr. Dar, "you tell me you have now driven 7,500 miles in my country, visiting cities, towns, and villages. What is your liveliest impression of the Indian people?"
>
> "I think," I said, "it is their moving gentleness. In my country, people believe in getting tough." "Mr. Barr," said Mr. Dar, "I wish you had been in Delhi seven years ago, when all night and every night you would have heard the screams of victims while gentle Hindus and gentle Muslims murdered each other by the tens of thousands."[1]

As in India, if we examine any nation's history, there is some period of violence, usually during times of change and centering on religious, ethnic, or political differences: Armenians were slaughtered by the thousands under the Turks, Kurds by the Iranians and Iraquis, Catholics and Protestants kill each other in Northern Ireland, Nazis murdered millions

of Jews, Slavs, and others, and the Japanese murdered millions of Chinese. However, Americans, while having similar periods in the whole-sale slaughter of Native Americans and lynchings of blacks, seem to have had a history of doing violence to one another without any special political, ethnic, or religious ax to grind. Thus, while the overall violence in America may not be that much greater than other nations, there seems to be a steady stream of it that is unlike any other fully developed, post-industrial society in the world.

American's peculiar institution of mass gun ownership goes back to the American Revolution and the ideals of a democratic society. If everyone had the right to bear arms, then an unwanted government—especially a foreign government—would not be able to take power. Then, as now, such a notion is radically revolutionary. The tradition of personal gun ownership was fostered through the period of westward expansion as Americans pushed further away from the East and organized communities. Hunting became an integral part of life on the frontier, as did fighting Native Americans. In the South, the gun was a primary instrument of maintaining slavery.

The real boost to the gun and violence in America came with the Civil War. Millions of arms were manufactured or procured in the North and the South; and after the war, men mustered out of the service kept their weapons, and war surplus arms were plentiful and cheap for the next generation of young men as well as those who fought in the war. In addition to being more plentiful, guns and ammunition were improved. Brass cartridges replaced the paper ones, and rapid fire and reloading made the weapons far more lethal. At the same time, ex-slaves and ex-soldiers were moving west to the new states seeking jobs in ranching and mining—generally known as "cowboys" whether they worked in mines or in the great cattle drives. Boom towns spread with the railheads where cattle were loaded and shipped East and in mining towns in the West. Organized law and enforcement, however, were unable to keep up with this new growth.

This combination of young men seeking their fortune, general availability of guns—especially handguns which were worn openly, and the lack of legal institutions—at least ones that were enforced—led to the first great violent crime wave with a peculiarly American touch. The violence was largely individualistic and interpersonal as opposed to political, racial, ethnic, or economic. Some exceptions may have existed, and the James Gang, led by Jesse James, saw itself as a political force of sorts. The James brothers along with their comrades had fought for the South during the Civil War and their initial outings tended to be justified by the Union's treatment of ex-Confederates in Missouri. They characterized their robberies as actions taken against the oppressive occupation by the Union army and government. In 1897, well after the heyday of the James Gang, Frank James commented, "If there is ever another war in this country, it will be between capital and labor. I mean between greed and manhood. And I'm ready to march now in defense of American manhood as I was when a boy in defense of the South."[2] This sentiment, while interesting evidence for the Neo-Marxist position in criminology, does not typify most of the violence during that era—even though it does some. Most violence erupted in bars and saloons over arguments resulting from card games or other petty matters, and someone would pull out the ever-handy gun and start shooting.

Unfortunately, many of the worst aspects and habits of the "cowboys" were eulogized and completely distorted in popular fiction of the time, giving them a romantic rather than a ruthless character. Today, what was romanticized as a "two-fisted man" would be seen as a psychotic mass murderer. For example, John Wesley Hardin murdered forty-four people, but was one of the "legends" that was passed down. Once Hardin killed a man in an adjacent hotel room for snoring too loudly![3] Likewise, Tom Horn was nothing but a professional killer hired by cattle barons to shoot anyone he saw fit—including sheepherders who the cattlemen believed to be encroaching on their domain. However, in a film on Horn, he was portrayed far more humanely.[4] The same is true of most of the other killers of the Old West—they are seen as having all the virtues of American individualism and fortitude and none of its vices.

The next epoch of Americans and violent crime came after World War I in the 1920s during Prohibition. By this time the Wild West was relatively tame, but the "hero mobster" emerged, and criminal gangs increased the murder and assault rate. Again, in the 1930s the murder rate went up, but rather than bootleggers, robbery gangs were the image of the "rugged individual." John Dillinger, Clyde Barrow and Bonnie Parker, Machine Gun Kelly, and Baby Face Nelson were the new "tough guys and gals." Faced with the "G-men" (FBI), equally armed with Thomson submachine guns, these characters represented individual willingness to solve problems with violence.

After World War II, violent crime subsided a bit, but at the same time, there was a growing amount of juvenile gang violence in the inner city, and even though these gangs were responsible for a large number of assaults and homicides they were romanticized in such productions as "West Side Story." In the 1960s the focus of attention turned to inner city violence and then a series of nonviolent and violent demonstrations and riots centered at first around civil rights, and then later anti-war protests. During this period, however, and into the 1970s the real violence was interpersonal violence. There was a connection, though, between the highly "mediaized" collective violence and individualistic violence. For example, after the 1967 black riots in Detroit, the sale of handguns soared, and during the period *after* the riots, the homicide and deadly assault rate rose dramatically. This post-riot violence was essentially noncollective, nonpolitical, and like most of the interpersonal violence intra-racial—whites killing whites; blacks killing blacks; browns killing browns.

The romanticized history of violence in America tells a story of cowboys on Main Street and gangsters and machine guns, glorified and distorted. The real history of violence is in the high rate of interpersonal assaults and homicides and ready availability of guns. However, virtually none of it is glorified or even told. In order to come to a more realistic picture of violence in America, we will begin with the demographics of assaults and murder.

The Statistics of Assault and Murder

Josef Stalin was credited with saying that a thousand deaths were a statistic while a single death is a tragedy. In this section we will examine violent crime statistics. In particular we want information about the social characteristics of assaults and murder.

First in comparison with other nations, the United States has a relatively high murder rate. In 1979, for example, the U.S. homicide rate was 9.7 per 100,000 population in comparison to Japan's rate of 1.6; Britain's 1.3 and West Germany's 1.3.[5] However, in the early 1970s the United States murder rate per 100,000 was 9.1, Canada's was 2.3, and Mexico's was 14.3.[6] Thus, while the rate is significantly higher than Canada's, it is significantly lower than Mexico's. Although the differences are clear, the reasons for the differences are not. Over the years, the United States has had a generally higher homicide rate than European countries and lower than most South American ones. General "cultural" explanations for these differences are only partially successful in explaining the patterns. The Latin American "machismo" ethic emphasizing the use of violence against personal affront may be of some explanatory usefulness, but considering Cuba's low rate of 3.7, it tends to fail to provide an adequate explanation. Also, since the rate of homicide in the United States had been the highest in the Southeast, and a relatively low population of Latin American immigrants lived in that part of the country, except for Cubans whose rate is relatively low to begin with, the Latin "machismo" would be a weak reason to use in explaining homicide in the United States. Further, in looking at rates of assault, while Hispanics do have a higher victimization rate than non-Hispanics for assault—27.4 per 1,000 to 25.6 per 1,000—the difference is not statistically significant.[7] In other words, the Hispanic-Americans have assault rates closer to Americans than Latin Americans.

Race and Ethnic Patterns in Violence

Perhaps the most important feature of assault and homicides is the fact that people tend to attack those of the same ethnic background and race. Table 10.1 shows the breakdown of assaults involving black and white victims and offenders.

Table 10.1 Racial Composition of Aggravated Assaults	
White offender/white victim	23.9
White offender/black victim	1.8
Black offender/white victim	8.4
Black offender/black victim	65.9
Total	100

Source: Christopher S. Dunn, *Assault Incident Characteristics*. (Washington, D.C.: U.S. Department of Justice, 1976), p. 12.

We begin to see significant differences when we examine the proportion of victims and offenders by ethnic/racial background. As we saw when we examined common crimes in Chapter 8, blacks, who make up only 12 percent of the population, tend to be victimized and to be the offenders far beyond their proportion of the population. In Table 10.1, we can see that blacks are offenders *and* victims in 65.9 percent of all aggravated assaults. In homicides, blacks consisted of 54 percent of the victims and 45 percent of the offenders (1979, based on police figures.)[8] However, while blacks do appear to bear the brunt of assaults and murder—both as victims and attackers—the figures are by no means wholly conclusive. In a 1977 victimization survey, blacks were victims of all kinds of assaults at a rate of 27.9 per 1,000 population compared to the white rate of 26.8—an insignificant difference, but the rate for *aggravated assault* compares at 13.9 to 9.6 per 1,000 for blacks and whites respectively.[9] Therefore, while blacks are about as likely to be the victim of an assault as are whites, they have about a 45 percent greater incidence of being victims of aggravated assaults.

Sex and Age of Victims and Attackers

Another clear difference we find in assaults and homicides is the sex and age of both victims and attackers. Women have an assault victimization rate of 16.9 per 1,000 while men have a rate of 37.5, and men's victimization rate of aggravated assault is three times that of women.[10] In assaults with single offenders, men comprised 87.5 percent of the offenders, and in multiple offender cases, 77.9 percent were men, with 13 percent being both male and female offenders.[11] The assault figures follow closely with homicide figures. In 1979, 77.6 percent of the victims were men and 23.4 percent women.[12] This 3 to 1 ratio follows exactly the *aggravated assault* proportion, suggesting further evidence that most homicides are aggravated assaults where the victim died.

When we consider age, there is an almost inverse relationship between assault victimization and age. Table 10.2 shows this breakdown.

Table 10.2 Age of Assault Victimization

Age of Victim	Rate of Victimization
12–15	44.0
16–19	55.5
20–24	52.5
25–34	34.8
35–49	15.1
50–64	8.4
65 and over	4.0

Source: U.S. Department of Justice, *Criminal Victimization in the United States, 1977.* (Washington, D.C.: U.S. Government Printing Office, 1979), p. 23.

When we look at the arrests for aggravated assault and murder, we see that about half are committed by persons under 25 years of age. Table 10.3 shows the cumulative arrest percentages for assault and murder for persons under 25.

Table 10.3 Aggravated Assault and Murder Arrests

Age	Aggravated Assault	Homicide
Under 15	4.2	1.1
Under 18	15.5	9.3
Under 21	31.0	24.2
Under 25	49.9	44.2

Source: Federal Bureau of Investigation, *Crime in the United States, 1979.* (Washington, D.C.: U.S. Government Printing Office, 1980), p. 198.

Another 30 percent of the homicide and aggravated assault offenders fall into the age bracket between 25 and 34 years of age.

Again, as we saw with common crimes, the young are more likely to be involved, but the age of people engaged in aggravated assaults and murders is slightly higher. The peak age of people who commit aggravated assault is 18 and that of homicide, 22, but we have to take the entire age group of between about 17 and 24 to pinpoint the age during which people are most likely to commit these crimes. This is still slightly higher than the peak age of common crimes, but it is still relatively young and far disportionate to this group's representation in the total population.

Young Males and Violence

The pattern of violent crimes is that of young males—under 25. While blacks have a greater involvement either as victim or offender, there is a stronger predictor in sex and age than race or ethnic group. Again, we can seek an explanation to this pattern in the age and sex role of those involved, but while it is a simple thing to point out that young males are in situations where violence is expected or even demanded, it is important to remember that *very* few are ever involved in aggravated assault or murder. Therefore, if we say that the "male role" encourages violence, it is only in comparison to the female role and not a general condition of being male. Were it the case that males are actively "pushed" to do violence, there would be far more than there is. Likewise, with age, while the young may be more mobile and less committed to the conventions of society, it is only a small proportion who ever attack people with deadly force or kill them.

Subculture of Violence

One interpretation of the patterns of violence is a subcultural one, put forth by Marvin Wolfgang.[13] Noting that violence—particularly homicide—is predominantly by young males and is overrepresented in certain lower-class minorities, Wolfgang suggests that such violence represents a value system or **subculture of violence**. Essentially, those groups who have low rates of violence adhere to a value system that denounces the use of interpersonal violence, and they are restrained from using violence because they embrace such values. On the other hand, groups with a high rate of violence have a "value system that views violence as tolerable, expected, or required."[14] The more one is integrated into the subculture of violence, the greater the chances of that person engaging in actual violence.

As we will see in examining gang violence later in this chapter, the violence by gang members can be directly linked to gang membership, and to the extent a gang holds a coherent set of beliefs justifying violence as a means of conflict resolution, we can refer to them as a violent subculture. Furthermore, as we saw above in looking at the patterns of violence, there were certain groups that rarely became involved in assaults or homicides and other groups where it was far more prevalent. The problem, though, in asserting a "subculture of violence" hypothesis lies in showing that the violence was due to the belief system. To say that groups with a relatively high rate of violence reflect a "subculture of violence" may do nothing more than give a name to a pattern and do little to explain why that group is violent. Moreover, as we will see in the following section, violence occurs predominantly only in certain situations and not in others, suggesting something other than an overall value system of violence.

Circumstances of Violence

Given the general social characteristics of people who are involved in aggravated assaults and homicide, we must next ask, "Under what circumstances will a person use deadly violence?" People who do use deadly force on occasions other than those that are socially acceptable (such as war) do not generally attack or kill under just any circumstances, but rather define only a few as appropriate. In order to examine the circumstances of violence, we will first examine situations of personal violence—the major source of killings—and then impersonal violence.

Personal Violence

In a study of violence between people who were "intimate" (well known to one another or related), it was noted:

> . . . some people may fear and avoid walking down dark streets alone at night because they believe this setting puts them in danger. By contrast, many individuals feel relatively safe at their jobs during the day or in their homes at night. It may well be, however, with respect to certain types of crimes, that these perceptions are inaccurate.[15]

What the study was referring to is the high incidence of violence between "intimates." About a quarter of all aggravated assaults involved intimates, and of those who were related 70 percent occurred in or near the home.[16] Thus, the place people consider the most secure, the home, is the setting for a large proportion of violence.

Family Fights

One of the most common reports received by police who handle violent crimes comes under the innocuous title **family fight**. In California, police logged these as "415 Domestics"—translated as "Disturbing the Peace."[17] Most other states and police do the same. However, many of these "squabbles," in other circumstances, would be considered aggravated assaults, and when someone happens to die in these "little spats," it is murder, and a very common type of murder. In 1979, almost half the homicides were because of "arguments" and many of these arguments were between family members or persons living together.[18]

Many "family fights" simply involve loud arguments and the neighbors call the police, but others involve both simple and aggravated assault as well as murder. The following are examples of some of the more violent altercations:

1. A man and woman were arguing over who got to eat the last banana in their apartment. During the argument, the woman threw the banana out the window, and the man then threw her out the same window, killing her when she landed several stories below.

2. A husband came home after drinking heavily. He and his wife got into an argument, and started hitting one another, he with his fists and she with a crowbar. By the time the police arrived, both were still fighting, and had to be separated. Neither wanted to file criminal charges against the other, their fighting being a long-standing pattern.

3. A father became angry at his wife and daughter, and began beating both of them, causing the daughter to bleed profusely from the side of the face. The mother and daughter escaped by jumping into the family car, but not before the father smashed the front windshield with an iron bar. The woman told the police that it was a "family matter" and did not want them involved.[19]

Other than the murder, the police were unable to use any of their law enforcement powers effectively. Since those involved in such altercations are unwilling to testify against one another in court, the prosecutor's office will not take the case, and so other than attempting to separate the combatants, there is little the police can do. Moreover, for the police, such incidents are dangerous, and next to responding to robberies in progress and attempting arrests, family disputes are the situations in which most police officers are killed.[20]

Bar Fights

The other major generic category of personal assaults and murders is the "bar fight," where someone takes a swing at an adversary and soon an individual or mutual assault ensues. Like the "family fight," the "bar fight" is typically between people who are either intimate or acquainted, but bar fights differ from family fights in that often strangers are involved. One study found that 15 percent of all homicides occurred in a bar or tavern, but the figure of homicides occurring in a "bar situation" is probably higher, since many homicides occur in the parking lot or sidewalk outside the bar.[21] The following observation illustrates an assault in a bar situation:

A large farm laborer was in a bar in the early evening, very drunk and annoying patrons. However, he was extremely large and generally friendly and so no one was overly concerned with his boorish actions. Later a motorcycle gang that frequented the bar came in, and the drunk began bothering them. They attacked him, knocking him to the ground and kicking him and hitting him with pool cues until he was unconscious. Later, the drunk was revived and taken home by two patrons.[22]

Even though the assault by the motorcycle gang is atypical, in that most such incidents are not related to criminal groups, it is typical in that it has all of the features of typical bar fights: 1) alcohol, 2) behavior defined as offensive, and 3) definition of the situation as one where physical assault is necessary.

Loose Occasions

A characteristic of both family and bar situations is that they are **loose**.[23] On a continuum from very formal (tight) to very informal (loose), family and bar fights are on the loosest end of the scale. In **tight** situations, behavior is highly regulated and there is a well-defined, sharply restricted line of action for participants in the situation. For example, funerals tend to be very tight occasions with strictly defined roles and expectations for behavior. Likewise, work situations are also tightly bounded and prescribed. However, when we go home, we feel freer to express our feelings and "let our hair down." Families, lovers and roommates—who would never scream and shout at one another in formal occasions—do not feel so constrained at home in their house or apartment. Similarly, a bar has the atmosphere of looseness and relaxation coupled with alcohol, which further breaks down inhibitions that control one's behavior.[24] Since the boundaries of appropriate behavior are not as well defined, the possibility for inappropriate behavior—behavior resulting in assault and murder— are more likely. In a study of the situations where police were called, it was found that the vast majority were relatively loose—situations such as bar gatherings, family evenings at home, and parties.[25]

The Social Process of Homicide

To understand how assaults and homicides occur, we will examine the stages of interaction between people in situations where interpersonal conflict results in murder. The same process occurs in aggravated assaults, but either the victim survives or the violence is terminated before one of the participants is killed. Using illustrated cases from a study of homicide we will examine how each stage develops and what dynamics of interpersonal contact are involved.[26]

STAGE I.   The first step in the transaction leading to assault and murder is when one person offends the **face** of another. That is, the situation is defined in such a way that someone feels insulted. The nature of the offense can be of several types, all of them being defined as such by the person offended and dependent on such a definition. Therefore, what may be defined by some as "offensive" would be defined by others as "nothing," "a joke," or in some other nonoffensive way. The following illustrates a situation where a man took offense to his girlfriend:

Case 10   *When the victim finally came home, the offender (in the homicide that followed) told her to sit down; they had to talk. He asked if she was "fooling around" with other men. She stated that she had, and her boyfriends pleased her more than the offender. The offender later stated that "this was like a hot iron in my gut." He ripped her clothes off and examined her body, finding scars and bruises. She said that her boyfriends liked to beat her. His anger magnified.*

STAGE II.   The second stage involves a definition of the initial offense as personally offensive and not something more general. That is, there is a clarification of the offense as being directed *personally* at the individual and not accidental. Sometimes, the offended party will ask for clarification from others as to the meaning of the defined offense. The following case illustrates this second stage involving assistance in defining the situation.

Case 20   *The offender and his friend were sitting in a booth at a tavern drinking beer. The offender's friend told him that the offender's girlfriend was "playing" with another man (eventual victim) at the other end of the bar. The offender looked at them and asked his friend if he thought something was going on. The friend responded, "I wouldn't let that guy fool around with (her) if she was mine." The offender agreed, and suggested to his friend that his girlfriend and the victim be shot for their actions. His friend said that only the victim (man) should be shot, not the girlfriend.*

In other cases, the meanings were imputed on the basis of past incidents involving interaction between the victim and offender. The history of the interaction was used as an interpretive scheme for understanding what was occurring in the fatal encounter. The following is an example:

Case 35   *During a family quarrel the victim had broken the stereo and several other household goods. At one point, the victim cut her husband, the offender, on the arm. He demanded that she sit down and watch television so that he could attend to his wound in peace. On returning from the bathroom he sat down and watched television. Shortly after, the victim rose from her chair, grabbed an ashtray, and shouted, "You bastard, I'm going to kill you." As she came toward him, the offender reached into the drawer of the end table, secured a pistol, and shot her. On arrest, the offender told police officers, "You know how she gets when she's drunk? I had to stop her, or she would have killed me. She's tried it before, that's how I got all these scars," pointing to several areas on his back.*

STAGE III. This stage is a crucial one in terms of deciding what to do about an affront. The person offended can decide that the offender was drunk, crazy, joking, naive, or any other possible excuse for being offensive. However, if the situation cannot be normalized in a face-saving manner, the offended party either has to lose face and back down or take some kind of retaliatory action. In homicides, the latter course of action is taken. The following two cases show two different forms of interaction leading to retaliation.

Case 12 *The offender, victim, and group of bystanders were observing a fight between a barroom bouncer and a drunk patron on the street outside the tavern. The offender was cheering for the bouncer, and the victim was cheering for the patron, who was losing the battle. The victim, angered by the offender's disposition toward the fight, turned to the offender and said, "You'd really like to see the little guy have the shit kicked out of him, wouldn't you, big man?" The offender turned toward the victim and asked, "What did you say? You want the same thing, punk?" The victim moved toward the offender and reared back. The offender responded, "OK, buddy." He struck the victim with a single right cross. The victim crashed to the pavement, and died a week later.*

Case 54 *The offender, victim, and two neighbors were sitting in the living room drinking wine. The victim started calling the offender, his wife, abusive names. The offender told him to "shut up." Nevertheless, he continued. Finally, she shouted, "I said shut up. If you don't shut up and stop it, I'm going to kill you and I mean it."*

In the first case the retaliation was physical and in the second case, at this stage, the retaliation was a verbal threat. In Case 12 the climax was reached very quickly, while in Case 54, there was still an opportunity to de-escalate the violence by re-defining the situation.

STAGE IV. If the victim is not killed in the third stage, the fourth stage becomes the mirror image of the third. At this point in the transaction an offensive action has occurred, the offense has been defined as personally directed, and there has been retaliation against the original offender. Now the person who made the original offense has been struck back— physically or verbally. If the person decides that things are now even— one offense for another—the violence can end, but in assaults and homicides, it simply calls for another round of choosing to back down and lose face or do something about the retaliation—a counter-retaliation. In continuing Case 54 from above, the original offender counter-retaliated, leading to his death.

Case 54 *The victim continued his abusive line of conduct. The offender proceeded to the kitchen, secured a knife, and returned to the living room. She repeated her warning. The victim rose from his chair, swore at the offender's stupidity, and continued laughing at her. She thrust the knife deep into his chest.*

The victim (the one who died) was the original offender, and to an extent we can see the transaction as "victim precipitated."[27] Had the victim walked away from the encounter or simply not started the fight to begin with, he or she would not have been killed.

While the situation leading to violence is escalating, there is often an audience present—a husband, wife, child, bystanders, patrons in a bar, etc. In homicides, the audience is either neutral toward or actually encourages the escalation of the violence. The following case illustrates how the audience defined the appropriate course of action for the killer.

Case 23 *The offender's wife moved toward the victim, and hit him in the back of the head with an empty beer bottle stating, "That'll teach you to (molest) my boy. I ought to cut your balls off, you mother fucker." She went over to the bar to get another bottle. The victim pushed himself from the table and rose. He then reached into his pocket to secure something which some bystanders thought was a weapon. One of the bystanders gave the offender an axe handle and suggested that he stop the victim before the victim attacked his wife. The offender moved toward the victim.*

STAGE V. If both parties are still alive at this stage, there is a consensus or working agreement to do battle. Both parties have defined the situation as one from which they cannot back down without losing face, and it is a character contest.[28] Both are bound to a course of action neither may personally want, but to quit at this point means to lose face. The situation the combatants are a part of and instrumental in creating demands mutual attack or loss of face—greater than the loss each may suffer physically in the battle.

It is during this stage that weapons are secured. Sometimes the parties will have weapons with them—in about 36 percent of the cases offenders carried handguns or knives into the setting. In the remaining 64 percent of the cases, the offender either had to leave the situation to obtain a handgun or knife or transform some available prop such as a beer mug, telephone cord, or baseball bat into a lethal weapon.

Once weapons were at hand, either the offender killed the victim in a single shot, thrust, or series of blows, or there was mutual assault until one of the combatants fell and died. The death of the victim signaled the final stage of the transaction.

STAGE VI. The last stage of a homicide situation is marked by a series of decisions made by the killer and/or audience. In over 58 percent of the cases, the killer fled, leaving the victim and audience. In some cases the audience encouraged the offender to flee and actively worked to cover up evidence of his/her involvement, while in other cases the audience restrained the offender from leaving. Sometimes, especially in cases where the killer and victim were intimates, the offender remained on the scene until the police arrived, often calling the police himself.

At his point, no matter what the audience or offender had been thinking during the initiation or escalation of the violence, with the death (or near death) of the victim, they understood that now the situation was one where the police would be involved. There does not appear, from what Luckenbill and others have found in these kinds of homicides, that intervention by the criminal justice system—or any social control agency outside the situation—is relevant at the time of the deadly transaction. However, once the transaction results in death, it is suddenly clear that the police will be notified, whether they believe the killing was justified or not. Even those who actively encouraged the escalation of violence where the outcome favored their champion *now* understand that the action transcends the situation that has just transpired. In Goffman's analysis of encounters, he points to "rules of irrelevance" in face-to-face transactions.[29] During the violence, the police and the wider rules of society are not part of the "frame" of the encounter, but as soon as the victim dies, the rules of irrelevance, along with the situation, dramatically change, so that now outsiders are not only relevant to the events, but the dominant concern.

In and of itself, such a state of affairs would appear to be of only analytical interest, but it is a vital point in understanding the role of law in typical homicides. To the extent the law and the criminal justice system are situationally irrelevant, they have no effect. Therefore, the laws can be either harsh or lenient in dealing with murderers of this kind, but they will have little influence on the homicide rate because during the violent transaction, the laws are simply not part of the situation.

Impersonal Violence

Another kind of assault and murder is committed by people who are not only strangers but have no particular animosity toward one another. As we saw in Chapter 8, robbers who beat up or killed their victims did not do so for some personal vendetta. Likewise, hired killers often do not even know the people they kill, other than by the description given them by their employers. Finally, juvenile gangs will do battle with a rival gang, not over a personal dispute between individual gang members, but because one gang happens to be at odds with another gang—sometimes for no other reason than the gangs have always been adversaries with no one knowing exactly why. These kinds of killings account for an uncertain proportion of homicides since they fall into the category of "unknown motives" in the reporting scheme. However, they are different from personal homicides and assaults, and in this section we will look at these differences.

Hired Killers

Our knowledge of hired killers is incomplete and sketchy, and public images of these men who will kill anyone for hire tends to be linked to organized crime. The stereotype of the hired killer or "hit man" is assumed to be a part of the underworld who is assigned by organized crime to kill rival gang members or uncooperative noncriminals—such as businessmen who refuse to pay "protection" money. To be sure organized crime does have hired killers, and Murder Incorporated was not a figment of fertile journalistic imagination.[30]

The roots of murder for hire in the United States do not, however, lie in the Sicilian Black Hand or Mafia. Rather, as we pointed out at the be-

Evidence of the existence of professional killers is often through testimony of organized crime members. Pictured giving such testimony in New Jersey is an unidentified hired killer who was a "hit man" for organized crime.

ginning of the chapter, if we go back to the Old West, we find that "hired
guns" were very real, and while some of the hired killers were supposedly
"crime fighters," such as the Earp brothers of Tombstone, Arizona, others
were simply hired to kill at their employer's whim. In one of the most no-
torious hirings of paid killers, the Wyoming Stock Growers Association, a
group of wealthy cattle barons, organized a group of twenty-two gunmen
to "clean-up" Johnson County, Wyoming in 1892.[31] Supposedly the gunmen were only to kill cattle rustlers, but since many of the small ranchers
in the area were considered "rustlers" by the cattle barons, they went beyond the law even as defined in the lawless West. The hired killers were
to receive $50 for every "rustler" killed, regardless of who did the killing,
and so the designation of "cattle detective" given to the gunmen was a
farce. What followed became known as the "Johnson County Wars," and
while the entire affair ended after the cattle barons' hired guns had murdered some innocent cowboys and trappers, and the group of cattlemen
and their killers were besieged and almost annihilated by a group of angry small ranchers, it serves to illustrate that hired killers were not introduced at the time of Prohibition and the bootlegging gangs of the 1920s.

Contemporary Hit Men

The character of hired killers really has not changed since the nineteenth
century, in that the financial arrangements and motives appear quite similar. That is, certain men are willing to pay others to have a rival murdered for any number of reasons. The status of the hired killer appears
to have changed, however, in that a fine talent for killing—a quick draw
and steady aim—are not as vital as was once the case. Many hired killers
are simply men who have "tough" reputations, not ones who are considered especially skilled. For example, one junkie-mugger was offered
$4,000 to kill two men. He was given a gun and descriptions of the vic-
tims. He was told to throw the gun away if he used it, but to bring it back
if he did not. He explained the killings as follows:

*So I went to this street where these two dudes lived. They were black dudes and they
had done wrong, I guess. I laid for them one at a time. I caught the first one in
the hallway, and I cut his throat. It was very fast.*

*I laid for him (the second victim) the same way. I caught him from behind in an-
other hallway and did the job with a hammer. I left fast. I didn't even remember
seeing him hit the ground.*

*The man (who hired him) was impressed, real impressed that I didn't use it (the
gun). He asked if I wanted to do other jobs. I said no. I didn't want to be a hit man.
I didn't feel there was any future in it.[32]*

Unfortunately, the above account, as well as others that are available, may
be of dubious validity. However, since the research necessary on hired

killers is difficult to obtain—especially from active killers—there is little else on which to base such a discussion.

Juvenile Gang Murders

In 1980 there were 351 gang-related homicides in the Los Angeles area.[33] Most of the killers and victims were juvenile gang members, but a large proportion were nongang members. Likewise in other urban areas where juvenile gang violence exists, a high percentage of all murders and non-homicide assaults involves inter-gang violence. In a study of cities with gang violence, about a quarter of *all* juvenile homicides were found to be gang related. Table 10.4 shows this breakdown.

Table 10.4	Juvenile Homicides and Gang-Related Killings		
City	Year	Number	Percent Gang Related
San Francisco	1974	18	72
Los Angeles	1973	92	42
Philadelphia	1972	127	30
New York	1973	268	15
Chicago	1973	188	10
Five Cities		693	24

Source: Walter Miller, *Violence by Youth Gangs and Youth Groups as a Crime Problem in Major American Cities*. (Washington, D.C.: U.S. Department of Justice, 1975), p. 31.

The variation between cities is considerable both in terms of the number of killings and proportion attributed to juvenile gangs; however, it is one cause for juvenile homicides.

Unlike killings for hire or personal homicides, gang killings are a combination of a tradition of gang violence and increased use of guns in gang warfare. Gangs and gang violence in the United States can be traced back to the American Revolution, but the use of a professionally manufactured gun on a mass basis is relatively new. A report from the mid-1970s pointed out:

> The prevalence, use, quality, and sophistication of weaponry in the gangs of the 1970s far surpasses anything known in the past, and is probably the single most significant characteristic distinguishing today's gangs from their predecessors.[34]

Four different but interrelated motives can be identified: 1) honor, 2) local turf-defense, 3) control, and 4) gain. *Honor* relates to the reputation of gangs and gang members. Establishing or defending honor is defined in terms of a willingness to stand up to violent physical confrontation; so in order to make or maintain a "rep" violent encounters are expected.[35] Similarly, local turf-defense is a matter of using physical force to keep outsiders out of one's territory, or alternatively, to raid a rival's area. However, violence for control and gain appear to be increasing causes of assaults. In extending their influence outside of the neighborhood, gangs attempt to exert control over educational and recreational areas through violence. Likewise, they have increased the use of violence to extort money from peers and rob juveniles and adults. As a result, a high proportion of the victims of gang violence are nongang members.[36] The best estimate at this time is that about 40 percent of all gang victims are nongang.[37]

Forms of Gang Violence

Besides assaults on nongang members for the purposes of gain—muggings and "shakedowns"—the most common forms of gang violence are the **rumble** and **foray**. The "rumble" is a fight between assembled members of rival gangs wherein each gang shows up at a designated location and proceeds to fight one another. This form of gang warfare may be on the wane, since not only are such encounters easily broken up by the police before they get started, but tactically they are becoming less efficient. Rumbles involving knives, chains, and clubs are essentially melees, with a larger gang usually emerging the victor. However, with the increased use of manufactured guns (as opposed to homemade or "zip" guns), such gangs of youth provide larger targets; in fact even a relatively small gang could hold its own against a large one if it was sufficiently armed. The newer form of gang violence is the "foray."[38] Using mobile, hit-and-run tactics, a small band from a gang will attack isolated members of rival gangs, or take a shot at a group of rivals and speed off. In California, the most common kind of foray is a **drive-by**, consisting of three or four gang members driving by a rival gang and shooting the victim, his house, or car. The following is a typical such incident observed by the author in 1981:

Members of the Shelltown gang were having a party in their own barrio when four members of the Spring Valley gang drove by. Shouting the name of their gang, the Spring Valley group began firing into a group of three Shelltown boys who were standing by a car outside the party. One of the boys was hit three times by rifle fire and died on the way to the hospital. In talking to Shelltown members after the shooting, it was learned that the boy who was shot did not have any personal dispute with the other gang, and the only reason they could come up with for the shooting was that the rival gang was trying to make a name for itself.[39]

Felony Violence

A final category of assaults and murder is what we will call **felony violence**—violence that occurs in the course of a felony crime. In examining
the number of homicides occurring in this context, we can see that it accounts for a fairly stable proportion of homicides. Table 10.5 shows felony homicides from 1976 through 1979.

	Table 10.5 *Felony Homicides*			
	1979	**1978**	**1977**	**1976**
Robbery	10.5	10.2	9.9	10.3
Narcotics	1.9	1.7	1.7	1.8
Sex Offenses	1.6	1.4	1.7	1.8
Other Felony	2.9	3.3	3.4	3.8
Total	16.9	16.7	16.7	17.7

Source: Federal Bureau of Investigation, *Crime in the United States, 1979.* (Washington, D.C.: U.S. Government
Printing Office, 1980), p. 12.

Looking at these figures, we can see that other than robbery, the felony
homicides make up a relatively small proportion of the killings in the
United States. Further, as previously noted in Chapter 9, very few result
in the death of the victim; and while violence is used in robberies, it is
usually when the robbery employs a nonlethal weapon.

The other felony homicides occur in narcotic disputes, rapes, and occasionally a burglary where the victim catches the burglar in the act of
some other felony. However, a person is far more likely to meet his or her
death at the hands of an acquaintance, friend, or relative in an interpersonal dispute than they are in the course of a felony. The public fear,
though, is of nocturnal fiends intent on rape, robbery, or insane blood
lust.

SUMMARY

To a great extent we can trace violence in the United States over a period from the American Revolution on up to the present. The unique character of American violence, however, is not its volume, but its nature. Other societies have similar amounts of violence, but they are relegated to periods of social conflict involving rival political, ethnic, religious, or economic factions. Violence in America tends to be a constant element, revolving around interpersonal conflict and the use of firearms. Relatively little involves organized political, ethnic, or religious groups against rival groups. In fact, most violence is intra-ethnic rather than across racial and ethnic lines. The individual ethic is a more important force than a group ethic in most violence.

Where there is a group orientation in violence, it centers around gangs of criminals rather than ideological lines. The race riots and anti-war confrontations of the 1960s and early 1970s, while often violent, contributed to a very small proportion of the violence in society as a whole. Even during the peak of the anti-war and race violence of the period, it never reached the volume of interpersonal violence at that time. Violence by apolitical juvenile gangs, for example, was responsible for far more deaths and injuries than were even the most violent racial or anti-war clashes.

Finally, felony violence, while certainly a form of assault and murder that cannot be ignored, plays a relatively small part in the maiming and death of people. This is not to minimize the violence in rape or robbery, for those and other violence felonies are clearly harmful and even fatal, but rather, to emphasize in the overall context of violent crimes, felony violence plays a minority role. The main emphasis in violent crimes must be in the area of family fights and barroom and sidewalk brawls. It is in these situations where the most violence and death occurs.

Glossary

Drive-By   A common form of intergang violence involving members of one gang driving by a rival gang and shooting at them. (See also *Foray*.)

Family Fight   A situation where family members or people living together come into violent conflict, sometimes resulting in homicide.

Felony Violence   Violence committed in the course of another crime, most typically robbery.

Foray   Hit-and-run violence common in contemporary juvenile gang conflict.

Impersonal Violence   Violence used by hired attackers against unknown victims. Used in organized crime killings, loan shark collections, and similar situations where the attacker has no personal grudge against the victim.

Loose Occasions   Situations where the norms governing the gathering are vaguely defined. Such situations are the most common for violence.

Offense to Face   Offending a person's self-image. Such offenses are the first stage of homicide situations.

Rumble   Fight between two violent juvenile gangs involving several members from each side. This form of gang fighting has been replaced by the more mobile tactics used in the FORAY and DRIVE-BY.

Subculture of Violence   Concept explaining violence in terms of a belief system that considers violence appropriate or necessary in certain circumstances.

Tight Occasions   Formal situations with clearly defined norms and role expectations, such as work and school. Relatively little violence is found in such occasions.

Questions

1. What are unique characteristics of American violence in comparison to other societies?

2. What groups are most likely to be involved in homicides as both killers and victims?

3. What is the nature of "personal violence," and why is it the major type of violence that leads to death?

4. What kinds of situations are most likely to lead to violence? Why do some situations lend themselves to violence more than others?

5. What are the stages in a typical homicide? What role does the audience play in homicides?

Notes

1. Stringfellow Barr, "Violence and the Home of the Brave," in Irving Horowitz, ed., *The Troubled Conscience*. (Palo Alto, CA: Freel, 1973), pp. 3–6.

2. Paul Trachtman, *The Gunfighters*. (Alexandria, VA: Time-Life, 1974), p. 87.

3. Trachtman, 1974, 176.

4. Trachtman, 1974, 201.

5. *Time*, March 23, 1981, p. 33.

6. World Health Organization, *World Health Statistics Annual, 1972*. (Geneva, 1975), p. 234.

7. "The Hispanic Victim: National Crime Survey Report," (Washington, D.C.: U.S. Department of Justice, Advance Report, June, 1980).

8. Federal Bureau of Investigation, *Crime in the United States, 1979.* (Washington, D.C.: U.S. Government Printing Office, 1980), pp. 8–9.

9. *Criminal Victimization in the United States, 1977.* (Washington, D.C.: U.S. Department of Justice, December, 1979), p. 24.

10. *Criminal Victimization*, 1979, 22.

11. Ibid.

12. FBI, 1980, 10.

13. Marvin Wolfgang, ed., *Studies in Homicide.* (New York: Harper & Row, 1967), pp. 3–12. Marvin Wolfgang, "A Sociological Analysis of Criminal Homicide," *Federal Probation* **23** (March 1961): 48–55. Marvin Wolfgang and Franco Ferracuti, *The Subculture of Violence: Towards an Integrated Theory in Criminology.* (London: Tavistock, 1968).

14. Ibid.

15. U.S. Department of Justice, *Intimate Victims: A Study of Violence Among Friends and Relatives.* (Washington, D.C.: U.S. Government Printing Office, 1980), p. 5.

16. Ibid.

17. William B. Sanders, *Detective Work: A Study of Criminal Investigations.* (New York: Free Press, 1977), pp. 165–189.

18. FBI, 1980, 12.

19. From unpublished field notes by the author. For general findings of study from which notes were taken, see William B. Sanders, "Police Occasions: A Study of Interaction Contexts," *Criminal Justice Review* **4** (Spring 1979): 1–13.

20. FBI, 1980, 310.

21. David F. Luckenbill, "Criminal Homicide as a Situated Transaction," *Social Problems* **25** (December, 1977).

22. Personal observation by author, December, 1973.

23. Erving Goffman, *Behavior in Public Places.* (New York: Free Press, 1963).

24. Sherri Cavan, *Liquor License.* (Chicago: Aldine, 1966).

25. Sanders, 1979, 10–11.

26. The formulation and cases in this section are all from Luckenbill's (1977) study of homicide, unless otherwise noted.

27. Marvin F. Wolfgang, "Victim-Precipitated Criminal Homicide," *Journal of Criminal Law, Criminology and Police Science* **48** (June 1957): 1–11.

28. Erving Goffman, *Interaction Ritual.* (Garden City, NY: Doubleday, 1967).

29. Erving Goffman, *Encounters.* (Indianapolis: Bobbs-Merrill, 1961).

30. Hank Messick and Burt Goldblatt, *The Mobs and the Mafia.* (New York: Ballantine, 1972), pp. 142–146.

31. Trachtman, 1974, 206–223.

32. James Willwerth, *Jones: Portrait of a Mugger.* (Greenwich, CT: Fawcett, 1974), p. 256.

33. These figures were presented at the Gang Task Force meeting, San Diego, CA (February 1981).

34. Walter Miller, *Violence by Youth Gangs and Youth Groups as a Crime Problem in*

Major American Cities. (Washington, D.C.: U.S. Government Printing Office, December 1975).

35. Ruth Horowitz and Gary Schwartz, "Honor, Normative Ambiguity and Gang Violence," *American Sociological Review* **39** (1974): 238–251.

36. Miller, 1975, 43.

37. Miller, 1975, 39.

38. Miller, 1975, 38.

39. William B. Sanders, "Forms of Gang Violence," Paper presented at the Annual Meeting of the American Sociological Association, Toronto, Canada (August 1981).

11

Rape

What to Look For:

The social perceptions of rape and the view of victims.

The relationship between the role of women in society and conceptions of rape.

The different frameworks for the study of rape.

The patterns of rape situations and what these patterns imply about rapists.

The process of rape assaults and the interaction between the victim and rapist.

How rape is an assault on self and why rapists might be best viewed as "wimps."

Introduction

OVER THE LAST DECADE there has been a new awareness of rape and its implications in society. At one time, rape was considered a half-humorous affair that involved an over-romantic Romeo and a teasing woman who "asked for it." However, with the women's movement came new perceptions and insights into the victim's plight and the nature of rape. New questions were raised about rape, and research was conducted to better understand the full dimensions of this crime.

In this book, it is treated as a unique crime apart from "violent" and "common" crimes because it requires special attention and understanding. Rape is different from other violent crimes both because of the way it is executed and, in part, because of the massive misunderstanding people have had of rape. Thus, we need a clarification of what rape is as a form of criminal behavior in the context of criminological knowledge, and at the same time to dismiss many historical misconceptions of rape.

We will begin by examining societal views, past and present, about rape, rapists, and rape victims. Then, we will examine the rape situation to see exactly what rapes are like—in part to disspell misconceptions and in part to analyze rape assaults. Next, having seen what rape assaults are like, we will look at the rapists in the context of the male role in society. Finally, we will look at the victim and the effects of a rape assault on her.

Societal Views of Rape

Rape has always had a dual character in the public view. It has been seen as a truly forceful sexual assault on women who have in no way encouraged the assault and are victims of madmen or conquering armies. Part of the booty of conquering armies has always been the vanquished's women who are raped and then either killed, thrown aside, or kept as slaves or wives.[1] The "mad rapist" is another public image of rapes where innocent women are assaulted. In this imagery, a woman, preferably a virgin snatched from her home in the middle of the night and brutally beaten, is raped after a brave but futile attempt to defend her virtue. Even some laws projected the madman image of rapists. Part of the laws regulating cocaine were directed at black men in the South who were supposedly driven to rape (white) women under the spell of the drug—they went mad with lust.[2] A more recent version of the "uncontrolled" mad rapist has been that males have certain testosterone levels that are quite impossible to control, making all males potential rapists.[3] Of these two versions, rape by conquering armies and at the hands of the "mad rapist," only the former can be verified in terms of the typical patterns of rape; but the for-

256

mer, of course, is limited to times of war. To be sure there are "mad rapists," just as there are "mad killers," but the incidence of rapes due to untethered compulsions is about the same as is the incidence of mad killers, and as we saw in the last chapter, that incidence is quite exceptional. The "Jack the Rippers" in the annals of crime are oddities and have no place in the development of explanations of general patterns, except to point out their rarity.

Blaming the Victim

To be a victim of a lustful army or monster rapist is to be an **innocent victim**, one to whom no blame can be assigned, only pity. On the other hand, if a victim is raped in circumstances where there is not overwhelming evidence of an army or a madman, the public stereotype often brings into question the victim's moral character. For example, victims who are raped while on dates, while hitch-hiking, or while dressed in what is considered a "provocative" manner are subject to suspicion as to the validity of their claims of rape. Also, they are considered partially responsible for the rape by either putting themselves in a position inviting sexual assault or actually having "egged on" the rapist. The "tease" who is raped is considered to have had what was coming to her.

WOMEN'S ROLE IN SOCIETY AND SEX. Woman's traditional role in society regarding sex has been passive and highly restrictive, while the male role has been virtually the opposite. Ideally women are to have sex only after they are married and only for love, not pleasure. Without a doubt that image has changed, and women are freer as to their sexual choice and discretion than before, but the residue of that traditional role is very strong, and in comparison to men, women are still relatively restricted.

However, while the traces of Victorian morality linger, the actual patterns of behavior are changing. For very practical economic reasons as well as self-fulfillment, more and more women are choosing careers, both before and during marriage, which take them outside of the home. Due to the career prerequisites of a college education, the proportion of women going to college, either returning after some noncareer activity or directly from high school, is high. This new situation puts women in positions where they are both more independent and at the same time living away from both fathers and brothers as well as husbands, the traditional protectors of women.

At the same time that women are enjoying more personal freedom and fulfillment in nontraditional careers, they are less restricted in sexual matters. Therefore, fewer women consider virginity an important criterion for marriage. However, while women are more sexually active than before, they are still restricted in their activity lest they be labelled "promiscuous" or "easy," a label not applied to men. Likewise, initiating sexual activity is still considered the male prerogative, and accepting or declining, the female. Put another way, women are not supposed to be aggressive in chasing men and men are expected to automatically favor having sex.

In the context of rape, women are caught between moralities. On the one hand, since women are freer than before, sex is more acceptable and common. At the same time, though, women are supposed to have final say in whether they will have sex at any particular time. On the other hand, the old stereotypes and repressive morality, along with all their implications and assumptions, are still present. Therefore, when a woman is raped, the old dogma of sexual contact and new realities clash. The freer lifestyle is used as a context to "show" that the victim was "asking for it," and her sexual activity provides further "proof" of her complicity in her assault.[4]

New Women's Consciousness of Rape

More than any single force in society, the women's movement has provided new interpretations and understandings of rape. Not only was the role of women in society as a whole redefined, but there was finally a coherent philosophy for women. Most important of the works on rape from the new feminist perspective was Susan Brownmiller's *Against Our Will: Men, Women and Rape*. Brownmiller's research ranges from the history of rape to the mistreatment of the victim by the criminal justice system. Overall, the work provides a new basis for interpreting the respective social roles of men and women and, more specifically, the impact of these roles on rape. Subsequent works have given empirical testing and clarification to many of Brownmiller's ideas; and while much has been critical of the initial assertions, the work still stands as a benchmark in modern conceptualizations of rape, for it redefined the meaning of such assaults.

RAPE AS A VIOLENT CRIME.   One of the most important points made by feminists is that rape was not some version of sex made illegal, but rather it is violent crime in league with murder and assault. The label "sex crime" seemed inappropriate, since rape has about as much to do with sex as a bank robbery does with cashing a check. The insistence on rape as a crime of violence instead of something less placed the blame squarely on the rapist. It took away the innuendos and implications that the victim may have somehow been responsible (thereby making the rape justifiable), and characterized the rapist as a violent criminal who attacked the victim in the same way a mugger attacks his victim. The fact that the rape victim was not beaten to a pulp no more suggests that she had been "asking for it" than does a bank teller who gave up the bank's money suggest that he/she had "asked" to be robbed.

A new women's consciousness on rape has taken the topic into the open. No longer is rape something victims are expected to hide, but rather a crime they should join other women in fighting.

Another important understanding that was brought about by the reformulation of rape as a violent crime was that of the plight of the victim. Rather than seeing the typical victim as someone who was either prowling the streets "looking for it" or a vestal virgin ravaged by a madman or an army, the rape victim was portrayed as an average woman doing average things. Initially, most of the evidence for this reformulation was anecdotal, but since the traditional stereotypes were equally ungrounded in research the new ideas served as a catalyst to re-examine existing research findings and focus new research.

AMBIGUITY ABOUT RAPISTS. In the feminist writings about rape, the rapist has occupied an ambivalent position. On the one hand, he was a reflection of all men in society, and on the other, a sexual deviant. To the extent that all men are potential rapists, rape is hardly "deviant"—the norm defined by patterns of behavior and not simply the prohibitions. The two positions, while not totally contradictory or incompatible, are in need of clarification.

The position that rape is closely linked to cultural standards and sex roles is probably the most widely held by the feminists. One author contends:

Anyone can be a rapist, and there is no group of men with whom women should automatically feel safe from the possibility of sexual assault.[5]

At the same time, though, there is clear evidence that, like other violent and common crimes, rapists are 1) younger—between 15 and 24, 2) single, 3) from a lower socioeconomic status, 4) disproportionately black, and 5) of the same race of the victim.[6] Thus, while "anyone" can be a rapist, only certain groups generally are, and since, by the same token, "anyone" can be a prostitute, robber, or skyjacker, it is pointless, and generally inaccurate, in criminology to contend that all people of a general category are "potential" criminals.

Another criminological interpretation of rapists comes from the social psychiatric sphere. From a psychiatric perspective, rape is viewed as having three components: 1) power, 2) anger, and 3) sexuality.[7] The rapist is typed as being one of the following:

1. **Power-assertive**. He regards rape as an expression of his virility and mastery and dominance.
2. **Power-reassurance**. He commits the offense in an effort to resolve disturbing doubts about his sexual adequacy and masculinity.
3. **Anger-retaliation**. Rapist who commits rape as an expression of his hostility and rage towards women.
4. **Anger-excitation**. Man who finds pleasure, thrills, and excitation in the suffering of his victim.[8]

Of these four types, the majority (64.9 percent) have been diagnosed as "power rapes" and the remaining as "anger rapes." The least common being the "anger-excitation" rapist (6.01 percent). Rape and rapists viewed from this position are clearly a deviant group, rape being a pathological form of deviance rather than simply an expression of culturally defined sex roles. The problem with this approach, however, lies in the theoretical assumptions about the meaning of the data, namely psychiatric interviews. Since psychiatry assumes pathology in the form of some prior biographical experience of the offender, the interviews tend to draw out accounts that reify the assumptions.[9] Therefore, rather than being a reflection of what rapists may have been thinking during a rape, it is a depiction of what the rapists think the analyst wants to hear.

The extremes of these two positions show the range in criminological literature concerning who the rapist is and what causes men to rape women. However, there is a common thread in these two polar positions—that of power. The **cultural role** position argues that men have always been in more powerful positions relative to women, and rape is a reflection of that differential. Rape is a means of keeping women in their subservient role, and it is an expression of either lust or power. The **de-**

viant role position also sees power as an important element in rape, but instead of being a reflection of larger cultural conditions, it is one of deviant biographies resulting in an abnormal need for power expression relative to women.

Patterns of Rape

In this section, we will examine both the general and specific patterns of rape assaults. First, we will look at the data from police reports and victimization surveys to get an overall picture of rape. Next, we will look at the rape itself and study the patterns in rape assaults, including the situations where rape occurs and the patterns of interaction between victim and rapist.

According to the FBI's figures, in the last decade (1970–1979), rape increased more than any other index crime.[10] The number of reported rapes rose to 75,990 in 1979, double the 1970 figure, with a rate increase of 84.5 percent from the beginning to the end of the decade. However, there were strong regional differences in the rate of rape. In the Western States, the rate was the highest at 49.1 and lowest in the Northeast at 25.9 per 100,000 population. In comparing rural and urban rates, metropolitan areas had a rate of 41.1 while the rate of rural areas was only 15.1.[11]

However, the data based on the FBI figures probably reflects an increasing willingness of women to report rape more than an actual increase in rape. During the years for which victimization data is available, we can see that there were virtually no changes in the rate of rape over the years. In 1973 the victimization rate was 0.9 per 1,000 (or 90 per 100,000) and in 1977 and 1979, the figure was exactly the same, 0.9.[12] Therefore, rather than there being a dramatic increase in actual rapes, there have been changes in women's attitudes toward rape, law enforcement's vast improvement in helping victims, more women police officers, various victim assistance programs, and increased police awareness of rape. All these factors have swelled the FBI's numbers.

In looking at available data on the racial and ethnic background of victims and offenders, we find that there are few differences between white and black victims—0.9 for whites and 1.0 for blacks—but Hispanics' victimization rate is about double that of black and white victims at 1.9 per 1,000 population.[13] However, white females tended to be a target of rape disproportionately to the racial makeup of the offenders, even though most rapes are intraracial. Table 11.1 describes this breakdown.

In comparing the intra- and interracial rapes with those arrested for rape, we find that 50.2 percent are white and 47.7 are black, with the remaining being Native Americans, Chinese-Americans and Japanese-Americans.[14] Given the high proportion of black rape offenders and the tendency of rapists to rape women of their own race, black women should

Table 11.1   Race of Victims and Offenders in Rapes

Victim	Offender		
	White	*Black*	*Other*
White	67.8%	19.3%	9.2%
Black	9.0	91.0	0.0

Source: *Criminal Victimization in the United States, 1977.* (Washington, D.C.: U.S. Department of Justice, December 1979), p. 43.

Table 11.2   Victim Race and Strangers

Offender a Stranger		Offender Not a Stranger	
Black	*White*	*Black*	*White*
1.6	.6	.6	.2

Source: *Criminal Victimization in the United States: 1973–1978 Trends.* (Washington, D.C.: U.S. Department of Justice, December 1980).

be expected to have a much higher rate of rape. Table 11.2 shows that in fact they do have a higher rate of rape assaults.

Thus, while there is a higher percentage of white victims overall, there is a higher *rate* of victimization of black women—more than double that of whites.

Rape Situations

Having examined general patterns of rape, we will now look at rape assaults in terms of the kinds of situations in which they occur. This will tell us whether they are patterned or random, and if patterned, something about the nature of rape. First, we will look at the general situation the victim was in when a rape assault occurred.

As can be seen in Table 11.3, the majority of rapes occur when the victim is in transit, and the bulk of the remaining rapes while the victim is at home. We will briefly examine each situation to see how rapes typically occur.

TRANSIT SITUATIONS.   **Transit situations** are those where a person is going from one place to another, usually leaving or returning home, such as to and from work or school, shopping, visiting friends, and just going for a walk. Consider, for example, the following transit situation:

Table 11.3 Rape Situations	
Situation	**Percent**
Transit	53.3
At home	16.7
Bedtime	15.6
Socializing	8.9
Date	4.4
Other	1.1

Source: Reprinted from William B. Sanders, *Rape and Woman's Identity*, p. 42, © 1980 Sage Publications, Inc.

Case 53 *The victim was dropped off at a parking lot by friends where her car was parked. They left, and she walked to her car but was attacked before she got there. The rapist jumped her from the rear grabbing her arm and saying, "Be quiet, get in the car." Sitting in the back of the car, the rapist made the victim drive to an isolated driveway and told her to get out and undress. He then raped her on the ground.**

As in most transit situations, the victim is vulnerable since she is in between "safe" places such as home, school, work, or at a companion's. Hitchhikers are common rape victims, being doubly vulnerable in that they are isolated in the car that can transport them to further isolation.

AT HOME. Women at home during normal waking hours are relatively less vulnerable than women in transit situations, for they may be able to call on the assistance of a roommate, pet, friend, or neighbor. Thus, while there are fewer rapes in such situations, they do comprise a large proportion of sexual assaults. Unlike transit situations where the victim is more open to contact, such contact in one's home requires special entrance requirements or breaking into the house. The following two cases illustrate two different modes of entrance and contact:

Case 36 *A man came to the victim's apartment taking a survey on rent reductions, and after interviewing her asked for a glass of water. When the victim went to get the water, the man grabbed her from behind and dragged her into the bedroom at knife point. He then taped her eyes and hands in front of her and made her orally copulate and masturbate him. Then he raped her.*†

*Reprinted from William B. Sanders, *Rape and Woman's Identity*, p. 43, © 1980 Sage Publications, Inc.

†Ibid., p. 45.

Case 90   *The victim was taking a shower when rapist entered through an unlocked sliding glass door. He entered the shower nude and said, "I don't want to hurt you, I've never done this before." The victim began screaming and the suspect fled.**

In both cases, the rapist isolated the victim in her own home during waking hours and raped or attempted to rape her. Unlike the transit situation, rapes in the home occur in a "protected" social area. However, it is the very privacy of the home, once violated, that is in favor of the rapist. Since what happens in a person's home is considered his or her own business, the social norms regulating interference by outsiders, even neighbors, provides protection against intrusion by those who might assist the victim.

Thus, while the victim is less vulnerable in her home in one respect, she is more vulnerable in another. In transit situations, there is the possibility that her appeals for help may be met by someone passing by, but in her home, such pleas may be misinterpreted as something other than an actual assault. For example, cries for help may be "heard" as a domestic argument, a party, or play. One victim explained that she had been advised to cry "Fire!" in case of a rape assault, since people would be more likely to rush to help put out a fire than interfere in what may turn out to be "play."

BEDTIME.   Another situation in the home where victims were raped was during normal sleeping hours. In these cases, the rapist broke into the victim's home and woke and raped her. The same social norms protecting people from intrusion during waking hours at home applied more so during bedtime situations. Not only are most people asleep at this time, but there are special norms at this time of night to discreetly ignore any noises emanating from a bedroom. Thus, the rapist who attacks victims in the middle of the night takes advantage of social norms protecting individual privacy. The following is a typical bedtime rape assault:

Case 35   *After entering through an open back door, the rapist took off his clothes in the living room. He climbed into bed with the victim and then awakened her, saying that he was going to have sex with her. She simply told him he had mistakenly come to the wrong place and that she was not going to have sex with him. Then she began screaming and the man put his hand over her mouth. He made the victim take off her pajamas and tried to rape her but could not achieve an erection; so he made her orally copulate him until he did. Then he raped her.*†

---

*Reprinted from William B. Sanders, *Rape and Woman's Identity*, p. 76, © 1980 Sage Publications, Inc.

†Ibid., p. 47.

At this point it should be noted that over 85 percent of the reported rapes occur in one of three situations—transit, at home, and bedtime. In each, the victim is vulnerable and isolated. This suggests a certain rationality of the rapist instead of a compulsive urge to commit rape. If a rapist were truly the "madman" depicted in popular stereotype, we would not find this kind of planned assault, but rather a random pattern across several situations. Instead, we find only a few situations used by the rapist to maximize his chances of completing the rape.

OTHER RAPE SITUATIONS.   The remaining rape situations reported to the police may be underrepresented in the official data on rapes. This is because the victim is more likely to know the rapist, sometimes having been recently introduced, but other times having known him for some while. The following examples illustrate rapes that occur in "socializing situations" of a general nature, and "date rapes," where the victim and rapists are together for the purposes of a date.

Case 77   *The victim, victim's brother, and another man were together at the victim's house drinking. When the victim's brother left, the victim asked the other man to leave, but he refused, demanding she have intercourse with him. She refused, and he began slapping her and then raped her.**

Case 4   *A blind date had been arranged between the victim and the rapist. The couple went out to dinner, and then for drinks with another couple who had introduced them. Leaving the other couple, the rapist took the victim by his apartment on the way home to "get something." At the apartment, the man began making overtures to the victim, and she declined. Then the suspect started slapping her, and took her into the bedroom and raped her.†*

Many of the social beliefs surrounding male–female relationships and sex roles make it very difficult for rape victims to report rapes where a rapist known to the victim is responsible. This is especially true if the victim has dated the rapist or he is a part of a circle of her friends. Likewise, women are still held up to a double standard of sexual relations, and women who have sex with several different men are still considered "loose," while men who have multiple sexual encounters are considered "studs" and generally held in a positive esteem. Furthermore, most state laws do not define sexual assault by husbands as being rape.

As societal views concerning sexual relations change, so too will conceptions of rape, but at this time, "date rapes" and similar sexual assaults are

---

*Reprinted from William B. Sanders, *Rape and Woman's Identity,* p. 49, © 1980 Sage Publications, Inc.

†Ibid., p. 51.

still very much subject to a double standard. This is true even among the young. In a survey of Los Angeles high school students aged 14 to 18, 54 percent of the boys and 42 percent of the girls said there were situations where "forced sex" was justifiable.[15] That is, about half the survey considered rape to be acceptable under certain conditions. The following cases were considered possibly justifiable for such assaults:

1. The girl says "yes" and then changes her mind.
2. She has "led him on."
3. The girl gets the boy "sexually excited."
4. If they have had sex before.
5. If he is "turned on."
6. If she has slept with other boys.
7. If she agrees to go to a party where she knows drinking or drugs will be.[16]

In the context of the crime of rape, there is a good deal of confusion between "rape" and "sex," confusion not present in other crimes. Consider the circumstances were we discussing a "bank loan" and "bank robbery." If we used the same list of "justifications" for robbing a bank, it would appear absurd. For instance, we would say, "Robbing a bank is acceptable under the following conditions":

1. The bank says "yes" to a loan and then changes its mind.
2. The bank has led the applicant to believe he/she will receive a loan.
3. Through advertisement, the bank has got the loan applicant "excited."
4. The bank has given the person a loan before.
5. The applicant "really needs" the money.
6. The bank has loaned other people money.
7. The loan officer goes to a party with the applicant where he knows drinking and drug use will be going on.

Since there is not the same confusion in the public stereotypes of crime between taking a loan from a bank and robbing it as there is between having sex and raping a woman, the second list is ridiculous. However, the extent to which society clearly differentiates between sexual relations and rape, the first list is equally banal. Thus, while the law makes any forced sex a crime (with the exception of a husband assaulting his wife), the public does not, leading to a confused understanding of rape.

Interaction in Rape Situations

Having examined the general structures of rape, we will now look to see what occurs in the interaction between victims and rapists in rape situations. We will move from the structure to the process of rapes to see how the interaction develops and leads to a rape assault. First, the following is the typical sequence found in rapes:

1. Contact through innocent presentation.
2. Isolation of victim.
3. Revelation of intentions.
4. Rape assault.[17]

This sequence describes the general order of interactions occurring in rapes, but oftentimes the entire sequence is collapsed so that the victim is isolated from the outset, the rapist's intentions are clear, and the assault occurs. For example, in cases where the victim is home in bed, she is isolated, and as soon as she is awakened by the rapist she is aware of his intentions either in his statements, presence, or gestures, and the assault is immediate. As can be seen in Table 11.4, in almost half the cases, the sequence is condensed in this way.

Table 11.4   Initial Presentation of Rapist

Front Used	Percent
Rapist	45.8
Masked intentions	38.5
Met at event	8.3
Known to victim	7.3

Source: Reprinted from William B. Sanders. *Rape and Woman's Identity*, p. 66, © 1980 Sage Publications, Inc.

In cases where the rapist first presents himself *as a rapist* the definition of the situation is one and the same from the outset of the interaction, the first step completely bypassed. However, in the other situations, the rapist must first present himself in some other fashion to contact the victim, and then later redefine the situation. For example, rapists who pick up women hitchhiking first present themselves as "helpers" or "assisters"—someone giving aid in the form of transportation. Later, they redefine their role and the victim's in the rape assault. The following example illustrates the complete sequence:

Case 73 *The victim went for a ride on a motorcycle with a man she met in a bar. He offered the ride for the fun of it and not to transport the victim anywhere in particular. He took the victim to his house and introduced her to some of his friends who offered her some marijuana. She declined, and the man and victim left, going to a remote canyon where he stopped the motorcycle. He said he would have to wait* *a half hour before he could get it started again. Then he began making advances toward the victim which she resisted. At that point he said he was going to rape her, and there wasn't anything she could do about it. He threatened to slap her around, and she finally did what he wanted her to. After the man raped her, he showed her his motorcycle wasn't really broken and gave her a ride home.**

Victim Reactions

At the point in the interaction sequence the victim realizes she is being sexually assaulted, she has a number of options. She can submit, fight, run, call for help, try to talk her way out of it, or take various other lines of action. Table 11.5 shows what the victim did in response to rape assaults:

Table 11.5 Victim Reaction to Rape Assault	
Victim's Behavior	**Percent**
No resistance	55.8
"Struggled"	8.4
Screamed	16.8
Hit, bit, kicked	5.3
Broke and ran	8.4
Other	5.3

Source: Reprinted from William B. Sanders, *Rape and Woman's Identity*, p. 74 © 1980 Sage Publications, Inc.

As can be seen, the most common reaction to the realization that rape was intended was to do nothing. By and large, the victim was frightened into a kind of "rape paralysis." That is, the overwhelming fear generated by the rapist caused the victim to fear for her life. Instead of thinking "I don't want to be raped," victims reported that all they could think of was surviving—"I don't want to die." There was an overwhelming sense of helplessness and all of the images of the "mad rapist" in victims' minds that have been supported by the popular stereotype.

It is this kind of reaction that rapists depend upon. If victims do not submit, they either have to fight them or run off. As in robberies, the weapons are not to be used so much as they are tools to intimidate the victim so that there will be no resistance. The idea that rapists enjoy a good fight and it further excites them seems to be pure fantasy—just as it

*Reprinted from William B. Sanders, *Rape and Woman's Identity*, pp. 67–68, © 1980 Sage Publications, Inc.

is fantasy to imagine that a robber wants a good fight. The rapist wants to control the situation so that he can rape the victim, and from the reactions of most rapists to resistance, especially a resolved fight, it is clear that rapists will run from a fight. Table 11.6 shows whether a rape is completed or attempted based on victims' reaction:

		Victim's Reaction				
Rape Assault	None	Struggled	Screamed	Fought	Ran	Other
Complete	96.3	62.5	56.2	40.0	25.0	20.0
Attempt only	3.7	31.5	43.7	60.0	75.0	80.0

Table 11.6   Victim's Reaction and Completion of Rape

Source: Reprinted from William B. Sanders, *Rape and Woman's Identity*, p. 75. © 1980 Sage Publications, Inc.

We can see by Table 11.6 that the extent to which women did something other than nothing, rapes were more likely to be only attempted—that is, the rapist gave up trying to rape the victim. If the rapist truly became more excited by resistance, we would expect a higher proportion of completed rapes with those who resisted, but this clearly is not the case. The more the resistance, the less likely the rape was completed.

Interactionally, this process can be understood in terms of the concept "definition of the **situation**" or "frame."[18] The sense of what to do in a situation depends on how the situation is understood and defined and the acceptance of that understanding and definition. Depending on the accepted definition of the situation, those in the situation have certain interaction roles. The situation's "frame" is the overall sense based on the dominant definition. To the extent the rapist is able to dominate that definition by his words and deeds, the victim's role is understood to be that of a *victim*. That is, if a situation can be defined as a rape, the frame of the situation demands the victim to be raped for that is a victim's role in a rape situation. However, the extent to which the rapist's definition is not accepted by the words and actions of the victim, especially the actions, the situation has a different frame. The victim states, in a sense, "This is not a rape, and you have no right to make these demands. You are violating the situational norms by your actions."

Such an analysis may at first seem to be an oversimplification and to ignore the entire aspect of violence used by the rapist to overpower the victim; however, since a large proportion of rapists who had the physical means to overpower the victim in situations of resistance did not do so, we cannot explain their reluctance simply by suggesting that violence was the only resource operating in rape assaults. Situational norms are at work as well. What happened was that when the rapist found that the victim would not accept his definition of the situation, he often fled, sometimes even apologizing. It is something like a person who mistakes a situation of one sort for another and after making the discovery that he has incorrectly assessed the nature of the occasion, apologizes and leaves. The rapist, in effect, says, "Oh, I thought this was a rape. My mistake, sorry," in the same way the someone mistakes a storefront church for a bar and realizing his mistake says, "Oh, I thought this was a bar. My mistake, sorry." The following cases illustrate this form of interaction:

Case 92   *The victim was on the way home from night school hitchhiking. A man picked her up, telling her he would give her a ride home. Once they were under way, the man pulled out a knife and told her to pull her pants down. She grabbed the knife and screamed. The man apologized and said he would take her home. When they stopped at a light, she jumped out of the car and ran.**

Case 100   *The victim was returning to a laundromat, sitting in her car when the rapist jumped in beside her. He grabbed her breasts and crotch and said, "I want to screw you." The victim screamed and the suspect put his hand over her mouth. She pulled his hand away and screamed more. The suspect muttered, "Oh shit," and ran off.*[19]

In all cases where the victim resisted, the rapist did not react this way, however. In some cases, he simply kept up his attack until he overcame the victim's resistance, forcing his definition of the situation on her through continued coercion. The pattern of rapists' reaction to victim resistance, though, shows that the rapes, to a large extent, depended on the situation being defined as a rape.

Resistance and Victim Harm

Given that victims who resisted rape were less likely to be raped than those who did not, we must now inquire into the problem of victims being harmed (beyond the rape itself) when they resist. Overall, only a very small proportion of rape victims are harmed to the point of requiring hospitalization, and an even smaller proportion are murdered in rape assaults. However, the stereotype of rape resistance is based on this tiny proportion. In 1979, homicides related to sex offenses made up only 1.6 percent of all homicides, and in only 0.4 percent of all reported rape assaults was the victim murdered. There is no evidence that shows murdered victims were killed because of resistance.

In examining data that compared the victim's reaction to rape and the

*Reprinted from William B. Sanders, *Rape and Woman's Identity*, p. 76, © 1980 Sage Publications, Inc.

extent of harm, we find that there is no correlation between resisting and being harmed. Table 11.7 shows this relationship:

Victim's Action Harm	None	Struggled	Screamed	Fought	Ran	Other
			(Percentage by Column)			
None	70	29	64	33	50	100
Slight	21	14	21	67	25	0
Moderate	9	43	0	0	25	0
Severe	0	14	14	0	0	0

Table 11.7 Victim Resistance and Physical Harm

Source: Reprinted from William B. Sanders, *Rape and Woman's Identity*, p. 145, © 1980 Sage Publications, Inc.

As can be seen in examining the data in Table 11.7 those who are most likely to be harmed beyond the rape itself are those who "struggled." Of the victims who were harmed, many were those who were known to the rapists—an acquaintance or date—and the "struggling" was often nothing more than pushing the rapist away. Moreover, "struggling" is a passive mode of resistance, and while it is clearly resistance, it is relatively ineffective.[20] The rapist has little to fear and feels he can use more force—slapping or hitting the victim. However, victims who fought—those who hit, bit, or kicked the rapist—were not taken so lightly and at worst suffered only minor harm—a slap or shove. Moreover, in looking at the type of executed force, we find very little was actually used. The threat of force—in the form of brandishing a weapon or verbal threat—was present, but not a great deal of execution in terms of severely harming the victim. Table 11.8 shows this pattern.

Type of Force	Percent
None	33.3
Drag/throw/push	45.1
Slap/hit	8.6
Moderate/severe beating	12.9

Table 11.8 Physical Force in Rapes

Source: Reprinted from William B. Sanders, *Rape and Woman's Identity*, p. 73, © 1980 Sage Publications, Inc.

Most of the harm beyond the rape occurred when a victim was pushed, dragged, or thrown down, and most of the injuries were minimal. The real harm is in the rape.

The Crime Against Self

Rape has been characterized as essentially a violent crime, which it is, and likened to a property crime—treating women as property and taking something illegally.[21] However, the real harm in rape is not physical, for we saw that only a small proportion of rape victims are subject to brutality other than the rape itself. Likewise, as a property crime, being raped generates a sense of loss much different than having property stolen. Rape is far worse than that for it violates a woman's choice. To the extent choice is taken from a person, their self-determination is taken. Since societal norms place a great deal of importance on how women conduct themselves in sexual matters, when rapists take that choice away, it is a direct assault on the self. Long after any signs of physical harm have healed, deeper scars remain: one's confidence and self-image have been damaged. Additionally, given the societal stereotypes of rape and confusion between sex and rape, the victim does not have the support of the community and

Women counselors help rape victims and victims of other physical abuse. An important role for the counselor is to help the victim reestablish a sense of self-worth.

often not even her friends and relatives. Therefore, the damage caused by rapists, while violent in its execution, goes far beyond mere physical harm to assault the victim's identity.

The Rapist As Wimp

While male sex roles may certainly call for more use of physical violence than women's, it is not the case that men are socialized into being brutish louts. Even concepts of "machismo" set limits to the use of violence; and in male sex role development, boys learn from an early age "not to hit girls." Whatever sexual discrimination there may be in protecting the "weaker sex," it is part of male role development. Since rapists use such violence and threat of violence against women in rapes, they violate male role expectations. In effect, they "hit girls" and that is something only wimps and sissies do.

This conceptualization of rapists is less flattering than that of their being truly "violent men"—men to be taken seriously, dangerous men not to be trifled with. It is also a good reputation for rapists since it scares the victims into submission. However, it is inaccurate. The greater the resistance of women in rapes, the more likely rapists will be to be run off. In the world of violent men, rapists are considered punks and generally low life. We find this in prison, where the status hierarchy is based on personal violence. Robbers, killers, and other violent characters who make up the prison population hold rapists in very low esteem, about one rung above child molesters who are at the bottom of the heap.[22] Even nonviolent criminals such as check forgers, confidence men, burglars, and thieves are held in higher esteem as "real men" than are rapists in prisons. If rapists were truly "violent men" or even men with an overwhelming sex drive, they would be accorded a higher status by those with whom they are locked up. However, because they are not, rapists may be enjoying a status in society not accorded them in circumstances where violent men make the rules. Further, most rapists tend to have a criminal background in property crimes more so than in other violent crimes.[23] This is not to say that rape is not violent, especially viewed from the victim's perspective and in terms of consensual sexual relations. Rape certainly is violent. However, in the context of violent crimes, the true harm in rapes is not the mere violence so much as it is a stab to the victim's self. While rapists at best are viewed as bullies of women, whom they terrorize, they are considered weaklings by men, since not only do they "hit girls," but they have to rely on physical force for sex, since they lack any kind of male attractiveness in terms of appearance, intelligence, or charm. Thus, while rapists loom large as fiends and overpowering monsters to women, they loom small to men, more mice than monsters.

Recent studies have shown that rapists are likely to be childhood victims of sexual abuse themselves, and most rapists are insecure individuals whose lives are marked by unhappiness.[24] This also supports the contention that the social evaluation by peers and self-images of rapists would be something less than "macho." However, such explanations, while partially useful in explaining rapists' behavior, ignore the larger context in which rapes occur and the nature of the situated interaction of rapes.

SUMMARY

More than most crimes, rape is misunderstood and misconstrued. In examining the patterns of rape, we find that, like other common and violent crimes, disproportionately the rapist is a young minority as is his victim, even though the majority of victims are white. Rape usually occurs in a rational context and evidentially is not the crime of the stereotypical "madman fiend." Instead, it is planned; occurs through a series of rational steps; and can be successfully thwarted by self-defense measures. Physical violence beyond the rape itself is typically minimal.

The major harm in rapes is the violation of self and not simply the violence; therefore, it is best understood as a "crime against self" rather than a violent crime. Typical rapists are stigmatized as weaklings and wimps by other men, especially violent criminals in prison. Ironically, many rapists have suffered the same kind of sexual abuses as they heap on women; and so those who were victimized themselves at one time create victimization for others.

Glossary

Anger-Excitation A psychiatric category of rapists who find pleasure and thrills in the agony of their victims.

Anger-Retaliation A psychiatric category of rapists who rape as an expression of hostility and rage toward women.

Crime against Self A crime where the major harm is against one's self-image.

Cultural Role A general set of behavior expectations of a given category of persons in society. It is used to explain the different sex roles in society and possible explanation of rape.

Deviant Role A category used to describe those who violate role expectation. In a deviant role, the expectations are to deviate.

Innocent Victim A characterization of rape victims who are seen to have no responsibility in their being raped.

Power-Assertive A psychiatric category for rapists who regard rape as an expression of virility.

Power-Reassurance A psychiatric category for rapists who rape to resolve doubts about their sexual adequacy and masculinity.

Situational Norms The rules governing a particular set of circumstances or situation.

Transit Situation Traveling to and from various places. It was found to be the most common situation where rape occurred.

Questions

1. What social prejudices about rape and rape victims lead to questioning the validity of claims of rape? Compare rape victims to robbery victims in terms of "victim culpability."

2. According to social psychiatric perspectives, what motives lie behind rape?

3. In what kind of situations are rape assaults most common? Why are such situations most likely to be chosen by rapists?

4. What is the sequence of a typical rape assault? What rationality is there to such a sequence of events, and what does this suggest for explanations looking to "compulsion" as a major cause?

5. What is the relationship between victim resistance and harm to the victim? What does this suggest as to the kind of man a rapist is?

Notes

1. Susan Brownmiller, *Against Our Will: Men, Women and Rape.* (New York: Simon & Schuster, 1975), pp. 23–118; Cornelius Ryan, *The Last Battle.* (New York: Simon & Schuster, 1966); Michael Herr, *Dispatches.* (New York: Avon, 1977).

2. David F. Musto, *The American Disease.* (New Haven, CT: Yale University Press, 1973).

3. Pepper Schwartz, "Rape, Battery and Incest," Presentation at the 34th Conference on World Affairs, University of Colorado, Boulder, Colorado, April 5–10, 1981.

4. William B. Sanders, *Rape and Woman's Identity.* (Beverly Hills: Sage, 1980).

5. Lee H. Bowker, *Women and Crime in America*. (New York: Macmillan, 1981), p. 182.

6. Sedelle Katz and Mary Ann Mazur, *Understanding the Rape Victim*. (New York: Wiley, 1979).

7. A. Nicholas Groth, Ann W. Burgess, and Lynda L. Holmstrom, "Rape: Power, Anger and Sexuality," *American Journal of Psychiatry* **134** (1977): 1239–1243.

8. Ibid.

9. Thomas Scheff, *On Being Mentally Ill*. (Chicago: Aldine, 1966).

10. Federal Bureau of Investigation, *Crime in the United States, 1979*. (Washington, D.C. : U.S. Government Printing Office, 1980), p. 327.

11. Ibid.

12. U.S. Department of Justice, *Criminal Victimization in the United States, 1977*. (Washington, D.C. : U.S. Government Printing Office, 1979); *Criminal Victimization in the United States: A Comparison of 1973–1974 Findings*. (Washington, D.C.: U.S. Government Printing Office, 1975).

13. Criminal Victimization, 1975, 24–25.

14. FBI, 1980, 200.

15. Lois Timnick, "Forced Sex Acceptable to Some Teens," *Los Angeles Times*, September 30, 1980.

16. Ibid.

17. Sanders, 1980, 68.

18. Peter McHugh, *Defining the Situation*. (Indianapolis: Bobbs-Merrill, 1966); Erving Goffman, *Frame Analysis*. (New York: Harper & Row, 1974).

19. FBI, 1980, 12–13.

20. I am grateful to Nancy Jo Jahnke for pointing out the difference between a "passive" and "active" form of resistance.

21. See Duncan Chappell, Robley Geis, and Gilbert Geis, eds., *Forcible Rape*. (New York: Columbia University Press, 1977) for an excellent collection of works detailing the various perspectives on rapes, both currently and historically.

22. Hans Toch, *Living in Prison: The Ecology of Survival*. (New York: Macmillan, 1977).

23. Menachem Amir, *Patterns of Forcible Rape*. (Chicago: University of Chicago Press, 1971).

24. Nicholas Groth and H. Jean Birnbaum, *Men Who Rape: The Psychology of the Offender*. (New York: Plenum Press, 1979).

12

Crimes in Occupations

What to Look For:

The meaning and extent of occupational crimes.

The problems in researching and policing occupational crimes.

Explanations of occupational crimes.

The relationship between business ethics and consumer fraud.

How professionals engage in occupational crimes.

Introduction

I N THIS CHAPTER we look at what has been called "white-collar crime," "upper-world crime," and "unconventional crime."[1] Such crime involves people in legitimate positions in society who use their positions to illegally enhance themselves. This may involve anything from charging for auto repairs that were never made to illegal price-fixing by corporations. Here we concentrate on those crimes committed by people in the course of their legitimate jobs. Included will be not only employees who steal from, or for, their employers, but also small businesses and professionals who either defraud their clients, insurance companies, or the government. Both blue- and white-collar occupations on the lower levels as well as small businesses and professionals, such as physicians and attorneys, are in this category. In Chapter 14 we will deal with the higher levels of this sort of crime in examining corporate executives and governmental officials who do the same thing on a much larger scale and in a somewhat different context.

The differences in the offenses to be discussed here depend on a *position* within a legitimate occupation, and so the divisions in this chapter will reflect these different positions and opportunities available for these crimes. While we have divided this chapter into a number of sections relevant to the topics we wish to cover, it should be noted that these topics are intended simply to set off the different forms of crime, and not to call for different theories for each type of offense.

We will examine these offenses in terms of the various explanations available as part of general theories of crime, rather than attempting to develop special "white-collar" or **occupational crime** theories. As Geis and Meier point out,

A major difficulty in the search for explanation and understanding concerns the determination of behaviors that are to be regarded as homogeneous and those that are to be seen as heterogeneous; that is, what things are to be viewed as similar and what as different. In making certain kinds of distinctions, we may destroy the base upon which the most sophisticated understanding can be built. Hirschi provides a fine illustration of this point with the observation that typologists, persons who believe in grouping behaviors which have the appearance of similarity, may be engaged in self-defeating behavior. "They would have us believe," Hirschi notes, "that it is 'patently absurd' to attempt to explain with a single theory such diverse phenomena as the movement of the tides, the erect posture of trees, and the difficulty of writing on the ceiling with a ballpoint pen." Hirschi is suggesting that perhaps some day criminologists may be able to discover a law such as the law of gravity, which explains all of the phenomena listed in the foregoing quotation.[2]

This is not to say that categorization is wrong per se, for all sciences develop categories—such as the plant phylums in botany—but rather, there is a difference between developing a theory for each category and having a single theory for certain underlying patterns.

The Extent of Occupational Crimes

A major problem in studying occupational crimes is the lack of available data. Throughout this book there have been numerous charts and tables showing the extent of all kinds of crime based on police data, victimization surveys, and other statistical and qualitative sources. However, when it comes to occupational crimes, there is very little, and what there is, is based on rough estimates. For example, an estimate made in 1960 by Norman Jaspers suggested that white-collar employees stole about $4 million a day.[3] In 1974, the Chamber of Commerce of the United States said that pilfering by white-collar criminals amounted to $40 billion annually.[4] These figures are based on the amount of **shrinkage** in businesses—losses that can be anything from shoplifting to misplacement of goods to employee theft. In one study in 1940 using lie detectors it was found that 76 percent of the employees in certain Chicago chain stores were taking money or merchandise—at a time when Americans were supposedly less dishonest.[5] Therefore, while there is little doubt that occupational crimes cost a lot of money, the exact amount is unknown. Furthermore, we know little about the people who commit such crimes: only a few are caught and those caught are usually fired or reprimanded rather than officially prosecuted. For instance, Montgomery Ward fired 3 percent of its employees one year for stealing merchandise (roughly 120 people).[6] Additionally, since firing is considered sanction enough they were not reported to the police, thus their crimes were omitted from the FBI statistics. Likewise, since we have little self-report or victimization data on these crimes, it is necessary to rely heavily on those few studies that have attempted to look at this phenomenon.

The Criminal Justice System and Occupational Crimes

One of the unique features of occupational crimes is their lack of enforcement. John Conklin referred to the various business crimes as being "illegal but not criminal"—an apt depiction of how the laws regulating these crimes are applied.[7] Conklin's characterization was aimed more toward corporate crimes, but it is equally applicable to occupational crimes. Simply put, there are criminal laws that apply to **employee theft**, business fraud, embezzlement, and other business crimes, but they are not enforced to the extent or in the same way as are common crimes.

Since if employees are caught stealing, there is no criminal report by the victim, it is not the fault of the law or criminal justice system that no criminal sanctions are applied. On the other hand, there is a tendency to treat criminal violations by occupational criminals as civil cases rather than criminal ones.[8] If treated as a criminal case, the focus is on some kind of punishment for guilty offenders, but civil cases typically involve payment of damages and restitution to the victim. If the victim is not interested in sending the violator to prison but primarily in gaining monetary restitution, the criminal court will be of little help. Any fines in the criminal court will go to the court and not the victim; therefore, the most practical approach from the victim's perspective is the civil court.

Another problem with enforcing laws regulating occupational crimes is the organization of the criminal justice system itself. Victims of burglaries, for example, can call the police and be directed to the "burglary detail" where a detective will be assigned to investigate their case. However, if a person believes he or she has been overcharged for a fraudulent auto repair or unnecessary medical operation, there is no unit in most police departments to handle such cases—no "auto repair fraud detail" or "medical fraud unit." Some jurisdictions have special investigators in the prosecutor's office for these offenses but many people are unaware of such special units or are afraid to call them since they lack the mechanical or medical expertise to back up claims of criminal victimization. If people come home and find their house burglarized, they can clearly see and understand their victimization and know what to do—call the cops! However, if they are told their car needed a new generator or fuel pump and they suspect it did not, then they are usually not knowledgeable enough in auto mechanics to know otherwise. However, were there a police unit that would investigate the claim—a unit with investigators trained in uncovering such consumer fraud—then not only would such crimes have a higher likelihood of being reported, but also there is a much better chance of enforcement of the laws regulating this kind of activity. Similarly, employers who suspect employee theft usually hire private security firms to deal with their problems with occupational criminals rather than rely on public law enforcement or the criminal courts. In this way they can have full-time security rather than an occasional police officer drop by.

Criminal justice system incumbents claim that such crimes are 1) technically difficult to prosecute; and 2) the victims would rather have restitution than criminal conviction. As to the first claim, there may be some difficulty in prosecuting a case involving highly specialized forms of fraud or theft, but the same can be said for many other crimes typically handled by the criminal courts. Rapes are difficult to prosecute in cases where it is the victim's word against the defendant's. Likewise, burglary cases are difficult in that not only is it a problem for the police to solve the typical burglary, but also linking a defendant to a crime scene in court is equally problematic. However, in the typical occupational crime the suspect is immediately identified and most of the evidence is readily available for any-

Consumer fraud is not typically viewed as a "real crime," and so it is not as readily reported, even though it has the same effect as other property crimes in terms of real losses. Aggressive prosecution of such crimes can, however, increase the possibility of criminal sanctions against consumer fraud criminals.

one with the expertise to examine it. As for the victims wanting restitution more than seeing a criminal punished, that is probably true, but the same can be said for all victims of property crimes. Robbery, theft, and burglary victims rarely get their money or property returned, and given a choice between seeing a burglar go to prison and having their losses recovered, most victims would probably want the latter. Were it not for the insurance covering their losses, it is likely that many more victims of property crimes would choose the civil court route over the criminal. Thus, it is not so much true that criminal sanctions could not be applied in cases of occupational crimes—or civil trials for common crimes—but rather because of the traditional organization and routines of the criminal justice system, it is simply inconvenient to do so.

Occupations and Opportunities for Crime

In their theory of delinquency and opportunity, it is unlikely that Cloward and Ohlin saw legitimate opportunities to be equally fraught with the possibilities for illegitimate opportunities. However, since occupational crimes require a place in a legitimate position in society, the opportunity to commit such crime comes with what Cloward and Ohlin would have predicted to lead away from crime.[9] In a large part then, the extent that occupational crimes are common is a rejection of Cloward and Ohlin's explanation of crime. However, if we expand the concept of "opportunity" to include the possibility of commiting occupational crimes, then part of the opportunity structure becomes the legitimate positions in society.

Learning to Beat the System

Another approach to understanding occupational crimes is differential association theory. Sutherland applied principles of differential association to white-collar crime, simply pointing out that people in legitimate occupations learn all of the necessary methods and motives from others who are breaking the law in similar positions.[10] In the same way that a person who associates with pickpockets will learn to be a pickpocket, a person whose job puts him/her in a position to associate with employees who steal from their employer will learn both the method and rationalizations for committing such crimes. At first, this may seem to be a contradiction in differential association theory since taking a job in a legitimate position in society is a reflection of noncriminal values. However, differential association is not a matter of "all criminal values" and "no criminal values," but rather a matter of degrees. Robbers, for instance, may have learned that robbery is "acceptable" but would never consider child molesting. By the same token, an employee might learn that stealing from his employer is "all right" as long as he/she does not steal too much. Conklin explains this application of differential association:

> Sutherland resolves this apparent contradiction in his theory of differential association. This theory explores the *ratio* of definitions favorable to violation of the law to definitions unfavorable to violation of the law. In other words, the businessmen are exposed to a multitude of values and norms. Some values and norms support certain business crimes, and others condemn such crimes. In Sutherland's view, a business crime will occur when the ratio is weighted toward the definitions favorable to violation of the law, even though definitions unfavorable to violations of the law will also exist in the violator's mind.[11]

Even though Sutherland was focusing on explaining larger corporate violations, the same principles apply to occupational crimes, only the *content* of the learning is different.

Employee Theft: The Perks of Petty Jobs

Learning to steal from an employer is not so much a matter of technique as it is in learning the proper "vocabulary of motives" and "techniques of neutralization."[12] If employees learn that they are "underpaid" or that the higher executives in a firm have special "perks" in the form of expense accounts, their own thievery is simply a matter of taking what is rightfully their own. For example, one executive's motivation was explained as, "the promise of a salary raise that was fulfilled too late."[13]

It is important not to confuse "learning" criminal vocabularies of motives with "causes." In a critique of one work on white-collar thefts, Frank Hartung points out that some analysts take the "explanations" or "rationalizations" as causes.[14] That is, if we take the cause of employee theft as being low pay, lack of adequate advancement, or any other explanation being used to account for thievery, we confuse "learning excuses" with causes. The cause *is* the learning of rationalizations, and not what the rationalizations contain. For instance, child molesters claim little girls "egg them on" thereby "asking for it," but very few analysts would say that children are the cause of their own molestations. Such explanations by child molestors are techniques of neutralization. In the same way, an executive's saying he stole from a company because it did not give him his raise on time is not an explanation or cause of the thievery. Rather, learning that rationalization is. Therefore, the extent to which employees learn a vocabulary of motives allowing them to steal or defraud their employers stands as the cause; not the conditions they claim leads them to crime.

Another perspective on the same issue involves the structure of interactions and associations in an organization. Some criminologists point out that it is the insulation of businessmen from certain values that leads them to business crimes.[15] As applied to occupational crimes, to the extent employees are separated from interaction with the owners of the business, they are less likely to learn definitions favorable to obeying the law—not stealing from the business. Businesses where there is close contact, especially informal contacts between higher-level management and employees, should be less likely to encounter high levels of employee theft since they are more likely to be in contact with values that are against such pilfering. However, since there is a good deal of criminal values held by the owners and higher executives themselves—such as corporate tax and antitrust violations, to name just a few—employees may learn that while they are not expected to steal from the business, it is all right for the business as a whole to illegally pursue profits! Thus, while learning is the key principle in understanding criminality, the structure of an organization can influence the interactions and associations linked to patterns of learning criminal and anticriminal values.

Embezzlement

Embezzlement is a form of employee theft, except that the employee typically takes money instead of goods. It is defined in the Uniform Crime Reports as follows:

Embezzlement   Misappropriation or misapplication of money or property entrusted to one's care, custody, or control.

If an employee takes money that has been given to him/her before it has reached the employer, technically it is not taken from the employer—he never had it in his possession.[16] Thus, the employee did not commit theft, for to commit theft, it is necessary to take something from someone else, and if it were never in the victim's possession then it cannot be taken from his/her possession. However, when we look at the embezzlement laws, we find many different interpretations, including everything from what is normally considered embezzlement to forgery and confidence games. We will examine embezzlement using Cressey's definition. Cressey states that two conditions are required:

1. The person must have accepted a position of trust in good faith.
2. The person must have violated that trust by committing a crime.[17]

With this broader definition, we incorporate a far wider range of violators, but it does serve to focus the attention on *positions of trust,* and the *violation* of that trust.

In Cressey's study of embezzlers, one of the major findings was that they acted alone. In fact, Cressey concluded that the major reason for financial trust violation was having a **"non-sharable" problem.**[18] To the extent a problem is "non-sharable" there are no interpersonal contacts concerning the commission of a crime, so there is no learning of crime through criminal associations. That is, while employees may learn from one another all the techniques and vocabularies of motives for pilfering and even help one another doing so, the embezzlers in Cressey's study were not in that kind of situation. Consider the following case:

Case 242   *I had been reared in a home above average. I had been accustomed to good clothes, good food, a good home, a good car, and similar expensive articles. I was married to a young woman I met in Z. She was from a middle-class home and was much more careful in her expenditures than I was, and she often objected to my purchases on the grounds that we could not afford them. But I did not feel that I could drop below the standard of living to which I had been accustomed. My parents owned the home in which we lived and I had no rent to pay on that. My parents and my wife's parents helped us in other ways, also. It needs to be remembered that the cost of living in Y is extremely high, since practically everything is shipped in. Then, also a person who works in a bank is generally regarded as wealthy, no matter how small his salary. He is expected to subscribe to everything, and I do not think I ever failed to pay my share on every such subscription affair that came around. Also, a person who works in a bank must, because of this expectation, live on a fairly high standard. He is compelled to look prosperous for the sake of the bank. He has to "live up to his position." Probably many others may have had an income no larger than mine and cost of living as high and have not embezzled, but the im-*

portant thing was my individual tastes. In that sense, a good home contributed to my downfall. I was not trying to live cheap because I had not been reared that way. Then, also, everyone else was spending money lavishly and we felt we ought to keep up. It was in the air. Boom times were on then.[19]

Since the embezzler could not share his problem with someone else—or at least he perceived he could not—he saw no way to resolve his dilemma without embezzling money. In this case the man suggested his upper-class background "forced" him to embezzle. However, other embezzlers violate positions of trust for very different reasons. For example:

Case 233 *I do not think that there is much chance of preventing embezzlement by auditing and examinations. The big defalcations are made by old and trusted employees who suddenly go wrong. . . . there are so many thousand ways of beating a bank that no auditing system will do. One of the difficulties is the con man. He is always coming into banks when he gets short, trying to make a little amount, a thousand dollars or so, to get started again. He beats a teller or cashier on some game or other. The officer can go to the president and explain and get fired, which he is ashamed to do for no one likes to appear as a sucker, or he can make it up some way out of the bank funds and cover it up.*[20]

In this case, the embezzler took *no* money for himself but rather to cover up someone else's crime so he would not lose his job. Both, however, deal with nonsharable problems.

Since the embezzlers do not learn from other embezzlers, it may appear that they do not learn to be criminals as we saw with employee thieves and other criminals. Instead, they appear to develop a vocabulary of motives for their offense on their own. According to Cressey,

THE WALL STREET JOURNAL

"I took at the office."

Source: From *Wall Street Journal*, Permission—Cartoon Features Syndicate.

After a trusted person has defined a problem as nonsharable, the total pertinent situations consists of a problem which must be resolved by an independent, secret, and relatively safe means by virtue of general and technical information about trust violation. In this situation the potential trust violator identifies the possibilities for resolving the problem by violating his position of trust and defines the relationship between the nonsharable problem and the illegal solution in language which enables him to look upon trust violation 1) as essentially noncriminal, 2) as justified, or 3) as a part of a general irresponsibility for which he is not completely accountable.[21]

Essentially, the embezzler learns that it is "justifiable" to break the rules in "unfair" situations, and having defined his own actions as noncriminal, and basically unfair to himself, his offense is "justified."

Since embezzlement is one occupational crime for which there is national police data, we can get some idea of its incidence. However, like other occupational crimes, it is probably far under-reported since it is often handled informally. Furthermore, since the reporting of embezzlement almost always involves a known offender, the arrest figures virtually equate the crime report figures.

Table 12.1 Embezzlement 1970–1979		
1970	**1979**	**Percent Change**
6,314	4,124	−34.7

Source: Federal Bureau of Investigation, *Crime in the United States*, 1979. (Washington, D.C.: U.S. Government Printing Office, 1980), p. 190.

As can be seen, there has been a sharp decrease in *reported* embezzlements, and whether this is an indication of a decrease in actual embezzlement or reporting is unknown. However, given the very low figures in the totals compared to other crimes, there probably is very little reported or discovered in the first place. Nevertheless there was a dramatic increase in reported embezzlement for youths under 18—an increase of 228.2 percent (from 195 to 640 reported cases).[21] This suggests that more youth-employment will not necessarily decrease the amount of crime! It simply shifts it to another kind of offense.

Fraud: Stealing from Clients

Consumer fraud has been a major issue in the United States for the past two decades. Pioneering work in this area by such people as Ralph Nader alerted the American public that they were being robbed of billions. However, consumer fraud is not new: the present defrauding popularized by

Nader and such programs as "60 Minutes" had precedents in the "snake oil" medicine shows of hundreds of years ago.

In Sutherland's classic work, *White Collar Crime*, the following investigative report was noted:

> Investigators for *Readers Digest* in 1941 drove their car into many garages with a defect artificially produced for this experiment. A proper charge for attaching the wire which had been loosened might be twenty-five cents. But 75 percent of the garages misrepresented the defect and the work which was done; the average charge was $4 and some garages charged as much as $25. Similar frauds were found in the watch-repair, radio-repair, and typewriter-repair businesses.[22]

Today we find the same practices, but very few criminologists have bothered to study this, and most of the exposures of consumer fraud are journalistic efforts, much like the 1941 *Readers Digest* investigation. Also, in various Congressional hearings reports of consumer fraud are brought to light, and consumer groups and "watchdog" organizations, such as the Better Business Bureau, have data on reported complaints. Unfortunately, the systematic collection of data on this area of crime has been haphazard. Therefore, much of this section will simply provide description and conjecture, illustrating some major ways in which small businesses defraud their clients.

Caveat Emptor

As a client–business relationship, **caveat emptor** (let the buyer beware) leaves much to be desired by the consumer. As an "accepted" relationship, it presumes that the consumer should not trust the businessperson, and if he/she does, then any fraud committed by the business is justified. (The reverse ethic however is not accepted—the customer stealing from the business.) To the extent a business ethic does exist in society, we can point to it as a cause for such offenses. That is, if "anything goes" in business, whether it is misrepresentation, fraud, or cheating, then business values are "taught" in a way that is criminal. However, since many businesses rely on return customers, they cannot be wholly irresponsible and misrepresentative in their dealings. Thus, the "practical ethic" of some businesses mitigate against routine fraud. The following are some examples of common forms of theft from clients and fraud.

Special Price. Customers are led to believe they are buying an item far below what it normally sells for in the "special low price" fraud. Some schemes are so routine that many customers are aware at the outset that the "special deal" is part of an ongoing pitch and pay little heed to it. Others, however, are not and will buy something on the basis of the "special price." In one such scheme, a company operating in Arkansas told homeowners that they had "chosen" their home as a "model" for aluminum siding, to be used to show prospective customers. The company would sell the siding to the homeowners at a "special price," $1,000 below cost, since they wanted to show off their product, and in addition, they would pay them $100 for every customer they showed the "model" house to who bought the siding. Not only was the siding in reality not at a "special price," but the material put on the house was also of inferior quality and poorly installed. So much so that many of the houses looked better before the siding was installed. Also, no one ever received the $100 bonus for customers who were shown the "model house"—all of the customers were told their's was the model house.*

Those who are most susceptible to such schemes are the poor and illiterate. By the simple expedient of checking different prices before buying, it could have been learned that the "special price" was not special. However, the ignorant tend to be the most trusting and naive and believe in the sales pitches. In the Arkansas aluminum siding fraud, the salesman invoked the client's "trust in God." One victim explained,

> "Well, then, he said one thing that kind of struck me," the homeowner later recalled. "He said to say a little prayer and pray to the Lord and let Him guide us as to whether to sign the contract." Touched by this display of humility, the man and woman signed a contract for $1,480 and gave Mr. G. a downpayment check for $200.†

It may seem to be the height of stupidity to fall for that kind of line, but to people who base the majority of their relationships on trust, it is evidence of sincerity. Businessmen who are bilked by confidence men and women view such tactics as unethical even though they may employ the same ones in their business. Thus, while there are many ethics protecting businesses, there seem to be few protecting consumers.

BAIT AND SWITCH.   Another kind of consumer fraud is **bait and switch** advertising. In this scheme, a store advertises a product at a very low price, and when the customer comes to buy it, they are led to something more expensive. Sometimes customers are told that the advertised item has "sold out" and was not a very good product anyway, leading them to a more expensive model of the same thing. New laws have been enacted that require that advertisers publish the number of such items actually in stock, and if no such limit is published, customers must be given a credit slip that allows them to buy the product at the advertised price at a later

---

*From the book, *The Dark Side of the Market Place* by Senator Warren G. Magnuson and Jean Carper. © 1968 by Warren G. Magnuson and Jean Carper. Published by Prentice-Hall, Inc., Englewood Cliffs, NJ, pp. 9–14.

†Ibid., p. 10.

date. However, this law is often violated, and unless the consumer is aware of the law, he or she may believe they either have to buy another model or nothing. The following excerpt illustrates the thinking behind this scheme.

> An appliance store advertises, for example, a 17-inch screen TV for $90, but woe to the salesman who actually sells it. Said one store manager, referring to an advertised GE portable, "Any guy who lets that set go out the door goes with it." This merchandise is, in sales lingo, "nailed to the floor," and it is the salesman's job to knock it, to disparage it in any way, and to switch the customer to a more expensive model.*

Not only are the sales personnel expected to sell customers more expensive items, enriching both the sales person and the store, but there can be severe sanctions for not cheating customers. In other words the *norms* of the business are to maximize profits, regardless of the customer's best interests. To the extent such illegal values (ethics) exist in business, there is the basis for a criminal subculture opposed to values supporting the law. In Chapter 14 we will go into this in more detail.

LO-BALLING.   Another common form of consumer fraud is **lo-balling**. The practice is most common in the auto repair business. The company advertises a service at an extremely low price and performs the service. However, this is done only to get the car. Once they have the car, they then convince the customer that he/she needs unnecessary repairs:

> The lucrative routine goes this way, as illustrated by the experience of a man in Washington, D.C. He responded to an advertisement promising to reseal his car's transmission for labor charges of $22 plus any extra charge for needed parts. He was promised one-day service. When he left the car, it was functioning properly except for an oil leakage, which was to be corrected by resealing the transmission.
>
> "About 4:15 the same day, I went back and they had a transmission lying on a work bench, and they said: 'This is your transmission and here are some parts of metal that were found in it and the pump is completely shot and needs replacing.' So I talked to the manager and said, 'What will that cost?' He said, 'Well, it would cost about another $42,' which raised the cost of the job to about $76."
>
> "So I told him to go ahead with it, take the things that were torn down and if they needed a new pump, to put it in. He said it would be ready the next afternoon."
>
> "Well, I called the next morning to find out if the car would be ready and he examined it further and said: 'All the bushings are shot and need replac-

---

*From the book, *The Dark Side of the Market Place* by Senator Warren G. Magnuson and Jean Carper. © 1968 by Warren G. Magnuson and Jean Carper. Published by Prentice-Hall, Inc., Englewood Cliffs, NJ, p. 16.

ing.' I said, 'What is that going to cost?' He said, 'Well, the total job is now $107."*

This kind of fraud is possible because people have to rely on the specialized skills of mechanics. However, the fraud is often doubly deceitful, for not only are unnecessary repairs made and parts charged for, but as the following example illustrates, the "new" parts are often not new:

> In Columbia, South Carolina, for example, three officers and employees of the local Aamco franchise were charged with conspiring to obtain money under false pretenses after a carefully marked 1959 automobile was left with them by state investigators for repairs. The transmission had previously been rebuilt, the parts marked by a competent mechanic, and was in good working order. Only the governor was defective. Aamco employees, however, tore down the transmission, declared it "burned up," and rebuilt it at a charge of $189.17. Subsequent examination of the transmission by a mechanic hired by the state revealed that some of the "new" parts listed on the bill were in fact the old parts which had been marked. Only two of the old marked parts reportedly had been replaced; the defective governor and a front seal valued at $2.25.†

Medical Fraud

To begin our examination of medical fraud, it is important to understand that medicine, as practiced in the United States, is proprietary. That is, medical practice is a business, just like repairing cars or selling appliances. Aside from oaths, ethics, and the popular image of physicians as demigods in American society, medicine is a thriving, lucrative way to make a lot of money. Like any business, it is necessary to sell something in order to make money, and since medical "service" is sold, there is a possibility to defraud the consumer just like any other business. Further, since the services vary in price, depending on their type and number, there is the temptation to sell the higher priced service and add unnecessary services or charges for services not performed. To the extent money is valued over professional ethics, there will be some kind of fraud. Like auto repair fraud, since most patients are unfamiliar with the causes of their disease or injury, they rarely question the service. The same general framework exists in other aspects of medicine, such as dentistry and pharmacy. For example, the following case illustrates deadly malpractice where there is the possibility of fraud in diagnosing a disease for profitable surgery:

---

*From the book, *The Dark Side of the Market Place* by Senator Warren G. Magnuson and Jean Carper. © 1968 by Warren G. Magnuson and Jean Carper. Published by Prentice-Hall, Inc., Englewood Cliffs, NJ, pp. 17–18.

†Ibid., p. 18.

A hospital has charged a doctor with 25 counts of unprofessional conduct. These incidents cost the lives of six patients.

*In one operation he unnecessarily removed both adrenal glands from a woman, causing her death. After opening up another patient for cancer, he found none. Without the patient's permission he proceeded to remove a kidney, so negligently as to cause gangrene and kill her. During a tumor operation he ignored warning that a sponge was missing. The patient later died of an internal abscess resulting from the sponge.**

Such acts of carelessness are not the main issue here, for even though they are as lethal as murder, physicians do not condone or support this kind of unprofessional work in their norms. They may involve both fraud and outright negligence. On the other hand, in cases where physicians, either in cooperation with other practitioners or alone with the tacit approval of the informal norms of their colleagues, perform unnecessary operations and/or pad expenses for medical services, there is clear fraud, and this is the main point to be examined.

The amount of fraud in medicine is generally unknown. Figures from medical organizations indicate that there is a good deal of "unprofessional" physician activity.[23] One estimate is that at least one physician in 20—about 5 percent—has a severe disciplinary problem and up to 11 percent are repeatedly guilty of practices described as "unworthy to the profession."[24] Most of this abuse of the profession is considered "unethical" rather than prosecutable such as substandard care, abandonment, and overcharging. However, it is estimated that between 2,500 and 7,500 are actually breaking the law through narcotics violations, frauds, and other felonies.[25] Since this estimate is fairly broad, it is difficult to say how accurate it is and what proportion actually represents fraud.

A study of pharmacist prescription violations showed that to the degree to which pharmacists were oriented toward their profession, they were not involved in prescription violations, and to the degree to which they were oriented to business, they were.[26] This is because making money to them was more important than following the law and ethics of their profession. Table 12.2 shows this breakdown.

Like physicians, pharmacists are oriented toward two different roles in their occupations—professional pharmacist and businessperson. This creates possible role strain, in that the professional role calls for maximum client orientation and the business role calls for maximum profits. The study hypothesized, "that retail pharmacists resolve the dilemma of choosing between different occupation roles—professional and business—by adapting to an **occupational role organization**. Occupational role organ-

*From the book, *The Dark Side of the Market Place* by Senator Warren G. Magnuson and Jean Carper. © 1968 by Warren G. Magnuson and Jean Carper. Published by Prentice-Hall, Inc., Englewood Cliffs, NJ, p. 18.

Table 12.2 Relationship Between Prescription Violation and Occupational Role Organization

Prescription violation	Occupational Role Organizations							
	Professional		Professional/ Business		Indifferent		Business	
	N	%	N	%	N	%	N	&
VIOLATORS	0	0	5	14	3	20	12	75
NONVIOLATORS	13	100	31	86	12	80	4	25
TOTAL	13	100	36	100	15	100	16	100

X = 28.6   df = 3   P< .001

Source: Richard Quinney, "Occupational Structure and Criminal Behavior: Prescription Violations by Retail Pharmacists," *Social Problems* **11** (Fall 1963): 179–185.

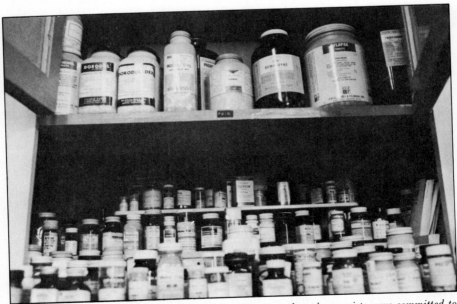

Illegal prescriptions were found to be linked to the extent that pharmacists were committed to a "business" orientation. Those pharmacists with self-images of a "professional" did not prescribe drugs illegally.

ization refers to the relative orientation of the retail pharmacist to both the professional and business roles."[27]

Thus, while some kinds of crimes have been explained in terms of lack of access to the legitimate opportunity structure represented by business, other kinds of crime occur because of such access. However, since both professional and business-oriented pharmacists have access to the same opportunity structure, we must explain the differences in their tendency toward crime by their value orientation to either their profession or business.

Computer Crimes

As finance becomes more and more dependent on computers for everything from bookkeeping to transfer of funds, stealing from business takes on a new dimension. This is especially true today as more people are using microcomputers in business, school, and even the home. What twenty years ago took up several rooms of storage space can now sit atop someone's desk, and even "big" computers (those with a great deal of memory storage) can fit in a broom closet.

As an area of research for criminologists, **computer crimes** are relatively new. What we do know, however, staggers the imagination. First of all, the average computer crime nets about $450,000.[28] If we consider what the average property crime costs—especially the common ones— computer crimes top the list in what can be stolen. In the same way that computers allow financial institutions to handle large sums, they also allow crooks to steal large sums. Computer criminals can burglarize a bank without prying open a door or digging a tunnel under a vault—they simply "access" the electronic funds in an "electronic safe," transferring them to their own account, withdrawing the money and doing with it what they please. Many cases of computer crimes are committed by trusted employees—embezzlements— the only difference being that the amount taken tends to be larger and the scheme more difficult to discover than ordinary embezzlement. In other cases, an employee will supply the computer criminal with a key code for accessing the computer, and then from his home—or anywhere—the crook will transfer funds to an account he controls. A sophisticated computer criminal can access funds, make the desired transfers, and then tell the computer to forget the transaction ever occurred, making the crime virtually undetectable.

Computers can be used by institutions themselves to commit crimes. In one of the largest such crimes, known as the Equity Funding scandal, a company used the computer to generate bogus insurance accounts. Of a total of $3.2 billion in life insurance policies claimed by Equity Funding, $2.1 billion was ficticious, and of the company's $737 million in assets it claimed one year, $185 million was bogus.[29] Not only did the fraudulent creation of policies increase the value of the company's stock, the company pocketed $1,175,000 from reinsurers for bogus claims. In addition, employees of Equity Funding, compounding one crime with another, took an additional $144,000 for themselves from the company![30] The victims of this crime were the company's customers, who had either bought mutual funds in the company or policies.

Who Are the Computer Criminals?

In looking at this kind of crime, we do not ask if such criminal activity is the result of lack of legitimate opportunities or if the criminals are suffering from low IQ scores—certainly not the latter! Some researchers have characterized computer criminals as "usually bright, eager, highly motivated, courageous, adventuresome, and qualified people willing to accept a technical challenge. They have exactly the characteristics that make them highly desirable employees in data processing."[31] One researcher commented, "The common denominator in nearly all cases of computer fraud has been that the individual is very much like the mountain climber—he or she must beat the system because it is there."[32] However, Jack Becker, the director of the National Center for Computer Crime Data, points out that many computer crimes are not that sophisticated and require very little knowledge of computer technology or programming.[33] The average bank employee, for example, uses computer terminals all the time, and while he or she may know little about computers, he/she has to know about *using* the computer in banking. For example, in a $21 million computer crime committed against Wells Fargo Bank that came to light in 1981, the main suspect in the case simply took advantage of a five-day delay between the time the computer transferred funds to the bank and the time it was actually debited against the account. By keeping the electronic transfers ahead of the "debit," the embezzlers were able to amass a fortune.[34] In another case, a "computer criminal" simply pressed the "repeat" button on the computer when it was processing his check. Nevertheless, there is not enough known at this time to say exactly what the typical computer criminal is like.

SUMMARY

In this chapter we have examined crimes that occur in occupations either against employers or clients. These crimes occur in the context of success and legitimate opportunities by people of relative social advantage. The "opportunities" for such crime depend on access to legitimate success channels, the very channels some criminologists have predicted to lead away from crime. However, in the same way that other law breakers learn to define their criminal behavior as "appropriate" in common crimes, occupational criminals learn their behavior too is appropriate. Therefore, there is a common thread of differential association in these crimes as well as the others discussed up to this point in the book.

Nevertheless, there are occupational criminals, such as embezzlers, who do not learn directly from others the necessary skills and vocabularies of motives *for* embezzlement. They commit their crime in isolation from fellow embezzlers, and while they may learn techniques of neutralization for problems of a general nature, then apply those rationalizations to the situation of embezzlement, they do not associate and learn directly from fellow criminals.

As for occupational criminals who defraud the public, there is in the "business ethic" certain short-term ideas concerning profit and the role of the consumer. These ideas are interpreted to mean that any actions that will increase profit, whether they are fraudulent or not, are legitimate. Therefore, within the "business culture," consumers are treated as fair game and any "cheating" is because the customer is less astute at business than the business person. Likewise, in the medical profession, to the extent the practitioner is oriented toward the practice as a business rather than a profession, he or she is likely to defraud the consumer or engage in other illegal activities that increase profits.

Finally, on a higher technical level, the computer criminals are the new embezzlers, burglars, and thieves whose crimes reap incredible illegal gains. However, their behavior can be explained in the same way as other criminals, the only difference being the use of the computer to multiply the gain. Romantic versions of the computer criminal "beating the system," hardly stack up with the evidence—they are simply men and women who use the computer to access funds—no more or less "adventuresome" than the robber who steals money with a sawed-off shotgun.

The greatest problem in the study of occupational crime is the lack of research. As with other white-collar crimes, no one has taken much sustained interest in it to really develop the kind of data necessary to understand it either as a type of crime in general or as a subtype with its own unique characteristics. However, with a fuller awareness of the incredible costs of these crimes, especially compared to common crimes, it is clear that more needs to be understood about them and their causes.

Glossary

Bait and Switch   A type of consumer fraud where a company advertises an item at a low price and then attempts to sell a higher-priced item when customers come to buy the cheaper product. Oftentimes, they will have only a few of the lower-priced item, and sell it out before the bulk of the customers enter the store.

Caveat Emptor   A Latin phrase meaning "let the buyer beware."

Computer Crimes   Crimes, usually some form of embezzlement, committed with the aid of a computer.

Consumer Fraud   A type of criminal fraud. It involves fraud in the advertising or sale of products.

Embezzlement   Taking money from an employer, usually from a position of trust.

Employee Theft   Taking goods or services from an employer by an employee.

Lo-Balling   A type of fraud involving unrealistically low estimates for services that are later inflated after the customer has agreed to have the service done.

Nonsharable Problem   A financial problem encountered that a person felt he/she could not share with others and saw the only alternative to be the violation of trust of position, usually culminating in embezzlement.

Occupational Crimes   Crimes occurring in the course of a legitimate occupation for self-gain.

Occupational Role Organization   The relative orientation to one's role as professional or business.

Shrinkage   The total losses in inventory due to carelessness, shoplifting, and employee theft.

Special Price   A form of consumer fraud where the buyer is led to believe that he/she is receiving an unusually low price for goods or services while in fact they are paying higher prices for inferior goods or services.

Questions

1. What is the difference between developing different categories of crime and different theories for each category? Why is a unified criminological theory important?

2. From the best estimates, how widespread and serious are occupational crimes?

3. How does differential association theory explain occupational crimes when the bulk of the associations do not support such crimes as robbery, burglary, and other common crimes?

4. How does the criminal justice system treat occupational criminals? Why don't the bulk of known occupational crimes ever come to the attention of the criminal justice system?

5. What are the rationalizations employed by occupational criminals? Compare delinquent "techniques of neutralization" with "reasons" for occupational crimes.

Notes

1. Gresham Sykes, *The Future of Crime*. (Washington, D.C.: U. S. Government Printing Office, 1980), pp. 44–48.

2. Gilbert Geis and Robert F. Meier, *White-Collar Crime,* rev. ed. (New York: The Free Press, 1977), pp. 16–17.

3. Norman Jaspers, *The Thief in White Collar*. (Philadelphia: J. B. Lippincott, 1960), pp. 11–12.

4. Chamber of Commerce, *White-Collar Crime*. (Washington, D.C. Chamber of Commerce of the United States, 1974), p. 5.

5. J. P. McEvoy, "The Lie Detector Goes into Business," *Forbes* (January 15, 1941): 16.

6. "Retailing: The Thieves Within," *Newsweek* **86** (November 1975): 103.

7. John Conklin, *Illegal but Not Criminal: Business Crime in America*. (Englewood Cliffs, NJ: Prentice-Hall, 1977).

8. Edwin Sutherland, *White Collar Crime*. (New York: The Dryden Press, 1949).

9. Richard A. Cloward and Lloyd Ohlin, *Delinquency and Opportunity*. (New York: The Free Press, 1960).

10. Edwin Sutherland, "White Collar Criminality," *American Sociological Review* **5** (February 1940): 10.

11. Conklin, 1977, 84.

12. C. Wright Mills, "Situated Action and the Vocabulary of Motives," *American Sociological Review* **6** (December 1940): 904–913; Gresham Sykes and David Matza, "Techniques of Neutralization: A Theory of Delinquency," *American Sociological Review* **22** (December 1957): 664–670.

13. Jaspers, 1960, 26.

14. Frank E. Hartung, "A Critique to the Sociological Approach to Crime and Correction" *Law and Contemporary Problems* **23** (1958): 722–725.

15. Conklin, 1977, 84.

16. Jerome Hall, *Theft, Law and Society*, 2nd ed. (Indianapolis:Bobbs-Merrill, 1952), pp. 62–79.

17. Donald R. Cressey, *Other People's Money*, rev. ed. (Glencoe, IL:The Free Press, 1953) p. 20.

18. Ibid.

19. Cressey, 1953, 56–57.

20. Cressey, 1953, 44.

21. Federal Bureau of Investigation, *Crime in the United States, 1979*. (Washington, D.C.: U.S. Government Printing Office, 1980), p. 190.

22. Sutherland, 1949.

23. Howard R. Lewis and Martha E. Lewis, *The Medical Offenders*. (New York: Simon and Schuster, 1970), p. 22.

24. Lewis and Lewis, 1970, 25.

25. Ibid.

26. Richard Quinney, "Occupational Structure and Criminal Behavior: Prescription Violations by Retail Pharmacists," *Social Problems* **11** (Fall 1963): 179–185.

27. Ibid.

28. W. Thomas Porter, Jr. "Computer Raped by Telephone," *The New York Times Magazine*, September 8, 1974, p. 40.

29. Thomas Whiteside, *Computer Capers*. (New York: Mentor, 1978), pp. 16–17.

30. Whiteside, 1978, 15.

31. Jay Becker, "Who Are the Computer Criminals?" *New Scientist*, March 13, 1980.

32. Ibid.

33. Ibid.

34. Christopher Byron, "Dropping By to Keep His Hand In: How the Wells-Fargo Bandit Beat the System," *Time*, March 9, 1981, p. 64.

13

Criminal Organization

What to Look For:

The basic organizational concepts used to explain criminal organization.

The difference between an organization and simply organization in crime.

The nature of delinquent gang organization.

Various types of professional criminals, the concept of independent interdependence, and the changing nature of professional crime.

How criminal syndicates are organized to maximize profit and minimize risk in criminal operations.

Introduction

RGANIZED CRIME COVERS a broad spectrum of criminal behavior. Indeed the previous discussion of occupational crimes could be considered organized crime in certain circumstances. However, the organizations in which the crimes occur are not structured primarily for crime. Thus, this chapter is focused solely on criminal organizations. **Criminal organization** refers to any organization whose primary goal is to commit crime.[1] That covers more than just the Mafia and criminal syndicates. Individuals organized in very small groups, such as a group of pickpockets, also constitute forms of organized crime.

Specifically, in this chapter organized crime will be viewed on a continuum from loosely to highly organized criminal groups. Beginning with simple division of labor with two or more people working together with the goal of committing crime to the full-blown criminal syndicate, we will see how each level of organization increases the profits of crime and reduces the chances of criminal sanction.

Basic Organization in Crime

In examining criminal organization, we must begin with the primary elements of any organization: 1) division of labor, 2) goals, 3) specialized areas and roles, and 4) rules for operation. We then simply apply general sociological concepts of organization to crime.

DIVISION OF LABOR   First of all, organizations have a **division of labor**. This involves the parceling of a large task into many smaller ones relating to a given goal. In its simplest form, two people working together can organize themselves to perform the task of shoplifting. One person acts as a "lookout" and the other acts as the "lifter." The lookout keeps an eye on the store clerks so that the lifter's chances of being caught are less and the lifter can concentrate on stealing. As we look at more sophisticated forms of organization, the division of labor becomes more complex and more efficient. Nevertheless, even the most sophisticated criminal syndicate has the same conceptual division of labor as the shoplifting pair.

ORGANIZATIONAL GOALS   A second major feature of **organizations** is their **goal(s)**. A university's goal is to educate, a hospital's goal is to heal, and a criminal organization's goal is to commit crime. Most criminal organizations have property crimes as their goal—how much they can steal. The shoplifting organization's goal is to shoplift, and it is organized to that end. Its simplicity does not detract from the fact that it *is* structured toward the goal of making shoplifting more profitable and safer.

SPECIALIZED AREAS AND ROLES   Part of Weber's classic formulation of bureaucracy was the inclusion of **specialized roles**.[2] It was reasoned that if people specialized in a single set of specialized duties, they could become far more adept at that specialization than if they tried to learn several different roles which they could perform at a mediocre level. Larger criminal syndicates have finer degrees of specialization—from dealing with legal questions to hijacking—but simpler organizations, such as our shoplifting pair, also follow the principle of specialization. The lifter becomes adept at taking things and concealing them, and the lookout becomes adept at spotting security personnel, and either signaling the lifter or creating a diversion. The lifter's expertise makes it possible for the lookout to develop his/her skills and vice versa.

RULES FOR OPERATIONS   The *rules of an organization* are constructed for its rational functioning. That is, rules are practical devices that will assist the organization in meeting its goals. Most rules specify how different roles will be carried out and the general organizational conduct of its members. For example, a university's rules state the various requirements for graduation as part of the student role, and a hospital has different rules for physicians and nurses. Likewise in criminal organizations, the rules specify the roles of the members and general expectations for everyone. For instance, the Mafia has general rules requiring that anyone arrested for a crime does not reveal organizational secrets or implicate others in the organization. At the same time, there are organizational rules that require the Mafia to supply legal aid to its members who are arrested. These rules help the Mafia protect itself from criminal sanction.

In order to have an overview of criminal organization, Fig. 13.1 shows the basic components graphically. By adding more features to the basic organizational unit, the criminal organization becomes more and more effective and efficient. Fig. 13.2 shows the authority structure of a Mafia (or

Fig. 13.1   Basic Criminal Organization

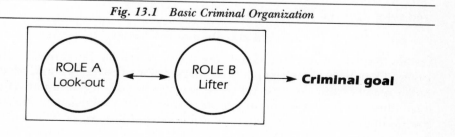

Fig. 13.2   Authority Structure of the Mafia

Boss
|
Staff positions
|
Underboss
|
Lieutenant
|
Staff positions
|
Soldiers

★ ★ ★ ★ ★ ★ ★ ★ ★ ★

Workers

Customers

Source: Donald R. Cressey, *The Theft of the Nation.* (New York: Harper & Row, 1969), p. 146.

La Cosa Nostra) "family." However, criminal organization does not automatically mean a criminal syndicate. In order to examine the full range of criminal organization, we will begin by looking at "outlaw" groups, then "professional" criminals, and finally criminal syndicates. First, though, it is important to differentiate between "organization" and "*an* organization."

Criminal Organization and a Criminal Organization

As we saw with the shoplifting pair, there was an organized, coordinated effort to breaking the law. However, there was not *an* organization. That is, the shoplifting pair did not constitute a minicriminal syndicate, but instead we are assuming that two or more people, such as juveniles, worked together to make shoplifting more profitable and less risky. (It is possible for an ongoing syndicate to organize itself around shoplifting, but typically shoplifters who work in organized coordination do so only occasionally.) Likewise, in examining the professional criminal, we will see that there is a good deal of organized efforts in their crime work, but they do not belong to a single organization in the same way as a juvenile gang member, outlaw biker, or Mafia soldier does. When we talk about *an* organization, we refer to a single, ongoing entity with a limited and recognizable membership; and when we talk about "organization," we simply refer to crime that occurs with a division of labor, criminal goals, specialized roles, and rules for interaction.

Criminal and Delinquent Gangs

On the less organized end of the continuum of criminal organization are *gangs*. They have the elements of an organizational structure and identifiable membership, and we can refer to them as *an* organization. However, the nature of that organization is somewhat problematic. The following definition by Miller, though, is a good starting point:

A gang is a group of recurrently associating individuals with identifiable leadership and internal organization, identifying with or claiming control over territory in the community, and engaging either individually or collectively in violent or other forms of illegal behavior.[3]

Miller's definition was developed around youth gangs, but it is broad enough to include far more criminal organizations. For the purposes of our analysis, we can use Miller's definition to differentiate gangs from the looser organization of professional criminals and the tighter organization of criminal syndicates. Key to Miller's definition of gangs is that the group is in recurrent association—that is, they hang around with one another most of the time. This element differentiates gangs from other criminal groups in that professional criminals and members of criminal syndicates are not in daily or even frequent contact with the association as a whole or a large segment of it. For example, a Mafia member may run the refuse collection business in a given city and be a recognized member of a Mafia "family"; however, since a single family can be spread over several cities—even states—not only would a daily gathering be logistically difficult, it would be dangerous for business. On the other hand, one of the

The fellowship of the gang is its major attraction, but the same strong ties often lead to violence. An offense against one member is taken to be an offense against all, leading to attacks on rival gangs.

major attractions of a gang is the recurrent association and fellowship of members.

In order to simplify matters, our discussion of gangs will focus on two major forms of criminal gangs—delinquent youth gangs and motorcycle gangs. Both groups fit into Miller's definition, and they constitute the main types of criminal groups on this level of organization.

Criminal and Violent Behavior

One of the most important features of gangs is their violent behavior. As we saw in Chapter 10, gang violence is often a means of establishing or maintaining a "reputation." Gangs are also involved in rapes, and they tend to engage in violent property crimes, mainly robberies/muggings, more so than professional criminals or syndicates. To a large extent this is due to the fact that gangs are not organized around property crimes or maximizing profits so much as they are around mutual interests—such as motorcycles—or neighborhood propinquity. There is minimal organization in their criminal activities, and most gang warfare usually consists of either hit-and-run attacks or melees.

The most organized types of criminal gangs do involve a more sophisticated kind of crime. For example, some gangs become involved in the smuggling and sales of drugs. One branch of the California Hell's Angels motorcycle gang has been involved in the national shipment and sales of amphetamines and heroin. Similarly, older members of some San Diego and Tijuana gangs are involved in international drug trafficking. To some extent, a gang will reflect the surrounding adult criminal milieu. In Spergel's study of gangs, he found that juvenile gangs in stable communities with organized rackets would emulate their adult counterparts and focus on organized property crimes, while youth in disorganized communities where there were little or no adult criminal syndicates, would tend to develop more individualistic marks of distinction by engaging in gang fights.[4]

Gang Organization

The defining organizational features of a gang are functional role-division, chain-of-command, and identifiable leadership.[5] However, there is so much variation in gang structure that even the defining features fail to adequately cover all the gang styles. Some biker gangs have an organizational structure and meeting format that is almost a model of Roberts Rules of Order, and others, while clearly a gang in association and behavior patterns, have only informal leaders at best and virtually no structure at all. Similarly with juvenile gangs, some gangs reflect a good deal of structure, and others very little. However, the typical gang has a relatively vague organizational structure. Keiser described a more organized gang structure in the Vice Lord Nation, a black Chicago youth gang:

Vice Lords' Organization

1. *President* Presides over meetings, sometimes decides whether to fight a rival gang, responsible for leading raids. Symbolizes group's power and is main target of rivals in gang warfare.

2. *Vice-president* President's assistant, takes over if president is arrested or incapacitated.

3. *War counselor* Gang's version of Secretary of Defense. Main figure in decisions to fight other gangs, initiates full scale fights, and main advisor to president in all matters involving fighting.

4. *Other officers* The gang also has a secretary-treasurer, gunkeeper, and sergeant-at-arms. The gunkeeper's (sometimes called "armorer") job is to take care of and hide the gang's weapons.[6]

The Vice Lords' organization changed, however, and was governed by a "board" of executive officers, absorbing all of the previous officers' positions. Other gangs appear to be less structured, especially those on the West Coast.

The most useful way to understand gang structure is in terms of neighborhood groupings. Juveniles living in a given neighborhood or "barrio," are part of that area's group. Some in the area "claim" or identify with a gang or more violent and criminal element of the neighborhood. Certain other groups in other areas are defined as enemies—for any number of reasons—lending cohesion to the gang and a "protection" rationale for its existence. The most active or "core" members are those who spend the most time with the gang, commit the most crimes, and are involved in the most violence. Various cliques within the gang identify with certain informal leaders, giving the gang multiple leadership and nonrival factions. Age and sex groupings tend to be nonstratified in that younger members and girls can be accorded the same status as the older male members. For example, Keiser quotes one of the older Vice Lord members:

The roughest boys I ever met, they were between the ages of 13 and 15—Lil' Lord, Rough-head and them. They was the Midgets—the Midget Lords. And these were the baddest boys I ever went up against! What happened, they beat up one of the Senior Lords, a stud called Dough Belly. And Cave Man wouldn't even mess with the Midget Lords 'cause they had so many guns. We didn't know where they got the guns, but they used to bring them around and give them to us.[7]

Thus, unlike some organizations, where seniority is given status, in some gangs, the younger members compete for status with the older members—and often achieve a higher status than the older members.

One of the more interesting aspects of gang organization is the nature of leadership. Most researchers agree that there is more than a single leader in most gangs, but there are important differences in interpretations of what this multiple leadership signifies. On the one hand Yablonsky argued that the multiple leadership represented the inability of gangs to organize an efficient gang structure.[8] Miller, on the other hand, saw multiple gang leadership as a survival feature. If one leader were arrested, killed, or in some other way incapacitated, another leader could take over and maintain the gang. This, Miller suggests, is a strength in the gang's organization, reflecting not disorganization and instability, but rather an understanding of the gang's survival requirements.[9]

As a final observation on gang organization, Miller differentiates between **street groups** and **gangs**. The former is an unstructured clique involved in petty crimes of a nonviolent nature, while the latter is a more structured group, with strong territorial claims and a willingness to engage in violence, especially against other gangs.[10] This distinction, while important to clarify the nature of gangs as opposed to any group of juveniles who engage in delinquency, is still a bit too formalized to be accurate. Barrio groups in Southern California engage in violence, identify with their group as a "gang," and generally do everything else other gangs do. However, they tend to be almost wholly unstructured; membership while not unrestricted is apparently "open" to anyone in the barrio and there are varying degrees of involvement with the "gang" depending on the situation. Thus, while some gangs have a good deal of structure, other ones that meet all other criteria for a gang tend to be loosely structured. This does not mean that gangs with a loose formal structure are weak, for the gangs often operate on the basis of a strong tradition in the neighborhood or barrio. Rather, it simply means that something other than formal structure is the basis for the gang's solidarity.

Territoriality

Another feature of gangs is their loyalty to a given area—their "turf," "dirt," "barrio," "set," or "place." This is especially true with juvenile gangs, whose area of operation is relatively small and clearly bounded. Older gangs—particularly motorcycle gangs and car clubs—have a looser conception of territory, and being highly mobile, cover a more general area and do not have the same restrictions on outsiders. However, for the typical gang youth, the territory is the main focal point of their gang activity. Findings from Moore's research on Chicano gangs in Los Angeles indicated that "barrio" had the dual meaning of both "neighborhood" and "gang."[11]

Organizationally, then, gangs tend to be grouped around ecological areas. Gangs, therefore, tend to be comprised of a single ethnic/racial group and there may even be familial ties in gang membership. The same ecological/cultural forces worked in the formation of many adult criminal organizations. The Mexican Mafia and Nuestro Familia as well as the Italian Mafia had similar roots in youth gang territory loyalties. However, the adult organizations shed neighborhood loyalties in their structure, while for youth gangs it is a major part of their group. (However, adult organizations do carve out general areas of operations.)

Professional Criminals

The group of law violators known as **professional criminals** is a difficult one to pinpoint. Most criminologists define a professional criminal as "anyone who makes the majority of his/her living from crime." However, such a definition would include every type of criminal from junkies who steal everything they can to buy dope to Mafia chieftains. A more important element of professional crime is what Edwin Sutherland referred to as participation in a criminal behavior system. Such a system was described as follows:

> The behavior system of crime may be described by its three principal characteristics. First, a behavior system in crime is not merely an aggregation of individual criminal acts. It is an integrated unit, which includes, in addition to the individual acts, the codes, traditions, espirit de corps, social relationships among the direct participants, and indirect participation of many other persons. It is thus essentially a group way of life. . . . Second, the behavior which occurs in a behavior system is not unique to any particular individual. It is common behavior. Third, while common and joint participation in the system is the essential characteristic of a behavior system, it can frequently be defined by the feelings of identification of those who participate in it. If the participants feel that they belong together for this purpose, they do belong together.[12]

Sutherland's depiction of a behavior system, while important for one part of a professional criminal's life, is still too broad: as we saw in our discussion of gangs, gang members are clearly part of a criminal behavior system too.

Besides their participation in a criminal behavior system we will focus on professional criminals in terms of: 1) specialized skills, 2) training or apprenticeship, 3) status; and 4) organization. First, a professional criminal has specialized skills in some kind of crime such as safe-cracking, fencing, forgery, or some other nonoccupational or noncorporate crime. Secondly, professional criminals have had training in their line of crime by a more experienced criminal. Third, a professional is recognized as such by other criminals in the behavior system. Finally, professional criminals are part of a well-structured system of communication among other professional criminals.

Specialization

A prime characteristic of the "professional" criminal has been his specialized abilities to commit certain crimes. For example, confidence men and women have incredible skills in "conning" people out of their money. Occasionally the newspapers will run stories about people who gave confidence men and women their life's savings, and will ask, "How could anyone be so stupid?" However, it is the skill of con artists to gain others' trust and take advantage of any weaknesses they have. For example, the "pigeon drop" is a favorite of the confidence women. Basically, it involves setting up the victim by having one confidence woman drop a wallet in front of the **mark**. When the victim picks up the wallet, a second confidence women comes along and "finds" the wallet at the same time as the victim. The confidence woman then convinces the mark that they should try and find the owner of the wallet, but failing that they should split up the money in the wallet—a considerable sum. However, in order to "show good faith," the mark is talked into withdrawing an equal sum of money from his/her savings account for the con woman to hold. After some fast talking and switching of money, the victim is left holding the wallet full of shredded newspaper, never to see the con artist again. Such a scheme seems so flawed that it would rarely work, but it works all the time since the con men and women perfect it and their skills in executing it. Similarly, cracking safes, forging currency, checks, and art takes considerable skill.

There is some evidence, though, that the specialized professional criminal is being replaced by the **hustler**. Research on professional criminals indicates that professional criminals are becoming disillusioned with the state of the "art"—said one, "Professional theft is just like the rest of the world: kind of falling apart."[13] Rather than specialize and go through extensive training or apprenticeship, the new orientation is opportunistic and situational. Gould describes it as follows:

> To "hustle" is to be persistently on the lookout for an opportunity to make an illegal buck. A criminal "on the hustle" will do pretty much whatever is required; he will consider whatever comes up.[14]

Because of opportunity the hustler has replaced the specialist. In specializing, a professional criminal will miss many opportunities to make a score, not only in terms of what he or she may encounter directly, but also in terms of contacts. If a professional criminal is known to specialize only in certain crimes, he or she will not be contacted to participate in a lucrative crime outside that specialization. Therefore, while there is still a respect and need for specialized skills, the broader those skills, the more a professional criminal can make. As Walker notes,

Hustling does not necessarily mean simply looking for something to steal. It means moving around bars and making connections, contacting other professionals to see "what's up," reading the papers to see if there are any obvious criminal opportunities, contacting fences to see if any special orders have been placed, and so on. To hustle is to use every bit of knowledge about crime and criminals, and to "straight" world and "straight" people, in order to make money—with no holds barred.[15]

Organization

Along with a change in specialization, the organization of professional criminals may have changed as well. Earlier studies of professional criminals indicate more cohesion, described by Mauer as a **mob**. Walker characterizes Mauer's conception as,

". . . neither a permanent group nor a group pulled together for a specific set of acts. It might be characterized as a "group in flux." Membership tends to be stable, but members may drop out at will or may be jailed, and they are replaced with other individuals from the racket. Members must be loyal to the mob, but this loyalty is business-based and independent of whatever personal bonds might prevail among members.[16]

However, the modern professional criminal has a much looser organization. In describing the "organization" of professional criminals, Harry King, a former "boxman" (safe-cracker) explained it in terms of "attachments." Professional criminals knew one another by reputation, connections through other professional criminals, and prison contacts. In discussing these contacts, King explains,

Thieves have attachments every place. If I have some stuff to sell I can't drop it with a fence in the East unless I know somebody. Well, I know a guy that works for a syndicate in Kansas City. One other guy I know don't work for the syndicate no more but is connected with it because he used to and the fence would accept his word. He lives in Cleveland. I'd just go to him and tell him, "Hey, Pete, I got some ice here I want to dump. You can make a few bucks, if you want."[17]

Similarly, the hustler, while connected to a network of fellow hustlers, is not part of a single organization—or syndicate. Since the "mob" concept implied loyalty to a certain group, it no longer applies to professional criminals:

"present-day relationships between professional criminals . . . are not structured by strong ongoing group relationship, but are structured primarily by the crimes that professional criminals commit."[18]

The most accurate depiction of professional criminals' organization is an **independent-interdependence**. Professional criminals are independent of a single organization, but they are dependent on one another for information and specialized skills. For example, in describing the others he worked with in cracking safes, Harry King explained that he used a "point-man" and a "fence." The point-man's role was to provide King with information regarding a target, including the contents of a safe, its probable value, when it was most likely to be full, a diagram or blueprint of the building, and security arrangements. Harry's role as the boxman was to open the safe and steal the contents, and then sell noncash valuables to the fence. The fence would pay the boxman for the merchandise and sell it for a profit.[19] Each was independent of the other, but at the same time dependent on the other, thus an "independent-interdependence."

> *Point-man* (Sets up the score)
> *Boxman* (Makes the hit)
> *Fence* (Buys the stolen goods)

Each is independent but part of an organized effort.

Types of Professional Criminals

There are several different types of professional criminals, each having his or her own speciality. The hustler may have many such skills. We will briefly examine the most common types of professional criminals.

THE THIEF   The term "thief" actually applies to different types of burglars and thieves. At the top of the hierarchy is the "boxman"—one who has skills in opening safes; and at the bottom is the "booster" or shoplifter, who is only rarely considered a "professional" by other thieves. Thieves generally prefer to specialize in certain areas. For example, one boxman preferred to operate supermarket safes, while another may prefer private residences. Others will specialize in stealing stocks, bonds, and securities, while others prefer jewels, automobiles or appliances. However, with an increase in "hustling," more thieves are branching out to a wider variety of targets and goods stolen.

THE CON ARTIST   The confidence "man" is becoming more the confidence "woman," but among professional criminals, the con artist of either gender is held in fairly high esteem.[20] In Mauer's study of confidence games, two major types of operations were noted. First is the "big con" or "big score" that involves a long-range plan to take a mark of several thousand dollars. Typically, the big con involves several confidence men and women working together to convince the "mark" (victim) that he or she can make a lot of money at little risk, usually involving something a little shady. For example, the con artist will convince the mark that he or she has "inside information" on a pending stock transaction, a fixed horse race, or some similar fast money scheme. The con artist manipulates the mark into asking, even begging, to be included in the scheme and giving the confidence man or woman large sums of money to "invest." After the con artist has bilked the victim, the victim is "cooled out"—made to believe that the con artist lost money as well, and for some reason beyond everyone's control the deal "went sour." This often keeps the victim from reporting the crime since he or she is unaware that a crime has been committed.[21] However, even in cases where the victim is aware of the con, they will often feel so stupid for being suckered, they will not report it.

"Short cons," on the other hand, are confidence games that are—as the name implies—of a short duration, involve minimal skills and planning, and yield relatively little. For example, a popular short con involves two con artists entering a cafe. The first will buy a cup of coffee and pay for it with a large bill on which he has written some note. A second con artist will then do the same thing, except pay with a small bill, and claiming he had given the cashier a larger bill, citing the note written on the larger bill left by the first con artist, pocket the extra change. Since these short cons require minimal skill and training, those who practice them are rarely considered "professional."

THE STICK-UP MAN   The stick-up man is a professional robber. However, according to one professional criminal, the stick-up man is quickly losing his professional status due to the rash of armed robberies of liquor stores, small markets, and gas stations where the take is small and the risk almost as high as a more favorable target. Those stick-up men who rob supermarkets, banks, and similar targets where a large "score" is likely, and are generally successful in doing so, are considered "professional."

FORGERS AND COUNTERFEITERS   The final category of professional criminals is a more difficult one to classify. First, writing bad or forged checks is practiced by all different kinds of professional criminals, regardless of their specialty.[22] Therefore, many different kinds of professional criminals practice it, and it is especially characteristic of the hustler. Second, in studies of forgers, Lemert found that they were not a part of the world of professional criminals, but most were typically "loners" who worked neither with other forgers nor depended on the specialties of other professional criminals. This is not to say that "professional" check forgers do not exist, but rather it is more likely to be either part of general hustling or committed by loners, who, while "systematic," are not a part of the professionals' world.

Counterfeiters, on the other hand, are considered professionals in that they have unique skills in creating bogus money and are part of the net-

Because of the skills involved in counterfeiting money, counterfeiters are considered "professionals." Here, a Secret Service agent examines sheets of one such professional's handywork.

work of professional criminals. They rely on their assocations for passing the counterfeit bills, usually "selling" the bogus money for real money.

As a final comment on the "professionals," Donald Cressey's observations are important. Cressey noted that the term "professional" has been misused to the point of including numerous careers, from hairdressers to police officers; we may, as a result, do a disservice to not only the language, but also the reality of crime by referring to career criminals as "professionals."[23] What we are really dealing with are men and women who are slightly better at committing crime than the "common" criminal.

The "skills" involved, while clearly skills to those who do not know of them, are relatively minimal. Learning to steal, cheat, and lie on a regular basis, while certainly not limited to the career criminal, is hardly something that should be overdignified with the label "professional."

The Crime Syndicate

Outside of corporate crime, the highest level of organized crime is the **crime syndicate**. Its organization, operation and profits make it the most powerful criminal group there is. What it is and how it operates is the topic of debate in criminology. Criminological discussion of the Mafia has brought charges that the researchers are prejudiced against the Italians. At the same time, lack of research on crime syndicates has created criticism that criminologists are negligent in their research efforts. However, noting that the Mafia is composed mainly of Italians, especially those of Southern Italian and Sicilian heritage, is simply an observation of fact and no more prejudicial than pointing out that the Ku Klux Klan is predominately composed of white, Anglo-Saxon, Protestants (Wasps). Most WASP Americans have nothing to do with the Klan as most Italian Americans have nothing to do with the Mafia. As for the criticism of ignoring the Mafia, criminologists have not so much ignored it as they have been unable to gather data about it. One of the ways in which the Mafia and other criminal syndicates protect themselves is to keep information from outsiders. However as Gordon Hawkins has noted,

> In the end, it is difficult to resist the conclusion that one is not dealing with an empirical phenomenon at all, but with an article of faith, transcending the contingent particularity of everyday experience and logically unassailable; one of those reassuring popular demonologies that, William Buckley has remarked, the successful politician has to cherish and perserve and may, in the end, come to believe.[24]

In other words, if criminologists characterize the Mafia as "unresearchable," they can postulate various facts about the Mafia based on little empirical evidence. There is not sufficient data to reject the idea of a national crime syndicate such as the Mafia, and on the other hand, there is confusing evidence as to exactly what the Mafia is. From the piecemeal evidence we have, however, there is some kind of criminal syndicate variously called the "Mafia," "Cosa Nostra" and simply "The Outfit." We will concentrate on how the organization operates in terms of its structural components, leaving aside some of the finer details regarding its cohesion and the individuals involved.

The Hierarchy of a Criminal Syndicate

To begin our examination of criminal syndicates, we will look at an organized crime "family," and discuss the various roles involved. Fig. 13.3

Fig. 13.3 An Organized Crime Family

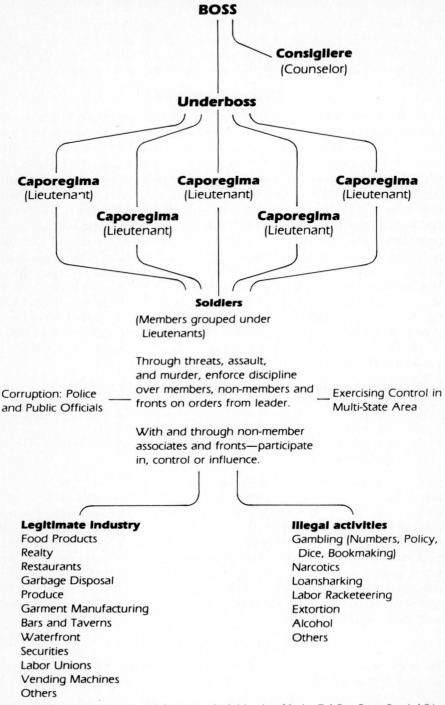

BOSS

Consigliere
(Counselor)

Underboss

Caporegima
(Lieutenant)

Caporegima
(Lieutenant)

Caporegima
(Lieutenant)

Caporegima
(Lieutenant)

Caporegima
(Lieutenant)

Soldiers
(Members grouped under
Lieutenants)

Corruption: Police
and Public Officials

Through threats, assault,
and murder, enforce discipline
over members, non-members and
fronts on orders from leader.

Exercising Control in
Multi-State Area

With and through non-member
associates and fronts—participate
in, control or influence.

Legitimate Industry
Food Products
Realty
Restaurants
Garbage Disposal
Produce
Garment Manufacturing
Bars and Taverns
Waterfront
Securities
Labor Unions
Vending Machines
Others

Illegal activities
Gambling (Numbers, Policy,
   Dice, Bookmaking)
Narcotics
Loansharking
Labor Racketeering
Extortion
Alcohol
Others

Source: President's Commission on Law Enforcement and Administration of Justice, *Task Force Report: Organized Crime.* (Washington, D.C.: U.S. Government Printing Office, 1967), p. 9.

shows how a Mafia family is organized, and the various legal and illegal activities it controls.

Given the organization in Fig. 13.3, we see several levels of control, beginning with the "Boss" at the top, and moving down to the individual "soldiers" who are the bosses of their own little rackets. The organizational hierarchy controls who will be involved in the various legal and illegal enterprises and how territories will be divided up to settle disputes. This structure minimizes losses due to fights over the control of rackets, infringement on territory, and the overall negative publicity and accompanying law enforcement attention that comes with organized crime warfare.

The important aspect of organized crime, though, is in the positions and roles that make criminal syndicates rational organizations. By examining the various levels of rationality for a successful criminal organization, we will see how these syndicates accumulate wealth and power.

The Commission

On a national level, organized crime maximizes control and coordination over its operations by the existence of a commission made up of representatives from the various individual syndicates. The commission operates in the same way that an individual boss controls the operations of a single crime syndicate. The commission's main function is to see that the various crime syndicates do not come into conflict with one another, leading to gang warfare. By being able to tap the power of several crime syndicates, the commission has power over any single syndicate that attempts to usurp power over another syndicate.

The commission's role is a purely practical one in terms of maximizing profits. Like a cartel made up of legitimate businesses, the criminal cartel represented by the commission reduces competition and conflict that diminishes profits. If the various crime syndicates are fighting, they cannot control outside competitors—whether legitimate or illegitimate—from moving in on their enterprises. Accordingly, they risk coming to the untender attention of high levels of law enforcement.[25]

The Corrupter

The next important role in crime syndicate is that of the corrupter. Cressey describes the corrupter as follows:

> The person occupying this position bribes, buys, intimidates, threatens, negotiates, and sweet-talks himself into a relationship with police, public officials, and anyone else who might help "family" members secure and maintain immunity from arrest, prosecution, and punishment.[26]

In terms of a position in a rational crime organization, the corrupter makes crime safe for the syndicate by greatly reducing the chances that a member will be arrested. More important, perhaps, the organization can operate such lucrative illegal operations as gambling without being raided or having their customers fear arrest. Corruption of public officials not only helps the organization avoid prosecution and investigation for its crime, but also by having corrupted public officials, syndicate-controlled "legitimate" businesses can obtain lucrative public contracts.

The corrupter works in many ways. Most typically, a corruptee is simply "bought" through bribery, but also the corrupter uses every other possible means of persuasion from charm to blackmail. A number of office holders were put into office by the crime syndicate, either through financial contributions or organizing votes. Once in office, they support legislation, contract placement, and anti-crime campaigns in a manner beneficial to the crime syndicate.[27]

The Enforcer

One of the problems with criminal organizations is that they are full of criminals, and the syndicate must have some way of controlling its members. Like any other organization, the Mafia has a set of rules and guidelines for its operation. Cardinal rules include not stealing from the organization or informing on fellow members or the organization as a whole. However, since the organization is involved in numerous lucrative businesses, it is tempting for its members to steal. Similarly, even with the protection afforded by corrupted law enforcement officials and public office holders, members of the organization are occasionally arrested, often by Federal law enforcement officers who have not been corrupted. Once arrested, there is the temptation to "make a deal" with the prosecutor's office in return for leniency. The deals usually include providing information damaging to the syndicate.

The **enforcer** makes certain that the rules are followed. He does this by punishing rule-violators.

There is not the same legal protection afforded by the criminal courts, and punishment—ranging from fines to beatings and killings—is swift and certain. Thus, while syndicate criminals think nothing of breaking the laws of larger society, they are very cautious in breaking the rules of the organization. As a result, the position of the enforcer helps to keep the organization's operation profitable by enforcing the rules.[28]

Strategic Planner, Tactical Planner, and Task Force Guide

To summarize the positions in a criminal organization they include a "public affairs or lobbying department (corrupter–corruptee), a justice department (enforcer), and a 'trade' or 'industry' department (confederation)," the last governed by a commission.[29] None of these positions, however, really deals with actually planning or carrying out crimes—they all involve controlling and protecting the criminal syndicate. This next set of roles are positions for actually committing crime in a rational and profitable manner.

STRATEGIC PLANNERS   To commit crimes that are both safe and lucrative, it is necessary to plan a strategy that will take the organization on a course that avoids crimes such as residential burglaries and small robberies, which are unsafe and arouse public resentment. Organizations with strategic planners can better pursue the safe and lucrative kinds of crime. For example, gambling is a safe and lucrative crime, since those arrested for the offense are rarely given stiff fines or penalties and it is profitable. Once the strategic planner has found the best kinds of crime for the organization, he looks for other ones that are similarly safe and lucrative. Organized crime activity which deals with forged and stolen stocks, bonds, and securities is an example of strategic planners having found new areas where crime is safe and profitable. Senator Charles H. Percy of Illinois testified ". . . that $1.2 billion in securities are either stolen or missing and that the bulk of them are being utilized in illegal operations throughout the world."[30] One of the reasons organized crime became involved in the theft of securities, besides their value, was that the strategic planners found that there was a ready market for them by legitimate bankers. Senator Percy further noted in testimony concerning the theft and fencing of stolen securities:

> From the standpoint of requiring assistance and cooperation from the banking institutions, one man, Wuensche, testified that he had a network of 25 what he called friendly bankers spread throughout the country who would accept his stolen securities and use them as collateral for loans.[31]

Since such a criminal enterprise would not be readily noted by the average crook, strategic planners play a vital role in criminal organizations in discovering and exploiting such illegal ways to make hugh profits with minimal risks.

TACTICAL PLANNERS   Tactical planners are similar to operation managers.[32] Whatever crime is chosen by a criminal organization, based on the assessment of the strategic planner, the tactical planner's job is to determine how that crime can be committed in the safest and most profitable manner. He plans the operations, chooses those to be involved and decides what the target will be. Cressey explains the role as follows.:

> . . . anyone holding a tactical planner position continually tries to improve the odds, no matter how favorable they are. For example, tactical planners have learned enough about the vagaries of law enforcement and criminal justice administration to know that the law looks with disfavour on a robber

who fails to do a good, clean job of it. In assembling a crew of robbers then, they are likely to take into account the fact that when a robber puts off an appearance of a coolness, toughness, and business efficiency, waves his club or gun in a menacing manner, and as a result receives the loot, criminal justice officials are not likely to drop all other pressing business in order to find him, and are likely to reward him with a light sentence in the unlikely event he is caught and convicted.[33]

Thus, while the strategic planner finds the general area of crime that is the safest and most profitable, the tactical planner finds the means to best commit the crime.

TASK FORCE GUIDE   The bottom level of a criminal organization is the task force guide. The person in this position actually leads or guides a task force in committing a crime to see that everything goes according to the outlines set forth by the tactical planner.[34] Sometimes the tactical planner doubles in the role of the task force guide, but the positions are analytically separate. The task force guide is equivalent to the "foreman" in the same way that the tactical planner is analogous to the "operations manager." By having a task force guide, the organization further reduces the chances of being caught because someone did not do their job properly.

Making Crime Pay

The old adage "crime doesn't pay" is only applicable in situations where the crime is disorganized, common, and irrational. Robbing convenience stores does not "pay," since the risks of getting caught are great and the profit small. Going to prison for ten years for robbing $30 from a small market is simply stupid. However, running a multi-million dollar gambling operation under circumstances where the police will not make raids, the prosecutors will not prosecute, and the judges will not sentence is not only profitable but also smart.

The origins of organized crime in America help tell us how and why it is successful. During Prohibition, the forerunners of the contemporary crime organizations made their stake on illegal alcohol. The public—the "average citizen"—poured billions of dollars into organized crime by patronizing "speakeasies" (illegal drinking places). Thus, because of the willingness of a large number of citizens to buy the goods and services of organized crime was it possible for the crime syndicates to grow and gain power. After the repeal of Prohibition, organized crime turned to other offenses that the public would support financially—prostitution, gambling, and drugs. They also began taking over various legitimate businesses, gaining virtual monopolies in the area of refuse collection and in some cases vending machine operations; however, their base remained illegal enterprises that were safe and profitable.

Today, organized crime still flourishes, and it is done on the basis of a certain hypocrisy. Legislators and the public seem to be content to keep laws on the books prohibiting behavior in which a large portion of society is willing to partake. These illegal monies are used to corrupt public officials and the justice system, further strengthening organized crime. Ultimately, the "average citizen" who finances organized crime is responsible for it. Crime syndicates depend on the working man and woman who not only spend money on the illegal goods and services they offer but also vote to keep these goods and services illegal. The so-called legitimate businessman, who buys stolen merchandise from organized criminals at a "good price," and the banker who uses stolen or forged securities for collateral also support the crime syndicate. Therefore, even though we cannot say that organized crime is the "fault" of the public, were it not for their financial support, it could not exist.

SUMMARY

In this chapter we have looked at the many levels of criminal organization: the gang, the professional criminal network, and the crime syndicate. Like any other organizations, criminal ones are generally more efficient and profitable than lone criminals. Delinquent gangs can do more violence than a single bully, networks of professional criminals can steal more than lone thiefs, and crime syndicates amass far more power than even the most frightening and talented criminal.

In the context of criminal organizations, crime becomes very much a "social" phenomenon, to be studied and understood in much the same way as any other group or organization. The "bureaucratization" of criminal organizations makes them more rational and efficient in the same way an organization that makes television sets, bathtubs or automobiles has higher profits through good organizational practices. Since power is usually linked to money, the better structured a criminal organization, the more power it wields in both legal and illegal spheres.

Perhaps the greatest irony is that the highest levels of criminal organization thrive on the willing cooperation of their victims. The "straight citizen" who pours money into illegal organized crime enterprises is victimized by corrupted police departments, prosecutors' offices, court systems, and political bodies. In this respect, the citizenry "gets what it deserves."

Glossary

Commission   The governing body of several organized crime "families."

Corrupter   A role in organized crime to bribe law enforcement and/or legislative officials for the benefit of a crime syndicate.

Crime Syndicate   An organization whose primary goal is to make profits by criminal means.

Criminal Organization   Any group that uses a division of labor, specialized roles, and a set of rules for the purpose of committing crime.

Division of Labor   Breaking down a larger task into component parts that are accomplished by individuals working in concert with one another.

Enforcer   A role in organized crime that ensures that the rules of the organization are followed. Typically, the enforcer uses coercive measures.

Gangs   A loosely organized group, in recurrent association, that claims dominance over territory and engages in criminal activity as a major group activity.

Hustler   A newer type of professional criminal who does not specialize in any particular crime but in several different ones. Hustlers are more opportunistic in choosing crimes than the traditional professional criminal.

Independent-Interdependence   The relationship among professional criminals, wherein each is independent but works in concert with other professional criminals.

Mark   The intended victim in confidence games.

Mob   A group of professional criminals that commits crimes together on somewhat regular basis.

Organizational Goals   The stated objectives of an organization.

Professional Criminal   A criminal who specializes in a given crime, has had training in committing crimes, and has refined skills in that crime.

Specialization   A feature of professional criminals. Refers to becoming proficient in a single crime.

Street Groups   A relatively disorganized clique, typically juvenille, that is involved in petty crimes. It is distinct from a gang in that such goups do not claim territory or engage in violence.

Territoriality   Claiming dominance over a certain area. This is characteristic of gangs.

Questions

1. What are basic elements of organized crime? How can these concepts be applied to all levels of criminal organization?

2. What characteristics define a gang? How is gang association linked to violent crime?

3. How have the characteristics of the professional criminal changed? Why wouldn't the hustler be considered a professional criminal by older standards?

4. What is meant by an "independent-interdependence" among professional criminals? How does this form of organization compare to crime syndicates?

5. What roles in the Mafia and similar crime syndicates make it the most profitable of all criminal organizations?

Notes

1. Donald R. Cressey, *Criminal Organization: Its Elementary Forms*. (New York: Harper & Row, 1969).

2. Max Weber, *The Theory of Social and Economic Development*, trans. by A. M. Henderson and Talcott Parsons. (New York: Oxford University Press, 1947).

3. Walter Miller, "Violence by Youth Gangs and Youth Groups as a Crime Problem in Major American Cities," (Washington, D.C.: U.S. Department of Justice, December 1975).

4. Irving Spergel, *Racketville, Slumtown and Haulberg*. (Chicago: University of Chicago Press, 1964).

5. Miller, 1975.

6. R. Lincoln Keiser, *The Vice Lords*. (New York: Holt, Rinehart and Winston, 1969), p. 17.

7. Keiser, 1969, 16.

8. Lewis Yablonsky, *The Violent Gang*. (Baltimore: Penguin, 1963).

9. Walter Miller, "White Gangs" *Trans-action* (September 1969): 11–26.

10. Joan Moore, *Homeboys*. (Philadelphia: Temple University Press, 1978), p. 35.

11. Andrew Walker, "Sociology and Professional Crime," in Abraham S. Blumberg, ed. *Current Perspectives on Criminal Behavior*, 2nd ed. (New York: Alfred A. Knopf, 1981).

12. Edwin Sutherland and Donald R. Cressey, *Criminolgy*, 10th ed. (Philadelphia: Lippincott, 1978).

13. Harry King, *Boxman*. (New York: Harper & Row, 1972).

14. Leroy Gould *et al., Crime as a Profession*. (Washington, D.C.: U.S. Government Printing Office, 1966), p. 25.

15. Walker, 1981, 166.

16. Walker, 1981, 161.

17. King, 1972, 89.

18. Gould *et al.*, 1966, 34.

19. King, 1972.

20. King, 1972, 70.

21. Erving Goffman, "On Cooling the Mark Out: Some Adaptations to Failure," *Psychiatry* **15**:415–463.

22. King, 1972.

23. Cressey, 1972, 44–45.

24. Gordon Hawkins, "God and the Mafia," *The Public Interst* **14** (Winter 1969): 24–38, 40–51.

25. Cressey, 1972.

26. Cressey, 1972, 36–37.

27. Ibid.

28. Ibid.

29. Cressey, 1972, 52.

30. Senator Charles H. Percy, "Organized Crime in the Securities Market," in John E. Conklin, ed., *The Crime Establishment*. (Englewood Cliffs, NJ: Prentice-Hall, 1973).

31. Ibid.

32. Cressey, 1972.

33. Cressey, 1972, 66–67.

34. Cressey, 1972, 68.

14

Corporate and Governmental Crime

What to Look For:

The concepts of corporate and governmental crime and how the two are interrelated.

How the Sherman Antitrust Law was an attempt to preserve free enterprise.

The nature of laws regulating corporate behavior and how these laws are administered.

Ways in which corporate crime might be controlled.

How the government commits crimes and the different motives for such crimes.

Introduction

OMEONE IS CLEARLY AWARE of their victimization in a mugging, and even in confidence games and occupational crimes, a person usually realizes that he or she has been "taken." However, the kind of crimes we will discuss in this chapter only rarely come to light. For the most part, the public is victimized and never realizes it. These are corporate and governmental crimes which involve a multitude of very costly expenses—crimes that take money from victims the same way as do muggings, burglaries, and forged checks. For example, during one corporate crime spree that lasted almost a decade, an illegal price-fixing cartel robbed the American public of millions. They did so by setting artifically high prices, which dropped by 62 percent when the crime was uncovered.[1] Other crimes we will discuss in this chapter rob citizens not of money, but of their rights. These are governmental crimes, offenses by the very structure that makes and administers laws.

Before getting into the numerous corporate and governmental crimes, we will first have to define what we mean by each. This is especially important for differentiating occupational crimes from corporate crimes, for while there is a good deal of overlap between the two there are important fundamental differences.

CORPORATE CRIMES: We will define **corporate crimes** as those crimes that are committed by large corporations for the enrichment of the corporation and not individual employees. This definition excludes occupational crimes such as embezzlement and employee theft, but it would overlap with certain offenses we described as occupational crimes such as consumer fraud. Also, there is a gray area when a company is small enough that the owner acts as an employee, such as a gas station where the owner is also a mechanic. Therefore, corporate crimes involve large corporations where the employees derive no direct benefit from the crimes.

GOVERNMENTAL CRIMES: Defining **governmental crimes** is somewhat more complex than defining corporate crime. This is because there is an intermixing of crimes by individuals for their own benefit and crimes by governmental organizations for the organization. For example, a Congressman who takes a bribe so that he can buy a new swimming pool takes advantage of his position in government for self-benefit. On the other hand, a police officer who beats a confession out of a rape suspect breaks the law, not for his own benefit but for what he sees as the benefit of law enforcement. In both cases, the law has been broken by governmental

328

representatives but for entirely different reasons. Therefore, we will define governmental crimes as being those that are committed by incumbents of public positions, either individually or as part of an organizational policy, for personal or organizational gain. As we will see, the "gain" can be defined in many different ways, from a flat monetary gain to an ideological gain.

Corporate Crime

Most of Edwin Sutherland's classic work on "white collar crime" dealt with what we are calling "corporate crime." The whole point of corporate crime is to make more money and thereby increase an organization's power. Since the business of business is to make money, it is important to understand why there are laws that restrict what legitimate businesses can do in pursuit of monetary gains. Sutherland's analysis of the development of some of these laws is still the most cogent.

Basically, Sutherland connected the existence of laws regulating the practices of corporate business with the ideology of free enterprise. Anything that threatened free enterprise and competition was seen as bad for the part of American ideology that values an open and free expression of capitalism. As Sutherland noted,

> The Sherman Antitrust Law, for example, represents a settled tradition in favor of free competition and free enterprise. This ideology is obvious in the resentment against communism. A violation of the antitrust law is a violation of strongly entrenched moral sentiments. The value of these laws is questioned principally by persons who believe in a more collectivistic system, and these persons are limited to two principal groups, namely the socialists and the leaders of Big Business. When the business leaders, through corporate activities, violate the antitrust law, they are violating the moral sentiments of practically all sections of the American public except the socialists.[2]

It is unlikely that either the notions of collectivism or the beliefs concerning the role of government as a reflection of the popular will are the same for business tycoons and socialists. However, rhetoric from the megacorporations has accused government of interfering with free enterprise and competition, and the conservative politicians have promised less government and *more* free enterprise. Since the **antitrust laws** were enacted to preserve a free and competitive market, the conservative position on government regulation would be more collectivistic according to Sutherland.

The point, though, is not so much that the antitrust laws and other laws regulating the conduct of business are anticollectivistic. Instead, this legislation is aimed to prevent large corporations from smothering competitive businesses and thereby dominating the economy. Other laws regulating business were developed to protect the public from fraud committed by businesses—just like the laws that protect individuals from fraud by other individuals. Similarly, environmental laws were passed to protect the public from the effects of a destroyed ecology. This "interference," or legislative regulation, has been no less unreasonable than other criminal laws that prohibit theft, fraud, burglary, rape, and murder.

The Law and Corporate Crime

Most of the laws regulating corporate crime have relatively minor criminal sanctions. Unlike many of the laws regulating common crime, the basis of the laws governing corporate behavior are seen as legislatively created rather than emerging from a public sentiment. The common laws are based in the concept of *mala in se*. That is, an act is prohibited because it is evil in and of itself. Corporate crime laws, on the other hand, are *mala prohibita*, an evil only because of the law saying so—something like the 55 MPH speed laws. (See Chapter 2 for a full discussion of these concepts.) Therefore, there is not the same sense of natural evil in the corporate crime laws. For example, Conklin notes:

> When asked about business crime in a survey, people may condemn such violations. However, they are rarely indignant or militant in the expression of their condemnation of business crime. They take their own exploitation for granted and feel they are helpless to rectify matters.[3]

Further, since the laws are not considered terribly serious, they are for the most part defined as misdemeanors—regulatory rather than "really criminal." Again, much like the traffic laws. Finally, criminal intent or *mens rea* is presupposed in conviction of corporate crime. It is assumed that intent is present and the action itself only needs to be proved.[4]

Along with the permissive and lenient laws regulating corporate behavior, there are relatively minor penalties for violating the law. They tend to be remedial rather than punitive. Newman's description of the penalties and their administration nicely sums up what will happen to corporate criminals should they be caught:

> Since laws proscribing *mala prohibita* are remedial in nature, they are liberally construed, so that the goal remains prevention or correction of existing illegalities rather than repression or punishment of violators. In this respect, various sanctions other than the criminal punishments or imprisonment, probation, and fines are used by the enforcing agencies. Violators of such laws may be subjected to warnings; injunctions; consent decrees; seizure and destruction of products; civil suits for damages, like the treble-damage suits sanctioned in the case of OPA violations during the wartime emergency; license revocation, where applicable; and similar informal or civil processes. Legislation also provides for the use of more traditional sanctions by criminal courts, however, in cases warranting such action. The discretion to press criminal charges rather than civil action is another function of the enforcing

agency. Sutherland's survey of the records of seventy large corporations showed a total of 980 adverse decisions against these companies, 158 of which were criminal proceedings, 298 made by civil courts, 129 by equity courts, while the remainder were administrative actions discussed above.[5]

Thus, while it is possible for the harsher criminal sanctions to be brought to bear against corporate criminals, they are rarely imposed. However, since most of the violations are treated as misdemeanors, even in a criminal court the punishments will be minimal. Other sanctions, such as cease and desist orders, simply require a company to discontinue an illegal practice. It would be analogous to telling a convicted burglar to stop committing burglaries and send him home. Thus, the massive governmental "interference" claimed by corporations is actually very little in terms of both possible and actual legal sanctions.

Types of Corporate Crime

A single law, the **Sherman Antitrust Law**, encompasses most of the legal sanctions against corporations *as* organizations. Basically, the law is an anti-monopoly law that keeps competition open and prevents a single corporation from usurping a single sector of the economy. In part this law has resulted in the formation of giant conglomerates—corporations that have pieces of several sectors of the economy but not a monopoly on any single sector. Other important laws include the National Labor Relations Law, Federal Trade Commission Law, and the Pure Food and Drug Law.[6] More recent consumer protection and environmental laws are also relevant to corporate crime. In order to examine the different types of crime, we will classify them by legal violation.

Antitrust Violations

One of the most common ways corporations attempt to evade anti-monopoly laws is to secretly form illegal **cartels**. Cartels are groups of corporations that agree to fix their prices so that the public cannot benefit from the law of "supply and demand" and open competition. Corporations who agree to enter a cartel have many different ways of manipulating the price of goods in a "free market." One method is simply to agree to sell consumer goods at the minimum price forcing customers either to pay the artificially high price or go without. For several years drug stores, using the ironic slogan "Fair Trade," agreed to sell prescription drugs at a set price. When this cartel was broken up and the public became aware of the generic formulas for drugs (basically what was in a prescription or drug) the prices dropped drastically. At the same time, truth-in-advertisement laws prevented drug manufacturers from making false claims that their drugs were any better than much cheaper generic drugs. Companies advertising aspirin, for example, could no longer claim that their brand of aspirin was any better *inherently* than another brand. The so-called "brand names" that many thought were superior were simply advertised more—the extra costs were due to the advertisement, not the preparation of the drug.

Another kind of illegal cartel exists when companies not only agree to fix prices, but also agree on who will get a certain contract to sell services or goods at those prices. The most famous (and lucrative) of such cases was the electrical company cartel that went on a decade-long crime spree. It involved price-fixing of heavy electrical equipment. Each of the companies involved, with General Electric and Westinghouse being the largest, agreed to fix their prices on heavy electrical equipment that was sold to utilities and municipalities. They then divided up the sales, deciding who would get what share of the market so that none of the companies would feel cheated and bolt from the cartel. Geis describes how the companies met and planned their division of sales:

> At the meeting, negotiations centered about the establishment of a "reasonable" division of the market for the various products. Generally participating companies were allocated essentially that part of the market which they had previously garnered. If Company A, for instance, had under competitive conditions secured 20 percent of the available business, then agreement might be reached that it would be given the opportunity to submit the lowest bid on 20 percent of the new contracts. A low price would be established, and the remainder of the companies would bid at approximately equivalent, though higher, levels. It sometimes happened, however, that because of things such as company reputation or available servicing arrangements, the final contract was awarded to a firm which had not submitted the lowest bid. For this, among other reasons, debate among the conspirators was often acrimonious about the proper division of spoils, about alleged failures to observe previous agreements, and about other intramural matters. Sometimes, depending upon the contract, the conspirators would draw lots to determine who would submit the lowest bid; at other times, the appropriate arrangement would be determined under a rotating system that was conspiratorially referred to as the "phase of the moon."[7]

The important aspect of this case is that is was done by and for corporations. The individuals involved were not committing the crime for themselves directly. They were doing it for the company they represented. To be sure, if a corporation executive participated in the cartel, he would be able to enhance company profits and therefore his own standing with the company, but the illegal millions reaped by those involved went to the corporation, not the individuals.

As to the "causes" of this kind of corporate crime, the answers are very similar to other crimes we have examined. In the corporations, they learned about price-fixing from their associations with others in the same kind of jobs. As Geis explains,

> The defendants almost invariably testified that they came new to a job, found price fixing an established way of life, and simply entered into it as they did into other aspects of their job. This explanatory scheme fit into a pattern that Senator Philip A. Hart of Michigan, during the subcommittee hearings, labeled "imbued fraud."[8]

Such explanations are similar to those pointing to a "criminal subculture" and "differential association." Likewise there were "techniques of neutralization" forgiving their offenses. For example, the executive of one company involved in the electrical company conspiracy said:

> *One faces a decision, I guess, at such times, about how far to go with company instructions, and since the spirit of such meetings only appeared to be correcting a horrible price level situation, that there was not an attempt to actually damage customers, charge excessive prices, there was no personal gain in it for me, the company did not seem actually to be defrauding, corporate statements can evidence the fact that there have been poor profits during all these years. . . . So I guess morally it did not seem quite so bad as might be inferred by the definition of the activity itself.*[9]

Thus, in the same way as delinquent boys "neutralize" theft from a big company on the basis it "really won't hurt them," big companies also neutralize price fixing on the basis that "it really won't hurt the public."

Fraud

Fraud by corporations is a form of consumer fraud, but often the victim is the retail outlet, distributor, or prime buyer; therefore, we will treat it as a different kind of "consumer" fraud than what we discussed in Chapter 12. For example, an automobile manufacturer may lead the car dealers to believe that the vehicles they are selling to customers are of a quality that is misleading as to the car's actual value. Therefore, a dealer, in good faith, may lead the consumer to believe something that is not true—consumer fraud, not by the dealer but by the manufacturer. Similarly, in cases where the "prime buyer" is a special consumer, usually the government, fraud by corporations takes on a somewhat different texture.

In the play, *Death of a Salesman*, the protagonist, Willy Loman, sold the government defective airplane parts for wartime use, and as a result several pilots lost their lives. A real-life parallel to the fictional one almost occurred when a large rubber company attempted to sell defective brakes to be used on a military aircraft—the fraud occurred but no one was killed before the fraud was discovered. The company received a subcontract from an aerospace corporation to build 202 brake assemblies, a relatively small contract, but one which would be very lucrative in terms of future sale of replacement parts and new brakes when the plane was updated and improved. This particular contract was extremely important to the company since the last such contract they had was lost due to an unsuccessful brake. As a result, everyone wanted to do it right and make sure nothing went wrong.

One of the main reasons the company had received the contract was that its brake was very light in weight, an important consideration in aircraft design. However, as the company began testing the brake on its simulator, it was soon learned that it was too light, and additional brake disks would have to be added. The calculations of the head engineer had simply been inaccurate, but the company did not want to admit this mistake and neither did the head engineer. In order to keep the contract, instrumentation engineers were instructed to falsify the test results so that the company would be able to deliver the brake on schedule. According to one of the instrumentation engineers, given these instructions,

> . . . I felt, deep down, that somewhere, somehow, something would come along and the whole thing would blow over. But Russell Line had crushed that hope. The report was actually going to be issued. Intelligent law-abiding officials of B.F. Goodrich, one of the oldest and most respected of American corporations, were actually going to deliver to a customer a product that was known to be defective and dangerous and which could very possibly cause death or serious injury.[10]

The really amazing aspect of this entire affair was that the brake was to be flight-tested by the Air Force, and since the brake had been shown to be faulty in simulated tests, the company would certainly be caught in its attempted fraud. This, of course, is exactly what happened.

> His face was grim as he related stories of several near crashes during landings— caused by brake troubles. He told me about one incident in which, upon landing, one brake was literally welded together by the intense heat developed during the test stop. The wheel locked, and the plane skidded for nearly 1,500 feet before coming to a halt. The plane was jacked up and the wheel removed. The fused parts within the brake had to be pried apart.[11]

The bungling coverup of the fraud can be compared with amateurs attempting a low profit, high-risk crime. Not only was there a disregard for human life, which would appear to be cause enough to provide an honest report, but there was a blind disregard for the procedures of testing that would surely lead to the discovery of the doctored reports.

Crime and Punishment

Usually if people or corporations break the law only a single time, we do not consider them to be true criminals. However, people who repeatedly break the law, especially those who are arrested and convicted for several crimes, generally are viewed as "real criminals," or "career criminals."[12] From Sutherland's classic work examining seventy large corporations, it appears that a good many corporations fall into the "career criminal" category. The average number of adverse decisions per corporation was fourteen—that's like someone who has a "rap sheet" with 14 convictions. In other words, the average corporation is a repeat offender criminal.[13]

Given the high rate of criminal violations, one might assume that the penalties would escalate to the point where it would be unprofitable to commit crimes or at least to be saddled with such a stigma that no one would do business with a "criminal corporation." However, corporate recidivism results in individual punishment, if any at all, rather than organizationally imposed sanctions. Furthermore, the individuals punished for involvement in corporate crime, rather than being shunned by others, including other corporations, receive light sentences or fines and are either kept on by the involved corporation or hired by another firm.

In the two examples we examined, the criminal sanctions imposed on the corporations were relatively light. In the case of the electrical com-

THE WALL STREET JOURNAL

**"I realize I'm allowed one phone call . . . so
I'd like to call my publisher."**

Source: From *Wall Street Journal*, Permission—Cartoon Features Syndicate.

pany cartel all of the twenty-nine companies involved in the conspiracy entered a plea of guilty to the major indictments. A total of $2,000,000 in fines were imposed and seven executives went to prison—none for more than six months and twenty-three others were given suspended jail sentences. The largest fine was imposed against General Electric, totaling $437,500.[14] Considering the millions illegally taken by the company, the fine actually showed a profit—analogous to fining a bank robber who took $2,000 only $100. Later civil law suits cost the companies more, but the *criminal* sanctions were uniformly light. As for the executives who went to prison, they suffered for their companies' sins, but most simply went back to work for the same companies after their release, some even receiving their normal salary while imprisoned. However, one executive who was not paid while in prison, resigned his vice-presidency at one company and soon became the president of another at a salary of slightly less than $74,000.[15]

In the case involving the falsification of the airplane brake reports, the company denied any intentional tampering of reports, and blamed the "misinterpretation" of results on inexperienced engineers—the very engineers who were forced to go along with the falsification by the company. The company then made a five-disk brake for the Air Force plane (the brake the young engineers had originally suggested) and was able to keep the contract, and so even with a bungling crime, the corporation was not ultimately hurt either by criminal sanction or by the loss of business. Only the engineers who were forced to lie about the test results were hurt, in that they were depicted as inexperienced or inept by the company.[16]

Controlling Corporate Crime

The difficulty in controlling corporate crime lies in the power of the organization to overcome traditional sanctions either in their legislation or application. However, in a study of corporate crime control by Marshall Clinard and his associates, there were several suggestions that would make corporate crime less attractive and profitable. Three basic approaches can be examined: 1) changing corporate attitudes or structures; 2) strong intervention by the political state through forced changes in corporate structure and legal sanctions; and 3) effective consumer and public pressures.[17]

VOLUNTARY CHANGES IN ETHICS AND STRUCTURE As naive as it may at first seem to seriously suggest that corporations voluntarily change their ethics and structure of rewards to reduce corporate criminality, such morality is the basis of any long-range crime control. Elsewhere in this book, it has been suggested that values are at the base of other kinds of crimes—criminal subcultures, for example. As Clinard and his associates note:

The inculcation of ethical principles forms the very basis of all crime prevention and control, whether ordinary, white-collar, or corporate. Deterrence affects only the small proportion of those who rationally choose to avoid "pain" by not violating the law. Any attempt to reorganize corporate structures (or to institute a federal chartering for corporations) must inevitably rely upon a broad compliance with the law. Persons in the corporate realm, whether management or boards of directors, must recognize that the very nature of laws that regulate antitrust, pollution, unfair labor practices, product safety, occupational health and safety, taxes, and other areas represent a compelling force for compliance.[18]

Without some ethical force behind changes in the law and structure of corporations, there is no reason to believe that corporate powers would not be employed to "buy" the avoidance of sanctions as they have in the past. By instituting a code of ethics and teaching business school majors such codes, along with the overall importance of such ethics in relation to society, there could be some movement to fill the ethical vacuum in which most corporations operate.

GOVERNMENT INTERVENTION While ethics are an important part of compliance with the law, we do not expect that other values would be uniformly upheld without criminal sanctions against burglary, robbery, and other common crimes. In the same way, it is necessary to institute clear and effective criminal sanctions against corporate crime. Currently, Clinard and his associates point out:

It has generally been conceded among knowledgeable persons that penalties for corporate offenses are far too lenient. . . . Administrative actions such as warnings and consent agreements are used too often. Civil and criminal actions are infrequently utilized, and monetary penalties, frequently because of statutory limitations, are often ludicrous in terms of the corporations' assets, sales and profits.[19]

In the same way that many states have passed "use a gun—go to prison" laws to reduce violent crimes, new laws against corporate crime should have strong sanctions. Suggestions include:

1. Strong remedial actions connected with consent decrees. For example, if a corporation is convicted of price-fixing, it should be made to pay the victims of overpricing either directly or by reducing their prices below cost to make up what they illegally made.
2. Increased sanctions for repeat offenders, just as with common crimes.
3. Fines based on corporate assets and not a set figure. Thus, a billion dollar corporation would be fined in the millions while a million dollar corporation in the thousands.

4. Mandatory prison sentences for corporate executives who allow corporate crime—not just the lower-level employee.

5. Outlawing corporate support of convicted executives—disallowing paying their fines.

6. Depriving convicted executives of resuming position for set period of years.

7. Publicizing corporate offenses at the corporation's expense.[20]

These sanctions are strong, and while it is unlikely that all of them will be instituted, given the political–corporate relationship, if there is any hope of controlling such crime, they are necessary. Furthermore, it is important to furnish the law enforcement and prosecutorial personnel to apply the sanctions.

PUBLIC PRESSURE Given the history of ethics and official sanctions against corporations, there is not a great deal of evidence that either will change rapidly unless there is public pressure for change. If politicians are elected who depend on corporate finances to put them in office, laws will never be enacted to control corporate crime. On the other hand, if the public demands representatives who enact corporate crime laws—just as other politicians have run on strong "law and order" platforms—there is a much greater chance of combatting corporate offenses. Likewise, if consumers boycott unsafe products and/or the products of criminal corporations, there is a good business reason for corporations to comply with the law. Consumer cooperatives in other nations, such as Sweden and Switzerland, are able to dictate the quality of products they are sold, and if such cooperatives were organized in the United States, they could wield tremendous influence over corporate behavior.[21]

Under the current conditions with light sanctions against corporations for very profitable crimes, there is little deterrence, either criminally or socially. As long as it is more profitable to break the law—as it clearly is in the case of corporations—it is doubtful that they will mend their ways. There is no social stigma attached to their law violations, and what there is can be overcome with public relations campaigns and accusations that "government" interference in business hurts the economy—a denial that the laws are legitimate. Thus there exists a strong criminal subculture among the corporations in that there is a shared understanding that violating the laws is not "criminal" but "smart business."

Crimes by the Government

Perhaps the ultimate crime is that which involves the very bodies that create and administer the law—the government. Governmental crime, however, is a tricky phenomenon to understand, for the government also interprets the law through the courts—courts often staffed by governmental appointees. Judges, who are appointed by one political party, for example, may have one interpretation of the laws for the party that appointed them and another for the opposition party. If an action taken by government is not interpreted by the courts as illegal, can we say that it is *really* criminal even though the official stance is otherwise? Probably not, even if there is evidence of blatant corruption. For instance, the Nixon administration used "national security" as a reason to bug telephones, break into doctors' offices, and a number of other crimes that were ultimately interpreted as being criminal. However, if the courts did accept the crimes as reasonable and justifiable under the provisions of national security, they would not have been crimes.

However, some crimes by the government, or by incumbents in governmental positions, are so blatantly illegal that even the most convoluted interpretation of the law fails to cover the crime. In this section, we will attempt to examine the various kinds of governmental crimes, concentrating on those that are clearly criminal violations.

Corruption

In 1980 the FBI conducted an undercover operation known as **ABSCAM**. The operation involved an operative posing as a wealthy Arab who offered to bribe Congressmen for helping him obtain a resident's visa. In order to assure that there would be no misinterpretation as to the intent or culpability of the crime, the briberies were secretly filmed. When the ABSCAM story broke, those involved attempted to explain away their crimes by claiming everything from attempting to obtain money for their district to conducting an undercover operation of corruption themselves. There were even grumbles from Congress that the FBI had overstepped its bounds by "entrapping" the Congressmen. However, the videotapes of the scenes showing Congressmen stuffing bribes into their clothes or briefcases was so convincing that all of the offenders were eventually prosecuted and convicted.[22] (Later appeals reversed some convictions.)

The extent of such political corruption and corruptibility is largely unknown, for even though there are almost constant stories and rumors of political bribery, there is little research or concrete evidence on this phenomenon. On the one hand, it is difficult to prove bribery has occurred; much of it is covered in the form of campaign contributions or cash payments that leave no trace of culpability. However, the ABSCAM operation did show us that bribing elected government officials—even by aliens—is relatively simple. Had ABSCAM's budget been larger, they would not have had to stop as soon as they did, and it was clear that more Congressmen were willing to "help" the rich Arab for a "consideration." On the other hand, criminologists have not really developed a great deal of theoretical interest in this area of crime nor has the government seemed interested in funding such research projects. Thus, while it would not be too difficult to replicate something like ABSCAM for research purposes, given the funding to do so, there is neither the apparent interest nor the available money for such a project.

By examining the structure of political power and vested interests relating to that power, we can see how and why elected officials are susceptible to bribery and corruption. First, large organizations, from the Mafia to General Motors, have a vested interest in what laws are passed and how they are administered. For example, if the government passes laws regulating exhaust emission, those laws affect how much it costs General Motors to manufacture a car and the profits it can make. Likewise, the Mafia is concerned about investigations into its activities and anti-racketeering laws. Secondly, politicians need money and votes to be elected. The money buys everything from television commercials to salaries for hired campaign workers. A fact of political life is that it costs money to run for office, and the candidate with more money has a better chance of winning. Of course, no politician of any sense runs on the basis of representing the Mafia or some large corporation—he or she runs "for the people." In fact, many politicians who were found to be involved in criminal activity ran on an "anticrime" platform. Nixon is a prime example of a "law and order" candidate who himself was forced to resign from office for the alleged crimes committed in his administration. Elected officials are "lobbied" by various interest groups when bills affecting their interests are being debated. These interests have their power base in high membership, strong organization and/or as was the case with the so-called "Moral Majority" in the 1980 elections, large organizations with lots of money to help in re-election. Since moral crusades of the left and right often come and go with changes in the social climate, they tend to be a risky star on which to hitch a political career. Large business organizations, on the other hand, tend to be relatively stable in both their existence and consistent interest—higher profits. Therefore, when questions of self-interest for the politician arise, they tend to listen to those lobbies that can back up their argument with long-range financial support. Thus, it is a major force in the corruption of public office holders.

Low-Level Corruption and Lawlessness

While there is little research on higher-level corruption, there is an abundance on lower-level corruption of governmental representatives, especially the police. Like other forms of crime and corruption, police corruption and that of minor officials occurs in a certain context. On the one hand there is a "cultural" context where an established norm exists for taking bribes, beating confessions out of suspects, or other forms of "ac-

Interest groups have considerable amounts of money and/or members to influence elections. The 1980 elections were strongly affected by Jerry Falwell's "Moral Majority."

ceptable" law violation. In perhaps the best-known instance of police corruption, that of a police officer named Serpico, an honest policeman was continually urged to take payoffs from gamblers, bookmakers, pimps, and drug dealers—not only by the crooks but by other policemen.[23] Like other forms of criminal subcultures, there are techniques of neutralization "excusing" the criminal behavior such as citing low pay, higher-level corruption, and the inability of the criminal justice system to deal effectively with criminals. These motives for breaking the law are passed on from one group of police officers in a corrupt department to the next via differential association. Since police officers tend to associate primarily with other police officers, not only is the learning through association strong, sanctions for not going along with the norm of law violation can be severe in the form of ostracism.[24]

On the structural level police corruption can be seen to be a matter of relative power. One of the points repeatedly made in Peter Maas's book on Serpico was that any investigation into corruption would only be directed against the police at the bottom levels—not against the higher level police administrators or the politicians, judges, and attorneys who also shared in the graft.[25] In later investigations carried out by the Knapp Commission, this is exactly what happened—the bulk of convictions and sanctions were against the lowest-level police officers and the higher-level police and other criminal justice incumbents either were let off totally or received only minor sanctions.[26]

In John Daly's examination of police corruption in an elite narcotics unit, it was found that the corruption started at a much higher level and filtered down to the police. The narcotic officers arrested wholesale heroin distributors in New York, only to see them receive bail and leave the country before their trial. According to Daly's account, there was a good deal of corruption among judges, bailbondsmen, and others in the criminal justice system, and the heroin trade was so lucrative that the dealers could afford to lose a half-million dollar bail and return to South America without fear of extradition. The courts kept the forfeited bail, and so the courts also made a profit. The police officers' work became meaningless since they knew that their arrests would rarely result in a conviction, and even the impounded evidence—often several pounds of heroin—would disappear from the police property room. At a certain point, the police saw no reason why corrupt judges, attorneys, and bailbondsmen should be making huge sums off their arrests and the felon released. Thus, they shortcircuited the entire system of graft by taking the drugs and money themselves and releasing the dealer. Sometimes the drugs would be destroyed so that there would be no evidence of police involvement in corruption, or they would be sold, often more than doubling profits. When the payoffs were discovered, only the police were tried and convicted, but again this sanctioning was not applied against crooked attorneys, judges, and bailbondsmen.[27] To be sure, citing higher-level corruption as a structural cause for lower-level corruption appears to justify the very techniques of neutralization and rationalizations of the police. However, the structural elements provided the point of reference for the excuses used by the police, and while it does not justify the police behavior, it does explain the situational elements that lent credibility to their rationalizations.

Another structural explanation of police criminality is found in James

Q. Wilson's study of the styles of police organization. In some police organizations, described as "watchman" style organizations, there is little room for advancement, low pay, and minimal expectations for police. As long as publically noticeable street crimes and vagrancy were absent, then there would be little public pressure on the political structure to make reforms. Both petty and major organized criminals took advantage of this kind of police organization by paying police officers to leave them alone. Since most of the organized crime activities involved the cooperation of the public, such as gambling, it was not the kind of crime that concerned incumbents in the political organizations, who themselves were enriched through graft.[28]

Other Government Lawlessness

The police are not the major governmental representatives who break the law, only the most researched. Other violations of the law by the government are not noted—either because of lack of detection or publicity, or because they affect only specific targets. For example, one governmental employee, A. Ernest Fitzgerald, was concerned about the astronomical cost overruns on the Air Force's C5-A cargo jet—some $2 billion more than the original amount for which they were contracted. He was called before the Joint Economic Committee's Economy in Government Subcommittee and instructed by Senator William Proxmire to prepare 100 copies of a written statement concerning the cost overruns. Fitzgerald was told by his superiors not to prepare the reports, but Fitzgerald did anyway as he was legally required. After his testimony was given, Fitzgerald's job tenure was revoked by the Air Force and in 1970 his job was "abolished."[29] Since a section of the federal criminal code clearly states that it is unlawful to threaten, influence, intimidate, impede, or injure a Congressional witness, as was done in the Fitzgerald case, the government had broken the law.[30] However, no action was taken against the government or those responsible—only Fitzgerald suffered. While Fitzgerald's case is unique in that it received publicity, government crimes against individuals are not. Besides illegal job dismissal other crimes include: prosecution of individuals under laws not enforced against other violators, faking or supressing evidence to secure convictions, unlawful sentencing and denial of procedures guaranteed by law.[31]

On a more general level, the government involves itself in other forms of illegal behavior as well. Most of the law violations occur, ironically enough, in the context of either enforcing the law or preserving national security. For example, the Central Intelligence Agency illegally intercepted mail from the early 1950s up to 1973.[33] Under certain circumstances it is legal to open mail, as long as national security is at stake and the proper procedures are followed.

However, in a CIA memorandum, it was noted:

> Since no good purpose can be served by an official admission of the viola-
> tion, and existing Federal Statutes preclude the concoction of any legal ex-
> cuse of the violation, it must be recognized that no cover story is available to
> any government agency. . . .[33]

Thus, it was not the case the CIA was unaware that its actions were illegal
and simply in an excess of exhuberance went beyond the law. Rather it
knowingly broke the law and discussed covering up their crime. There
was no personal gain for breaking the law, and there can be no question
that the CIA believed its actions were in the best interests of national security and the good of the people as a whole. However, many groups,
whether revolutionaries or reactionaries have the same "pure" motives.
Likewise, police who beat confessions out of accused criminals certainly
have the "best interests" of the community. Killers may believe their victims will go to heaven, a noble cause for insane homicides. The motive,
whether selfish or collective, is not the issue, but rather breaking the law
is; and in the case of the CIA, as well as other law enforcement agencies,
whether local, state, or federal, whenever they break the law, they engage
in the very behavior they are mandated to enforce.

A final area where the government breaks the law is in Constitutional
law that simply has been broken by custom. It is a kind of **reverse case
law**—the Supreme Court has never decided against the action, but the
routine practice of the violation gives it a certain legitimacy. One of the
areas where this occurs is in the presidential impounding of funds. If
the Congress has allocated money for a purpose, the administration is
supposed to use the money for the purpose mandated by Congress. However, since about 1941, Presidents have impounded such funds for various purposes—not so much for use elsewhere but because they did not
believe the monies were appropriated properly.[34]

Similarly, in campaigns, other than the Watergate affair and certain
other scandals in campaign practices that were too big to cover up, there
have been routine violations of the law. Attorneys General have not prosecuted, either because to do so would put members of their party in jail
or, if aimed against the opposition, would put pressure on them to investigate their own party—not to mention embarrassing those who made
illegal contributions. For example, according to Jethro Lieberman,
the American Medical Association routinely breaks the law requiring
full reporting of campaign contributions, and they are never prosecuted
for it.

> The American Medical Association donated some $7,000,000 to groups
> throughout the United States. Most contributors actually abide by the law
> and file reports with Congress revealing the candidates to whom the money
> was given. Not the AMA. The Association has set up an intermediary organ-

ization called the American Medical Political Action Committee (AMPAC), which has established state affiliates to which it gives the money. The AMA then simply reported to Congress that it gave so much to each AMPAC affiliate—for instance, $42,000 to the California affiliate. AMPAC itself claimed not to be connected with the American Medical Association; it must be by coincidence, then, that all members of AMPAC's board belonged to the AMA. In 1970, only the Indiana affiliate of AMPAC filed a contribution report with Congress. The other affiliates, since they made contributions in only one state, ignored the filing requirements.[35]

By ignoring such law violations, there is a double crime: the crime of breaking the law and the crime of not enforcing the law.

SUMMARY

In discussing common crimes, it was relatively simple to come up with statistics and even dollar values of crime. However, billions or even trillions of dollars may be a realistic estimate of the cost of corporate and government criminality. Whatever the figure, though, it is certainly an area where sociologists and criminologists need more theory and research.

The laws regulating corporate crime, while as precise as any other criminal law, have relatively minor sanctions; additionally the corporations can spend a great deal on legal talent to find or manufacture loopholes in the law. As a result, it costs the government a great deal to prosecute such cases, and oftentimes it is simply less expensive to overlook many violations than to take them to court. Moreover, since the prosecutor's office is political, either directly or indirectly, there is always the possibility that an overzealous prosecutor will find his party voted out of office due to heavy backing of more "cooperative" opposition parties by corporations. Likewise, congressmen elected into office with corporate backing—or in fear of such backing for their opposition—are not inclined to pass especially harsh laws regulating corporate activities, either closing loopholes or stiffening penalties.

The overall result of the corporate and governmental crimes is a continual loss both financially and in terms of democratic institutions to the public at large. Campaign laws requiring stricter reporting of financial backing and contributions are a step in reducing such crimes, but until there is some kind of active prosecution of those who break the campaign laws, they have little effect.

Glossary

ABSCAM   An undercover operation by the FBI that uncovered corruption by government officials.

Antitrust Laws   Laws aimed at organizations to prevent monopolies and preserve competition and free enterprise.

Cartels   Groups of organizations that work together to fix prices illegally.

Corporate Crimes   Law violations by large organizations for the benefit of the corporation.

Corruption   A type of governmental crime in which a public official accepts payment for favorable action towards an interest group or individual.

Governmental Crimes   Law violation by governmental representatives.

Reverse Case Law   Actions that are illegal in that they violate either a specific law or Constitutional law, but have never been ruled upon by appellate courts. As a result, the illegal behavior sets a precedent.

Sherman Antitrust Law   The major antitrust law aimed at preventing monopolies and cartels. (See ***Antitrust Laws***.)

Questions

1. How are corporate crimes defined as uniquely different from occupational crimes?

2. What was the purpose of the Sherman Antitrust Law? Why is this law important to free enterprise and competition?

3. Who are the victims in corporate crimes? How do costs of corporate crimes compare with the cost of common crimes?

4. What are the different kinds of corporate crimes, and what happens when one is uncovered? Who is punished for these offenses?

5. What are several kinds of governmental crime? Explain why some governmental crimes do not involve financial payment and others do.

Notes

1. Richard Austin Smith, "The Incredible Electrical Conspiracy," *Fortune* **63** (April 1961): 132–137.

2. Edwin Sutherland, *White Collar Crime*. (New York: Holt, Rinehart & Winston, 1949, 1961), p. 45.

3. John E. Conklin, *Illegal But Not Criminal* (Englewood Cliffs, NJ: Prentice-Hall, 1977, p. 18.

4. Donald J. Newman, "White-Collar Crime: An Overview and Analysis," in Gilbert Geis and Robert Meier, eds., *White Collar Crime* (New York: Free Press, 1977), p. 53.

5. Newman, 1977, 54.

6. Newman, 1977, 34–35.

7. Gilbert Geis, "The Heavy Electrical Equipment Antitrust Cases of 1961," in Marshall Clinard and Richard Quinney, eds., *Criminal Behavior Systems*. (New York: Holt, Rinehart & Winston, 1967), p. 143.

8. Geis, 1967, 144.

9. Geis, 1967, 145.

10. Robert Heilbroner, Morton Mintz, Coleman McCarthy, Sanford Ungar, Kermit Van Diver, Sol Freidman, and James Boyd, *In the Name of Profit*. (New York: Doubleday, 1972), p. 18.

11. Heilbroner et al., 1972, 19.

12. Howard S. Becker, *Outsiders*. (New York: Free Press, 1963).

13. Sutherland, 1949, 20–22.

14. Smith, 1961.

15. Geis, 1976, 149.

16. Heilbroner, et al., 1972.

17. Marshall Clinard, with Peter C. Yeager, Jeanne Brissette, David Petrashek and Elizabeth Harries, "Controlling Corporate Crime," *Illegal Corporate Behavior*. (Washington, D.C.: U.S. Department of Justice, 1979).

18. Ibid.

19. Ibid.

20. Ibid.

21. Ibid.

22. ABSCAM articles and television stories were numerous, from local stories concerning individual congressmen to nude pictorial story/interview in *Playboy* of one former Congressman's wife.

23. Peter Maas, *Serpico*. (New York: Viking Press, 1973).

24. John P. Clark, "Isolation of the Police: A Comparison of the British and American Situations," *The Journal of Criminal Law, Criminology and Police Science* **56** (September 1965): 309–319.

25. Maas, 1973.

26. Ibid.

27. John Daly, *Prince of the City*. (Boston: Houghton Mifflin, 1978).

28. James Q. Wilson, *Varieties of Police Behavior*. (Cambridge, MA: Harvard University Press, 1968).

29. Jethro Lieberman, *How the Government Breaks the Law*. (Baltimore: Penguin, 1973), 29–33.

30. Ibid.

31. Ibid.

32. *Report to the President by the Commission on CIA Activities Within The United States*. (Washington, D.C.: U.S. Government Printing Office, June 1975), Chap. 9.

33. Ibid.

34. Lieberman, 1973, 167–173.

35. Lieberman, 1973, 177–178.

15

The Police

What to Look For:

Why police discretion is a key concept in the study of crime.

How the legal criteria for arrests are subject to social interpretations.

Major variables in police discretion and how these variables affect official crime rates.

The meaning of proactive and reactive police organization.

The different types of police organizations and units within a police organization.

Introduction

HAVING EXAMINED DIFFERENT kinds of crimes, we shift now to the reactions to crime. As was noted in our discussion of labeling theory in Chapter 7, being a criminal depends on society officially separating that person from the rest of society and marking him or her a criminal. Likewise, unless there is an official reaction to crime, even though a law may be on the books, it is not treated as a crime. Therefore, in order to fully understand all aspects of crime, we must now look to the societal reactions to events and people defined as criminal. Special attention will be paid to the way in which some people and events are chosen to be labeled while others are not. Since there are far more criminal acts noted by societal members than are officially acted upon, for the most part it is not a matter of innocents being accused of crime. Rather, we must look to see the ways in which the societal reactions are patterned toward law violations and violators.

One of the more perplexing roles in the criminal justice system is that of the police officer. The police have a great deal of power to make arrests, use coercive force, and define who will and will not be considered an official criminal. However, relative to other positions in the criminal justice system, the police have little social status, little control over the general policies of their departments, and they are greatly limited (beyond the lower socioeconomic classes) in the extent of power they are able to exercise.

In this chapter we will examine the role of the police. Specifically, the overall perspective will be on what is called **police discretion**—decisions by police officers regarding whether or not to make an arrest when there is legal probable cause to do so. First, we will examine the legal criteria for arrests and the interpretive processes involved in deciding on legal standards. Next, we will look at the broader organizational context of police discretion. We will see that arrests are largely a function of the form or "style" of a police organization. Third, we will examine several different variables that exist in situations where the police must decide exactly what to do with a suspected law breaker. We will refer to these as discretion situations. Fourth, in regard to discretion, we will look at the operations of various specialized units in law enforcement and show how the existence (or nonexistence) of various organizational components affect who will come to the attention of the police. Finally, we will consider the social stereotypes of police and discuss how these stereotypes affect police and their work in enforcing the law.

Before beginning our discussion of the police, it should be pointed out that there are many different kinds of law enforcement agencies. Most familiar are city police and county sheriff deputies. Also, state troopers or highway patrol are typical police officers. However, various other agencies on the state and federal level are also police—the best known being the Federal Bureau of Investigation (FBI). Lesser known police agencies include state investigative agencies such as Illinois Bureau of Investigation and state marshalls. On the federal level, the Drug Enforcement Agency and the Alcohol, Tobacco, and Firearms Agency specialize in their respective areas. Agencies such as the Securities and Exchange Commission police banking practices, and units of the Environmental Protection Agency police for violations that damage the ecology. There are hundreds of such policing agencies throughout the country, but we will concentrate on the local police and sheriff departments, since most citizen calls for law enforcement involve these local organizations.

Legal Criteria for Arrests

The single most important feature of police work is the power to make an arrest. By arrests, we mean the ability to use **coercive force** to take a person into custody. This does not mean that a person is physically wrestled to the ground when arrested (although that may sometimes happen); rather it refers to the legal power of the police to use coercion to take a person into custody. However, before a person can be arrested, the law requires that there be **probable cause** that a specific person has committed a specific crime. Basically, this means that there is good reason to believe someone committed a crime.[1] For example, if a policeman knows a bank has just been robbed, and he sees a man running down the street with a bag bearing the bank's name, he has probable (or reasonable) cause to believe that the man robbed the bank. This does not mean that the person is guilty of a crime; for a teller could be running to the bank with a bag of money to replace the one that was just stolen or it could be someone running to return the stolen money that has just been found. However, it is reasonable to assume that the person in this case is the robber. There is a good deal of **case law**—laws based on judicial decisions and not legislative enactment—that provides strict guidelines for probable cause, but ultimately probable cause rests on assumptions and commonsense understandings. The following is an example of a somewhat elaborate probable cause used by police detectives in a burglary arrest:

A suspect was arrested on a warrant based on circumstantial (indirect) evidence. The detective who made the arrest explained that a burglary victim had given him a list of ex-employees, and from this list the detective had deduced a suspect. The physical evidence indicated that the point of entry was a window that had been broken.

*Since the window was relatively small, so, too, would the suspect have to be. Second,
the burglary alarm switch had been turned off, from which it was deduced that the
burglar was someone familiar with the alarm system. Money was the only item taken;
this also pointed to an ex-employee who knew where the money was stored. Finally,
the fingerprints taken at the scene were smudged, but indicated a whorl pattern on the
left hand. The suspect had whorl patterns (a type of distinguishing configuration
used in fingerprint identification) on his left hand.*[2]

None of these items by themselves could/would constitute probable cause;
for example, millions of people have whorl patterns on their left hand.
However, taken together, it was possible to construct a reasonable account
of probable cause.

Assessing and Defining Situations

Because probable cause is a concept requiring the interpretation of both
the meaning of the situation and the law, it is inherently vague in practical everyday use. That is, there is always more than one interpretation regarding probable cause, and each case depends on how the police officer
interprets the situation. Therefore, it is important to understand how the
interpretive work is done.

For the most part police officers rely on commonsense assumptions
about the world or "what everybody knows."[3] To explain fully why they
had reasonable cause to make an arrest, they depend on others seeing the
same kinds of circumstances essentially as they do. This process was best
described by Sacks as **procedure by incongruity**.[4] When police officers observe elements that do not fit, it is cause for suspicion—for example, a
person wearing a coat on a warm day. Commonsense reasoning suggests
to the police officer that any person wearing a coat on a a warm day does
so to hide something—a sawed-off shotgun or stolen goods. The incongruity between the weather and coat would be the probable cause. As police officers become more and more experienced, they tend to see more
and more subtle clues that serve as probable cause to stop persons and
search them for evidence of a crime.

Specialized police units working with delinquent gangs learn to recognize clues to gang membership that nonpolice and nongang members
would not see. One characteristic of gangs in Southern California is hand
signals that have special meanings to gangs and the police. A police officer seeing such a signal may use it as "probable cause" to question, search,
and arrest a youth for a crime involving the gang.[5] The problem, however, is that these signals are not generally recognized by outsiders; therefore, "any reasonable person" would not see a hand signal as a good reason to make an arrest. Thus, it is necessary to establish "expertise" in the
area of this kind of specialized information, much like fingerprint experts
who can determine whether or not a suspect was at the scene of a crime.

Gang "colors" often attract police attention, and youths whose appearance conforms to police images of possible law violators are most likely to be stopped and questioned.

The problem in defining situations as having probable cause is the large number of possible suspects. For example, the following case was noted by La Fave as falling within the commonsense realm of "reasonable cause," yet it might be seen as being rather flimsy to make an arrest:

A patrolman came upon a man walking in a residential neighborhood late at night. The community in question was experiencing a particularly serious wave of nighttime

*offenses. Although the man could identify himself, he did not live in that neighbor-
hood, and his explanation for being there was equivocal. The officer placed him under
arrest.*[6]

On the one hand, commonsense reasoning would concur with a police officer's suspicions in those circumstances; but, on the other hand, it is clear
that being outside of one's neighborhood is hardly a good reason to arrest
someone. Race often will play a role in who "belongs" and who does not
"belong" in certain areas. Blacks living in white middle-class areas are
more likely to be stopped than whites in the same area. Given the racial
homogeneity of most neighborhoods, such actions are not "unreasonable"; however, they can cause resentment and charges of discrimination.

The problem of establishing probable cause for an arrest is based
largely on experiences of police, and what can be seen as a good reason
to stop a person and make an arrest broadens with experiences. As a result, probable cause comes to be *seen* as arbitrary or discriminatory when
in fact it is a matter of operating on a set of commonsense assumptions
about the world. As the assumptions change, so too does the sense of reasonable or probable cause.

Police Discretion

Given the legal requirement of probable cause before an arrest is made
and given the vague nature of what constitutes probable cause in terms of
actual situations, the issue of police discretion becomes central in discovering who is arrested. However, we are not dealing simply with the legal
requirements of probable cause; for most police discretion occurs when
there is sufficient probable cause from the standpoint of a court. Most instances of police discretion are ones in which there is probable cause to
make an arrest or issue a citation, but the officer chooses *not* to do so. In
order to examine all of the salient features of police discretion, we will
begin on the broadest level—the organizational level—to see how the arrangement and policies of organizations determine a police officer's decision of whether or not to make an arrest.

Police Organization: The General Context

What a given police officer will do in an arrest situation would seem to be
mediated more by the law and the nature of the situation than by the organization. After all, the organization is not out on the streets to control
hundreds of police officers. Or is it? In some ways the organization
touches everything police officers do, and, while there is some independence in police organizations because of the dispersed nature of police
work, the organization can determine the very situation in which a police
officer finds him/herself. For example, some police departments have
traffic divisions, and either a formal or informal norm regarding the

number of traffic citations to be issued.[7] Accordingly, the organizational context may: 1) increase the probability that a traffic stop will be made and 2) influence the officer's decision in the situation. The very existence of a traffic unit means that certain police officers will be concentrating on traffic violations, and the criteria for doing a good job in such units is measured by the number of citations—effectively reducing leniency in discretion not to give a ticket.

We need to ask, however, "Why do certain departments have one organization while others have a different one?" What determines the nature of a police organization? Is the department primarily organized to respond to requests for assistance or is it organized to drum up its own business? For these answers, there are several avenues of inquiry. We will begin by looking at the history of the police and their establishment and then contemporary studies of police organization.

Origins of the Police

Modern police organizations are generally traced back to the Metropolitan Police in London, created in 1829. The establishment of the police was controversial; even though London was experiencing high urban crime, riots, and disorder, the British feared the kinds of dictatorships that existed in Europe. The English did not want an occupying home army, and so one of the provisions of the Metropolitan Police Act that is still true today was that the police would not carry guns.[8] However, London's crimes were not new, and given the general public resistance to a police force the development of the police organization may not have been a reflection of general social interests. Rather, the police may have been a reflection of special interest groups, mainly the economic elite in Britain, and in subsequent development of police organizations in other Western societies.[9] Therefore, it cannot be said that the development of police forces were simply a response to crime. According to Lundman:

> Elites take control of the law creation and enforcement machinery of the state when the actions of the powerless threaten the position of elites. By making certain actions illegal and by creating law enforcement agencies, the powerless are brought under the control of the state.[10]

Lundman and others argue that, if the establishment of a police force was based on the extent of crime, law enforcement agencies would have emerged much earlier in the development of cities. Again, Lundman notes:

> The same is true of the impact of public riot, public intoxication, and the dangerous classes notion. None either automatically or even quickly resulted in the founding of organized police. In the summer of 1780, London was

controlled by mobs during the Gordon Riots; professional police did not appear for another forty-nine years. Public drunkenness was a serious nuisance in Boston as early as 1775, yet professional police did not materialize until 1838. And the existence of the dangerous classes was widely acknowledged well before the dawn of professional police.[11]

Lundman, then poses the question of why urban problems festered for so long without a police, and why the elite are credited with the development of the police if those same problems affected the poor as well? Furthermore, if the elite feared the mass uprising of the working class, there would seem to have been a need for a police force from the outset of industrialization.

By and large, those who advocate the position that the elite were the prime beneficiaries of police organizations claim that the early crime and riots never touched the elite. They were not living in the urban slums where the riots occurred and where crime was rampant. It was only when the workers began organizing seriously and threatened to take power that the elite felt it necessary to establish a police force.[12] The fact that the police were used as strike breakers and that the great majority of those arrested by the police tended to be in the lower classes bolstered this position.

Proactive and Reactive Police Organization

Policing in a democratic society requires some kind of popular base. To the extent that police respond to citizens' requests for assistance, they reflect the direct wishes of those whom they police. On the other hand, to the extent that police go about arresting people on the basis of either a narrow department policy or the wishes of a few, they are the tool of an elite. For example, if a community is concerned with burglary, but the police department allocates most of its resources to traffic citations to bolster the city treasury, the police do not reflect the popular will. The issue is not whether or not a department exclusively responds directly to citizens' requests for assistance or only goes after selected offenders on their own initiative. Clearly all departments spend some time and resources responding to citizens and going after offenders whose behavior has not been brought to their attention by citizens. The primary issue is how the police are organized.

We can conceptualize the two different types of police activities as being **reactive** and **proactive**.[13] Reactive policing occurs when the police "react" to a citizen's call for help. Proactive policing is when the police go off on their own and go after someone without a direct request from a citizen. A typical example of the former is when the police rush to the aid of a liquor store owner who has called to say that he has been robbed. Typical proactive policing includes traffic stops and drug cases. We will now examine the evidence and arguments regarding both types of police organization.

Proactive Organization

The argument that the police are essentially a proactive organization is summarized by Skolnick and Woodworth as follows:

> Imagine, as an example, a social system where criminality could be accused only if a citizen complained that a law was being violated. In such a system we would have a grossly different conception of police from the one commonly held, at least in the United States. In such a system, police would be men who sit in rooms and investigate only when accusing citizens are moved to complain by the occurrence of events regarded as violation of law. Under such circumstances we would not have, for example, surveillance by traffic police. If an automobile were speeding or if its driver made an illegal left turn, it would be up to some other citizen to make a complaint against him, which would be duly investigated and prosecuted by appropriate officials. Awareness of criminal violation would be the responsibility of the citizen, and there would be no concern on the part of police for increasing their capacity to become aware of infractions.[14]

This conception represents what an ideally reactive department would be like. Police awareness and information would be limited to only those infractions reported by citizens. Compared to typical modern police departments with undercover officers, informants, electronic surveillance, and other information enhancements, the reactive ideal is a stark contrast to reality.

The discretion in a proactive department would emanate from the top and filter down to the police officer. If those in control of the department (whether they be elites, local politicians, or police chiefs and sheriffs) wanted certain laws enforced or ignored, the decisions of the officers in arrest situations would be oriented toward the desires of those at the top and not the complainant. For example, a local city councilman was driving to work when he had to swerve to avoid hitting a bicyclist. After the incident, he called the chief of police and demanded that something be done about enforcing the traffic laws for bicycles. The chief sent down an order that every patrol officer issue one citation per shift. As a result, patrol officers began actively looking for traffic violations by bicyclists and issuing citations to them.[15] Their discretion had been determined by the city councilman in the context of the police organization.

To some extent, those in power will reflect the wishes of the population; therefore, even a highly proactive department can be reactive in the sense that it is responding proactively to community wishes. For example, parents in a community may be very concerned about heroin traffic, and, if the police set up special undercover drug units to deal with heroin in response to local community pressure, they are in effect reacting to the wishes of the citizens. The New York City Police Department was roundly criticized for *not* actively pursuing drug traffic in poverty and minority areas of the city because the ghetto community wanted the police to react to the availability of heroin in their area. Thus, the extent to which proactive police work is in fact purely proactive depends on the degree to which the police are organized to meet general community demands and not simply the availability to specific citizen calls for service.

Reactive Elements

Another view of police operations holds that police departments are essentially reactive—organized to respond to individual citizen complaints. Albert Reiss, Jr., studied police patrol in several major cities and found that 87 percent of all patrol mobilizations were initiated by citizens.[16] That is, in all but 13 percent of the cases where the patrol took some kind of policing action, it was done so because a citizen had called and asked them for assistance. Reiss argues that it would be absurd for police officers to sit around a room and wait until somebody "called the cops" instead of patrolling the areas where citizens live. The response to a call for assistance is much quicker from a patrol car that is in the area from which the call originated than from central headquarters. To be sure, police do extend their awareness of public behavior, but uniformed officers in clearly marked police cars are hardly the best disguises for prying into the private sector as suggested by Skolnick and Woodworth. Typically, the private world of the citizen is available to the police only at the invitation of the citizen.[17] Thus, the extended awareness into citizen privacy—while uninvited in cases of undercover operations, telephone taps, and the like—is usually at the insistence of the citizen.

Since citizens typically mobilize the police, citizens have the greatest influence over police discretion. The very call for police assistance is discretionary in that it determines what the police will do on their patrol. Once the police answer a call for help, police decisions concerning whether or not to make an arrest are also very much in the hands of the citizen. For the most part, the police will go along with what a citizen wants, especially when leniency is called for. As Donald Black summarizes:

> *Arrest practices sharply reflect the preferences of citizen complainants*, particularly when the desire is for leniency and, though less frequently, when the complainant demands arrest. The police are an instrument of the complainant, then, in two ways: Generally they handle what the complainant wants them to handle, and they handle the matter in the way the complainant prescribes.[18]

Police patrol, however, is only one part of a police organization. The investigative or detective units comprise the other major, albeit smaller, line force of police departments. In examining the allocation of resources, we also find that most investigative units are predominantly reactive.[19] While vice, intelligence, and drug details are a part of most police departments and are proactively organized, the bulk of the organizational resources are given to reactive units such as robbery, homicide, rape, burglary, fraud, and similar investigative divisions. Furthermore, the bulk of the cases the investigators handle originate with citizen complaints relayed either directly to the detectives or through patrol.[20]

In understanding the police willingness to go along with the citizen's wishes in arrest situations, it is important to consider the practical considerations of the police officer in terms of what will happen to a case. Since the complainant is usually the primary witness in a trial and is essential from the prosecutor's point of view in filing of information (filing charges), the police officer *must* consider what the complainant wants done. If the police officer relies wholly on his or her own discretion, the officer will be making arrests only to see the suspect released. This looks bad on the officer's record, and it takes a great deal of time writing reports that will result in no conviction.

Organizational Styles

In addition to looking at how a department is organized for gathering and using information, we can assess organizations in terms of their "styles" of policing. The style of a police organization not only affects it in terms of discretion, but it also is a reflection of the local political and social institutions. We will look at three major forms of police organizations as described by James Q. Wilson: 1) **watchman**, 2) **legalistic**, and 3) **service**.[21] We will briefly describe each style and then look at the consequences of each style on police decision making.

Watchman Style

The watchman style organization described by Wilson exists in cities with heavy political patronage, corruption, and little response to community needs. The organizations tend to be "flat" and "narrow." They are flat in that there is little opportunity for upward mobility within the organization, and they are narrow due to relatively little differentiation in the types of work that they do. The pay is low even at the higher ranks, there is little expectation for the officers to do anything other than show up for their jobs, and there are few rewards for doing a good job. Advancement is a function of "connections," and there is virtually no training or education for the officers. As a result, the department is characterized by officers who are patronage appointees, and the existence of corruption (payoffs) is rationalized by the low pay and poor chances for advancement. Wilson describes the consequences of watchman departments from an organizational standpoint:

> . . . there will be few places in which he can be transferred in the department and few incentives to seek transfer there. Most men will spend most of their police lives on patrol; unless they make detective, they will be in uniform driving a car or walking a beat all their lives—even after making sergeant, in most cases. In Albany, a patrolman could get assigned to the traffic division, but that means riding a motorcycle or standing at a traffic intersection during long icy winters. If there are few rewards to be sought outside the patrol force, there is little incentive to work hard to get out.[22]

WATCHMAN DISCRETION   Since not much is expected of the police and supervision is minimal, they have a wide range of discretion. Aside from major crimes, their orientation is toward order maintenance, and they tend to handle matters informally rather than invoking their arrest powers. Keeping drunks off the streets, occasionally rousting them, and maintaining a general appearance of order is their prime orientation.

Where corruption is high—as it is in many watchman organizations—there are investigative and proactive efforts at police work primarily to secure bribes or to make sure the police are getting their share of illegal earnings from gambling, prostitution, narcotics, or some other crimes the police "protect." Thus, discretion is used in corrupt watchman departments as much for shakedowns and bribes, as for enforcing the law.

Legalistic Style

The reaction to watchman style police departments, with their inefficiency and corruption, are the legalistic departments. "Good government" or "reform" political administrations take over local government such as city manager plans, and the old patronage system is replaced by one that is based on training, education, and merit. A new chief is hired to restructure the department, and the old watchman organization is completely revamped. For example:

When . . . a reform chief took over the Oakland Police Department, he promptly abolished the precinct stations and centralized the entire department into one headquarters building, he created the position of departmental inspector to investigate alleged police misbehavior and a planning and research section to gather and analyze data from the voluminous reports patrolmen were required to file, he launched a nationwide recruiting program (after first having abolished the local residence requirement for patrolmen), he established an elaborate and lengthy training program, and he held inspections to check the appearance and equipment of the men.[23]

Police-operated fencing operations have been very successful in appre-hending burglars and thieves as well as in recovering victims' property. Some critics have suggested that this kind of operation is a form of "en-trapment," but court decisions have upheld their legality.

In legalistic departments, control is maintained over the individual of-ficer's behavior to the extent that virtually every matter is treated as a law enforcement problem, no matter how commonplace.[24] For every call on which a patrol officer is sent, he must make a report explaining his ac-tions—particularly in situations subject to corruption. For example, if an officer makes a traffic stop, he first calls in and reports the car and its license plate number and the reason for the stop. If no citation is issued, he must explain his reason for not doing so, and if insufficient, he is subject to disciplinary action, including firing. This kind of control minimizes the opportunities and temptations to take bribes from drivers; likewise, in other situations where corruption is possible, strict supervision is maintained such that, if an arrest is possible but not made, the officer is held accountable.

In addition to having strict supervisory controls in legalistic departments, they also have greater opportunities for advancement and incentives for the type of police work the department wants. By creating new administrative positions and broadening the line positions, there is increased vertical and horizontal mobility in the department. The new positions carry with them far better pay and an incentive for doing a good job. Since performance is measured by a set of unambiguous criteria laid out by law enforcement (e.g. giving traffic tickets and making arrests), the officers know the prerequisites for career advancement. The old informal ways of the watchman organization are no longer tolerated, and even what by standards of "community commonsense" would be an order maintenance problem is redefined as a law enforcement problem. For instance, one sergeant explained:

It's Chief X's philosophy that the case is either unfounded or you had better have charged them with the offense they are suspected of having committed. When we come across a group of kids scuffling after a basketball game, there's no such thing as "messing around" in his eyes. Either there's no trouble and no reason to stop them or you had better bring them in.[24]

The result of such a policy is a rapid increase in arrests for activities that would have been handled informally under a watchman organization. For example, when one department went from watchman to legalistic style, the number of juvenile arrests went from 77 to 507 in a single year.[25]

LEGALISTIC DISCRETION   As might be imagined, in such a department the individual officer has little discretion. If headquarters dispatches a call, there is a departmental record of it. If an arrest is possible and officer did not make one, the officer's supervisor will demand to know why. Since there is a heavy "paper trail" in reports and dispatch logs that follows the officers, they have little room to decide whether or not to make an arrest—in most cases they have no choice. Furthermore, since there are incentives for arrests, the officer's own self-interests also instigate the formal procedure of arrest rather than an informal alternative. Thus, instead of relying on an officer's assessment of the situation and taking actions in terms of his/her common sense, the strict regulations and control give the organization almost total discretion.

The legalistic departments, while relatively narrow and severe in the margin given individual officers, are by far the most equitable. As Wilson notes, in discretionary situations there is a trade-off between the leniency of watchman organizations and the equality of legalistic organizations. In arrest decisions, watchman officers are far more likely to let someone go with just a warning, but their patterns of arrests tend to discriminate against minorities and the poor. The legalistic style, on the other hand, does not discriminate patterns of citations or arrests—everybody receives the same harsh decision.

The Service Style

The third style of policing described by Wilson attempts to combine the efficiency of the legalistic style and the broad informal discretion of the watchman style. Wilson describes it as follows:

> In some communities, the police take seriously all requests for either law enforcement or order maintenance (unlike police with a watchman style), but they are less likely to respond by making an arrest or otherwise imposing formal sanction (unlike the police with a legalistic style.) The police intervene frequently but not formally. This style is often found in homogeneous, middle-class communities in which there is a high level of apparent agreement among citizens on the need for and definition of public order, but in which there is no administrative demand for a legalistic style. In these places, the police see their chief responsibility as protecting a common definition of public order against the minor and occasional threats posed by unruly teenagers and "outsiders" (tramps, derelicts, visiting college boys). Though there will be family quarrels, they will be few in number, private in nature, and constrained by general understandings requiring seemly conduct. The middle-class character of such communities makes the suppression of illegal enterprises both easy (they are more visible) and necessary (public opinion will not tolerate them), and it reduces the rate of serious crime committed by residents; thus, the police will be freer to concentrate on managing traffic, regulating juveniles, and providing services.[26]

Organizationally, the service style reflects the dispersed precincts of the watchman organization; however, the purpose of the decentralization is to maintain a sense of "local" community oriented police and not the partisan political dispersion of the watchman forces. It is political only in terms of good community relations—not patronage.[27] The service in these departments is defined in terms of what the community sees as its major crime problems, burglary, for instance, rather than in terms of any priorities set by the department or the law. For example, in one service style department, high priority was given to runaways and lost children—not because of any law violations involved in running away from home, but rather because a missing child is a major cause for concern.[28] Since the organization does not measure performance solely on the basis of law enforcement activities, but rather on how appropriately a situation is handled by an officer, there is no effort to maximize the number of arrests except in those areas of community concern. However, there is a maximum effort to provide service. All calls for police help are handled as quickly as possible, either as order maintenance, law enforcement, or simply service (e.g., finding lost children). Thus, individual officers are evaluated by the promptness and appropriateness of their responses and not by the narrow legalistic criteria of handling the situation as a law enforcement problem.

SERVICE DISCRETION   An officer's discretion in service organizations is tied to the nature of the community. The very nature of most communities where service organizations are found makes discretion relatively simple in that there is homogeneity—there is a common understanding of what is appropriate under a given set of circumstances. On the one hand, this gives the officer a good deal of discretion. He/she decides the correct course of action on the basis of his/her understanding of community mores. On the other hand, this limits the choices to those mores. To a great extent (as we saw in discussing reactive organizations) the discretion rests with what the citizen wants done—either directly in a situation or in terms of more general police department policies. In this context, then, discretion refers more to being attuned to community values than to decisions made on the basis of an officer's individual values.

Situational Elements of Arrest Decisions

We have seen that the organizational context determines discretion on a departmental level; but the situation in which a crime occurs also has several variables that determine whether or not an arrest will be made. In this section we will examine the major variables that affect an arrest. It should be pointed out again, however, that the typical encounter between a police officer and a citizen does not end in an arrest or citation, and most discretion is the decision *not* to make an arrest when there is probable cause to do so.

Seriousness of Crime

Above all else, the most important variable in whether or not a police officer will make an arrest is the seriousness of the crime. Major felonies such as homicide and robbery virtually always result in an arrest regardless of other variables involved—including organizational policy, previous record, demeanor, and the race of the suspect.[29] All of the variables we have discussed before and all of those we will discuss are less accurate as predictors of arrests than the seriousness of the crime.

What is considered to be a serious crime varies both in time and interpretation. However, once a given offense is defined as being a serious crime, arrest is fairly automatic. There is a reflexive connection between the course of action taken by the police and the characterization of the offense—if an arrest is made, the offense is considered serious and a serious offense warrants an arrest. The offense justifies the arrest, and the arrest points to the seriousness of the offense.[30]

Previous Record

A suspected offender's previous record plays a mixed role in arrests. Generally, if a suspect has a previous record, he is more likely to be arrested than someone who does not.[31] The problem, however, as noted by Piliavin and Briar, is that most police patrol officers do not have a suspected offender's record on hand when deciding to make an arrest.[32] Thus, while such a record may determine whether or not an arrest will be made, it is not readily available and therefore is not that significant as a variable.

In small jurisdictions where the police come to know who does and does not have a record, it will play a larger role, and, even in large metropolitan police departments, specialized investigative units *do* have access to records, and they use them. For example, the gang detail of one city used its extensive files (including previous arrests) on gang members for determining the course of action to take in arrest situations. However, since most of the crimes they investigated were serious ones usually involving homicide, attempted homicide, robbery, and assaults, the seriousness of the crime was the main consideration in an arrest;[33] but there can be a trade-off with previous records and arrest. Sometimes offenders with previous records will act as informants for the police, and this may even lead to an inverse relationship between arrest and previous record. Those with previous records have the most information to offer and so are in the best position to make a deal with officers for their freedom.[34]

Demeanor

Of all the situational variables, **demeanor** has been the most widely studied. In one of the earliest such studies, Piliavan and Briar found that demeanor was directly linked with the arrest of juveniles. To the extent that juveniles who had committed petty crimes were cooperative with the police, they were not arrested; those who were uncooperative were taken into custody.[35] In further studies of demeanor and arrests, the relationship was not as strong, and it became clear that while the police did use demeanor as one indicator in deciding to make arrests it was not as strong as was suggested by Piliavan's and Briar's study.

In a study by Black and Reiss, it was found that, while antagonistic suspects were slightly more likely to be arrested than those who acted in a civil or very deferential manner, the difference was not significant.[36] In a replication of the Black and Reiss study by Lundman, Sykes, and Clark, similar patterns were found. However, unlike Black and Reiss, Lundman, Sykes, and Clark found that those who were very deferential were the most likely to be arrested, and those with a civil demeanor were far less likely to be arrested.[37] A further replication by Sanders found essentially the same thing to be true.[38] One of the problems with these studies is that the police themselves said that they used an **attitude test** (i.e., an assessment of an individual's demeanor) in making determinations in arrest situations. Since the findings contradicted what the police themselves claimed—and especially since the police said their own behavior was *not* objective—the findings are somewhat perplexing.

A partial explanation was discovered by Reiss. Specifically, he found that the complainant's preference had considerable weight in the decision of whether or not to arrest.[39] Thus, if a suspect was especially antagonistic, a citizen's unwillingness to file a complaint accounts for nonarrest patterns. The nature of a suspect's antagonism toward the police also appears to influence officers' arrest decisions. In many police encounters, particularly domestic disputes, all parties (those involved in the altercation) are generally antagonistic. The antagonism is not directed toward the police officers, rather there is a "general antagonism." As a result, the police do not perceive themselves as the primary target of the antagonistic behavior, do not take it personally, and do not typically exercise their arrest option.[40]

Specialized Police Units

Much of the research on police has centered on routine patrol, and, while there has been some research on investigative units, it seems slight by comparison to the number of patrol studies. The romanticized view of police detectives—Sherlock Holmes, Sam Spade, Kojak, and similar characters of fiction and film—distorts the basic operations of these units. Some specialized units such as the traffic division are accurately portrayed to the public, and the undercover "narcs" who investigate drug cases are also familiar. However, the basic work of the other mainline units within police departments are not as familiar, so we will briefly review their roles in police work and discretion.

The Detectives

There are several different subdivisions of detectives or "investigators," as they are usually called in police departments. Large departments have very fine divisions of responsibility while smaller departments have more general groupings. To simplify matters, we will discuss investigations in four general categories: 1) major crimes, 2) property crimes, 3) juveniles, and 4) morals.

MAJOR CRIMES   Major crimes usually include crimes of violence such as homicide, rape, assault, kidnapping, and robbery. The investigators who deal with these offenses are considered the best, and positions in such units are the most sought after. Compared to officers in other units, especially juvenile, these officers are considered to be dealing with "real crime" and "real criminals"—whose arrest is not typically subject to question.

Given the nature of the crimes and those involved in them, there is relatively little discretion once a suspect has been identified—he or she is almost always arrested. However, there is discretion at another level. Most of the cases investigated by major crime detectives are received from patrol reports. The supervisors go over the reports and decide which ones will receive investigative resources. Cases considered petty such as assaults where both parties appear to have been responsible (e.g., bar fights) will receive little or no investigative resources, while homicides will virtually always be investigated.[41] Even with homicides, the police sometimes exercise "discretion by interpretation." For example, one homicide detail had reports of seven homicides in a single week, one being a very difficult quadruple homicide. During the week a case was received in which another "possible homicide" had occurred. It involved a report that a man and a woman were having a fight in a back bedroom. A shot was fired. The woman came out of the room and told her daughter that the man had just shot himself and to call an ambulance. The man died before he arrived at the hospital. Such a report usually would be investigated as a possible homicide, but given the pressure to solve seven other murders the officers involved decided it "sounded like a suicide." No investigation was pursued.[42] Thus, one of the criteria in investigative discretion is the work load. The greater the work load, the more discretion is exercised not to make an investigation.

PROPERTY CRIMES   Property crimes are so numerous and routine in comparison to major crimes that the procedures for investigating them are done by a formula. Most typical of detective units investigating property crimes are burglary detectives. On a daily basis they receive reports of several burglaries of both residences and businesses. Here discretion is exercised in a far more general manner than in major crimes. The typical burglary is not investigated extensively. Usually the investigation consists of no more than a phone call to the victim or a single visit to the crime scene. This is not because of laziness on the part of the investigators, but because most burglaries have very few investigative leads. Even though the crime is considered serious in the context of all crimes, there are simply too many to handle—and time is allocated to those with the best leads and largest loss. It may be true that if every burglary were investigated thoroughly that leads could be developed, but given the resources of most departments there simply is not enough time to do so. It is deemed better to spend time on cases that will lead to an arrest than to waste time on cases that are not likely to be solved.[43]

JUVENILE INVESTIGATORS   In the pecking order of police investigators, the juvenile detectives are at the bottom. Referred to as "Kiddie Kops" by their colleagues, their work is considered trivial.[44] This stereotype is inaccurate; juvenile officers typically have the most varied types of cases, and there is a high rate of crimes committed by juveniles. Discretion in investigating cases in these units is handled very much as other investigative units are handled, with one exception. While major-crime and property-crime details have "serious crime" criteria (i.e., the more serious the crime the greater the likelihood that it will be investigated), the juvenile detail operates on a slightly different basis. With the exception of runaway cases, the more serious offenses (based on general public views of seriousness) are given the highest priority. Runaways are given top priority even though they are considered trivial by the public at large. Because of the pressure brought on the department by parents of runaways, these cases are automatically investigated.[45]

MORALS INVESTIGATORS   The term "morals" here refers to vice, narcotics, and similar consensual crimes. These units operate very much on the basis of a proactive model, and, even though there are citizens who call and complain about prostitutes, drug addicts, and other characters who are viewed as immoral, the general work of these details is based on policies generated within the department.[46] Thus, the organizational style and type of leadership within the police department largely determines how cases are handled by a given morals detail. Citizen crusades to clean up vice will often prompt action by such units. Filtered through the political and departmental structure, such campaigns can indirectly affect discretion; however, such movements are typically shortlived, and the police can always claim that while they take care of moral crimes the bulk of their resources is by necessity directed against violent crimes and property crimes.

SUMMARY

The discussion of the police has focused primarily on arrest decisions. Under a purely legalistic definition, in all cases where the police have probable cause to make an arrest for a crime, an arrest will be made. However, since the typical interaction between police and criminal suspects results in no arrest, it is important to understand more than just the legal criteria for taking suspected criminals into custody. By examining several sociological variables in police discretion, we can better understand the observed patterns.

The first consideration in examining discretion is the organization in a sociopolitical context. Depending on the kind of departmental organization and political structure, different kinds of discretion patterns emerge. Since the most sweeping consequences in patterns of discretion can be seen by comparing different forms of police organization, and by understanding the different kinds of organizations and policies, it is possible to account for the vastly different arrest rates from department to department.

At the same time, we find discretion is patterned along the lines of the interaction situation. One of the most important determinants is citizen discretion which effectively passes the discretion from the officer to the citizen. While the effect of most variables on arrest decisions varies by context, the seriousness of the offense appears to consistently affect law enforcement activity.

The final element of discretion is found in the detective division where the discretion lies in whether or not to investigate a case. Basically, the same general parameters—the seriousness of the crime, the wishes of the victim, etc.—are used by detectives in deciding whether or not to investigate a case. However, unlike patrol officers, detectives rely more heavily on investigative leads in their decision whether or not to carry out an investigation.

Overall, it is important to understand that the police do not make arrests solely on legal criteria. Like all social encounters, those situations where police make decisions are also social, and they are affected by community norms, organizational structure, and all the other social forces affecting nonpolice.

Glossary

Attitude Test   A police term to denote if a defendant has a positive or negative demeanor. (See DEMEANOR).

Case Law   Appellate court decisions that interpret the precise meaning of a law stemming from a particular case which will then apply to all similar cases.

Coercive Force   Using physical force. Refers to the legal ability of police to use such force in arrests, even though it is typically unnecessary.

Demeanor   The general behavior of a person in terms of respect or lack of respect. Demeanor has been an important variable in studies of police discretion.

Legalistic Style   A type of police organization using strict departmental policies for enforcing the law, treating most situations as law enforcement cases rather than peace-keeping ones.

Police Discretion   The decision by police officers to make or not to make an arrest (or issue a citation) in circumstances where they have legal cause to do so.

Proactive Policing   Actions by the police to enforce the law in situations where they have not been called by a complainant. Drug enforcement is usually proactive.

Probable Cause   A legal requirement that police officers must have a good reason to believe a specific person committed a specific crime before making an arrest.

Procedure by Incongruity   Looking for items and events that do not "fit" in a particular situation. Used by police to pick out possible law violators.

Reactive Policing   Police mobilizations that respond directly to a citizen's request for services.

Service Style   Police organization typically found in homogeneous communities where there is a high consensus as to what the police should do. The police respond to all calls, but they are expected to exercise discretion based on community norms and not on a strict interpretation of the laws.

Watchman Style   A form of police organization with little mobility, low pay, and minimal expectations of police officers. Most situations are treated as order maintenance and not law enforcement.

Questions

1. What is the importance of studying police discretion in explaining patterns of crime?

2. What are the legal criteria for arrest? When decisions to make arrests are made, why is it that the decision usually is not to make the arrest even though there is sufficient legal cause to do so?

3. What are the different interpretations of the origins of police organizations? What is the extent of police power?

4. What are aspects of proactive and reactive elements in all police organizations? What social, organizational, and political forces influence whether a police department is more proactive or reactive?

5. Of the several variables in police discretion, why is seriousness of the crime always the most important? How does the definition of the situation affect a crime's seriousness?

Notes

1. Wayne LaFave, *Arrest: The Decision to Take a Suspect into Custody.* (Boston: Little, Brown, 1965), p. 245.

2. William B. Sanders, *Detective Work: A Study of Criminal Investigations.* (New York: Free Press, 1977), p. 68.

3. Harold Garfinkel, *Studies in Ethnomethodology.* (Englewood Cliffs, NJ: Prentice-Hall, 1967).

4. Harvey Sacks, "Notes on Police Assessment of Moral Character," in David Sudnow, *Studies in Social Interaction.* (New York: Free Press, 1972).

5. William H. Campbell, "Report on Young Gang Violence in California," (Sacramento: California Department of Justice, June 1981): 38–42. Prepared under the auspices of the Attorney General's Youth Gang Task Force.

6. LaFave, 1965, 249.

7. Richard J. Lundman, "Organizational Norms and Police Discretion: An Observational Study of Police Work with Traffic Law Violators," *Criminology* 17 (August 1979): 159–171.

8. The President's Commission on Law Enforcement and Administration of Justice, *Task Force Report: The Police.* (Washington, DC: U.S. Government Printing Office, 1967), pp. 3–12.

9. Richard Lundman, *The Police and Policing: An Introduction.* (New York: Holt, Rinehart and Winston, 1980).

10. Lundman, 1980, 31.

11. Ibid.

12. Lundman, 1980, 30–35.

13. Albert J. Reiss, Jr., *The Police and the Public.* (New Haven, CT: Yale University Press, 1971).

14. Jerome Skolnick and J. Richard Woodworth, "Bureaucracy, Information and Social Control," in David Bordua, *The Police: Six Sociological Essays.* (New York: Wiley, 1967), p. 100.

15. Research observation by the author, Florida, 1976.

16. Reiss, 1971, 11.

17. Reiss, 1971, 7.

18. Donald J. Black, "The Social Organization of Arrest," *Stanford Law Review* 23 (June 1971): 1087–1111.

19. Sanders, 1977, 49.

20. Sanders, 1977, 48–50.

21. James Q. Wilson, *Varieties of Police Behavior.* (Cambridge: Harvard University Press, 1968).

22. Wilson, 1968, 155.

23. Wilson, 1968, 184.

24. Wilson, 1968, 177.

25. Ibid.

26. Wilson, 1968, 200.

27. Wilson, 1968, 203.

28. Sanders, 1977, 137.

29. See LaFave, 1965; Irving Piliavin and Scott Briar, "Police Encounters with

Juveniles," *American Journal of Sociology* **70** (September 1964): 206–214; Reiss, 1971; Black, 1971; Richard E. Sykes, James C. Fox and John P. Clark, "A Socio-Legal Theory of Police Discretion," in Arthur Niederhoffer and Abraham S. Blumberg, *The Ambivalent Force,* 2nd ed. (Hinsdale, IL: Dryden Press, 1976), pp. 171–183.

30. Garfinkel, 1967, 45.

31. Piliavin and Briar, 1964.

32. Ibid.

33. Research by the author in progress, 1980–1981.

34. Jerome Skolnick, *Justice Without Trial.* (New York: Wiley, 1966).

35. Piliavin and Briar, 1964.

36. Donald Black and Albert J. Reiss, Jr., "Police Control of Juveniles," *American Sociological Review* **35** (February 1970): 63–77.

37. Richard Lundman, Richard E. Sykes and John P. Clark, "Police Control of Juveniles: A Replication," *Journal of Research in Crime and Delinquency* **15** (January 1978): 74–91.

38. William B. Sanders, "Police Occasions," *Criminal Justice Review* **4** (Spring 1979): 1–14.

39. Reiss, 1971.

40. Sanders, 1979, 12.

41. Sanders, 1977, 169–170.

42. Field research observations by the author, 1981.

43. Sanders, 1977, 150–164.

44. Skolnick and Woodworth, 1967, 116–121.

16

Prosecution and Adjudication

What to Look For:

The meaning and effects of proprietary justice.

How plea bargaining has become standardized into routine deals.

The nature of charging discretion and what criteria are used to file charges in cases.

How the process of plea negotiations operates.

The differences in patterns of outcomes with private and public defense attorneys and client perceptions of the different attorneys.

The difference between summary and jury trials.

Introduction

AFTER A CRIMINAL SUSPECT has been arrested by the police, that person then comes under the jurisdiction of the criminal courts. The process of what happens to the suspected criminal offender, the defendant, is the topic of this chapter. Our discussion will not be confined, however, to the idealized legal processing of criminals; instead we will discuss typical patterns of adjudication and prosecution in the context of the legal structure.

First, we will confront the fact that legal work in the United States is a business. That is, many criminal attorneys defend people primarily to make a profit. The extent to which profit affects the defense work is an important consideration we will discuss.

Secondly, just as the fate of the suspect is a matter of police discretion, the fate of the criminal defendant is a matter of discretion. The prosecutor has the power to decide whether or not to prosecute a defendant, even if he or she has the necessary legal requirements to do so. We will examine the decision-making process in light of both legal and sociological concepts to determine the extent to which the procedures are consistent with the Constitutional ideals of justice and how they can be understood as social issues.

Thirdly, we will examine the relationship between prosecutors and defense attorneys in the context of the legal structure. The focus will be on the extent to which the relationship is an adversary one (as envisioned in the Constitution) as opposed to a streamlined bureaucratic system for minimizing processing time at the expense of justice.

Finally, we will look at the process of the trial. A jury trial is the ideal of the criminal justice system, but since, as we will see, it is not typically used in the great majority of criminal cases, it will be left to the end.

The Legal Structure

From an ideal legal point of view, once a criminal suspect is arrested, the case is reviewed by a grand jury or public prosecutor to decide whether or not a defendant should be charged with the crime and brought to trial. If it is decided that there is sufficient probable cause to bring the defendant to trial, the prosecutor will represent the people, and the defendant will be represented by an attorney equally adept in criminal law.[1] The judge informs the defendant that, if he or she cannot afford an attorney, one will be appointed free of charge by the state. These are called **court-appointed attorneys** or **public defenders**.[2]

At this point, we must consider the ramifications for the defendant of paying for an attorney. If a person pays for an attorney, are the possibilities of getting a better defense greater than if one is appointed and paid for by the state? Since as a legal ideal a person is assumed innocent until proven guilty, to what extent does having the defendant pay for a defense counsel add an additional fine, especially if the defendant is innocent? Overall, how does the institution of paid legal representation affect the process of adjudication and prosecution?

Proprietary Justice

Since many criminal defendants are compelled to pay for defense attorneys, we must examine the extent to which our justice system is guided by proprietary interests over strictly legal ones. That is, how much does the interest in maximizing profits determine the actions of defense attorneys, prosecutors, and judges? To begin our examination, we will look at the outcomes of criminal cases where the defendant is represented by a public prosecutor or a court-appointed attorney as compared to a **private attorney** hired by the defendant. If the process is guided significantly by financial considerations, we would expect private attorneys to obtain better outcomes for their clients than public defenders.

Research on the effect of having a private attorney rather than a court-appointed lawyer or public defender suggests that there is no significant difference in the outcome of a criminal case.[3] A typical criminal defendant has an equal chance of being convicted whether represented by a private attorney or public defender. Table 16.1 shows the breakdown in outcomes.

Table 16.1 Type of Attorney and Outcome			
Attorney	**Guilty**	**Dropped**	**Not Guilty**
Prosecutor	48%	48%	4%
Public Defender	48%	48%	4%
Court Appointed	71%	29%	0%
Private Attorney	42%	52%	6%

Source: David B. Sten, Joseph M. Crevasse III, and Dennis Mosley, "Relationship of Prosecutor to Defense Attorney in the Criminal Justice System." (Unpublished research paper, University of Florida, 1976).

In examining the stages in the justice process where the defendant entered a plea of guilty, however, we find a very interesting difference. Those defendants represented by legal-aid or public defenders were advised to enter a plea of guilty much earlier than those with a privately retained attorney. Table 16.2 shows a clear pattern of privately retained attorneys suggesting their clients enter guilty pleas in the later stages of the process.

Contact	Private	Legal-aid	Assigned	Total
First	35%	49%	60%	40%
Second	44%	29%	17%	32%
Third	15%	13%	9%	13%
Fourth or more	6%	7%	11%	7%
No Response	0%	3%	4%	2%
Total	100%	100%	100%	*101 100%

Table 16.2   Type of Attorney and Stage of Guilty Plea

*Over 100% due to rounding

Source: Abraham Blumberg, "The Practice of Law As a Confidence Game, Organizational Cooptation of a Profession," *Law and Society Review* 1 (June 1967): 38. © Law and Society Association, 1967.

At first glance, it may seem that private attorneys try harder to free their clients, but on closer examination it was found that something very different was happening. According to Abraham Blumberg, the private attorneys "con" their clients into believing they are getting a special deal from the prosecutor for entering a plea of guilty.[4] Since most defendants who end up pleading guilty, receive pretty much the same adjudication decisions, private attorneys in most cases are not worth the fees they charge their clients. In order to convince their clients that they are worth the fees they charge, private attorneys often advise defendants to enter pleas of not guilty in the early stages of the adjudication and prosecution process. Simply put, to provide his client with tangible proof of his/her efforts, private attorneys tend to delay the time when they suggest that their clients enter guilty pleas.[5]

Charging Discretion

The decision to charge a criminal suspect with a crime is largely in the hands of the prosecutor. While it is true that grand juries hand down indictments, it is typically on the recommendation of the prosecutor that the grand jury makes its decision.[6] Therefore, in order to understand the dynamics of charging discretion, we must examine the criteria used by the prosecutor in his decision making.

Formally, the prosecutor determines if the information provided to him in a criminal case supports probable cause that a specific person has committed a specific crime (this is essentially the same criteria used by police officers). He must decide two things: 1) if the suspect should be charged, 2) what the charges should be.[7] However, informally or realistically the prosecutor must take into consideration several other elements and variables. Can the case be prosecuted? In essence this means, Can it be won? Is there pressure from the police or others to prosecute? Would justice be served by prosecution? These and other questions play a role in the prosecutor's decision.

WHAT TO CHARGE The prosecutor can **file an information** (file charges) against a defendant for many or few violations of the law. He can file for every possible charge if he believes the crime is especially bad. For instance, if a rape victim is badly beaten, a defendant may be charged with kidnapping and assault in addition to rape. Secondly, a prosecutor may charge a defendant with only one of several possible charges. A convicted felon, for example, who used a gun in a robbery may not be charged with illegal possession of a gun in addition to armed robbery. Thirdly, the prosecutor may charge the defendant with less than is possible. For example, for first-time offenders, a prosecutor may charge a man accused of burglary (a felony) with petty theft (a misdemeanor). Finally, a prosecutor may decide not to charge a person with anything at all, even though there is sufficient evidence to do so. This is called **nolo prosequi**, and is virtually as good as an acquittal.

What are the reasons a prosecutor would charge one person with all offenses and another with only a few or none at all? According to Kaplan, the following reasons are pertinent:

1. *Standing in the community.* To charge an upstanding person with a crime, let alone convict him, brings punishment far beyond what is necessary.

2. *Prior offenses.* In many cases, first-time offenders are not seriously committed to crime as a way of life.

3. *Age and health.* The rigors of processing may impose a severe hardship on defendants who are old or in ill health. Furthermore, when the physical condition of the accused substantially precludes the ability to maintain criminal conduct, the need for punishment is reduced.[8]

These criteria do not apply to all situations, particulary not to serious crimes such as robbery or murder. Even an upstanding, older member of the community would not be let off if his first offense were murder, but these criteria do apply for the typical petty offenses that come to the attention of prosecutors.

A more important element in the charging decision is that **full charges** are seen as a strategy for the general operation of the prosecutor's office and as a political expedience. In many cases the defendant will agree to plead guilty only if charges are substantially reduced. Since a "substantial" reduction is relative to the original charges, full maximum charges facilitate bargaining. For instance, if a defendant is charged with rape, assault, brandishing a weapon, and kidnapping, it is far easier to convince the defendant to plead guilty and that he is getting a deal if all the charges except rape are dropped. Three-quarters of the arrest charges sounds good—even though all the prosecutor really wants is a conviction on the rape charge. This pattern was noted by Newman in the following observation:

The other day the bargaining prosecutor came in and told us: "For God's sake, give me something to work with over there. Don't reduce these cases over here; let me do it over there or many of these guys will be tried on a misdemeanor." What he was referring to is, if we had graded a case at the lowest charge in the class of offenses in which it logically belonged, a defense attorney could conceivably get his man to plead to even lower crime, a misdemeanor, for example.[9]

Likewise, a prosecutor who has full charges can create the appearance of a tough prosecutor for political purposes if he/she believes such an image has mass public appeal.

There is a certain danger in getting too carried away with maximum charging, for such a practice can put a strain on organizational resources. Felonies take far more of the court's time and resources than do misdemeanors, and by reducing certain felonies to misdemeanors the cases can be handled relatively quickly.[10] Generally, the prosecutor's office would prefer to have a more serious charge reduced to obtain conviction than to go through a long drawn-out trial that may ultimately result in the defendant being convicted on the original charges.

Given the tactical reasons for having full charges and the practical exigencies for not carrying through with them, there are still patterns of full charging under certain conditions. The following circumstances typify the conditions in which one finds prosecution of full charges:

1. There is a strong desire by the community to separate itself from the offender. One who is seen as a persistent criminal in the community is more likely to be fully charged than a first-time or occasional offender.

2. There is a great deal of publicity surrounding the case. This can be due to an especially heinous crime, (such as multiple rape and murder) or the assassination or attempted assassination of a public figure (such as the case with John Lennon's killer and President Reagan's attempted killer).

3. Law enforcement agencies can be assisted by full charging. Generally, this is when full charging is used as a lever to obtain cooperation from a defendant in pleading guilty. It becomes a tangible threat held over the head of the defendant. For example, in cases where charges are reduced in return for cooperation by the defendant (such as offering testimony against codefendant) full charges will be brought against the defendant if the defendant reneges on the deal.

Routinized Justice

A major feature of adjudication and prosecution has been **bargain justice**, **plea negotiation**, and **assembly-line justice**.[11] As opposed to adversary justice, the major features of assembly-line justice include bureaucratic concern with fast processing over lengthy due process, routine reduction of charges, overcharging defendants with initial charges, and cooperation between the prosecution and the defense.[12] The cause for concern over bargain justice has been based on both the rights of the defendant and those of the victim. On the one hand, in a system where the defendant is seen to "cooperate" by entering a guilty plea, there is no assumption of innocence, and there is a greater chance that innocent suspects will be coerced into cooperating even though they have broken no law. On the other hand, if a criminal defendant is not convicted of the crimes he or she committed, the victim feels cheated and the criminal law is undermined. The ideal of a fair and impartial jury trial for all is largely a myth. While the prosecution and defense may appear to work on opposite sides, most of their efforts are cooperative with little concern for the rights of the defendant or the victim. The extent to which this kind of justice dominates American criminal courts can be seen in Table 16.3.

Table 16.3 Guilty Plea Convictions in Trial Courts

State (1964 Statistics Unless Otherwise Noted)	Total Convictions	Guilty Pleas	Percent of Total
California (1965)	30,840	22,817	74.0
Connecticut	1,596	1,494	93.9
District of Columbia	1,115	817	73.3
Hawaii	393	360	91.5
Illinois	5,591	4,768	85.2
Kansas	3,025	2,727	90.2
Massachusetts (1963)	7,790	6,642	85.2
Minnesota (1965)	1,567	1,437	91.7
New York	17,249	16,464	95.5
Pennsylvania (1960)	25,632	17,108	66.8
U.S. District Courts	29,170	26,273	90.2
Average (excluding Pennsylvania)			87.0

Source: President's Commission on Law Enforcement and Administration of Justice, *Task Force Report: The Courts* (Washington, D.C.: U.S. Government Printing Office, 1967) p. 9.

Assembly-Line Justice

Getting defendants through the front door of arrest and out the back door of disposition as fast as possible seems to be the preoccupation of adjudication and prosecution. The emphasis on speedy resolution endangers both the rights of the criminal defendants and their victims; shortcuts increase the possibility of convicting the innocent and releasing the guilty. The extent to which speed and efficiency have come to dominate the justice process can be seen in one urban drunk court where their average case took only 30 seconds![13] Likewise, in the lower courts, where 90 percent of all criminal cases are heard, speedy trials undermine justice. According to a Presidential Commission study:

> Speed is the watchword. Trials in misdemeanor cases may be over in a matter of 5, 10, or 15 minutes; they rarely last an hour even in relatively complicated cases. Traditional safeguards honored in felony cases lose their meaning in such proceedings; yet there is still the possibility of lengthy imprisonment or heavy fine.[14]

The courtroom itself is typically used only to formally announce what has been decided elsewhere. The conviction and disposition have been hammered out by the defense and prosecuting attorneys in their offices. Defendants and their attorneys enter the courtroom or the judge's chambers; they explain the agreement they have reached concerning the plea, charges, and sometimes sentence; and the judge simply formalizes the procedure in the courtroom by accepting the plea and handing down a sentence.

Sometimes, either inside or outside the courtroom, the defendant will not want to go along with the routine and will cause trouble for his attorney by refusing to plead guilty or accept a deal involving a guilty plea. The defense attorney (rather than any mythical cop in the back room with a rubber hose) will then wrest a guilty plea from his client. According to Blumberg, the defense attorney is most likely to first suggest a plea of guilty to the defendant and is most influential in getting the defendant to do so.[15] Blumberg points out:

> The overwhelming majority of accused persons, regardless of type of counsel, related a specific incident which indicated an urging or suggestion, either during the course of the first or second contact, that they plead guilty to a lesser charge if this could be arranged. Of all the agent-mediators, it is the lawyer who is most effective in manipulating an accused's perspective, notwithstanding pressures that may have been previously applied by police, district attorney, judge, or any of the agent-mediators that may have been activated by them.[16]

This cooperation by the defense counsel is essential in keeping things moving.

Typical cases do not involve jury trials, but rather "deals." However, in sensational cases, such as that of the "Hillside Strangler" in Los Angeles, both prosecuting and defense attorneys can gain a good deal of publicity by taking the case to court. The Hillside Strangler suspect, Angelo Buono, received a vigorous defense case from his attorney.

Recalcitrant defendants are not perceived by defense attorneys to be "standing up for their rights"—they are seen as troublemakers. In his study of a public defender's office, Sudnow notes:

> Some defendants don't buy the offer of less time as constituting sufficient grounds for avoiding a trial. To others, it appears that "copping out" is worse than having a trial, regardless of the consequences for the length of sentence. The following remarks, taken from P.D. files, illustrate the terms in which such stubborn defendants are conceived:
>
> "Defendant wants a trial, but he is dead. In lieu of a possible 995, D.A. agreed to put note in his file recommending a deal. This should be explored and encouraged as big break for Defendant. Chance of successful defense negligible. Defendant realizes this but says he ain't going to cop to no strong-arm. See if we can set him straight. Dead case. Too many witnesses and . . . used in two of the transactions. However, Defendant is very squirmy jailhouse lawyer and refuses to face facts."[17]

These remarks clearly indicate the defense attorney's desire for his client to "get with the program" and plead guilty. However, the defense attorney is not attempting to sell his client short, but in the context of the courthouse he is attempting to serve him. The defense attorney, based on his experience in court, is attempting to be realistic. As the public defender's notes indicated, one case had "too many witnesses," and taking such a case to trial would mean almost certain conviction. Therefore, entering a guilty plea was the most reasonable course of action because it would mean a lesser sentence for his client. At the same time, given the case load of public defenders (or the economic realities of private attorneys), it is a waste of time to go to a trial with a case that will be lost. Likewise, it is seen as a disservice to the courts to take their time with a case that could be expedited with a guilty plea. In this light, from the position of the prosecutor and defense attorney, assembly-line justice is seen as a fair, inexpensive, and realistic way of doing justice.

From Plea Bargaining to Standard Deals

One of the major reasons prosecutors are willing to reduce the initial charges against a defendant is to entice him or her to plead guilty. For the defense attorney, it is possible to get a lighter sentence for the client and save time and money in the process. Aside from various problems with this practice (such as railroading innocent defendants, undermining the law, and creating a negative image of the force of law), there is the question of equity. On the one hand, we saw that private attorneys and public defenders have about the same record in winning and losing cases, so for most criminal cases, there is equity in the sense that economics does not determine the outcome. However, there is another kind of equity. Will two defendants, both brought to court for their first offense, receive the same disposition if the same circumstances surrounded their offense?

This question has two sides, one legal and the other sociological. The legal issue involves the concept of **uniformity** under the law.[18] Uniformity simply means that everyone is treated equally under the law regardless of economic or social characteristics. Matza notes the following in relation to the idea of consistency:

> In its simplist form, justice in law consists in no more than taking seriously the notion that what is to be applied to a multiplicity or different persons is the same general rule, undeflected by prejudice, interest, or caprice. This impartiality is what the procedural standards known . . . as principles of "Natural Justice" are designed to secure. Hence, though the most odious laws may be justly applied, we have in the bare notion of applying a general rule of law, the germ at least of justice.[19]

The sociological issue of equity has to do with the sense that justice has been done—a link between the legal ideal and social expectations of the law. However, rather than being interested in equity for its own sake, sociologists see it as an important element in binding people to the law. If a person breaks the law, and he or she is punished, there is a sense of justice in that one individual's treatment under the law is the same as all others'. The extent to which there is a perceived element of inequity, there is a sense of wrongdoing in the legal institutions and a loosening of the bonds to the law. Matza summarizes this point as follows:

> The moral bond of law is loosened whenever a sense of injustice prevails. Law, whatever its guiding principle, trial by ordeal or due process, binds members of society to the extent that it maintains a semblance of even-handed administration. Guiding principles may vary, but, whatever their substance, persistent violation of their spirit occurs at the peril of alienating the subjects of law and order. A legal style based on trial by ordeal is tenable, but one in which the internal logic of that system is regularly violated would to that extent lose the loyalty of its subjects. The legitimacy granted to law would be withdrawn.[20]

In other words, if people do not feel the law is equitable, they are less likely to feel obliged to abide by it.

The Process of Plea Bargaining

Keeping in mind the necessity of equity in the law, we will now examine the processes involved in plea negotiation. To begin with, the reduction of charges does not occur in the context of an arbitrary system in which crimes coming to the attention of the prosecutor's office are randomly reduced. Instead, there is an institutionalized yet informal procedure for deciding how a case should be handled. In his study of a public defender's office, David Sudnow found that cases were typified as being of a certain category of **normal crimes**.[21] The actual circumstances surrounding a given crime were specific and unique, but in order to work with defendants in terms of some standard their offenses were "normalized," or placed in a set of similar crimes. Once the set or class of normal crimes to which a given offense belonged had been determined, it was possible to apply a routine formula to that offense. In explaining this process, Sudnow notes:

> I shall call *normal crimes* those occurrences whose typical features, e.g., the ways they usually occur and the characteristics of persons who commit them (as well as the typical victims and typical scenes), are known and attended to by the P.D. (public defender). For any of a series of offense types, the P.D. can provide some form of proverbial characterization. For example, *burglary* is seen as involving regular violators, no weapons, low-priced items, little property damage, lower-class establishments, largely Negro defendants, independent operators, and a nonprofessional orientation to the crime.[21]

It is not necessary that the act or actor fit the mold of the normal crime or criminal, for there is a way to typify a crime so that it can be treated as a normal crime of some sort. For example, in a case involving "assault with caustic chemicals" (Section 244 of the California Penal Code), the prosecutor asked a police detective if the case should be a "battery" (Section 242) or "aggravated assault" (Section 245). The detective pointed out that the crime was correctly characterized as a 244 since the victim had been assaulted with chemicals sprayed in his face, but the prosecutor insisted that it be treated as either a battery or aggravated assault since these offenses were routine and could be handled more efficiently.[22]

In addition to normal crimes, there are normal deals or **standard deals**. Once it has been decided what a crime really is—how it is most acurately characterized in terms of normal crimes—there is a standard deal to go along with it. Thus, in dealing with their clients, attorneys (especially public defenders who have to cut through a great deal of material quickly to expedite their case load) seek to determine the gross characteristics of an offense rather than the fine details that may differentiate it from other crimes. Sudnow points out:

> When a P.D. puts questions to the defendant, he is less concerned with recording nuances of that instant event . . . than with establishing its similarity with "events of this sort." That similarity is established, not by discovering statutorily relevant events of the present case, but by locating the event in a sociologically constructed class of "such cases." The first questions directed to the defendant are of the character that answers to them either confirm or throw into question the assumed typicality.[23]

Thus, the character of the crime as determined by the prosecution and defense is more than just the criminal statute; it is the statute (or statutes) plus a characterization of what the actor is really like—Did he commit the crime in the fashion of a professional or an amateur? and What actually happened in the crime? Was it planned or committed on spur of the moment? Taken together, there is a characterization of the offense and offender that can be placed into a prepackaged deal.

Likewise, in misdemeanor courts plea bargaining has been replaced by standard deals. In their study of one such court, Mendes and Wold point out:

> Plea bargaining in Division 81 is also virtually routinized. The participants in bargaining make deals not on an individualized basis but according to the current policies of the court. Deputies have only limited discretion when "dealing" with defense attorneys. Thus, "plea bargaining" in Division 81 is typically devoid of any real bargaining. As one deputy city attorney observed: "Ninety-eight percent of the stuff here is routine. There is a policy covering almost every charge." And one judge asserted that "bargains are almost always predetermined. I can look at the defendant's arrest report and prior record and know in advance what the bargain will be. The actual bargaining is over the number of days of jail time to be credited or other relatively minor questions."[24]

The major aspect of discretion in the entire juridical process, then, is the characterization of the offense. Once that is determined, everything else is more or less automatic.

Returning to our original question about equity in the courts, we find that there is indeed equity—not what was expected, perhaps, but a kind of equity nevertheless. To the extent that plea negotiation has become standardized, an individual who commits a crime in a given gross manner will be given a disposition similar to all others who have been classified in the same way. While there will certainly be exceptions to this pattern (with for example different judges having different ideas of what is harsh and what is lenient—variables that may lead to inequities), the general policy of the courthouse is one of equity as defined by a set of standard deals.

Justice by Consent and Cooperation:
The Demise of Adversary Justice

Rosett and Cressey have characterized the institution of standard deals as **justice by consent**.[25] The defense attorneys, prosecutors, judges, probation officers, and others working in the courthouse are cognizant of the ways in which the system operates, as are the repeat offenders. Only the

"Obviously, I couldn't say this in open court, but my client is a sorcerer, and in exchange for leniency he is prepared to grant your Honor three wishes."

Source: Reproduced by Special Permission of PLAYBOY Magazine; Copyright © 1980 by Playboy.

naive and first offenders believe in the full adversary system. Everyone works to the end of obtaining the defendant's cooperation in going along with the system of justice that has been informally instituted.

The ideal of justice, however, has been based on an **adversary system**—one in which the interests of society (prosecutor) and those of the defendant (defense attorney) are equally represented. If the prosecution and defense are working together to get a person through the system instead of mounting evidence for their respective sides, the possibility exists that neither society nor the defendant are adequately represented. On the one hand, the criminal laws along with the punishments that accompany the laws are ideally a reflection of society.[26] On the other hand, if the defense attorney is working not to mount a defense for his client but to obtain his or her cooperation to plead guilty, he is not necessarily working in the best interests of his client. He may be working in the interests of the courthouse bureaucracy. If defense and prosecuting attorneys come to see the best interests of justice as being met by the smooth, efficient operation of the courthouse machinery rather than adversary due process, a courthouse bureaucracy replaces legal safeguards and criminal sanctions.

Again, we return to the sense of justice in the criminal justice process. Do defendants who go through the system, even though objectively there is general equity, feel that justice has been done? Rosett and Cressey point this out in discussing the typical (but fictional) case of Peter Randolph:

> Americans who commit serious crimes usually share the values of law-abiding citizens, including the sense that crime should be punished, that the process of justice should be fair, and that its operation should be visible. Peter Randolph was offended by what happened in the courthouse, to say nothing of what happened to him in jail. The problem was not the matter of his guilt, it was his discovery that he was a case to be processed by a mindless machine. The system treated him as less than a person, as an annoyance to be gotten rid of. Nobody was interested in who he was and how he got into trouble.[27]

This overall perception is an accurate portrayal of how defendants view their experiences. In one study of defendants' perspective of their experiences in the criminal justice system, it has been found that most defendants maintained strong images of an adversary system of justice. Johnathan Casper points out:

> Sizable majorities—typically approaching 85 to 90 percent of the respondents—embrace images of private lawyers quite like Perry Mason. Most were not speaking on the basis of direct experience, for only about 4 of 10 respondents had actually been represented in the past by a private lawyer. Since the literature dealing with private criminal attorneys suggests that many are somewhat exploitative marginal practitioners who depend upon turning over large numbers of cases paying rather small fees, we do not ar-

gue that these images are "correct." Rather, what is striking is simply that defendants embrace them.[28]

On the other hand, defendants were very critical of public defenders, and, while we have shown that, overall, privately retained lawyers and publically appointed ones have the same kinds of outcomes, the defendants perceive private attorneys to better fit the adversary image. Table 16.4 shows a breakdown of these perceptions.

Given the general belief concerning private attorneys and public defenders among criminal court defendants, it is surprising to find that the

Table 16.4   Defendant View of What Most Lawyers Are Like

"In general, most (private lawyers/public defenders) . . . "

	Private Lawyers	Public Defenders
1. Fight hard for their clients	87%	42%
2. Want their clients to plead not guilty	84%	43%
3. Tell their clients the truth	85%	54%
4. Listen to what their clients want to do	85%	53%
5. Do not care more about getting a case over with quickly than about getting justice for their clients	64%	30%
6. Do not want their clients to be convicted	94%	69%
7. Want to get the lightest possible sentence for their clients	92%	53%
8. Do not want their clients to be punished	92%	71%

(N = approximately 812)

"In general, would you say that (private lawyers/public defenders) are on their client's side, on the state's side, or somewhere in the middle between their client and the state?"

	Private Lawyers	Public Defenders
Client	86%	36%
Middle	8%	15%
State	6%	49%

(N = approximately 812)

Source: Jonathan D. Casper, *Criminal Courts: The Defendant's Perspective,* Executive Summary, (Washington, D.C.: U.S. Department of Justice, February, 1978): p. 3.

data show that the two do not produce vastly different outcomes. However, defendants are true believers in "the system" in its ideal form. In fact, those who are *clearly* guilty of crimes feel their interests have been sold out by a public defender who acquires a charge reduction. The following comments by defendants summarize this situation:

> *You get what you pay for. (A) private lawyer tries to get you off so he'll get paid. Money talks. When you're paying a private lawyer, he will spend more time on your case and check out every little angle. I feel I would get that extra effort and service if I was paying a private lawyer. If I was paying him, I think he would give that little extra above the normal effort that could be the difference between being convicted and not.*[29]

This kind of thinking reflects a very real belief in the adversary system. As Casper notes:

> In a sense, I think that we can understand the defendants' distrust of public defenders as indications that they are in this respect simply "good" Americans. That is to say, they have internalized some general norms common to most people in American society. I think it fair to say that in our society most of us are taught that things that cost more are likely to be of higher quality than those that cost less or are free. Because private attorneys cost something, because they can command more in the marketplace, they are likely to be more desirable and valuable . . . . In this sense, then, defendants see a marketplace—the hiring of private attorneys—in which they do not and cannot participate, and they are inclined to believe that the "goods" available are likely to be of higher quality than those that come without cost.[30]

Ironically, while defendants do feel a sense of injustice due to lack of an adversary system, their perception is fogged by a naive belief in "the system." They feel that an adversary justice does exist outside of their economic means—one where a private attorney will fight for his client's aquittal—even if the defendant is guilty. Thus, the lack of an adversary system which is more obvious with public defenders is not the point of contention with defendants; they believe that another justice is available to those with the means to pay for it. The truth is, such an ideal justice is just that—an ideal, and in the modern criminal justice system courtroom trials and adversary relationships are an exception rather than a rule.

Criminal Trials

Virtually any day of the week it is possible to walk into a courthouse and view a criminal case being tried. A judge and jury are present, and the prosecution and defense are in the roles of courtroom adversaries. Given the routine processing of criminal defendants, it may be surprising to find

Much of the legal system is based on proprietary interests of attorneys. To earn a living, attorneys must attract business, and even innocent defendants have to pay to have their innocence proven. Most guilty defendants believe that they can "buy justice" with a private attorney.

any trials at all; but even though the criminal trial (other than the summary trial) represents an exception to the routine handling of criminal cases, it plays an important role in the criminal justice system. In this section, we will examine some of the features of criminal trials and the process by which one comes to be on trial. It is important to remember, however, that a relatively small proportion of criminal defendants will ever go the route of a criminal trial.

The Summary Trial

The most common criminal trial is called the **summary trial**.[31] Vagrancy and intoxication cases along with other minor misdemeanors are quickly run through summary trials; only in a computer printout of charges and dispositions do they even get to the prosecutor's office. The cases are handled so quickly that they never even reach the stage of plea bargaining, and the standard deals are simply a routine formula for sentencing. The entire process from initial appearance to sentencing all occur at one time and place, with virtually no legal counsel for the defendants. Often, the real decision is made by a court clerk who sits next to the judge and tells him what the standard sentence is for a given case and defendant. In examining the role of this liason worker, an interviewer found the following:

Interviewer: *"What do you do?"*
"Up here we act as a combination district attorney and public defender. We are more familiar with these guys than the judges are. The judges alternate. We have the previous arrest records. A lot of times, guys will give phony names. It may take us a while to catch up with them. We try to remember if we have seen a guy before."
Interviewer: *"How does a judge decide whether to sentence the men and, if so, for how long?"*
"We help him out on that. If a guy has been in three times in four weeks, they should get a minimum of 30 days. They need to dry out. You know, if a man has been arrested three times in four weeks, you ask yourself the question: 'How many times has he been drunk that he wasn't arrested?' Also, you look at the condition of a man—he may even need hospitalization."
Interviewer: *"You mean you can tell whether a man ought to be sent to jail by looking at him?"*
"Some of them look a lot more rough looking than others. You can tell they have been on a drunk for more than one day. They are heavily bearded. They have probably been sleeping in doorways or on the street. You can tell they have been on a long drunk."[32]

The criteria used to determine a sentence has nothing to do with innocence or guilt, but with the defendant's social characteristics—what he looks like, his social position, and previous appearances in court.[33] The charge of public drunkenness was applied in cases of homeless men, but was not applied a few blocks away where conventioneers staggered around in public, quite drunk, in the same city. Since lower-class homeless men were arrested for public drunkenness and those in the upper social strata were not, those from the lower classes tended to have previous records. One such defendant told the judge that he was not drunk when arrested, but that when the police in the paddy wagon "got to know you, you automatically get picked up."[34]

The atmosphere of these courts lacks the decorum of the higher courts. One observer noted the following in an urban drunk court:

Bailiff came in today and asked other court officers in voice audible to all, "When does the parade (of defendants) begin?" There is open flirting between a police matron and police officer before court starts. The Knocker and bailiff put a sign, "The Flying Nun," over the judge's name before court started. Removed it when judge appeared.

Judge comes in the front door of the court, walks very casually, often presides without robe. Unlike other courts, bailiff asks everyone to remain seated when judge appears. Judge is always five to ten minutes late.

Just as the judge was about ready to start, there was a gasp and a thud . . . One of the defendants had fallen over near the front of the line, and the other defendants stood there like this wasn't anything to get upset about. The judge asked, "What was his number?" and the Knocker told him. Then one of the court policemen said that he thought the guy was dead. "This man has had an alcoholic seizure. We're going to take him to the hospital," the judge said.

The bailiff asked what should be done about the man's case. The judge dismissed it. It was the only kickout that day.[35]

For the judge, and all others in the drunk court, the purpose is to get through as quickly as possible. Anything that inhibits the flow of defendants is seen as an unnecessary bother, including a defendant who enters a plea of innocent or any other troublesome aspect of due process. Often in drunk court, if a defendant who had had previous suspended sentences entered a plea of not guilty, the judge would dismiss the case and revoke a previous suspended sentence, sending the troublesome defendant to jail![36]

Given the perfunctory nature of summary trials, it may seem to be a poor example to discuss in examining the trial process; however, since the summary trial is the most common kind of trial (given the high number of arrests for petty misdemeanors as compared with felonies), it is more representative than the trial by jury. Furthermore, the summary trial is a microcosm of the criminal justice processing system. It is fast, relatively lenient for the charges, based on a set of disposition standards impersonally applied, and is only vaguely concerned with due process. Compared with the popular stereotype of "real justice" consisting of a jury, fine details in due process, and adversary relationships, the summary trial pales by comparison. As we will see in the following section, the ideal system may not be any more just, fair, or impartial than the informal system of plea bargaining and summary trials.

Jury Trials

Only small percentages of all defendants (between 2 and 5 percent, depending on the state and jurisdiction) will ever experience a jury trial. The great bulk of defendants will have their cases dismissed, or they will enter a guilty plea before reaching the trial stage. In order to see the path to the trial, we will provide a summary view of all of the steps along the way and briefly explain their legal and social significance.

Charging

The prosecutor or a grand jury decides if charges should be brought against a criminal suspect and what those charges should be.

Initial Appearance

The defendant is brought before a magistrate and informed of the crime he or she is being accused of committing. In some jurisdictions if the defendant is charged with a misdemeanor, he or she may be asked to plead at the initial appearance. Generally, however, bail is set after the defendant has been informed of the charges, and the defendant either pays the bail or goes to jail. In some jurisdictions defendants are released without bail to await trial.

Preliminary Hearing

This stage provides three basic functions: 1) "to determine whether there is probable cause to hold the defendant for trial, 2) to afford the defense and opportunity to learn about the state's case, and 3) to enable the state to preserve the testimony of witnesses who may later balk at testifying."[37]

Arraignment

The trial judge reads the charges and their consequences if the defendant is found guilty. At this time the judge asks the defendant to enter a plea to the formal accusations. He or she may plead guilty, innocent, or *nolo contendre* (no contest). Nolo contendre means the defendant is neither admitting guilt nor denying it. It is typically used when there are civil or other suits pending in a case, and the defendant does want to go on record as pleading guilty. However, in a criminal case, pleading nolo contendre generally is treated in the same manner as a guilty plea.

Criminal Trial

If the defendant enters a not guilty plea, he or she then is tried by a judge or jury. In the trial, the defense and prosecution present evidence that is legally admissible, and based on this evidence the jury decides the defendant's innocence or guilt. The judge acts as a referee in deciding the legal validity of materials presented in court.

Sentencing

If a defendant is found guilty, the judge or jury decide on the appropriate punishment for the defendant.

Structure of a Trial

As we have seen, it is rare that a case gets beyond the first few steps in this process. A trial can be broken down into six basic parts. Each part is designed to ensure a fair and equitable trial for both the state (the prosecutor) and the defendant.

1. A jury is selected from a panel of potential jurors. In what is called *voir dire,* the prosecution and defense have an opportunity to dismiss any jurors who show prejudice toward the case. In addition, they have powers of *pre-emptory challenges* allowing them to dismiss a certain number of jurors for no given reason. Both the defense and prosecution attempt to get people on the jury whom they believe would be sympathetic to their case.

2. The trial actually begins with summary statements by the prosecution and defense, each outlining their cases. The prosecutor denounces the defendant and the defense protects the defendant.

3. First, the prosecutor presents his case. He or she introduces evidence and witnesses that will support the contention the defendant is guilty. During this stage, the defense attorney has the opportunity to cross-examine the prosecution's witnesses attempting to discredit their testimony. After the prosecution has presented its case, the defense will usually ask the judge to dismiss the charges, claiming either that there is not enough evidence or that some or all of it has been gathered illegally. Sometimes the judge will dismiss the case if he or she believes there is insufficient evidence.

4. Next, the defense presents its case, much in the same manner as the prosecution. The prosecution has the opportunity to question the defense's evidence and to cross-examine its witnesses.

5. After the defense has brought forth all of its evidence, witnesses, and testimony and rests its case, both the prosecution and defense make summary closing arguments. Each attempts to convince the judge and jury of their respective positions. The judge then instructs the jury as to the points of law before the jury retires.

6. Finally, the judge or jury decide if the defendant is innocent or guilty. If no decision can be reached by jury (a hung jury), either all charges are dropped or a new trial is set. Whether a new trial will be set depends on the nature of the case, the evidence, and the expense of a new trial. The judge may reverse the decision of a jury in a finding of guilty, but not when a not guilty finding has been reached.[38]

All of these procedures are designed to find the truth in a case. The ground rules state that neither side may openly lie, thereby committing perjury, but the defense and prosecution are not required to reveal information that is harmful to their case. For example, if a defense attorney has clear information that his or her client has committed the crime, there is no requirement to enter that information in a trial—especially if that information is privileged, i.e., provided by the client. Thus, while it is against the rules to lie by inclusion, it is not to do so by omission.

There is evidence, however, that deception is part of the game in the courtroom, including outright perjury. The participants are coached to play deceptive roles, and there is an all-out fight to convince the jury of one's case. Included in these courtroom battles are the following tactics:

1. Attorneys coach witnesses before the trial, perhaps telling them precisely what to say and what not to say in response to formal questioning. In some cases, especially those involving dishonest lawyers, attorneys might even tell witnesses to provide false testimony.

2. Attorneys coach witnesses on how to deceptively manage appearances in court. For example, "he educates the irritable witness to conceal his irritability, the cocksure witness to subdue his cocksureness. In that way, the trial court is denied the benefit of observing the witness's actual normal demeanor, and is thus prevented from sizing up the witness accurately."[39]

3. Attorneys may work at controlling information that is unfavorable to their line of argumentation. The attorney, if possible, "will not ask a witness to testify who, on cross-examination, might testify to true facts helpful to his opponent."[40]

4. An attorney may bring in surprise testimony for which his opponent is unprepared. The point, of course, is to catch the adversary off guard; develop a line of information that the opponent cannot readily or methodically rebut.

To find whether or not a defendant has or has not committed a crime becomes a game or circus rather than a method of justice. The deceptive features themselves do little to encourage integrity and do much to undermine both the sense of justice and the justice system. Police officers, witnesses, and defendants are all coached by attorneys to present something other than what, even for the participants, are objective facts.

The referee for these proceedings is supposed to be the judge; however, even the judges tend to play favorites in a case. Studies of higher courts have found that depending on a judge's sociopolitical position in society he will tend to side with either the prosecution or defense—his own ideology coloring the outcome of the case.[41] Similarly, judges are affected by the political implications of trials, such as the opinions of local pressure groups.[42] In this kind of situation, it is impossible to have judicial objectivity, for the judge will favor motions by one side or the other by sustaining objections, dismissing cases, etc.

There also is evidence of judicial prejudice in certain kinds of cases. The most notable has been found in rape cases. In her study of rape,

Carol Bohmer found that the victim rather than the defendant was on trial. According to Bohmer, "the judges revealed that their central orientation in trying rape cases is to evaluate the credibility of the victim's allegation that forcible rape (as defined by law) occurred." As several of the judges stated, "Rape is the easiest crime to allege and the hardest to prove."[43] While rape is objectively difficult to prove, it is not any more so than other crimes where the matter often comes down to the victim's word against that of the defendant. The crucial point is that the judge considers the victim to be on trial as much, if not more so, than the defendant. If the social characteristics of the victim do not match the judge's stereotype of an innocent victim, then a rapist is likely to go free. In their study of the institutional reactions to rape, Holmstrom and Burgess found that the victim was badly treated in criminal trials. Many victims said after their experience in court that if raped again they would not call the police or go to court.[44]

While rape victims are not typical of complainants in the courtroom, criminal victims who go to trial are put into a fearful situation. Defense attorneys, a defendant's friends, and even the defendant will harass victims who insist on maintaining a complaint. In one case a burglary victim was called by friends and relatives of the defendant telling her how bad she was for getting the burglar in trouble—a burglar who broke in, took her savings, and then set her room on fire! After several delays, when the case came to trial, the defendant suddenly changed his plea to guilty, much to the relief of the victim who would then not be required to testify.[45] Victims and other witnesses also have to put up with extensive delays in court and taking off time from work whenever they are called to the courthouse (often only to find that the trial date has been delayed or their testimony will not be needed). For those victims who have been through the trial process, plea negotiations and standard deals are seen as a relief rather than a miscarriage of justice.

Juvenile Justice

The juvenile justice system is separate from the adult system, and it has a number of different formal features. For example, a juvenile who receives an official petition to court does not have the right to a jury trial, and there are "findings of involvement" rather than "findings of guilt." Furthermore, the child's family plays a much larger role in deciding disposition than is true in the adult system. In the juvenile court there is more official informality than in the adult system, giving the juvenile court judge several more options than are available in adult court.

The distinction between adult and juvenile court is more apparent than real however, on the formal level. As we have seen, standard deals are informal arrangements that have come to dominate adult prosecution and adjudication, and the trial, while still a significant formal difference, is employed for only a small fraction of the cases. The real difference between adult and juvenile court lies in the key actors. In the adult court, the prosecutor orchestrates the courtroom routine, while in juvenile court, it is the probation officer. In the following chapter, we will examine the role of the probation officer in juvenile court as well as the development of probation and the juvenile justice system.

SUMMARY

This chapter has attempted to show the processing in the criminal courts. For the most part, the Perry Mason concept of courtroom trials with brilliant defense and prosecution attorneys is no more realistic than Robin Hood criminals stealing from the rich and giving to the poor. There are relatively few trials outside of summary trials for petty misdemeanors. Instead there is a routine processing of criminal defendants on the basis of standard deals—pleas of guilty for standard reductions in charges.

Defendants are treated as guilty by the defense, prosecution, and judges. Those who claim their innocence are more likely to be seen as troublemakers than men and women standing up for their rights. Defense attorneys must cajole recalcitrant defendants who will not go along with the standard deals, and they more than any others in the criminal justice system are responsible for eliciting guilty pleas. This double-agent role is more obvious to the defendant in the case of public defenders, but privately retained attorneys are part of the same system—they are just better at evoking the appearance of doing more for the defendant than the publicly hired lawyers. As a result, defendants believe that better justice can be had for a price even though it is not true.

For those who get a trial, there exists only a ritual of prosecution and defense. In the context of an adversary game between the prosecution and defense, there is little concern for honesty. There is an attempt to win through deception, misrepresentation, and even perjury. However, in cases that are believed to be lost, especially those where the defense attorney has failed to convince his client to plead guilty, there are only the motions of an adversary confrontation, with the outcome a foregone conclusion of guilty—and if nothing else a lesson to those who do not cooperate by entering a guilty plea.

Perhaps the greatest irony of the criminal court system is that there may be more justice under the informal system than would be possible under the ideal system. Costs for defendants are kept down by guilty pleas, and victims do not have to spend as much time in court. Some punishment is meted out, and even though it may not be what is prescribed by law the pressure for pleas of guilty ensures some criminal sanction. Furthermore, the institution of the standard deal generally provides a greater amount of consistency than what a variety of juries are able to produce. To compound the irony, those most involved in crime have an almost naive faith in the ideal system of law and would probably receive greater punishment were their cases handled by such a system. Nevertheless, it is the *belief* in a proper system viewed as being undermined by bargain justice that gives rise to the sense of injustice and the perception of hypocrisy in the routine court operations. This perception, whether accurate or not, will continue to be a constant force in weakening the authority of the criminal justice system by both convicted criminals and the public at large.

Glossary

Adversary System An ideal system of adjudication where the prosecution and defense are equally qualified adversaries in representing the people or defendant.

Assembly-Line Justice A characterization of the court system that suggests that defendants are rushed in and out of the system as quickly and cheaply as possible with little regard for due process.

Bargain Justice A situation where the defense and prosecution bargain for reduced charges and guilty pleas.

Court-Appointed Attorneys Private attorneys who are paid minimal fees by the court to represent defendants who cannot afford to pay for private attorneys.

Filing an Information The decision by the prosecutor or grand jury to charge a defendant with a crime(s), often called filing charges.

Full Charges Charging a defendant with as many crimes as possible in a given situation. Often used as a bargaining tool by the prosecutor to pressure the defendant into pleading guilty to something less than full charges.

Justice by Consent A characterization of the adjudication and prosecution process that emphasizes the defendant being pressured to consent to the courthouse routine of pleading guilty to standard deals. (See ***Standard Deals***.)

Nolo Prosequi A Latin term referring to the decision of the prosecutor not to charge a defendant even though he has probable cause to do so.

Normal Crimes The typification of a crime into a standard category used by the prosecutor in deciding what to do with a case.

Plea Negotiation The interaction between a prosecutor and defense attorney in which the prosecutor attempts to get a guilty plea and the defense attorney attempts to get reduced charges.

Private Attorneys Lawyers who represent clients for a fee.

Public Defenders Defense attorneys who are paid by public funds to represent indigent defendants.

Standard Deals A routine reduction in charges for a plea of guilty. This procedure has replaced plea negotiation in that it has standardized the reduction in charges and sometimes the sentence in exchange for a guilty plea.

Summary Trial A trial presided over by a judge in which the entire adjudication process from initial appearance to sentencing occurs in a single hearing. These trials can take from a few seconds to a few minutes.

Uniformity An ideal in criminal justice that the laws apply equally to everyone regardless of social position.

Questions

1. What is meant by proprietary justice? How do financial arrangements between clients and attorneys affect the system of justice?

2. What criteria are used in charging discretion? Why are charges increased or decreased?

3. What kind of justice is there when the courthouse uses standard deals to decide cases?

4. What is meant by normal crimes? How does this concept explain bargain justice?

5. What are the formal features of jury trials? What are all of the ideal steps in the adjudication process leading up to a jury trial?

Notes

1. Frank Miller, *Prosecution: The Decision to Charge a Suspect with a Crime*. (Boston: Little, Brown, 1969).

2. David Sudnow, "Normal Crimes: Sociological Features of the Penal Code in a Public Defender Office, "*Social Problems* **12** (Winter 1965): 255–276.

3. Abraham Blumberg, "The Practice of Law As a Confidence Game," *Law and Society Review* **1** (June, 1967): 15–39; Sudnow, 1965; Johnathan D. Casper, *Criminal Courts: The Defendant's Perspective*. (Washington, DC: U.S. Department of Justice, February 1978).

4. Blumberg, 1967.

5. Ibid.

6. Miller, 1969.

7. Howard C. Daudistel, William B. Sanders and David F. Luckenbill, *Criminal Justice: Situations and Decisions*. (New York: Holt, Rinehart and Winston, 1979), p. 124.

8. John Kaplan, "The Prosecutorial Discretion: A Comment, "*Northwestern Law Review* **60** (May-June 1960): 174–193.

9. Donald J. Newman, *Conviction: The Determination of Guilt or Innocence Without Trial*. (Boston: Little, Brown, 1966): p. 81.

10. Daudistel et al., 1979, 135.

11. Arthur Rosett and Donald R. Cressey, *Justice by Consent: Plea Bargains in the American Courthouse*. (Philadelphia: Lippincott, 1976).

12. Daudistel et al., 1979, 124.

13. Jacqueline Wiseman, *Stations of the Lost: The Treatment of Skid Row Alcoholics*. (Englewood Cliffs, NJ: Prentice-Hall, 1970).

14. The President's Commission on Law Enforcement and Administration of Justice, *Task Force Report: The Courts*. (Washington, DC: U.S. Government Printing Office), pp. 29–34.

15. Blumberg, 1967.

16. Ibid.

17. Sudnow, 1965, 138.

18. Daudistel et al., 1979, 7.

19. David Matza, *Delinquency and Drift*. (New York: Wiley, 1964), p. 110.

20. Matza, 1964, 102.

21. Sudnow, 1965, 121.

22. William B. Sanders, *Detective Work: A Study of Criminal Investigations*. (New York: Free Press, 1977).

23. Sudnow, 1965, 130.

24. Richard Mendes and John Wold, "Plea Bargains Without Bargaining: Routinization of Misdemeanor Procedures," in William B. Sanders and Howard C.

Daudistel, *The Criminal Justice Process: A Reader*. (New York: Praeger, 1976), p. 193.

25. Rosett and Cressey, 1976.

26. Roscoe Pound, *Social Control Through Law*. (New Haven: Yale University Press, 1942).

27. Rosett and Cressey, 1976, 46.

28. Johnathan D. Casper, *Criminal Courts: The Defendant's Perspective, Executive Summary*. (Washington, DC: U.S. Department of Justice, February 1978), p. 3.

29. Casper, 1978, 4.

30. Casper, 1978, 5.

31. Daudistel et al., 1979, 150.

32. Frederic S. LeClercq, "Field Observations in Drunk Court of the Pacific Municipal Court,": 7. Unpublished memorandum. Cited in Wiseman, 1970.

33. Wiseman, 1970, 86–103.

34. Ibid.

35. Wiseman, 1970, 95.

36. Author's observations of West Coast Drunk Court, 1968.

37. Frank Miller and Frank Remington, "Procedures Before Trial," Annals of American Academy of Political and Social Sciences **339** (January 1962): 111–124.

38. Daudistel et al., 1979, 235.

39. Jerome Frank, *Courts on Trial*. (New York: Atheneum, 1969), p. 83.

40. Frank, 1969, 84.

41. Stuart Nagel, "Judicial Backgrounds and Criminal Cases," *Journal of Criminal Law, Criminology, and Police Science* **53** (September 1962): 333–339.

42. Alexander B. Smith and Abraham S. Blumberg, "The Problem of Objectivity in Judicial Decision-Making," *Social Forces* **46** (September, 1967): 96–105.

43. Carol Bohmer, "Judicial Attitudes Toward Rape Victims," *Judicature* **57** (February 1974): 303–307.

44. Lynda Lytle Holmstrom and Ann W. Burgess, *The Victim of Rape: Institutional Reactions*. (New York: Wiley, 1978).

45. Sanders, 1977, 150–164.

17

Probation and Parole:

Juvenile and Adult Processing

What to Look For:

How probation developed historically.

The role of probation in the juvenile justice system and the quasijudicial role of the intake officer.

The relationship between judges' decisions and probation recommendations.

How the probation officer fits into the plea negotiation process.

The process of granting parole.

The organizational concerns in revoking parole and the discretion of parole officers.

Introduction

THIS CHAPTER EXAMINES the often overlooked but extremely important processes of **parole** and **probation**. The most common sentence by the courts is some form of probation in both adult and juvenile courts, and the vast majority of men and women sent to prison serve part of their sentence on parole. In order to fully understand these processes, we will look at probation and parole separately. Since probation is such an important part of the juvenile justice system, we will discuss juvenile probation separately.

First, we will go into the background of probation and examine its roots as a general way of dealing with convicted offenders. Then, we will turn to the role of probation in the juvenile justice system—specifically the development of the juvenile court and probation. We will then examine the central role played by probation in juvenile justice and the nature of the juvenile justice system as a whole. Finally, we will look at the role of the adult probation officer in court.

Secondly, we will examine the process of parole. We will look at the decision-making process in the granting of parole by the parole board. Then we will discuss the work of the parole officer in the context of the parole bureaucracy and the goals of parole (what parole officers attempt to accomplish). Finally, we will examine the decision-making process in parole revocation.

In our discussion of the decision-making process, in both probation and parole, it is important to note that the very same criteria employed by the police in deciding whether or not to make an arrest are also used at this end of the criminal justice system. The main concern is still with the seriousness of the crime and not necessarily with any progress made while in prison, on parole, or on probation. There are to be sure other variables that are relevant, but the most important ones appear to be the same.

Background of Probation and Parole

Probation and parole developed out of a belief in leniency and an underlying belief on the part of society in Christian charity and forgiveness. To a great extent, probation was a means of giving first offenders a second chance to redeem themselves and to differentiate the real criminals from those who merely slipped up. For the most part, leniency was granted by suspending sentences of those who were considered first-time offenders. However, in a federal court test case of the suspended sentence which involved a typical situation where probation would later be applied, the court decided that it was illegal to grant such suspensions. The following events ensued in a 1915 case:

> . . . *Judge John M. Killits suspended "due to the good behavior of the defendant" the execution of a sentence of five years and ordered the court term to remain open for that period. The defendant, a first offender and a young man of reputable background, had pleaded guilty to embezzling $4,700 by falsifying entries in the books of a Toledo bank. He had made full restitution and the bank's officers did not wish to prosecute. The government moved that Judge Killits' order be vacated as being "beyond the powers of the court."*[1]

The Supreme Court ruled that it was indeed beyond the powers of federal courts to have indefinite suspended sentences. However, the purpose was as much to set the stage for legal reforms as it was to set limits on the power of judges. The Killits case became the background for a federal probation law, and even though Massachusetts had such a law in 1878, it was not until 1925 that there was a federal probation law.[2]

In establishing probation, the argument boiled down to leniency and a second chance versus "coddling criminals." Typical of the antiprobation sentiment at the time, a 1924 memorandum to the Attorney General read:

> It (probation) is all a part of a wave of maudlin rot of misplaced sympathy for criminals that is going over the country. It would be a crime, however, if a probation system is established in the federal courts. Heaven knows they are losing in prestige fast enough . . . for the sake of preserving the dignity and maintaining what is left of wholesome fear for the United States tribunal . . . this Department should certainly go on record against a probation system being installed in federal courts.[3]

Against these sentiments were two strong arguments for probation. First, there was the argument that, since reducing crime was a major concern, probation could provide *individualized* treatment in the community. Such treatment would better prevent crime than sending men and women to prison. Secondly, and of equal importance, there were the economic advantages of community probation. In 1923, 63 percent of the offenders were being sent to prison for the first time.[4] The housing, feeding, and maintenance of this large number of prisoners was seen as economically wasteful as well as a poor means of rehabilitation. Eventually, probation won out. Now, in all 50 states, the District of Columbia, and the federal courts there is some kind of probation.

The general provisions of the Federal Probation Act gave the federal courts more flexibility in dealing with criminal cases. Since it is a generic example of probation used in state and municipal courts, we will use it to illustrate what the courts can do with probation. The law, as summarized by Evjen:

. . . gave the court, after conviction or after a plea of guilty or nolo conten-
dere for any crime or offense not punishable by death or life imprisonment,
the power to suspend the imposition or execution of sentence and to place
the defendant upon probation for such period and upon such terms and
conditions it deemed best, and to revoke or modify any condition of probation or change the period of probation, provided the period of probation,
together with any extension thereof, did not exceed five years. A fine, restitution, or reparation could be made a condition of probation as well as the
support of those for whom the probationer was legally responsible. The probation officer was to report to the court on the conduct of each probationer.
The court could discharge the probationer from further supervision or ter-
minate the proceedings against him, or extend the period of probation.[5]

While the probation laws gave the courts an alternative to prison or
fine, it was not clear what probation officers were supposed to do by way
of rehabilitation or supervision. Money was appropriated to hire probation officers, and general guidelines were laid down for the kind of person desired; however, with no way to enforce the hiring and no guiding
philosophy, there was little idea of what to do with probationers. The ap-
pointments quickly became political. Evjen notes:

> Among those appointed as probation officers in the early years were deputy
> clerks, prohibition agents, tax collectors, policemen, deputy marshalls, dep-
> uty sheriffs, salesmen, a streetcar conductor, a farmer, a prison guard, and
> a retired vaudeville entertainer! Relatives of the judge were among them. A
> master's thesis study by Edwin B. Zeigler in 1931 revealed that 14 of the 60
> probation officers in service at that time had not completed high school, 14
> were high school graduates, 11 had some college work, 11 had graduated
> from college, and 9 had taken some type of graduate work.[6]

Since they were federal probation officers, their general quality was
probably higher than those of the state and local courts. However, over
the years, the quality of probation officers increased. Federal probation
set an example by instituting standards of personal characteristics and college graduate education.

However, the philosophy of probation never had a clear direction. In
1926, during a period when probation was strongly advocated as a new
way to deal with convicted criminals, Healy and Bronner noted, ". . . probation is a term that gives no clue to what is done by way of treatment.
. . ."[7] Many different ideas were put forth, but each was general and vague—and many were contradictory. For example, in 1966 the American
Correctional Association proclaimed:

> Probation's most important achievement is not control of the probationer
> under supervision but rather enabling the probationer to understand him-
> self and gain strength in independent control over his own behavior.[8]

On the other hand, in a 1976 article entitled, "Probation: Call It Control—and Mean It," Walter Barkdall, Assistant Director of the California Department of Corrections, noted:

> . . . The public image of getting probation means getting off. . . . While it may seem more semantic than real, it is time that we abandoned use of the present terminology of "granting probation." Instead we should be sentencing persons to a period of "community control" or some other phrase that connotes the realities of probation.[9]

While Barkdall was making a pitch for community acceptance of probation in the face of rising violent crimes and a general trend against lenient sentences, his point concerning the realities of probation, focuses on the general attempt of probation to foster control by *some* means. Whether it is control through counselling or through the threat of prison for violating probation, control has always been implicit in probation. The philosophy, however, was never clear as to how best to implement such control.

Probation in the Juvenile Courts

The juvenile court best exemplifies the course of probation over the years. In the same way that the prosecutor's and public defender's offices run the routines of the adult court, probation officers run the juvenile court. The role of the probation officer has been expanded far beyond the scope of the original intentions of keeping an eye on convicted offenders, and in the juvenile court a probation officer is involved with juveniles from shortly after arrest all the way through juvenile court disposition. In order to understand the role of the probation officer in juvenile court, we will first examine the juvenile court philosophy and operation, particularly in how it differs from the adult court; then we will look at the several roles played by probation officers in both prosecution/adjudication and treatment/supervision.

Parens Patriae

The origins of juvenile court can be traced back to the social conditions and the concerns of upper class around the turn of the century.[10] Arguments for both humane and more effective treatment became major parts of the juvenile court movement, but it was clear that better control over the urban-working and lower-class youth was of paramount importance to the movement's advocates. Delinquency was noted to be on the rise in urban slums where the lower classes lived; there was increasing immigration from Southern and Eastern Europe, and there was ample evidence that the traditional adult courts could not cope with the new problems.

Since treatment was popular as a reform alternative to punishment, the rhetoric was centered around both the practicality and humanity of something other than the strict punishment-deterrence model of the adult court. Under the proposed model of juvenile court, the court would be like a parent to an errant or misguided child—this was called **parens patriae**. What was "best" could be anything the court deemed necessary, giving it broad powers not allowed under due process in the adult court. Anthony Platt pointed out:

> The unique character of the child-saving movement was its concern for pre-delinquent offenders—"children who occupy the debatable ground between criminality and innocence"—and its claims that it could transform potential criminals into respectable citizens by training them in "habits of industry, self-control, and obedience to law." This policy justified the diminishing of traditional procedures and allowed police, judges, probation officers, and truant officers to work together without legal hindrance. If children were to be rescued, it was important that the rescuers be free to pursue their mission without the interference of defense lawyers and due process. Delinquents had to be saved, transformed and reconstituted.[11]

Thus, children who had broken the law as well as those who had not were to be subject to this new court. And under the mandate of *parens patriae*, there was little the court could not do. One juvenile court judge went so far as to suggest:

> It seems to have been demonstrated that the broad powers of the juvenile court can be helpfully invoked on behalf of children whose maladjustment has been brought to light through juvenile traffic violations. A girl companion of a youthful speeder may be protected from further sexual experimentation. Boys whose only amusement seems to be joyriding in family cars can be directed to other, more suitable forms of entertainment before they reach the stage of "borrowing" cars when the family car is unavailable.[12]

It is unclear just where the judge got the idea that the broad powers of the court had been "helpfully invoked," but his comments clearly show that the powers of the juvenile court were immense. Not only does his statement imply that girls who happen to be in a car with a male traffic violator become subject to the court's jurisdiction, but it is also a clear indication that the court's powers could be over all juveniles, whether they had been originally considered to be a problem or not.

In this context of treatment (and even meddling) the role of the probation officer emerges. Since the treatment and social work orientation of the probation officer fit well with the concept of *parens patriae*, not only was the probation officer the logical choice for post-disposition treatment, but he/she was also the most likely candidate to suggest court dispositions. Since the laws governing juveniles give broad powers to the juvenile court to "help" children and the judges and attorneys were primarily experts in interpreting the law and not in rehabilitation, there was a need for someone to determine what disposition would be most "helpful." This job was to be taken over by probation, making the juvenile court judge a legal, albeit powerful, figurehead in the court. The probation officer would play the role of prescribing treatment (typically placing the youth on probation) and then play the role of healer in supervising the juvenile placed on probation.

Assembly-Line "Treatment"

The remarkable features of juvenile court are not in the differences from adult court, but rather in the similarities. Not long ago, one could marvel at the lack of legal rights accorded defendants in juvenile court, but case law has given juveniles virtually every right given to adults and the informal processes in juvenile court also appear to be very similar. For example, **In re Gault** (1967) gave juveniles the right to counsel, the right against self-incrimination, notice of charges, confrontation, and the right of cross-examination. In most states, however, a juvenile is not accorded the right to a jury trial; since only a small number of cases brought to the prosecutor's office in adult court ever go to jury trial, this should not be seen as an important difference. Furthermore, the routines in juvenile court have the same assembly-line character as adult courts, only the names of the roles have changed.

Intake Officer

In the adult court, there is usually an assistant prosecutor whose major responsibility is to go through all incoming cases and decide if they should be dropped or filed. If the latter choice is made, he decides exactly what the standard deal should be given the circumstances of the case. Similarly, in juvenile court, a lone probation officer, usually a senior officer, will decide the fate of juveniles brought into his or her office, but perhaps with even more finality than in the adult court. In describing the role of the **intake officer** in juvenile court, Cressey and McDermott note:

> The design of the buildings and the rooms used for giving justice to juveniles hides the fact that the intake officer is the most important person in the juvenile justice system. This man's workroom is smaller and barer than the "chambers" of juvenile court judges, the suites used by Chief Probation Officers, and the offices of the probation department section chiefs, called supervisors. In his little cubicle there are no flags, no polished wood furniture, no paneled walls, no carpet, and no statue of the blindfolded lady. The cubicle is equipped with a cheap metal desk and a couple of straightbacked chairs. A few unframed prints and a diploma or two are temporarily taped on the walls. The intake officer doesn't wear a robe or a wig. He sits at his bare desk, often wearing an open-collared shirt, and does justice.[13]

Most dispositions in the juvenile court are handled by the intake officer, and even those juveniles who go to court are handled in a less formal manner than adults. The "parens patriae" philosophy of juvenile court rests on the basis that no punishment is involved, only "help" for the accused juvenile.

This statement reflects the concentrated responsibilities of a single role in the juvenile justice system, but it accurately characterizes both the operations of juvenile justice and the role of the intake officer.

To understand this role in its proper context, it is necessary to explain both the dispositions available to the court and the intake officer and the context in which these dispositions are made. First, the juvenile court can go through all of the stages of a hearing, much like a court trial, except a juvenile judge or referee presides, and there is no jury. If the formal hearing is held, the probation officer, using a "social history report," recommends what disposition should be taken. Typically, juvenile court judges go along with this recommendation—the probation officer virtually decides the disposition.[14] Furthermore, since the report is often introduced in the early stages of a hearing before there has been a finding of involvement (guilty), the probation officer's report decides the finding as well.[15] Since the probation officer is making these decisions anyway, it is small step between having a probation officer make these decisions in court or out. However, only a juvenile court judge is empowered to make the official disposition decisions, and probation officers are only in court as advisors. In order for the probation officer to become more fully involved in dispositions, a number of informal dispositions had to be employed. These dispositions are dealt out by the intake officer and they are the predominant ones in juvenile justice.

The various dispositions that developed came as a result of both cost consideration and rehabilitation measures. Whether the new dispositions were initiated because of financial or treatment considerations, most could be imposed by a probation officer without the necessity of a formal juvenile court hearing. Furthermore, other than having a juvenile incarcerated, the informal dispositions reflect almost exactly what is done in court; thus, only the serious cases had to go to court, and the rest could be handled by an intake officer. The following is a summary of the intake options, in order of the frequency of their use:

1. *Counsel, warn, and release* is the most commonly utilized option. This disposition is an almost automatic response to cases brought in via citations. The child is usually discharged after a warning, a lecture, or a short conference with him and his parents. The case is not carried in the official records as "dismissed," even though CWR is sometimes called "dismissed" rather than a disposition.

2. *Informal probation* is the option whereby, under Mountain State law, a juvenile might be placed on a maximum of six months' informal probation if he and his parents agree to it. In practice, the term of probation is rarely less than six months.

3. *Probation diversion units* may be used for the particular types of cases they have been established to receive. The intake officer may be required to refer certain cases (usually predelinquents or minor lawbreakers) to such a unit. In addition, or in some locations, he may opt to send other cases there. When a child is sent to a diversion unit, his case is officially logged as "dismissed." However, the child is strongly urged to participate in the special unit's program.

4. *Referral to another agency* (or to a person) is a common disposition of walk-in and phone contact cases. Such referral is an attempt to handle the case unofficially by sending the juvenile to someone who "is better able (qualified) to handle his case." This disposition is sometimes used for other than walk-ins by intake officers on night duty. These officers tend to be viewed by detention center staff members and the police as troubleshooters. Intake officers receive cases from them that have not officially come to the attenion of the juvenile justice system, and they dispose of them unofficially. It is questionable, then, if such referrals are dispositions, diversions, dismissals, or something else.

5. *Petition for an official hearing* before a juvenile court referee or judge is the classic disposition used in serious and last-resort cases. It is something like the filing of charges in criminal cases. The papers on the case are simultaneously filed with the court and with a regular probation officer

... who makes an investigation and reports back to the court, which then conducts a hearing.

6. *Dismissal* is the least-used option. It occurs most frequently when the intake officer decides there is not enough evidence to justify further action or when he believes the technicalities of the arrest were improper.[16]

Since the petition for an official hearing is one of the least used options, we can see that the intake probation officer and not the hearing is the key to understanding the juvenile justice system. Very much like plea bargaining is the key to adult court, the intake officer is the key to juvenile court. One may question the legal rights of juveniles in this system, but it is seen as far more efficient and equally as effective as sending a juvenile to court where he/she will then have an official record and be adjudicated a delinquent. Furthermore, since experienced probation officers serve as intake officers, the informal dispositions tend to be the same as what the juvenile would get if he/she were to attend an official hearing. Only those juveniles considered to be serious delinquents, such as multiple or violent offenders, are sent to court.

The Probation Officer in Adult Court

Like juvenile probation officers, adult court also has a role for probation officers; however, with the extensive use of plea negotiation and standard deals in court, the probation officer's role is considerably diminished. Ideally, the probation officer acts in the role of advisor to the judge. He or she prepares a presentence report: 1) to provide the court with sufficient information to make a rational decision; 2) as a guide to referral agencies that may be involved with the probationer (for example, alcoholic or drug rehabilitation services, and marital counselling); 3) as a resource for prison staff and administrators who plan a program for the person if he/she is sentenced to prison; and 4) as a device for parole agencies to understand the background of the offender.[17]

To this end of providing information for decision making by the judge and others who may become involved with the defendants, the following items are to be considered:

- Offense
    Official version
    Statements of codefendants
    Statements of witnesses, complainants, and victims
- Defendant's version of offense
- Prior record
- Family history
    Defendant
    Parents and siblings

- Marital history
- Home and neighborhood
- Education
- Religion
- Interests and leisure-time activities
- Health
  Physical
  Mental and emotional
- Employment
- Military service
- Financial condition
  Assets
  Financial obligations[18]

If the probation officer's presentence report contains all of the above information, it would appear to be a very thorough instrument for determining the best course of action for a particular case. However, there appears to be some class bias in the criteria used in the report. Beginning with family history, most of the other items in the format would appear to favor the more affluent over the less affluent—with exceptions perhaps in religion and military service. Supposedly people with a "good" family, neighborhood, education, and other social status symbols are treated differently from those with "bad" characteristics on the selected items. Moreover, these items are not inherently unequivocal, but are subject to the interpretation of the probation officer. For example, interests and leisure-time activities can be interpreted in any number of ways as being good or bad. A leisure-time activity of playing pool is usually considered a negative pastime, while playing football (a far more violent leisure-time activity) is seen in a positive light. Similarly, religion is more likely to be seen in a positive light if it is conventional, even though an unconventional (e.g., Hari Krishna) devotee may be far more sincere in his/her beliefs.

Not all criteria are weighed in the same way, however. In a study of what most affected the sentencing recommendation, it was found that two variables, type of offense and prior record, were the most important considerations in arriving at a recommendation.[19] As we saw with the police and the prosecutors, the same two criteria are primary in judicial decision making. To be sure, an offense of the same criminal code violation is interpreted to be more or less serious on a case-by-case basis—two automobile thefts, for instance, may be interpreted as completely different offenses (as joy-riding or theft for profit). Based on police reports, which are used as the major objective document in assessing cases, there does appear to be a consistent and shared interpretation of exactly what a crime is (i.e., its actual seriousness). Thus, there is a link from the initial decision by police officers to make an arrest, based on their interpretation of the events, to the probation officer's decision of what to recommend as a sentence.

Given the criteria used by probation officers in determining their recommendations, we must now look to see to what extent judges follow these recommendations. Studies have discovered that in about 95 percent of the cases in which probation officers recommended probation, the judges concurred. In cases where the probation officers recommended against probation, the judges went along in about 83 percent of the cases.[20] Fig. 17.1 shows the distribution of judges who followed probation officers' recommendations between 1959 and 1965.

Given the high percentage of judicial sentencing decisions that were consistent with probation officers' recommendations, it would appear that the probation officer has a great deal of influence in the court. However, it is possible that the recommendations reflected the ability of the probation officer to second guess the judge. That is, in order to have a high rate of agreement between the recommendation and sentencing, probation officers may have recommended what they believed the sentence would be anyway. Carter and Wilkins proposed four possible combinations:

1. The court, having such high regard for the professional qualities and competence of its probation staff, follows the probation recommenda-

Fig. 17.1

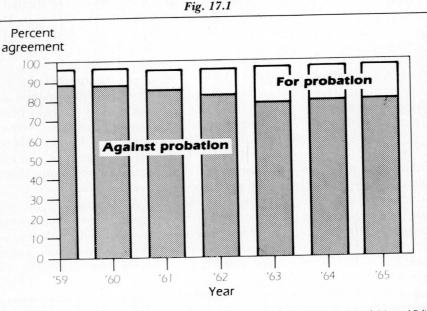

Source: State of California Department of Justice, *Delinquency and Probation in California*, 1964, p. 168 and *Crime and Delinquency in California*, 1965, pp. 98–99.

tion—a recommendation made by the person (probation officer) who best knows the defendant by reason of the presentence investigation.

2. There are many offenders who are obviously either probation or prison cases.

3. Probation officers write their reports and make recommendations anticipating the recommendation the court desires to receive. (In this situation, the probation officer is quite accurately second guessing the court disposition.)

4. Probation officers in making their recommendations place great emphasis on the same factors the court uses in selecting a sentencing alternative.[21]

Carter and Wilkins reject the idea that probation officers second guess judges. They conclude that the judge and probation officer either emphasize the same factors in making decisions or the court has a high regard for the probation officer's recommendation. The second-guess hypothesis is rejected mainly on the basis of the variations in recommendations for probation by different probation officers (from a low of 40 percent to a high of about 90 percent).[22] Since there was the same proportion of agreement between those with the low and high percent of probation recommendations in terms of the court's sentencing, it was concluded that the courts indeed do follow the probation department's recommendation.

The conclusion that probation officers have a great deal of influence in the courthouse has some merit; for, if nothing else, if something goes wrong when an offender is placed on probation, the judge can always share the blame with the probation department. However, given the contemporary structure of using standard deals, it is unlikely that the probation officer has anything other than a ceremonial role in the courthouse. If a prosecutor is to execute standard deals, and there is a high correlation between the probation officer's recommendation and what is done in court, then the probation officer must have some understanding of the plea bargain to maintain such a high correlation. Either the probation officer is knowledgable of the standard deals and tailors his/her presentence investigation to fit the deal or, as Carter and Wilkins suggest, he/she "place(s) great emphasis on the same factors as does the court."

Rosett and Cressey take a somewhat different view. They contend that the probation officer is more or less instructed as to the contents of the courthouse deals, but they go through a charade of preparing a presentence investigation to maintain the appearance of individualizing the sentences. The following illustrates this viewpoint:

Following his guilty plea, Peter Randolph spent another two weeks in jail awaiting sentencing. One day a probation officer called him to the lawyers' room. He seemed friendly, and he explained that he was writing a personal history of Randolph to be used by the judge in setting Randolph's sentence. Most of his questions were routine requests for the same information Randolph had already given to others. After ten minutes of such questions, Randolph was asked for his version of the crime. The probation officer seemed to listen carefully as Randolph explained that on the night of the crime he was feeling sorry for himself, disappointed, fed up, and drinking too much wine. On his note pad the probation officer wrote: "Subject says he doesn't know why he committed the burglary. Was drinking wine in the park and just wandered in the house. Inadequate personality." Then he asked Randolph what he thought a proper sentence would be. Randolph replied that a public defender had told him that a district attorney was going to let him out of jail and put him on probation. That seemed OK. The probation worker seemed unconcerned. He made some notes.

*   "That's the deal, ain't it?" Randolph asked.*

*   "The D.A. and the P.D. don't have the final say. That's up to the judge. He'll read my report and decide what to do . . ."*

*   At Peter Randolph's sentencing hearing the prosecutor addressed the judge first. "If it please the Court, since Your Honor has the presentence report in hand, the People at this time have no further statements or recommendations to make. Thank you. Your Honor." It was easy for the prosecutor to speak so briefly and with such confidence in the outcome. He had spent ten minutes with the probation officer before the report was written, describing the arrangements he had worked out with Randolph's lawyer. When he was given a copy of the final report, he glanced through it to make sure it recommended the disposition they had agreed upon. He skipped the parts dealing with Randolph's background, personality, and probation plan.*

*   Steven Ohler, the public defender assigned to Randolph at arraignment, made a slightly longer speech. "Your Honor, in the interests of justice, I would like to take just a minute to make a few remarks concerning my client, Mr. Randolph. I would remind Your Honor that this is my client's first adult conviction. He has never been in any really serious trouble before, and the offense he has pleaded to, unlawful entry, was committed in such a way that it is clear we are not dealing with an experienced criminal. In fact, I feel sure that in this case we are, so to speak, nipping a criminal career in the bud. I would also remind the court that my client has already served more than sixty days in the county jail. He has expressed to me a deep and sincere remorse for his behavior, and this is, more than anything, what leads me to believe that this is a case in which the mercy of the Court would be most appropriate and just." The judge then asked Randolph if he wanted to add anything. The bailiff motioned him to stand before the bench.*

*   "No, Your Honor."*

*   "Nothing to say?"*

*   "Well, Judge . . . I don't know, but I sure wish you would let me out."*

*   This the judge did, as everyone but Randolph was sure he would do. He sentenced Randolph to a jail term equal to the time already served, plus a year on probation.*[23]

Given the general situation surrounding the sentencing process, the probation officer seems to be more a cog in the wheels of the standard deals. It may be that the probation officer has influence in establishing standard deals, but once established, the presentence report appears to be little more than a formality.

Probation Supervision

If a person (adult or juvenile) is placed on probation, the program tends to be little more than periodic reports to the probation officer. In fact, most departments have no program at all—no probation officer school and little more than on-the-job training. Furthermore, most probation officer training focuses on how to properly fill out the correct forms and other paperwork. One department claimed to be eclectic in its approach, explaining that different probationers had different needs. As a result, they hire people with all kinds of backgrounds, from former police officers to ex-offenders, in addition to those with counseling, psychological, and sociological skills. However, there was no matching between the background of the probation officer and the client![24] Over 20 years ago, Lewis Diana found a similar pattern in probation. He reported:

> (Probation is) primarily a process of verifying the behavior of an offender: 1) through periodic reports of the offender and members of his family to the probation office and 2) by the incidence or absence of adverse reports from the police or other agencies. Secondarily, probation is a process of guiding and directing the behavior of an offender by means of intensive interviewing utilizing ill-defined casework techniques.[25]

Contemporary observations of probation have found nothing to alter Diana's observations of standard probation and probation work.

Effectiveness of Probation

The problem in evaluating probation is in measuring its effectiveness. Even supporters have noted that the degree of effectiveness of probation is uncertain, but it is clearly cheaper than prison. For example, it was pointed out:

> Probation has established itself as the new wave in corrections. . . . Successes have been claimed, but they are difficult to verify. As an alternative to imprisonment—less costly and probably as effective—probation offers great appeal, for it appears to answer the need for a sound and economical approach to corrections.[26]

Thus, the best that may be said is that, as far as rehabilitation is concerned, those placed on probation do not fare any worse than those placed in prison, and there is probably a lot less recidivism of those on probation. This may be due to nothing more than the fact that those who go to prison are typically more committed to crime than those who find themselves on probation.

The greatest problem with evaluating probation's effectiveness is still the diversity of activities that "count" as being somehow treatment oriented. As Diana pointed out:

In scenes such as this, probation officers and juveniles meet on a regular, usually monthly, basis. However, there is little actual control by the probation department, and such meetings usually consist of discussions of the youth's activities during the month.

> It is also highly probable . . . that the image that many probation officers have of themselves is a picture of a warm and understanding though objective person. . . . In any event, the influence of a clinical, casework ideology, along with its confused and contradictory elements, has been pervasive. . . .
> It is no more than what could be expected, then, if the probation officer feels that whatever he does and however he does it, it is treatment.[27]

Hence, any evaluation of probation's effectiveness should be based on what probation does specifically in addition to the fact that the person who is on probation is in the community instead of behind bars. At this time there is no reliable and valid data to evaluate probation effectiveness. This is an area in which new approaches in research and evaluation are sorely needed.

Parole

Parole, another form of community supervision, is not unlike probation. Instead of being a sentence from the court, however, parole is decided upon at the discretion of a **parole board**. Also, those on parole are actually serving the remainder of a prison sentence under parole supervision instead of behind bars. Thus, while probation can be likened to a sentence *before* the prison option is taken, parole is an action taken *after* the prison option has been taken.

In this section we will examine two crucial aspects of parole. First, we will look at the decision-making process in granting parole. Second, we will examine the parole supervision and revocation processes.

Granting Parole

Men and women in prison have the right to apply for parole after serving a portion of their prison terms. The parole board members, who are usually political appointees, may or may not have backgrounds in treatment and/or rehabilitation.[28] The presentence investigation report, correctional institution classification material, institutional progress reports, and pre-release plans are used by parole boards in making parole decisions, but it is not clear how the material is used and what interpretations are given to the materials.[29] For the most part, researchers have found that parole boards appear to use some method of "intuitive conclusion" based on ad hoc policies that are "unarticulated and not well developed."[30]

It appears that the most important criterion, as we have seen is true in all of the other critical decisions in criminal justice, is the seriousness of the crime.[31] On the one hand, there are "serious" crimes that have political repercussions (such as those involving well-known victims) or are sensational cases. For example, if a person is up for parole for a crime that received widespread attention in the press, local groups may lobby to make certain that parole is not granted. There are also the more mundane criteria for seriousness based on the type of crime originally committed. Such criteria belie the faith put into rehabilitation efforts, and a person who seems to have made little progress toward rehabilitation (e.g., by completing an education, learning a trade, resolving psychological problems) but who is not in prison for a serious crime, is far more likely to receive parole than one who has made a good deal of rehabilitative progress but whose original crime was considered serious. Such a state of affairs does not encourage prisoners' cooperation in rehabilitation programs. This fact is true for offenders who have committed the more serious offenses and who most need rehabilitation. However, for political purposes, it is considered more prudent to put a nonrehabilitated check forger back on the streets than to release a rehabilitated murderer; for if the check forger commits another crime it is unlikely to receive much public notice.

Parole Programs

When a convicted prisoner is granted parole, he or she is assigned to a parole officer who monitors his/her behavior to make sure that the person follows the provisions of parole and does not break the law. Parole provisions include such things as not drinking, staying away from other felons, and other conditions which vary depending on the specific case. If a parolee violates one of the parole provisions, he/she can be sent back to prison on what is called a **technical violation**. For example, parolees typically have to get permission to leave the state in which they are on parole. If a parolee visits relatives out-of-state without telling his/her parole officer, he can have his parole revoked and be returned to prison on a technical violation. On the other hand, if a parolee breaks the law, not only can he or she be convicted of the crime, but they might also be returned to prison to serve the remainder of the sentence for which he/she has been paroled.

The available programs for parolees are about as vague as those for probation. There is usually some kind of treatment or counseling orientation, but it tends to be unsystematic. Likewise, parole officers often have 100 or more cases, making individualized attention almost impossible. For the most part, parole officers simply attempt to keep track of what their charges are doing in terms of work and home as well as being informed as to any legal trouble their parolees may be involved in. In one study comparing parole caseloads of 15 and 100, there was no significant difference in the rates of arrest, conviction, and return to prison.[32] In a comparison of caseloads of 30 and 100, the same results were found.[33] However, a third study comparing caseloads of 35 and 90, there were significant differences between the smaller and larger caseloads in terms of breaking the law or violating parole. Parolees who were involved in the smaller units did better, particularly those who were considered medium risks (those considered not to be either good or bad risks).[34] It was concluded that parole effectiveness could be increased by placing medium-risk parolees with parole officers having smaller caseloads.

In studies comparing early parole to normal parole release time, again, there was no significant difference between those who were released early or those released on schedule.[35] This indicated that time in prison had little effect on how well a person would do on parole. The legal ideal of deterrence holds that the greater the punishment, the greater the deterrence; however, prison itself seemed to have little effect one way or the other, since those who were released from prison early did as well as those released on schedule. Further studies using Base Expectancy Scores, tests used to predict parole risks, placed low-risk parolees on minimal supervision, with the parole agents extending assistance only on the direct request of the parolee. The results showed that the minimally supervised group who were low risks did better than a mixed group (of high-, medium-, and low-risk) parolees with normal supervision.[36] This finding suggests that the characteristics of the parolee more than parole supervision is the main determinant of parole success.

The difficulty of adjusting to parole has both formal and informal dimensions.[37] On the one hand, the formal requirements of parole specify certain conditions to be met for successful parole. These expectations are based on written criteria which may or may not be realistic in terms of what a parolee can actually do. On the other hand, there are the informal expectations of parole officers and their orientation to their job. In general, the parole agents want their parolees to do well by following the guidelines of the formal conditions of parole, but it is not always possible to meet the overall goal of adjustment to legitimate society and formal demands. For example, one state specifies that before driving, a parolee must have permission from his parole officer. However, before permission to drive can be granted, a parolee must have a valid driver's license and insurance. Because parolees are considered high risks by insurance companies, their insurance rates are very high. To be able to afford the insurance, parolees must have jobs—and often to get a job they must drive, either to and from work or as part of their jobs. This dilemma is often overcome by illegal job-related driving until the parolee can afford the insurance.[38] The irony is that the parolee must break the formal conditions of parole in order to meet the overall goal of having self-sustaining legitimate employment.

Another adjustment problem for parolees is the provision not to associate with other ex-offenders. The idea behind such a parole condition is based on the assumption that criminal norms and actions are more likely to be generated if ex-offenders associate with one another. Often the only people with whom ex-offenders can associate are other ex-offenders. In part this is because of the stigma attached to convicts, but it is also because of the milieu of most ex-offenders. As one parolee noted:

What do they mean don't associate with ex's and guys with bad reputations? I don't know nobody who hasn't done time or been arrested many times. Where I was raised and live now, in the ghetto, there ain't nobody that don't have a bad reputation. And where am I gonna meet new people? Is the parole officer gonna take me into his home and introduce me to his friends?[39]

Thus, from the parolee's point of view, the conditions of parole often do not apply to the realities of parolees' lives although they may be reasonable from an ideal perspective.

Overall, the various parole studies suggest that parole has little direct effect on the success of released offenders. At the same time, they show that parolees are of little risk to the community. In summarizing the findings of major parole studies, Walter Burkhart concluded:

It is quite evident, for example, that large numbers of offenders do not constitute serious risks to the community, are relatively unaffected by the supervision process, and need not, and in fact should not, be on parole. In addition, there is no strong evidence that caseload size per se or any specific type of counselling or treatment is an effective rehabilitative or control measure. It is also recognized that the still largely subjective manner of

granting and revoking parolees, imposing parole conditions, and determining parole discharge has created serious problems in terms of equity, fairness, and both effective and humane criminal justice.[40]

Parole Discretion

Once a man or woman is granted parole, he or she is subject to parole
office supervision. Parole can be revoked for either a technical violation
or for further violation of the law. However, parole cannot be revoked on
the whim of a parole officer. In the 1972 **Morrissey v. Brewer** decision,
parolees were given several rights. The following is a list of guidelines en-
suring those rights:

1. Written notice of the claimed violations of parole.
2. Disclosure to the parolee of evidence against him.
3. An opportunity for the parolee to be heard in person and to present
   witnesses and documentary evidence.
4. The right of the parolee to confront and cross-examine adverse witnesses (unless the hearing officer specifically finds a good cause for not
   allowing this confrontation).
5. A "neutral and detached" hearing body, such as a traditional parole
   board, members of which need not be judicial officers or lawyers.
6. A written statement by the factfinders as to the evidence relied on and
   reasons for revoking parole.[41]

It does not seem to be the case however, that parole officers are men
and women who are attempting to have their clients "violated" and returned to prison; rather, they are attempting to help those under their
supervision. On the one hand, any return to prison of a parolee is a parole failure, and since the officers are responsible for the parolee it can be
seen as a parole officer failure as well. On the other hand, parole officers
like everyone else want to see their work done well. Even though part of
their work is keeping track of all parole violations, parolee success is seen
as doing a good job.

Parole work does not exist in an organizational vacuum—a parole officer is part of a bureaucratic organization having formal and informal
norms. Their operations reflect both the legal mandates of legislative and
case law and the organizational policies for dealing with parolees. It is in
this context that decisions about parole and its violation are made. While
this orientation protects parolees from individual whims and personality
traits of parole officers, it virtually rules out being able to "individualize
parole decision making.

In this organizational/legalist milieu, the individual parole officer comes
to see decisions as being realistic or unrealistic rather than fair or unfair.
This is because if an officer's decision does not correspond with depart-

mental policy or the legal institutions' formal and informal arrangements concerning parolees, the decision will not be carried out. As one officer explained decisions and fairness:

Realistic is a better word for it. First off, I don't make distinctions between guilty and innocent men. I'll help a guilty man beat a rap if I can if he deserves a break, and I'll watch an innocent man go down the tubes if I have to. It's not that I don't want to help, it's that I can't. I can make a certain amount of trouble for the State's Attorney but that's an unrealistic option. I'm only stalling off the inevitable. The State's Attorney's going to get my man anyway and I'm only making a powerful enemy by stalling. What I do in a case like that is cooperate. Maybe I even give the State's Attorney some moral support. Then I come out of it with a reputation for being fair. But that's not being fair, that's just being realistic.[42]

The conception of being realistic is based on parole officers' experience with the system and (as the officer's candid explanation above suggests) his own self-interest in furthering a career. Nevertheless, it is not a matter of a wholly cynical officer, looking to get ahead at the expense of his charges. Depending on the behavior of the parolee, the officer has a greater or lesser chance of effectively influencing the outcome of a case. Table 17.1 shows a breakdown of the situations parolees may get into and how much influence can be exerted by the parole officer.

Table 17.1	*The Degree of Freedom in Parole Officers' Decision Making*	
Situation	**Examples**	**Degree of Constraint on P.O.**
Absolutely hopeless	Murder/Narcotic sales	The P.O. has no freedom whatsoever. His behavior is totally constrained by the situation. If he "bucks the system," he will be denounced by his peers.
Marginally hopeless	Burglary/Simple robbery	The P.O. has relatively little freedom.
Marginally promising	Narcotic possession/ Simple theft	The P.O. has relatively greater degree of freedom.
Absolutely promising	All misdemeanors "victimless" felonies	Freedom is greatest. The parolee will not ordinarily be returned to prison in these situations unless his P.O. is forced to "sacrifice" him for some reason.

Source: Richard McCleary, "How Structural Variables Constrain the Parole Officer's Use of Discretionary Powers," *Social Problems* **23** (December 1975): 213.

As can be seen from the above table, it is not that the parole officer is making decisions about parolees who are involved in petty technical violations, but they are dealing with men and women who have been granted parole and then continue to break the law to the extent that they are again caught. Most of the decisions by parole officers appear to be the marginal cases where a parolee has committed some form of petty theft or burglary. There is some freedom, but the more serious the crime even in the marginal situations, the less the parole officer can do to save his client.

When parole revocation does occur, it involves two different kinds of decisions. First, the parole officer decides if a person deserves to have his parole revoked. If a parole officer does not think the parolee is really trying to reform and is likely to continue committing crimes, the officer may feel that a revocation is "deserved." On the other hand, if a parolee appears to be sincerely attempting to lead a noncriminal life but occasionally gets into trouble, he is not thought to deserve being sent back to prison, even for a serious violation. Secondly, parole revocation is considered in light of what can be done officially. This involves the legal and organizational limits of a parole officer's power. The first aspect is a "private typing" of parolees by the officer on the basis of his/her intuitive assessment of the parolee; the second is an official designation.[43] If an officer sees a parolee as deserving parole revocation, he/she will use official powers to revoke the parole in situations where there is a realistic case for doing so. Conversely, a parole officer will attempt to help those he/she privately considers to be sincerely attempting to reform, but the structural limitations are such that the private typings must be linked to official designations if the parole officer is to be successful in either keeping a parolee free or returning him/her to prison.

SUMMARY

This chapter has examined the work of probation and parole officers. The probation officer is both an officer of the court and a correctional officer. In the juvenile justice system the probation officer makes most of the disposition decisions that the court was established to make, while in the adult court, the probation officer's influence is minimal and the presentence report is little more than a reflection of what has been decided in plea negotiations.

As a supervisory technique, probation is vague and poorly grounded in either a clear theory or program. The treatment orientation is so broad as to include virtually anything done by probation as some form of rehabilitation. By and large, nonprofessional intuition is employed by probation officers to evaluate and supervise their clients. Parole is similarly vague as a device for corrections—from the parole board that uses the seriousness of a crime as the main criteria for making release decisions to the bureaucratically structured decision process that compels realistic decisions concerning parole.

Overall, the importance of probation and parole has been largely ignored in the criminal justice system. Probation is virtually synonomous with juvenile justice, and, while the probation officer's role in the adult court is largely diminished by the institution of standard deals, it does have the potential for structuring all sentences. Parole officers are clearly limited by the structure in which they work, but they do have the discretion to return people to prison. In the rehabilitative role, they can redirect offenders to noncriminal careers.

Glossary

In Re Gault   A 1967 Supreme Court decision that gave juveniles many of the rights adults have in court, including notice of charges, right to an attorney, and right to face the accuser.

Informal Probation   A type of probation where the defendant agrees to be placed on probation instead of receiving an official criminal/delinquent record.

Intake Officer   A probation officer who screens incoming suspects. In the juvenile court, this officer makes the majority of disposition decisions.

Morrissey v. *Brewster*   A court decision spelling out the rights of parolees.

Parens Patriae   Juvenile court philosophy giving the court substantial leeway in deciding what is best for a juvenile defendant.

Parole   Placing a convicted offender outside of prison for the remainder of his/her sentence.

Parole Board   A group of people who decide whether or not a prisoner should be granted parole. These boards often consist of political appointees with little background in social or psychological evaluation.

Probation   A form of supervision for convicted adults and juveniles as an alternative to incarceration.

Technical Violations   Breaking the rules of probation or parole while not committing any other crime.

Questions

1. Compare the role of the probation officer in adult and juvenile courts.
2. Explain why the probation intake officer does most of the justice in the juvenile justice system.
3. What is the problem in the philosophy of probation? Why is it important for successful programs to have a clear underlying philosophy?
4. What is the main criteria used by parole boards in granting parole?
5. What is the concept of realism used in parole office decision making? How do the organizational constraints affect parole officer discretion?

Notes

1. Victor H. Evjen, "The Federal Probation System: The Struggle to Achieve It and Its First Twenty-Five Years," *Federal Probation* (June 1975): 3.

2. Ibid.

3. Evjen, 1975, 5.

4. Evjen, 1975, 6.

5. Evjen, 1975, 6.

6. Evjen, 1975, 8.

7. William Healy and Augusta Bronner, *Delinquents and Criminals: Their Making and Unmaking.* (New York: Macmillan, 1926), p. 82.

8. American Correctional Association, *Manual for Correctional Standards.* (Washington, DC: American Correctional Association, 1966), pp. 107–108.

9. Walter L. Barkdall, "Probation: "Call It Control—and Mean It," *Federal Probation* (December 1976): 5–6.

10. Anthony Platt, *The Child-Savers: The Invention of Delinquency*. (Chicago: University of Chicago Press, 1969).

11. Anthony Platt, "The Triumph of Benevolence: The Origins of the Juvenile Justice System in the United States," in Richard Quinney, *Criminal Justice in America: A Critical Understanding*. (Boston: Little, Brown, 1974).

12. Edwin Lemert, "The Juvenile Court—Quest and Realities," in Task Force Report: Juvenile Delinquency and Youth Crime. (Washington, DC: U.S. Government Printing Office, 1967), pp. 91–97.

13. Donald Cressey and Robert McDermott, Diversion from the Juvenile Justice System. Project report from the National Assessment of Juvenile Corrections. (Ann Arbor, MI: University of Michigan, 1973).

14. Lemert, 1967, 93.

15. Lemert, 1967, 95.

16. Cressey and McDermott, 1973, 19–20.

17. Alvin W. Cohn, *Crime and Justice Administration*. (Philadelphia: Lippincott, 1976), pp. 361–362.

18. Division of Probation, "At the Selective Presentence Investigation Report," *Federal Probation* **38** (December 1974): 48.

19. Robert M. Carter, "The Presentence Report and the Decision-Making Process," *Journal of Research in Crime and Delinquency* **4** (July 1967): 203–211.

20. *Crime and Delinquency in California*. (Sacramento, CA: Department of Justice, 1965), pp. 98–99.

21. Robert Carter and Leslie Wilkins, "Some Factors in Sentencing Policy," *Journal of Criminal Law, Police Science and Criminology* **58** (1967): 503–514.

22. Carter and Wilkins, 1967, 512.

23. From pp. 31–33 in *Justice by Consent: Plea Bargains in the American Courthouse* by Arthur Rosett and Donald R. Cressey. Copyright 1976 by J. B. Lippincott. Reprinted by permission of Harper & Row, Publishers, Inc.

24. This was explained to the author by a probation officer working in an urban department.

25. Lewis Diana, "What Is Probation?" *Journal of Criminal Law, Police Science and Criminology* **51** (July-August 1960): 189–204.

26. Harry Allen, Paul Friday, Julian Roebuck and Edward Sagarin, *Crime and Punishment: An Introduction to Criminology*. (New York: Free Press, 1981), p. 416.

27. Diana, 1960, 203.

28. President's Commission on Law Enforcement and Administration of Justice, *Task Force Report: Corrections*. (Washington, DC: Department of Justice, 1967), p. 66.

29. Robert Carter, Richard McGee, and Kim Nelson, *Corrections in America* (Philadelphia: Lippincott, 1975), p. 206.

30. Vincent O'Leary and Joan Nuffield, *The Organization of Parole Systems in the United States*, 2nd ed. (Hackensack, NJ: National Council on Crime and Delin-

quency, 1972), p. 181. See also Peter Hoffman and Lucille K. Degostin, "Parole Decision-Making: Structuring Discretion," *Federal Probation* **38** (December 1974): 7.

31. Hoffman and Degostin, 1974, 12.

32. *Special Intensive Parole Unit, Phase 1, Fifteen Man Caseload Study.* (Sacramento, CA: California Department of Corrections, November 1956).

33. E. Reimer and M. Warren, *Special Intensive Parole Unit, Phase II Thirty Man Caseload.* (Sacramento, CA: California Department of Corrections, December 1958).

34. J. Havel and E. Sulk, *Special Intensive Parole Unit, Phase III.* CDC Research Division, Research Report #3. (Sacramento, CA: California Department of Corrections, March 1962).

35. John E. Berecochea, Dorothy R. Jaman and Welton A. Jones, *Time Served in Prison and Parole Outcome: An Experimental Study.* CDC Research Division. Research Report #49. (Sacramento, CA: California Department of Corrections, June 1973).

36. Joan Havel, *Special Intensive Parole Unit, Phase IV (High Base Expectancy Study).* CDC Research Division, Research Report #10. (Sacramento, CA: California Division of Corrections, June 1963).

37. John Irwin, *The Felon.* (Englewood Cliffs, NJ: Prentice-Hall, 1970), p. 152.

38. Irwin, 1970, 152–153.

39. Irwin, 1970, 154.

40. Walter R. Burkhart, "The Great California Parole Experiment," *Federal Probation* **40** (December 1976): 13.

41. National Advisory Commission on Criminal Justice Standards and Goals, *Corrections.* (Washington, DC: U.S. Government Printing Office, 1973), p. 407.

42. Richard McCleary, "How Structural Variables Constrain the Parole Officer's Use of Discretionary Powers," *Social Problems* **23** (December 1975): 212.

43. Robert C. Prus and John Stratton, "Parole Revocation Decision-Making: Private Typings and Official Designations," Federal Probation **40** (March 1976): 48–53.

18

Punishment and Prisons

What to Look For:

The development of the concept of punishment and prisons.

The concept of total institutions and adaptations to such institutions.

What changes came about when prisons went from a punishment to rehabilitation mode.

The nature of the prisoner's world and its effect on rehabilitation.

Common types of prison violence and its causes.

Evaluation of prison in terms of recidivism.

Introduction

THIS CHAPTER DEALS with punishment and the places men and women are sent to when they have been sentenced to incarceration. The philosophies behind punishment and prisons have changed over time, and different societies have varying conceptions not only of what is proper punishment but also what is an adequate prison. To understand the relationship between prisons and punishment, we will first examine how conceptions of punishment were developed.

Then we will look at prisons. Prisons are not merely reflections of society's idea of punishment—they are a type of *"total institution"*.[1] Within these kinds of institutions, an **underlife** develops as an adaptation to prison life. Often the underlife has more impact on the inmate than the prison program (whether benevolent or punitive). Therefore, we will examine this informal but very real world in which the offender lives, and we will examine the violence, both individual and collective, related to this underlife. We will examine violence as a feature of prisons that is not intended by society or prison administrators.

A final issue in the study of prisons is an evaluative one. How effective are prisons? We will re-examine the punitive and rehabilitative goals of prison, and see to what extent these goals are met or not met. Then, we will look at studies of recidivism to determine if sending men and women to prison has the desired effect of returning them to society as noncriminals.

Background of Prisons

The roots of prison can be traced back to ancient forms of punishment. Primitive religions held that people existed in two worlds, the earthly and the spiritual.[2] The gods controlled both of these worlds, and depending on how they viewed the earthly behavior of mankind they either rewarded or punished them through natural forces. The ancient Greeks, for example, had many gods whose wrath was visited on humans. Since the gods so obviously engaged in punishment, human beings' punishment of one another for offending the gods was justified. This was especially true if the gods, angered by one individual, brought natural forces to wreak vengeance on an entire community. By taking care of the punishment themselves, primitive man could ward off wholesale punishment by the gods. Early punishment however, was often the duty of the family or clan, and it was not until more sophisticated forms of government emerged that public justice came into being. Graeme Newman suggests:

Public justice may, of course, have evolved to satisfy other needs, such as the control of economic life, but it seems reasonable to consider that it also helped hinder the social process of feuding.[3]

Thus, while there is a difference between later public justice and the theories of deterrence, the idea of punishment can still be traced to primitive religion and the harshness of the gods. Consider the following "public justice" and the primitive manner in which it is carried out:

> That the traitor is to be taken from the prison, and laid upon a sledge, or hurdle, and drawn to the gallows or place of execution, and there hanged by the neck until he be half dead, and then cut down; his entrails to be cut out of his body, and burnt by the exectioner; then his head to be cut off, his body to be divided into quarters; and afterwards his head and quarters are to be set up in some open places directed, which usually are on the City Gates, on London Bridge, or upon Westminister Mall. And to render the crime more terrible to the spectators, the hangman, then takes out the heart, shows it to the people, and says, here is the heart of a traitor.[4]

The organs of the body were believed to be the source of the criminal activity, and so naturally they had to be punished specifically.

The publicity of the punishment was early theorized to be a better deterrent than private punishment. Indeed, a few modern commentators have gone so far as to suggest that public executions be held on television to show everyone exactly what happens to evildoers. The early affairs where they graphically showed the crowd exactly what happened to criminals seemed to attract the very people who were to be deterred. In England, when an execution was to be held, the procession to the gallows was described as follows:

> . . . No solemn procession, it was just the contrary; it was a lowlived blackguard merrymaking. . . . the whole vagabond population of London, all the thieves, and all the prostitutes, all those who were evil minded, and some, a comparatively few curious people made up the mob of those brutalizing occasions.[5]

In part, the role of the prison was for petty crimes or for these awaiting punishment. During the Inquisition, when people were punished for their religious beliefs, there was a finely tuned use of imprisonment and torture. One writer described the process thusly:

> Trained through long experience in an accurate knowledge of all that can move the human breath; skilled not only to detect the subtle evasions of the intellect, but to seek and find the tenderest point through which to assail the

conscience and the heart; relentless inflicting agony on body and brain, whether through the mouldering wretchedness of the hopeless dungeon protracted through uncounted years, the sharper pain of the torture chamber, or by coldly playing on the affections; using without scruple the most violent alternatives of hope and fear; employing with cynical openness every resource of guile and fraud on wretches purposely starved to render them incapable of self-defense, the counsels which these men utter might well seem the promptings of friends exulting in the unlimited power to wreak their evil passions on helpless mortals. Yet through all this there shines the evident convictions that they are doing the work of God. No labour is too great if they can win a soul from perdition. . . .[6]

Jumping ahead in history, the modern study of punishment has taken on a clinical detachment where terms such as "torture" have been replaced by new vocabularies including happier words such as **aversion therapy** and "negative stimuli." Most punishment research has been carried out on mice in laboratory settings. The conclusion is that mice, and therefore humans, will alter their behavior to avoid negative feedback. As Newman has noted, however, there are considerable differences between the laboratory and society—the latter having far more uncontrolled variables.[7] Overall, the research on *deterrence* is far from clear, even though there is evidence that it has some result. Newman summarized:

> In general, our conclusions are that although there are some mixed results deterrence has been shown to work for some crimes, especially if certainty of punishment is strong. The effects of increasing severity of punishment for crimes needs further study, but it appears as though severity is of lesser importance in suppressing unwanted behavior in the real-life situation of crime. This bears consideration since the majority of experimental studies have concluded that it is severity that is the dominant parameter of punishment.[8]

As we have seen throughout this book, punishment is as much a matter of discretion as it is of being caught. For those who are in fact punished by being sent to prison, there is no doubt some sense of inequity. Prison inmates not only know of others who have committed the same crime without punishment, but many who eventually do go to prison also have committed the same crimes before without punishment.

Over the years, the general revulsion toward torture, particularly that used by the Nazis on the people in concentration camps, has made imprisonment a favored punishment; for this torture is either invisible or not used at all. Despite the expense of prison, the growing concern over crime has led to a general mood of impatience with alternative measures. Humane measures are seen as ineffective, and harsh measures are repulsive. If nothing else, prisons have come to be seen as places where dangerous criminals can be incarcerated and kept away from the law-abiding populace. It is seen as a general deterrence to those who value their freedom.

Life in Prison

Ideally, from the punitive viewpoint, men and women who break the law for serious crimes are placed in a secure, confined setting where their incapacitation hurts them in return for the harm they have inflicted on society. If such institutions can also be used to educate them, to teach them a skill, and to help them resolve personal problems through therapy, so much the better; at least prisons keep criminals off the streets temporarily.

Such a vision assumes that the prison life is a reflection of whatever policy happens to be in force at the time—be it humane or harsh. By cutting inmates off from conventional social life, it is assumed that no social life exists. This is not the case. A full, although warped, social life emerges within the confines of the prison. To understand how this life springs forth, it is first necessary to see exactly the structure of life in prison. Conceptually, a prison is a **total institution**, defined by Goffman as:

> . . . A place of residence and work where a large number of like-situated individuals, cut off from the wider society for an appreciable period of time, together lead an enclosed, formally administered round of life.[9]

Within the total institution, Goffman points out two adjustments: 1) primary and 2) secondary.[10] **Primary adjustments** are those that are part of the institution's organized plan of operation. Prison inmates who participate in educational programs and rehabilitation efforts and who follow the rules can be said to have made primary adjustments. Likewise, the organization ideally rewards compliance with the program by granting privileges. In some institutions there is a systematic behavior modification program whereby inmates are given some token reward for a number of specific desired behaviors.

Secondary adjustments are unauthorized routines developed to get around the official policies (mainly to obtain forbidden goods and services). This type of adaptation also serves to preserve one's sense of identity in the face of the batch treatment in total institutions. We can view these adjustments either as greater or lesser *individual* achievements or as *collective* adjustment. To be sure, there are both collective and individual primary and secondary adjustments, but to the extent that secondary adjustments are collective, we can begin to see a whole new way of understanding the life in total institutions. This is explained by Goffman as follows:

> An interest in the actual place in which secondary adjustments are practiced and in the drawing region from which practitioners come shifts the focus of

attention from the individual and his act to collective matters. In terms of a formal organization as a social establishment, the corresponding shift would be from an individual's secondary adjustments to the full set of such adjustments that all the members of the organization severally and collectively sustain. These practices together comprise what can be called the underlife of the institution, being to a social establishment what an underworld is to a city.[11]

Primary Adjustments

To understand the underlife in prison, we first must see to what the underlife is an adjustment. By understanding how the prison is arranged to house, control, and preferably rehabilitate prisoners through the prison administration, we can understand the nature of the adjustments. This is neither a condemnation of prison programs nor an apology for the underlife that grows in relation to it. Instead, we are looking at general human forms of adaptation to a total institution. Remembering the various theories of criminal behavior, moreover, we are not interested in these forms of adjustment as reactions to housing criminal personalities in a setting and situation of total control. Our basic assumption is that most people in similar circumstances would probably do the same thing as convicted criminals do when they are sent to prison. Studies of prisoners-of-war have shown this to be the case, and in experiments simulating the relationship between the keepers and the kept it has been found that even supposedly enlightened college students quickly take on authoritarian roles. For example, in Zimbardo's study of a mock prison, those students who were assigned the role of prison guards took on harsh authoritarian roles and punitive attitudes toward their classmates who were assigned prisoner roles.[12] Likewise, the students in the prisoner roles began to look for ways to beat the system and to undermine the authority of the student guards. It was not the background of the students that was important, but the relationships that developed in the inmate–guard context.

When a prisoner first enters prison, he is placed in some type of screening unit to determine the type of program in which he or she will be placed. This involves determining level of education, the length of sentence (for long or short programs), background, and other factors (such as prison resources and needs). He/she is taught the rules of the prison, penalties for violating the rules, and privileges that can be earned by appropriate behavior. The prisoner is then assigned to a cell, possibly an educational program, and some kind of work detail. Some prison jobs include minimal pay—others do not—and most of the work is dull, requiring only unskilled or semi-skilled labor. Common prisoner jobs include work in the prison laundry or collecting litter from highways.

Some prisons, however, do have more advanced facilities for training

Prisoners in a women's prison are given classes in typing. Such programs hope to provide inmates with legitimate skills with which to earn a living after release.

and education. For example, California's Sierra Conservation Center, a medium-security prison, has training programs in carpentry, masonry, firefighting, and auto body repair. There are even more sophisticated programs such as computer science courses at Folsom prison in California and at the Massachusetts correctional institutions. Those who have successfully completed the Honeywell computer training program in Massachusetts (to the extent that they qualified for entry-level positions in the computer industry) have had only a 3 percent recidivism rate; the state as a whole has a 30 percent recidivism rate.[13] However, these programs are exceptions, and, even where they have programs to teach skills involving such high-status and high-paying jobs as computer programming, the facilities are minimal. One inmate who coordinates the Folsom computer program commented:

> "I'd be afraid of having an article come out in the prison paper saying there's an opening in a computer class because I think we'd probably get swamped." . . .
>
> Most of the students find out about the program through word of mouth. The class has a large waiting list now, and he believes it will eventually reach the point where they'll have to turn hundreds of prisoners away for lack of equipment.[14]

The interest in such things as computers for a prison population that is between 20 and 50 percent illiterate, the majority having less than an eighth-grade education, may seem strange; but in the context of the dull prison routine, it is a means of doing something that will both pass the time and provide a high-status skill.[15] The following outline of a prison schedule illustrates "time in prison":

6:00 A.M.	Wake up, get ready for breakfast, clean cell, be counted.
6:30 A.M.	Breakfast (march in column of twos, tallest in front, shortest in rear).
7:00 A.M.	Back to your cell.
7:30 A.M.	Sick call.
7:45 A.M.	Work call.
8:00 A.M.	Work
Noon	Lunch
12:30 P.M.	Back to your cell and be counted.
1:00 P.M.	Back to work.
3:00 P.M.	Lights flash. Time to quit work, line up.
3:15 P.M.	Back to your cell and/or to yard for recreation.
4:00 P.M.	Line up for supper.
4:15 P.M.	March to mess hall.
5:00 P.M.	Lock up for rest of the night. Be counted again.
7:30 P.M.	Bell rings. No more talking for the rest of the night.
10:00 P.M.	Lights out.
11:00 P.M.	Radio earphones off. Absolute quiet.[16]

In some respects, the above schedule appears to be similar to a nonprison workday with the exception of the early (3:00 P.M.) quitting time at work and evening lock-up. However, the "work" is usually dull, takes place in confined quarters and under tight security. Even though the work is dull, most prisoners would rather be working than locked up in their cells. The following typifies prison routine:

They get up in the morning, stand in line to be counted, then stand in line to eat breakfast. They go to work for a few hours, making license plates or metal furniture, shoes, or street signs. Then they line up to be counted again, line up to eat lunch, and go back to work again for a few hours. Or, an increasing number do no work, because there isn't enough to go around. So they stand around in the prison yard, sit idly in their cells or occupy themselves with arts and crafts. Before dinner there is an exercise period. Then they are counted again, eat a third meal and spend the evening watching television.[17]

An aspect of the prison routine that is difficult to quantify but which plays an important role is the metallic and concrete acoustics of prisons. It is extremely difficult to concentrate on reading, watching television, or even holding a discussion because the sounds intrude everywhere in the cell block. Clanging cell doors opening and shutting, guards and prisoners shouting or calling, and even the footsteps on concrete—all have a certain sound that reverberates far beyond what is found in normal settings. Thus, even the simple act of watching television in this setting is often an exercise in futility. It is part of "doing time" and an often overlooked aspect of the prison world.

The rewards for following the official rules and the punishments for their violation are often vague. As we saw in discussing parole board decisions, the main criteria for granting parole was found to be the seriousness of the crime for which a person was imprisoned. Since good behavior in prison is supposed to be a measure of rehabilitation and the ultimate reward for such behavior is early release, parole board practices often play against prison programs. If prisoners perceive their release to be linked not to their prison behavior but to their crime, it really does not matter what they do in terms of "programming" in the prison.

To overcome this defect, some states set up **indeterminate sentences** to be based on the extent of a prisoner's rehabilitation. In reality, however, the authorities appointed to determine extent of rehabilitation were as vague in their criteria as were the parole boards. In a critique of the indeterminate sentence, one anthropologist who studies prisons pointed out:

Ideally, within legal limits, the Adult Authority supposedly administers certain parts of the indeterminate sentence in a more scientific manner than the earlier parole board did. Within those limits, the Adult Authority has the power to determine the total time a prisoner is to serve in prison and on parole (conditional release from prison under the supervision of California Department of Corrections (CDC) presumably based on when the prisoner becomes rehabilitated. As an ideal example, a first termer usually becomes eligible for parole after serving one-third of his sentence in prison. If he is rehabilitated, he may be paroled from prison when eligible; but he must serve the remainder of his minimum sentence on parole.

. . . Unfortunately, these underlying ideals will never be achieved under the existing system because there is a basic defect in the way that the indeterminate sentence is administered. This basic defect has never been realist-

THE WALL STREET JOURNAL

"You mean we're being kept here for *display*?
And all this time I thought we were
being *rehabilitated!*"

Source: From *Wall Street Journal*, Permission—Cartoon Features Syndicate.

ically acknowledged or faced by CDC and the Adult Authority. In . . . the ideally functioning system, it is evident that the key factor is the point in time *when the prisoner becomes rehabilitated*. Unfortunately, the system in practice stands in bitter contrast to the theoretical system. The basic defect is that *there is absolutely no way to judge if a prisoner has become rehabilitated or not*. Prisoners have long been aware of this. However, with the cooperation of CDC, the Adult Authority has been able to effectively sidestep this issue. In lieu of admitting the impossibility of determining when and if a prisoner is rehabilitated, the Adult Authority has used its quasijudicial and administrative power to set up a system that ignores many of the ideals that supposedly underlie California's indeterminate sentencing system.[18]

Secondary Adjustments

The adjustments to official prison life can be extremely difficult in situations where there is a vague system of rewards. Since prisoners are denied the taken-for-granted amenities of normal social life, they manufacture their own, along with norms to sustain this life. Additionally, in total institutions, the self is merged as part of a batch of others in like circumstances. Not only is the self submerged, but it is also connected with a distasteful institution, the prison. The secondary adjustments, then, are not just a reaction to the material amenities of life, but they are a means of carving out some expression of self.[19]

To fully examine the secondary adjustments and the underlife in prisons, we will first examine the general relationship between the inmates and staff, which represents the official program of prisons. The adjustments to the staff (and the institution they represent) will be viewed primarily as the material underlife. Secondly, we will examine the roles and selves in the prison underlife.

Staff and Inmates

At one time there was a clear distinction between convicts and prison guards. The guards saw themselves and were seen by the prisoners as instruments of punishment. Adjustments by the prisoners were fairly uniform in their view of prison and the staff. The staff was the enemy, and the prisoners were united against them.[20] Norms developed among inmates that stressed unity and loyalty toward the prisoner cohort, and no one should attempt to gain by hurting another inmate. Noncooperation with the staff, in other words, was the norm. In this situation, the lines were clearly drawn, and unity was high.

With the advent of the indeterminate sentence and the concept of rehabilitation rather than punishment, this relationship changed. Davidson explains:

> An important change came about when emphasis on rehabilitation began many years ago. When implemented, the rehabilitative nature of the new programs became apparent to prisoners. They were now told by staff that they were in prison to be rehabilitated, not punished; the guards were "correctional officers" there not to administer punishment, but merely to keep the prisoners confined; that confinement was necessary to protect society while the prisoners were being rehabilitated. Prisoners began to wonder why they were in prison. Supposedly, the staff was no longer an enemy; it was a partner, who was helping the prisoners. The fierce opposition between prisoners and staff seemed to disappear, thus effectively destroying that intense unity among prisoners. Without an obvious opposition or enemy, most prisoners saw no reason for unity. Simultaneously, convicts (as a type of prisoner) seemed to fade into insignificance while a new type of prisoner appears—the inmate. . . . Under this system, prisoners did almost anything to prove to the staff that they were rehabilitated, regardless of how it would affect other prisoners. Since unity no longer existed among most prisoners, each inmate was a single individual, trying to get out as soon as possible. Inmates thought they could further impress staff into believing they had become rehabilitated by telling staff about the illegal and rule-breaking activities of other prisoners—activities in which prisoners have always engaged. This "law-abiding" snitching became wholesale and made it difficult for the relatively few remaining convicts to continue many of their activities; they were forced into even more convertness than before. For convicts, the staff was not the only enemy now. Inmates were a new enemy who could not be privy to convict activities, because they did not adhere to the convict code.[21]

The adaptation to the initial punishment-oriented institutions was one of the convict and the **convict code**, but as the institution changed (at least in name) to rehabilitation so too did the secondary adjustments. Whereas the convict was a unifying figure among all prisoners, the inmate was an individualistic adaptation attempting to gain release through cooperation with the prison program. However, as the rehabilitation process came to be seen as little more than a new way of controlling prisoners, the convict adaptation became dominant again. Davidson points out:

> With the passage of time, more and more prisoners began to question the validity of the rehabilitation programs and the sincerity of those who administered them. They came to recognize the general inability of programs inside a prison to affect rehabilitation programs and the hypocrisy of the indeterminate sentence system. In their new role, the "correctional officers" did more than merely confine the prisoners; they continued to harass, repress, and punish the prisoners as they had before. A general disillusionment began to grow among most prisoners. More and more prisoners recognized that their own illegal and rule-breaking activities were more important to them than the staff's rehabilitation activities. Although even convicts superficially played the game and programmed, the basic opposition between staff and prisoners became apparent to more prisoners.[22]

Thus, from the prisoner's point of view, the staff was not really interested in rehabilitation, but in control or security. Whether they were called "guards" or "correctional officers," they were simply doing everything they could to repress prisoners.

To a great extent the role and perspective of the staff has been ignored. However, it is not the conflict between staff and prisoner we must understand—it is the structure of the situation in which they find themselves together. Prison reforms have included better education and pay for prison staff, but even a better paid and more enlightened staff could do little to change the nature of staff–convict relationship in the context of the total institution. Regardless of the staff's background, they are responsible for keeping people locked behind bars. Therefore, there will always be a structurally produced strain between the two.

To the staff, the prisoners are men and women who have committed several crimes, and many of them are violent and sadistic. The staff sees the attempts to break the rules that are to be enforced and despite "prisoner unity," they see the inmates brutalize one another. When a convict claims he/she wants to be rehabilitated, the staff views this claim as an attempt to manipulate the system to gain special privilege or to gain release. It is not seen as a sincere effort to be rehabilitated. Thus, even in situations where prisoners, either individually or collectively, want programs to assist them in rehabilitation, the staff tends to be cynical. For example, in the Folsom computer course program, the administration believed the prisoners would possibly use computers to mastermind an escape plan or simply play games.[23] Such cynicism may appear to be banal and paranoid, but it is understandable in light of the fact that prisoners have used shop classes to fashion weapons, including rudimentary guns. This leads to a vicious cycle of distrust. Sincere efforts at rehabilitation are exploited by prisoners, creating cynicism among staff. Sincere efforts at reform by prisoners are met by the cynical staff, building distrust among prisoners of the sincerity of rehabilitation programs. It is not a matter then of good or bad staff or prisoners; rather it is a matter of the nature of the relationship they have to one another in the total institution.

The Prisoner's World

A key part of secondary adjustments is the economic world of prisoners. The legitimate economic system in prison allows for relatively little, as compared to the outside, so part of the underlife is a robust economic system where goods and services are exchanged. Basically, all prisoners enter into this sub-rosa economic system, and they do so to increase their luxury and pleasure.[24] More recently, the goods and services legitimately available in prisons include televisions, stereos, typewriters, musical instruments, books, and street clothing. To obtain these goods, prisoners must have money, and most cannot earn enough to buy these things through legitimate channels. Furthermore, forbidden items have greater importance in prison including mundane materials that are taken for granted on the outside. For example, common nutmeg is a highly desired prison narcotic.[25] There are other highly desired prison goods, as noted by Irwin:

> Prison contraband goes beyond the ordinary street items and includes many types of drugs, prison-brewed alcohol, and weapons. Together, the legitimate items and contraband have significantly raised the standard of living of many prisoners. Affluent prisoners eat more and better food, which they purchase through the canteen and sub-rosa market, occasionally or regularly consume drugs and alcohol, smoke good tobacco products, wear more comfortable and fashionable clothing, have cells where and with whom they choose, enjoy expensive appliances in their cells, attend extra prison activities (especially movies), have abundant books, or art and craft materials, and even buy prison sex.[26]

The status hierarchy in prison is based on one's ability to obtain these goods and services, and since this is only possible through the illegal economic system a prisoner's status is dependent to a great extent on being a part of this sub-rosa system.

The operation of the illegitimate economic system is tied to *rackets* and *prison gangs*. At one time, the prison economic system was fairly meager, and a few entrepreneurs operated individually. More recently, it is controlled by rackets and **prison gangs**, and their protection is necessary in

order to operate. Individual dealers who obtain prized goods and who
have no protection are robbed by racketeers. The following illustration
shows the vulnerability of the lone prison businessman:

> *When Earl arrived, T.J. uncoiled and squeezed an arm around Earl's shoulders, "Sit
> down here, boy," he said, "an' help us scheme on gettin' them narcotics." "How
> much has he got?" Earl asked. Black Ernie answered, "Half a piece. It come in on a
> visit a couple days ago and he kept it cool, just selling to some dudes over in the
> South block." . . . "Hunch on down here," Bad Eye said. "We'll run it to you. Ernie
> brought it to us because it's a white boy . . . and the motherfucker didn't throw us
> our end. We're the motherfuckers be fightin' when the rugs [black prisoners] start
> wasting people around here."*[27]

Prison Identities

Given this kind of economic orientation, the groupings in prison have
changed from the convict vs. guards/collaborators to either an independent orientation of retreatism or connection with a prison gang. Instead of
having a single convict group, there are splinter groups of violent gangs
whose energies tend to be geared as much against one another as against
the staff. The respected prisoner is no longer the "right guy" who treats
all other convicts who are loyal to the convict code with consideration and
stands against the staff. Instead, as Irwin points out:

> Today the respected public prison figure—the convict or hog—stands ready
> to kill to protect himself, maintains strong loyalties to some small group of
> other convicts (invariably of his own race), and will rob and attack or at least
> tolerate his friends' robbing and attacking other weak independents or their
> foes. He openly and stubbornly opposes the administration, even if this re-
> sults in harsh punishment. Finally, he is extremely assertive of his masculine
> sexuality, even though he may occasionally make use of the prison homo-
> sexuals or, less often, enter into more permanent sexual alliance with a kid.[28]

The breakdown of **prison identities** can be seen in relationship to the
new type of convict. Each of the following represents a type:

1. *Core gang member.* Ruling clique of a prison gang. These are the most respected and powerful of prisoner types.
2. *Near-core gang member.* Not a core member, but loyal to the core and as-
   pires to be part of it. Called upon frequently by core members to perform duty.
3. *Affiliated gang member.* Found in prisons where large gangs such as the
   Nuestra Familia or the Black P Stone Nation exist. Can be called upon in
   emergencies, such as gang wars, to fight with gang.
4. *Independents.* In the convict world, there are few independents, and those
   who exist do so because they have withstood attacks and won. They can-

not prevail, however, if they oppose the gangs. The odds are too great that they will be murdered. Therefore, they work within the sub rosa system, independent of gangs but not against them.

5. *Political organizers.* These men are outside of the illegitimate economic system and concentrate on political reform and creating unity among all prisoners with the goal of reforming prisons. They cannot, however, oppose the gangs or their economics. As long as they abide by the code of conduct, they will be left alone.

6. *Outside independents.* There are men who are outside the prison economic system and pose no threat to the gangs. They can exist as "characters" who are seen as harmless, "dings" whose mental capacity is obviously minimal, or the less desirable homosexuals who (unlike the younger more desirable kids) do not require gang protection.

7. *Organization men.* In larger prisons, certain groups such as the Muslims and Mafia do not subscribe to the violent gang activities, but are not bothered by the gangs since it is believed that their organization will crush anyone who harms them. They are active in the prison economics and politics, often taking a leadership role during times of disorder.[29]

Prison Violence

The first day I got to Soledad [prison] I was walking from the fish tank to the mess hall and this guy comes running down the hall past me, yelling, with a knife sticking out of his back. Man, I was petrified. I thought, what the fuck kind of place is this?[30]

When prison groups reunited after the brief spell of adopting an individual orientation toward the indeterminate sentence and the even more brief political unity in the early 1970s, the convict group was never quite the same group it had been before. The groupings were decidely antagonistic toward each other, they were ready to exploit fellow cons, and they employed far more violence than the earlier convict groups. They also maintained the antagonistic stance toward the prison administration. In looking at prison violence, it is important to keep these groupings in mind.

Interpersonal Violence

The most common form of prison violence is interpersonal. In one study, it was found that there are two primary kinds of prison homicides: those involving single assailants and those involving multiple assailants.[31] In cases involving individual assailants, the murder was typically a spur-of-the-moment affair, where one inmate killed another. A "falling out" in a homosexual relationship often led to this kind of homicide. In the multiple-assailant killings, however, the murders appeared to be planned.

These killings were, in all likelihood, gang-related killings for some infraction of the convict code or moves by an individual into a gang-controlled economic sphere.

Violence involving homosexual activity is connected to either "turning" a young inmate (forcing him to submit to homosexual activity), a lovers' quarrel, or fighting one man for another's lover. Many young prisoners join one group or another to avoid homosexual attacks, or (as the following illustrates) they suffer brutal consequences:

> . . . A young, clean-cut Anglo had just come to prison. He had some college background and felt that he really did not fit, so he chose to be a loner and have no friends. Apparently a few blacks thought him very attractive sexually. The first open encounter was a shouting match, but the Anglo adamantly refused to capitulate to the blacks' desires. About a month later, in a second encounter, he was socked in the jaw; but he did not give in. The third and final open manifestation occurred about a month later. He still refused to submit, so the blacks literally beat him to a pulp. The bulls bundled up his bruised, bloody, yet still living body and sent him off to another prison.[32]

According to Davidson, most prisoners avoid such attacks either by joining a clique, by carrying a homemade knife, or by virtue of being bigger than anyone who might attack them. Any attack on a clique member will bring the rest of the clique to his aid, thus leading to further violence.

The *machismo* ethic is a related underlying cause of interpersonal violence, especially among Chicano prisoners with violent backgrounds. In comparing black and Chicano prisoners, Davidson pointed out that blacks are more vocal than Chicanos and more likely to take on an "inmate" individualistic adaptation than a "convict" group adaptation. The Chicanos tend to be far more loyal to their group and strict group ideals, while the black inmates tend to look for means of "beating the system," even at the expense of other prisoners. The blacks tended to be flexible and the Chicanos rigid. The overall result of this kind of orientation is that black prisoners can better avoid violence, and when violence comes there is some advance notice that it is brewing. As Davidson points out:

> The Chicanos are quiet and reserved, keeping their ideas and emotions inside; and the blacks are quite verbal, often openly displaying their ideas and emotions. The Chicanos are action people; they do not back down on their few words and subtle actions; and when violence comes, it usually is without any apparent warning to outsiders. In contrast, the blacks are vocal people; they are able to verbally back off from almost anything they say; and when violence comes, there has usually been a long public prelude.[33]

Most violence is not between rival gangs, however, and especially not between different ethnic or racial groupings. Since conflict requires interaction, and most groups segregate themselves racially and ethnically, most

In both the Attica (top) and New Mexico State Penitentiary (bottom) riots, old scores were settled among inmates. However, most of the deaths in the Attica riot occurred when the police stormed the prison, while the deaths in the New Mexico riot were due solely to vengeance by inmates.

of the interpersonal violence is intraracial.[34] To be sure, interracial violence occurs, but it typically does not concern race. By avoiding one another, most prison groups also avoid interracial violence; but to the extent that gangs begin competing for control of prison sub rosa economic systems, interracial violence is likely to increase.

Inmate–Guard Violence

Until the early 1970s assaults on guards were relatively rare.[35] However, as part of the general radical politics of the late 1960s and early 1970s, the politicization of prison groups, the definition of guards as oppressors, and the rise in prison gangs, attacks became more frequent. The radical prisoner groups asserted themselves and defined more situations in terms of politics. The radical prison movement believed their incarceration to be political. These were the reasons:

> . . . They had committed crimes because of unnatural, unjust, and inhumane strains or pathological socialization, which stem from the relationships in a capitalistic society; they were pressured into economic crime as a means of surviving in an economically exploitative capitalist society; they were framed by police for crimes that they did not commit because of political activities; or they were actually conscious perpetrators of political crimes, such as acts committed in protesting the war, racial discrimination, or the capitalist society in general.[36]

This view among prisoners justified what they took to be self-protection in assaulting the guards. As a result, during the period when the radical prison movement was strong, numerous guards were attacked and several were killed.

At the same time the radical prisoner movement was gaining its power, there were several legal decisions regarding prisoners' rights that sharply limited the punishments taken. For example, the *Holt* v. *Sarver* case involved evidence from the Arkansas prison system that showed torture, rape, extortion, and assault to be a common measure used in the system. In addition, several graves containing the bodies of murdered prisoners were found. The Supreme Court ruled the Arkansas prison to be in violation of the Eighth Amendment to the Constitution.[37] Such decisions really did little to change the fundamental nature of total institutions, but they did show that the administration of at least some prisons was less than professional.

For unknown reasons, the radical prison movement fizzled. To be sure, those in prison administration did little to encourage political organizations, but it probably died for reasons similar to those in other radical movements of the period.

Women in Prison

Since 95 percent of the prison inmate population is male, our discussion has focused on men in prison.[38] Women in prison make primary and secondary adjustments to life in a total institution, and much of our discussion of male prison adjustments also applies to females. However, given the different societal roles of men and women, the adjustments and problems as well as the official orientation by administrators tend to be somewhat different.

Perhaps the most notable difference between male and female adjustments to prison is the relative lack of violence in women's prisons. This can be linked to the less violent nature of women's role and the status accompanying a tough image. Another related difference between men and women's incarceration is the nature of homosexual conduct. While homosexual relationships in male prisons are often violent and exploitive, they tend to be less physical and more emotionally supportive in female prisons. According to Rose Giallombardo, such relationships are substitutions for families and are attempts to simulate the family.[39] Sexual roles taken on by women in prison also reflect positions in the family—for example, "stud" and "daddy" are used for the male role and "femme" and "mommy" for female roles.

Official policy toward women in prison is also different. While rehabilitation programs for men stress preparation for noncriminal careers outside the home, most of the rehabilitation for women stresses the traditional domestic role. It has been argued that such a role is more desired by women inmates, but Sue Reid has pointed out that women are denied the possibility of an alternative to a predominately domestic role and career whereas it is available to men.[40] In many state prison systems, there is even less opportunity for higher education—four years of college are available to men while only two years are available to women.[41]

As we have seen in previous chapters, there has been an increase in female criminality, and if the trend continues there will be a larger female prison population. At this time, given the paucity of research on female prisons, we know little about them; however, as more women come to be a part of the prison population, more research will be required so that they can be understood at least as well as male prisons. In the meantime, we are limited in our understanding.

Prison Riots

The most popularized form of prison violence is the riot. For example, during the New Mexico State Prison riot, the national media covered the uprising with grim detail as negotiations for prison–guard hostages were in progress and the buildings were burning. When the riot was over, evidence of brutal murders with blow torches and other grisly torture came to light. The public was thrilled and horrified at the spectacle, and hearings subsequently were held to determine the causes of the riot. Time passed and the event was forgotten. However, given the periodic recurrence of riots, it is important to understand their underlying causes and how they develop.

For the most part, prison riots are not spontaneous uprisings—they are deliberately planned.[42] Indeed, the New Mexico State Prison riot was known to at least some staff members before it occurred, but nothing was done to prevent it. These riots are not simply a means to go on a drug-using spree or to take revenge on informers, as was the case in the early rioting in New Mexico, Attica, and other prison riots; rather most riots are to bring attention to prison conditions. After riots, better conditions in prison became available in the form of food, visiting privileges, and other scarce goods. Sometimes deplorable conditions will be brought to light along with archaic prison practices, and in some cases even the prison administration benefits from riots in that long sought after funds suddenly become available and the very changes the administration wants are made possible.

The course of riots is somewhat predictable. In the first stage the "gorillas" take control engaging in a drug and alcohol orgy and settling old scores against informers and rivals.[43] After the initial violence the "right guys" or convicts will take over and begin serious negotiations to improve conditions, end the riot, and perhaps gain amnesty for the rioters. During both the Attica and New Mexico riots, this pattern was followed. In New Mexico, however, the gorillas went a little too far for too long, and at Attica the state police assaulted the institution before the right guys concluded their negotiations; the result was the death of several guards and prisoners.[44]

Recidivism

The term **recidivism** refers to the extent to which prisoners released from prison return to prison because of further violations of the law. It is the primary measure of rehabilitation or reform, and despite the many weaknesses of using simple recidivism as the main measure of prison effectiveness it is the most important measure. The weakness of using simple recidivism as a measure of prison effectiveness is that it fails to consider the many variables outside of prison that will cause an ex-offender to be arrested. For example, if an offender is released into a supportive community program providing assistance in readjusting to freedom and in finding a noncriminal career, his chances of succeeding may be far better than if the same ex-offender were released in an environment with no such program. Other outside variables, such as family support, police attitude toward ex-offenders, background of the offender, and similar factors may all play an important role in whether or not an ex-offender will become a recidivist. Since these variables may only be marginally connected to the prison experience, it would be misleading to cite the prison as the significant causal variable in any change or lack of change in the ex-offender's behavior. By the same token, even if we study prisoners released into the same community environment, it is difficult to see what recidivism rates measure. It could be a measure of a prison's intended programs, or it could be a reaction to a prison's underlife. For example, if a prison has instituted a progressive educational and training program and recidivism goes down, the low rate of recidivism could be due to the programs; however, at the same prison, there might be an extremely violent underlife, and the low recidivism rate may reflect a fear of returning to the prison. It is almost impossible to tell, given the possible combination of variables, what recidivism rates reflect. Further, some criminologists have argued that recidivism is largely a measure of age and maturity, and regardless of what happens in prisons there will be lower recidivism among older ex-offenders than younger ones. Despite these shortcomings, recidivism is still the most widely used measure of prison success since it provides a simple device to evaluate prison performance.

Given the direction of the prison underlife, especially the violent content of that underlife, it is difficult to see how rehabilitation is possible in a prison environment. This is not to discount the different kinds of programs in prison or their effect on the underlife, but it is to point out the overall impact of a total institution on inmates' behavior.

In looking at the research on recidivism, the most complete study was conducted by Glaser.[45] By following the lives of a group of released prisoners, Glaser found that in the 10 years following release from prison, only about one-third were returned. This is not to say that only one-third ever committed another crime, but only one-third either: 1) went back into committing crime to the extent that they were caught and returned to prison or 2) violated their parole to the extent that they were returned to prison. Given the prison experience and the stigma attached to ex-offenders, the two-thirds success rate of ex-prisoners can be seen as quite good. The question, however, is why prisoners give up criminal careers after serving time in prison.

Research into the effectiveness of prison programs has not found them to be the major reason behind postrelease success. For example, in evaluating the effect of group counselling on inmate behavior, Kassebaum and his associates found the counselling to have no bearing on the recidivism rate of released prisoners.[46] It may be due to the lack of usefulness of counselling altogether or group counselling in particular, or it could be the countereffects of prison underlife. Whatever the case, it has not been shown to be effective.

The most useful predictor of postrelease success has been time served in prison. Several studies have shown that the less time prisoners are in prison, the more likely they are to succeed on the outside, regardless of the prison program.[47] These findings are not surprising—for several reasons. Usually, those with shorter sentences are less committed to crime, and there is less time to totally identify with the convict code. In our discussion of the underlife of total institutions, we saw that violence and allegiance to a convict gang are common secondary adaptations in prisons. The extent to which one becomes institutionalized to that way of life, he or she is less likely to make adjustments to a noninstitutionalized, noncriminal life.

At the present time, there is more that needs to be understood about the relationship between prisons and repeated criminal offenses. Studies have been fairly consistent in showing some minor relationships, such as time spent in prison and chances of success or that certain programs have no effect. Overall, we can only say that about one-third of the people who go to prison will be returned, and it usually will be during the first few years following release. In the meantime, research on recidivism is continuing.

SUMMARY

In times of rising crime or rising fear of crime, there is an urgent feeling of anger, hate, and desire for revenge. In ancient times, human reactions were modeled after nature—violent "punishment" appeased the gods. The punishment response has been refined into theory—from the classical theory of Becaria to modern-day deterrence theory. However, the peaks and valleys of crime do not follow the forms of punishment. It is the other way around—when crime goes up, there is fear and clamoring for more severe punishment. Thus, punishment does not seem to affect crime—crime seems to affect punishment!

The public reaction to executions, torture, and dismemberment was one of horror rather than deterrence, so these measures faded along with many of the superstitions that accompanied them. In their place was the prison. At first, it was nothing more than a place to lock up wrongdoers, but later there was a movement to turn prisons into places where prisoners could be rehabilitated. However, overshadowing whatever programs were developed in prisons, the underlife dominated the daily lives of inmates. The primary adjustments to the official programs were less important than the collective secondary adjustments which resulted in a world within itself. Over the years, the prison underlife changed: from high solidarity among convicts, to a breakdown in solidarity because of the introduction of rehabilitation, and finally formation of violent prison gangs opposed to both the prison administration and to each other.

The ultimate question of how successful prisons are either in deterring future crime through punishment or in changing prisoners through rehabilitation is as yet unanswered. Research on recidivism shows that one-third of those entering prison return; but we still do not know why the two-thirds who do not return gave up criminal ways of life. Given this overall situation, needed research continues in this area.

Glossary

Aversion Therapy   A type of treatment for prisoners that uses negative stimuli to remove unwanted behavior.

Convict Code   A secondary adjustment by prison inmates composed of a set of norms for behavior, generally in opposition to the institution's goals.

Indeterminate sentence   A sentence that does not specify a release date. Instead a release date is determined by the behavior of the prisoner.

Primary Adjustments   Adjustments to the official rules and regulations of a total institution.

Prison Gangs   Groups of prison inmates involved in illegal activities in prison, including violence to other prisoners.

Prison Identities   Self-images available in prisons. These selves revolve around various primary and secondary adjustments.

Recidivism   Returning to prison after having been released. It is used as a measure of the success of prison programs.

Secondary Adjustments   Adjustments to the informal inmate norms and a reaction to the institution's official policies.

Total Institutions   Organizations that control all aspects of an individual's existence.

Underlife   The informal patterns established by inmates in total institutions.

Questions

1. How were the ancient conceptions of punishment linked to the supernatural? What modern-day parallels can be found in forms of punishment?

2. What is a total institution? How effective are such institutions in rehabilitation and/or punishment?

3. What effect did indeterminate sentences have on inmate group solidarity?

4. In contemporary prisons, what are the major sources of violence?

5. What is the "natural history" of most prison riots? How do riots start?

Notes

1. Erving Goffman, *Asylums.* (Chicago: Aldine, 1961).
2. Graeme Newman, *The Punishment Response.* (New York: Harper & Row, 1978), p. 29.
3. Ibid.
4. J. Stow, *A Survey of London* (New York: London, 1912).
5. Newman, 1978, 126.
6. H. C. Lea, *The Inquisition of the Middle Ages.* (New York: Harper & Row, 1969). Originally published in *A History of the Inquisition of the Middle Ages,* 1887.
7. Newman, 1978, 245.
8. Newman, 1978, 245.
9. Goffman, 1961, 1.
10. Goffman, 1961, 188–189.
11. Goffman, 1961, 199.

12. P. Zimbardo, "Pathology of Punishment," *Trans-action* **9** (1972): 4–8.

13. Zimbardo (1972), 4–8.

14. Melissa Milch, "Computers Behind Bars at Folsom Prison," *Softalk* (August 1981): 51.

15. Ibid.

16. Tom Wicker, *A Time to Die*. (New York: Ballantine, 1975), p. 106.

17. Sue Titus Reid, *The Correctional System: An Introduction*. (New York: Holt, Rinehart and Winston, 1981), p. 242.

18. Theodore Davidson, *Chicago Prisoners: The Key to San Quentin*. (New York: Holt, Rinehart & Winston, 1974), pp. 35–36.

19. Goffman, 1961, 14.

20. Richard Kwartler, *Behind Bars: Prisons in America*. (New York: Random House, 1977), p. 4.

21. Davidson, 1974, 46.

22. Davidson, 1974, 47.

23. Ibid.

24. Milch, 1981, 51–52.

25. John Irwin, *Prisons in Turmoil*. (Boston: Little, Brown, 1980), pp. 206–207.

26. Irwin, 1980, 208.

27. Ibid.

28. Edward Bunker, *Animal Factory*. (New York: Viking Press, 1977), pp. 26–27.

29. Irwin, 1980, 195.

30. Irwin, 1980, 195–196.

31. Sawyer F. Sylvester, John H. Reed, and David O. Nelson, *Prison Homicide*. (New York: Halsted Press, 1977), pp. 71–74.

32. Davidson, 1974, 77.

33. Davidson, 1974, 79.

34. Reid, 1981, 202–203.

35. Irwin, 1980, 90–91.

36. Irwin, 1980, 96.

37. Irwin, 1980, 103.

38. Ruth M. Glick and Virginia V. Neto, *A National Study of Women's Correctional Programs*. (Washington, D.C.: U.S. Government Printing Office, 1977).

39. Rose Giallombardo, *Society of Women: A Study of Women's Prison*. (New York: John Wiley and Sons, 1966).

40. Reid, 1981, 294–295.

41. "Newsline," *Victimology: An International Journal* **1** (Fall 1976): 484–495.

42. Thomas Murton, *The Dilemma of Prison Reform*. (New York: Holt, Rinehart and Winston, 1976), pp. 80–81.

43. Donald R. Cressey, "A Confrontation of Violent Dynamics," *International Journal of Psychiatry* (1972): 118.

44. Wicker, 1975.

45. Daniel Glaser, *Effectiveness of a Prison and Parole System*. (Indianapolis: Bobbs-Merrill, 1969).

46. Gene Kassebaum et al., *Prison Treatment and Parole Survival: An Empirical Assessment*. (New York: Wiley, 1971.

47. Several studies by the California Department of Corrections have measured

time in prison and success on parole. See, for example, Dorothy R. Jaman, *Sentences and Offenses—One or More Than One: Time Served and Parole Outcome,* Research Report #54. (Sacramento: California Department of Corrections, 1974). See also, Don Gottfredson et al., *Four Thousand Lifetimes—A Study of Time Served and Parole Outcomes.* (Davis, CA: National Council on Crime and Delinquency Research Center, 1973.)

19

Dealing with Crime:

Criminological Research and Public Policy

What to Look For:

The way in which criminologists attempt to tie in theory with programs designed to improve crime prevention and rehabilitation.

The parameters of theoretical application in American society.

Research findings on the effect of capital punishment on deterring crime.

A model for using criminological theory and research to reduce crime.

Directions of criminology in the future.

Introduction

ONE OF THE MOST exasperating experiences for students taking their first course in criminology is to see the variety of problems existing in crime and the lack of solutions offered. At the beginning of this book we noted that most people have some idea of a sure-fire solution to the crime problem. Some solutions are geared toward elaborate programs while others are simple—some are humane, others brutal. In this chapter, we will examine how criminological research can contribute to solving some of the problems in dealing with crime. However, we will not turn a blind eye to the complexities involved. Instead, we are going to point out exactly the kinds of real-world obstacles that must be overcome in order to make a meaningful dent in crime.

In order to show how criminological research can be employed for crime control or rehabilitation, we will begin by examining the parameters for dealing with crime in American society. Next, we will examine one solution, capital punishment, as an example of a crime control mechanism. We will also discuss criminological research in this area to show how such studies can be employed in public policy decisions. Third, we will look at the role of criminological research in a larger social context. Finally, we will discuss the applications of criminological findings and the future of criminology.

Crime Control and Rehabilitation in American Society

No matter how much we believe in a given solution to crime control, the implementation of such a solution must be realistic in terms of what is legally, politically, economically, and socially acceptable. For example, if one is plagued by bicycle thieves, establishing the death penalty for bicycle theft is not a realistic possibility—even if such a solution could be shown to reduce bicycle theft. Likewise, a plan to rehabilitate offenders by assigning each offender his or her own caseworker probably would not be considered feasible—even if it could be shown to be cheaper and more effective than imprisonment. Neither example may be as farfetched as we might believe in terms of deterring or rehabilitating criminals, but both would fail on one basis or another in the context of the way society views itself and law violators. Let us now briefly examine the barriers to dealing with crime in a democratic society.

1. Legal Parameters

The first criteria one must examine in suggesting solutions to crime control is the law. Any solution to crime must meet due process criteria.

456

Thus, plans advocating the public execution of skyjackers the second they step off the hijacked aircraft, for example, are legally unrealistic. Torture or other cruel and unusual punishments fail to live up to Constitutional expectations. By the same token, certain rehabilitation programs, even ones with the best intentions, can deny offenders their basic rights as citizens. For example, forcing a person to cooperate in his or her rehabilitation might be seen as a form of brainwashing. Also, cooperating in counselling may run afoul of the right against self-incrimination.

The Constitution may appear to be an obstacle to crime control/rehabilitation, but in fact it protects innocent citizens against excesses. It is not something to curse, but rather to understand as an important limitation and safeguard in dealing with crime.

2. Economic Parameters

The economic costs of crime control are the most perplexing of all limitations. It is partly a matter of what the public is willing to pay and partly what a society can afford. Sometimes, the economics are a matter of quantity and quality. Until action by the 1967 President's Commission on Law Enforcement and Administration of Justice, the average police officer's education was about 12.4 years.[1] To improve the quality of police officers, educational programs were introduced for law enforcement personnel. This program cost millions of dollars, but it did serve to upgrade the *quality* of police. That money might have been used to increase the quantity of police. This is just one area where the economy affects what will be done. The institution of standard deals and plea bargaining in the courts has been cited as a problem because they mediate against deterring criminals; but if every case went to trial additional court personnel and, hence, an increase in taxes would be required. In turn, this would create a greater need for prisons, probation officers, and parole officers—all of which cost a great deal of money.

Any new or improved solution for dealing with offenders would have to be weighed in terms of its cost. If the overall cost to society for certain offenders is less than the economic costs of rehabilitation or punishment, the rehabilitation or punishment may not be feasible, even if it would reduce crime. This is not to say that it is cheaper to let murderers and rapists go free since it costs less money to do so, but unless a program is cost-effective, it is not likely to be instituted no matter how good it is. (Ironically, a crackdown on corporate crime would probably be the most cost-effective program possible, but other realities conflict with this idea.)

3. Political Parameters

By **political parameters** in introducing crime control programs we are referring to both legislative and administrative realities in implementing

ideas. On the one hand, the political climate will determine if needed legislation will be passed and approved by higher courts. On the other hand,
funding for programs will vary depending on the politicians in office. For
example, during the Carter Administration, the Justice Department sent
out teams of specialists to assist in prosecuting white-collar crimes. They
helped to uncover arson in Pittsburg, Medicaid fraud in Detroit and Philadelphia, fraudulent disaster-assistance loans in Houston, and voting
fraud in South Carolina. One white-collar crime specialist in Atlanta
helped to obtain indictments against operators of day-care, Head Start,
and child nutrition programs—alleging they were stealing from these chil-
drens' programs.[2] However, the Reagan Administration slashed funding
for the anti-white-collar unit, rendering it relatively ineffective. It was not
that the unit or its program was ineffective, but that the conservative political ideology of the Reagan Administration put less emphasis on crimes
by those in higher positions and more emphasis on lower-class, street
crimes. Likewise, cost-effective programs (in terms of controlling illegal
gains) against corporate crimes as well as laws regulating corporate behavior have taken a permissive turn in the conservative political climate.

4. Social Parameters

Social parameters, which are closely linked to political and economic
ones, refer to norms and values instead of power and money. For example, when proposing a new program to deal with crime, public acceptance
is important. Many halfway houses have had a great deal of difficulty
from people in the community or neighborhood who are resistant to having paroled offenders living in their neighborhood. In some cases, the
public may support a program's goals and methods, but is not willing to
provide the economic support required for the program to work. This is
especially true in volunteer programs. For example, the Neighborhood
Crime Watch programs require citizen participation to work effectively,
and only if citizens actively participate in the programs can they succeed.
Similarly, Volunteer Bed programs, designed as an alternative to detention for runaways and to provide a place to sleep for juvenile status offenders, have constant problems in getting and keeping volunteers.

Other social parameters of crime control and rehabilitation include the
larger social climate. During times when the public perceives a high rate
of crime, especially crime that is viewed as personally threatening, they
are less inclined to support rehabilitative programs. Likewise, during hard
economic times, people are less willing to pay for what they consider to
be unproven, but expensive programs (especially rehabilitative programs). These public concerns are translated into political realities, and
only low-cost or traditional programs tend to be implemented.

In the community, many residents oppose halfway houses in their neighborhoods since they see them as "coddling" convicted felons and endangering the people in the community. However, in the halfway house pictured, the director explained that kicking a drug habit is anything but pleasant and that the environment of the half-way house reduces the chances of repeated offenses and long-term danger to the community.

Capital Punishment

In order to examine how these various parameters operate, we will look at a controversial means of dealing with offenders—the death penalty. Sentiments and logic change along with changing social climates and changing crime rates; these parameters are also quite dynamic, and capital punishment serves to illustrate these issues in crime solution programs.

The greatest punishment society can impose on an individual is death. It can be argued that death is less cruel than certain forms of torture and imprisonment, but every other form of punishment, even the most hideous, always offers hope of freedom. We can view the death penalty in three ways: 1) as **retribution**, 2) as *prevention,* and 3) as **deterrence**. First, it can be seen as a form of vengeance by society. It is a way for society to take retribution. As such, it has been used to implement the Biblical proverb, "An eye for an eye, a tooth for a tooth," (and in the case of murder, "a life for a life"). Commenting on a study of the "justness" of "justice," Graeme Newman notes:

> In a recent report, *Doing Justice,* the results of several years' work by a very prestigious panel of lawyers, social scientists, educators, philosophers, and theologians concluded that the most "just" principle from the punishment of criminals is that of retribution, which in its simplest form means, "If you break a rule, you deserve to be punished in proportion to your offense, and that's the end of it." It is the law of "just deserts." But what is "just" about deserts? One of the members of that panel, Professor Leslie Wilkins, stated in an appended comment that, although he supported generally the principles laid down by the committee, it was really because all other alternatives appeared worse, not because he affirmed the principle of retribution itself. Professor Wilkins lamented that the committee embarrassingly had rediscovered sin.[3]

As retribution, the death penalty can only be indirectly assessed. Whether or not there actually is a collective feeling of doing justice by taking the life of a convicted criminal is unknown, but, on the face of it, it would certainly seem to be a way of gaining vengeance.

A second function of the death penalty is prevention. When the death penalty is carried out, it certainly does prevent a recurrence of the crime by the punished party. When a mass murderer is put to death, the community can rest assured that he will no longer commit crimes against them.

The third and most important aspect of the death penalty is its presumed deterrence effect. Rarely do we hear advocates of the death penalty demand blood vengeance; instead they offer clinical explanations of how it serves to prevent others from committing murder. (Publically and politically, it is wiser to advocate the death penalty as a means to prevent further crime than as a method of seeking revenge.)

One of the difficulties in evaluating the death penalty lies in the fluctuation of its use. For example, Table 19.1 shows figures from the 18th century and early 19th century in London and Middlesex, England.

Table 19.1	
Date	**Percent Executed**
1710–1714	35.0
1749–1758	69.0
1790–1799	29.5
1800–1810	13.0

Source: Adapted from Sir L. Radzinowicz, *A History of English Criminal Law.* (London: Stevens, 1943), pp. 151–157.

According to Graeme Newman, the increase in the percentage of people executed during the period from 1749 to 1758 reflects the impact of Henry Fielding's work, *Inquiry into the Late Increase in Robbers,* published in 1751.[4] However, there is no evidence that there was a decrease in crimes that led to the drop in the percentage of criminals executed by the turn of the century. In fact, given the number of cases for which the death penalty could be applied, very few actually were sentenced to die. This shows that the execution rate is not linked to the number of capital crimes.

In examining more contemporary studies comparing states with and without the death penalty, no difference in the murder rates seems to exist. In fact, if we do not divide the country into regions, we find that states with the death penalty tend to have higher homicide rates! However, this is because almost all southern states have death penalties, and that region of the nation traditionally has had the highest homicide rate.[6] A better comparison can be made between states in the same region. Fig. 19.1 shows the difference in homicide rates in Michigan (a state without the death penalty), Indiana, and Ohio (two states with the death penalty).

As can be seen, the homicide rates of these three states follow almost identical trends—climbing in the 1920s, peaking around 1930, dropping during the rest of that decade, and then following a jagged trend up to 1960. The existence of the death penalty in Indiana and Ohio does not appear to have an effect one way or the other on the rate of homicide as compared to neighboring Michigan. Likewise, if we examine states with the death penalty over time, we find that the execution rate is not related to the homicide rate. For example, in Ohio during the period between 1946 and 1950, there were 229 admissions to prison for first-degree murder. Of those criminals, 21 percent had death sentences, and 77 percent of those sentences were carried out. From 1961 to 1965 when there were

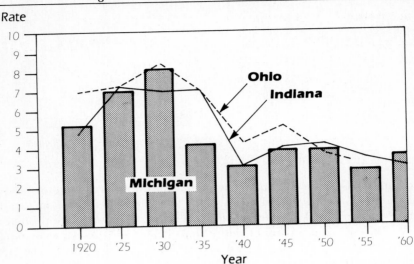

Fig. 19.1   Homicide Rate and Death Penalty

roughly half (117) that number of admissions for first-degree murder and 19 percent with the death penalty, only 21 percent were carried out. If the death penalty were a deterrent, we would expect a lower number of admissions for first-degree murder during the period in which a high proportion of executions took place. As we can see, however, the changes in the number of executions did not seem to stem the homicide rate. In fact, in comparing the periods from 1946 to 1950 and 1961 to 1965, the opposite seems to have been true.[7]

Over the past several years there has been a gradual decrease in death sentences. From the mid-1930s to the mid-1960s, there was a steady decline, and by the 1970s executions ceased altogether.

The use of capital punishment from the mid-1960s forward, declined because of the increase in litigation. Of particular importance was the **Furman v. Georgia** (1972) decision which ruled that the death penalty had been often applied in an arbitrary and capricious manner, thereby violating the Eighth Amendment to the Constitution. As a result of the *Furman* decision, all prisoners who were on death row awaiting execution were removed, and their sentences were changed to life imprisonment.[8] After the *Furman* decision, many states changed their execution laws to conform with the Supreme Court's decision, and executions have again been taking place.

During the decline in executions, there was strong public opinion against the death penalty: only two out of five participants in a public

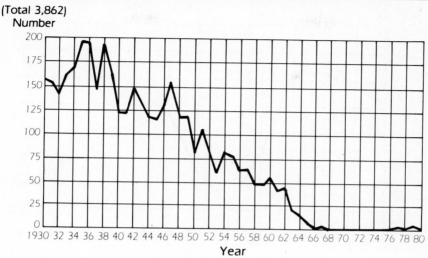

Fig. 19.2   Number of Persons Executed, by Year, 1930–80

(Total 3,862)

Number

opinion poll favored the death penalty. However, by the beginning of the 1980s, two out of three people believed the death penalty should be imposed.[9] The change in public opinion did not seem to change the number of executions, but the number of criminals on death row did increase substantially. Fig. 19.3 shows this trend from 1968 to 1980.

Whether or not the actual sentencing of convicted felons to death will increase along with executions is unknown. However, from the data that is available, it does not seem likely that an increase in executions will reduce the homicide rate. Other trends in society lead to increases and decreases in murders, and while it is unknown precisely what causes trends in homicides, it is fairly clear that the death penalty has no effect one way or the other.

The role of criminological research and theory in the capital punishment controversy has been mixed. On the one hand, criminologists have shown that there is no consistent relationship between the death penalty and the homicide rate, but at the same time they have been unable to explain the trends in the homicide rate. Similarly, there is a good deal of difference in theories relating to the death penalties. Deterrence theory has argued, as we saw in Chapter 6, that swift and certain punishments have a deterrent effect. Since capital punishment is both slow and uncertain (given the delays in appeals and uncertainty in terms of case law and public opinion), it is argued that we do not have valid evidence that the death penalty is not a deterrent. Others have argued that capital punish-

Fig. 19.3   *Number of Persons on Death Row, Yearend 1968–80*

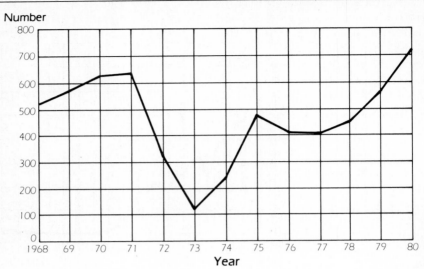

ment is a brutalizing force in society encouraging violence and murder. They cite evidence in the form we saw above showing an actual increase in homicides during periods where the execution rate was relatively high.

All such data are subject to how courts implement the law—e.g. whether there is a high or low rate of *convictions* on first degree murder— and criminologists find themselves honestly qualifying their findings because of the many intervening variables. In a matter such as capital punishment, certainty is necessary; for it involves the life and death not only of convicted felons but also of real and potential victims.

Developing Better Measures of Crime Control and Rehabilitation

Social control and rehabilitation can be seen as synonomous since rehabilitation is a form of social control, and social control is socially acceptable self-control. We talk about better measures of crime control and rehabilitation, but in fact we may only be asking about stopping burglars and rapists, never inquiring about developing better measures for stopping occupational and corporate crime. We must stop and ask for whom are we directing research. In the above discussion of capital punishment, we did not talk about the effect of capital punishment on those who make automobiles they know to be unsafe. For example, there is evidence that engineers knew that the Ford Pinto gas tank was positioned in such a way as to increase the possibility of explosion in a rear-end collision. This information was passed on to those responsible for producing the automobile. Attitudes toward the death penalty might be different if we included those who decided to let the Pinto go into production in our list of candidates for capital punishment. Similarly, if we included those responsible for legal violations leading to death through medical malpractice and negligence, those ignoring industrial safety laws, and others whose actions cause death because of failure to follow the law, the tone and character of the discussion about crime control and rehabilitation might change drastically.

The extent to which criminological research and theory is directed toward methodological issues centering around what we have called in this book common crimes, there is a tendency to ignore crimes by the middle and upper classes. If we study only the crimes of the poor and powerless, our findings will lead us to the erroneous conclusion, as is the case in several criminological theories, that the poor are disproportionately criminal. Therefore, in order for criminology to proceed either as an area of study in sociology and psychology or as a field in its own right, it will be necessary to broaden our data and methodology for gathering such data. The best data we have are for common crimes, and are improved vastly by the use of victimization surveys and self-report studies. In the same vein, it is necessary to develop methods to uncover both hidden and overt violations in occupational, corporate, and governmental areas. Investigative reporters, not criminologists, have developed the best techniques in this area, and they serve as a useful and valid model for research.

Further Development of Theory in Criminology

As was pointed out above, if we only ask questions about common crimes, our research and theory will reflect only a part of the total crime picture. Theory is the most important aspect of any discipline, and data is simply a reflection of either implicit or explicit theory. To proceed in crime control, our theory must reflect the full scope of crime. Development of theory must pose questions that encompass more than the common crimes.

The extent to which a criminological theory explains the general causes of crime, we are in a position to develop programs that will remove the causes. Herein lie the real dilemmas in crime control, particularly in terms of political, economic, and social realities. As we saw in a previous example, the Reagan Administration slashed funding for crime control aimed at white-collar offenders. If crime flourishes due to lack of enforcement, we can say that white-collar crime is due to certain political realities over which criminologists have little or no control. Further, as suggested by Matza, if lower-class crime is caused in part by a "sense of injustice" at seeing violations by the "upper world" unpunished, we have compounded the dilemma.[10] In other words, if crime in one segment of society is caused by lack of enforcement in another part, how is it possible for criminologists to develop crime control programs?

In this situation, there are two very different stances that can be taken by criminologists. First, they can simply stick to their theory and research, divorcing themselves from developing programs to reduce crime. This adaptation has been taken by "pure" theorists, leaving applications to those who have the power to implement the theories. Unfortunately, the "purity" of the theory is often tainted by political realities which fund research in one direction or another. The extent to which research money is available only for certain kinds of research (usually common crimes), there is less a possibility of developing a broad theory covering upper-world crime. For example, the federal government has solicited research to test/develop deterrence theory, but it is unlikely the same offer will be made to neo-Marxist theorists. Thus, the pure theorist who follows the path of funding can only find causes of lower-class crime and can never really have a full theory of crime.

A second approach taken by criminologists is an activist approach where in the important work is seen as the restructuring of society so that crime can be reduced through broader changes. The best example of this perspective is the critical approach. As we saw in Chapter 5, the critical theorists hold that crime is largely due to the structure of capitalism, and only by a fundamental change in this structure is crime control possible. Thus, the emphasis is primarily on society as a whole. The critical theorists focus on changing the laws that define criminal behavior; not only do they see restructuring society as the best means to control crime, but they also propose to redefine what is properly considered criminal.

Between the pure theorists and the activists, there is a group we might call **applied criminologists** who attempt to make changes in crime control through the structure of the current socioeconomic-political situation—whatever it happens to be. On the one hand, this represents a compromise between pure theory untainted by the various realities in applications and an activist approach that proposes to change those realities. On the other hand, it can lead to "grant chasing" to obtain funds for programs that may or may not be useful. It can lead to a form of **criminological entrepreneurship**, wherein the criminologist attempts to fit his/her theory and program to the current funding possibilities.

So far, a pretty bleak picture has been painted for the serious student interested in the causes and reduction of crime; but the reader must be familiar with the realities of meaningful change. The choices among a pure theorist whose work is very important but unused, an activist-revolutionary who tests unproven theory through radical change, or the applied theorist who chases after program funds are not an attractive set of alternatives. However, there have been programs, some successful and some not, that have been developed and executed along the lines of an ideal pattern. It is a model approach, one that can work in any society that is serious about reducing crime through criminology. The following section examines this model as an answer to the question, What can we do about crime?

A Model for Developing and Applying Criminology

A program to reduce crime in any society must be both systematic and applicable in terms of some social-legal-economic context. Given a particular context, the following model outlines the procedures for: 1) studying crime, 2) finding its causes, and 3) working out programs for removing the causes. This model is not original, inventive or radical; it simply follows fundamental scientific methods. The real difference lies in the effect social programs can have on a society in comparison to nonsocial programs.

- *Step 1: Develop Theory.*   No matter how good, realistic, or well intentioned a program is, its chances of success are slight without a tested theory. Therefore, the first step in a program to deal with crime is developing theory that isolates the causes of crime. This step includes extensive research with the best data and methods avilable. Theory should be pure in the sense that the ultimate goal is to locate the causes of crime and to develop propositions that spell out the conceptual variables and their interrelations. At this point, the practicalities of applications (funding possibilities or any other matter) are irrelevant to the goal of formulating explanations.

- *Step 2: Translating Theory into Programs.*   Having developed and tested a theory, the next step is to work out a **program** that will apply the theoretical concepts in such a manner as to remove the causes of crime. This must be done in the context of the social realities of the community in which the program is being applied. For example, if a theory showed that the use of a secret police and abridgement of Constitutional rights would reduce crime, it could not be implemented. At this point, then, the theorist and programmer must either look for ways to develop a program that will fit into the socio-legal context of a society or work to make changes in other aspects of the society so that the program can be used. This latter approach may include changing the laws—either by removing laws that needlessly create crime or by passing new laws that deal with new types of socially harmful behavior. It also considers improved procedures for dealing with criminal behavior. Usually, however, programmers attempt to find methods of dealing with applied concepts in the context of society as it is. For example, Cloward and Ohlin's differential opportunity theory was applied in New

York City in a series of Economic Opportunity programs in the 1960s. Those from the lower strata of society were given a more equal opportunity to obtain the goals of societal success through economic and educational assistance. The Office of Economic Opportunity administered the programs, covering everything from programs for preschool education to clinics for job interviews. By opening up the legitimate routes to success in the form of these various programs, the programmers hoped to see a reduction in lower-class crime and delinquency and a corresponding increase in social mobility. Although not a perfect fit with the theory, the program did attempt to operationalize concepts in an application to reduce crime.

The importance of this second step cannot be overemphasized. Most program planners and administrators have only a vague notion of what they are doing. It is similar to mixing chemicals together without the slightest idea of what the reactions will be. Theory must be used in chemistry and in social science to obtain the desired reactions and to avoid unwanted ones. Therefore, program planning must be backed by solid theory.

- *Step 3: Pilot Projects.* Having designed a program based on tested theory, the next step is to try it out as a small working program. This step is crucial since there may be a flaw in either the theory or the way the program has been designed around the theory. By testing it on a selected group, preferably with a comparison group not affected by the program, it is possible to determine the effect of the pilot project.

  If everything works as projected, the program can be implemented on a larger scale. If changes are needed, the pilot testing can continue. However, it is important that careful measurement be used in this step so that it is clear whether or not the applications are working.

- *Step 4: Evaluation.* The process of measuring the success of a program is called **evaluation**. It is similar to researching theory except that its focus is on an application of theory. In pilot projects, evaluation is most critical—a mistake here can cost a great deal, either by implementing a flawed program or by failing to implement a good one.

  Usually, in a pilot project it is important to use a variation of the experimental method. This involves having a control group and an experimental group.[11] The experimental group is exposed to the program while the control group is left in the regular system. If *after* going through the program the experimental group has less crime when compared to the control group, then the differences can be attributed to the effects of the program. It is important to make sure that the experimental and control groups are matched. For example, if the experimental group were mainly seasoned criminals and the control group contained first-time offenders, the results might be due to the difference in the two groups rather than the program.

Another key element in program evaluation is determining the extent to which the program actually has been implemented. Sometimes, various parts of a program do not get put into action, and as a result invalidate the entire program before it has a chance to work properly. Making certain that all parts of a program are in operation is particularly critical when it is linked to a theory that states the interrelationship between several variables. Omitting part of the program may omit one or more variables that have an important effect on the overall project.

- *Step 5: General Acceptance and Application of the Program.* The extent to which a criminologist can show that a given program will work will determine the degree of acceptance for that program. This is not always true, given the vagaries of the socio-political climate, but a program is certainly in a stronger position to gain acceptance if there is demonstrable evidence—not just rhetoric—that a given set of procedures will reduce crime.

Easy solutions to the crime problem, such as better street lighting, evade the real issues. The South Bronx in New York City is an example of a high-crime area, where the street lights are an ironic testimony to the ineffectiveness of such measures.

This last step involves lobbying, public relations, and several other efforts—it is not enough to be right. Most criminologists and sociologists are not accustomed to the role of politician, but it is an important role in relation to vested interests lobbying for their programs (some of which have questionable value in crime prevention, but are funded anyway). A case in point is the vast sums spent on street lighting despite lack of systematic research showing their value in crime prevention. There were effective campaigns in the mass media, particularly television, that led many to believe that more street lights would reduce crime. Such a suggestion runs counter to academic and scientific traditions since the *substance* is more important than *image*. Nevertheless, without some lobbying effort made on behalf of a well grounded and tested program, applied criminology will be in the hands of hucksters.

Most people have faith in institutions that have been around for a long time, even if they have never really worked. This is especially true in the case of rehabilitation. For decades, some sort of detention or prison has been the public fallback position on rehabilitation. Any new program, especially a community-based program, that promises rehabilitation must be proven through comparison to prisons. For sake of illustration, we will say that prisons are about 66 percent effective, based on rough recidivism measures. If one has a program operating in the community that is 80 or even 90 percent effective, there still will be difficulty in convincing people of its usefulness. Citizens can *see* the failure of any program based in their community or neighborhood. Even if a program is 90 percent effective, the question is always about the other 10 percent. One would think that citizens would prefer 10 percent recidivism over 33 percent, but prison recidivism is diffuse and divorced from a failure of prison programs, therefore the focus is on the individual who commits another crime rather than on the prison. On the other hand, even a single failure of a community-based program is focused on the *program* and not on an individual failure. Even in a highly effective community-based program, public relations are necessary to gain initial acceptance for the program, and there must be an ongoing program to placate the community when there are failures. As a result, any overall program must include some mechanism for dealing with public fears about new programs.

The Future of Criminology

The future of criminology, like all disciplines, is uncertain; but the challenges are clear. Just as the field of medicine strives to overcome cancer, the social sciences are faced with a monumental task of discovering the causes of crime. To dwell on the failures of the past and look bleakly toward the future misses the essential point of discovery—the problems are yet to be conquered, and like undiscovered worlds there is new territory to be explored. For the student of criminology, there awaits the possibility of fresh findings and creative theory, opening even more fields for exploration.

The discretion of criminology must stretch beyond the narrow confines of index crimes and juvenile and lower-class crime in general. This is necessary in order to develop a general theory of crime and to isolate the overall causes of crime. The levels of analysis, from the sweeping structural level to the minute social psychological level, are all important aspects of this broader focus of criminology. With research into these little-understood areas of crime, insights are possible not only in terms of upper-world crime but also in terms of other levels of crime and human behavior in general. In the last analysis, crime is simply a form of human behavior, and it is commendable when a criminologist can apply his or her findings beyond criminal activities in the realm of general social behavior.

In addition to broadening the scope of the crimes to be examined, criminology must look at the very subject it claims to study—crime. Most of the research in crime has focused on criminals, societal reactions to crime, and the legal framework defining crime. To be sure, these inquiries are essential and should continue, but there has been an almost dismal lack of research into what actually occurs in criminal situations. We tend to make assumptions about criminal acts and the moments when crime occurs, and the little research that has been done in this area suggests that our assumptions are often inaccurate. Therefore, in order to have complete and accurate theories of crime, it is essential that we understand the nature of the acts our theories explain as well as the people involved.

A final feature of future criminology will be in its application. Crime, especially large-scale crime by the powerful, can threaten the very foundations of society. Without a full theory of crime, there can never be an adequate application of criminological theory in practice—and without application there will never be a solution to the crime problem.

SUMMARY

This chapter has explored the ultimate purpose of criminology—its use as a tool to control crime. However, we saw that criminology does not exist in a vacuum; it exists in a sociopolitical context. Capital punishment provided an example of the social forces, generally independent of criminological theory, that mold societal reaction to crime. The changes in patterns of capital punishment followed legal decisions, with criminologists providing data showing its uselessness as a general deterrent.

The success of applied criminology has been spotty at best, but, given the economic, social, and political difficulties (not to mention the theoretical difficulties), faced by applied criminology, the task has not been a simple one. Thus, criminologists, like all others involved in social change—and attempting to control crime is very much a process of social change—must deal with more than simply finding the causes of crime and implementing programs based on theories. They also must engage in the work necessary to have their programs tested and implemented.

Criminology must continue to be a scientific enterprise because this is the one method that demands empirical proof of effective results. Moreover, since it requires extensive testing before implementation, it is the most economical manner of dealing with solutions to the problems dealt with by criminologists.

Finally, the future of criminology is full of opportunities and possibilities. The results so far may not be impressive, but, when compared to other methods of dealing with crime in a given social context, it is by far the most promising. It offers a broad horizon, and for the student of crime, the possibilities are limitless.

Glossary

Applied Criminology   Using criminological theories to control criminal behavior.

Capital Punishment   State-sanctioned killing of convicted criminals.

Criminological Entrepreneurship   Pursuing funds for research and programs regardless of their assumed value or consequences.

Deterrence   The prevention of crime by the examples of punishment to others.

Economic Parameters   The financial considerations that must be given to crime control/rehabilitation programs.

Evaluation   The assessment of how well a program meets its stated goals.

Furman v. Georgia   A Supreme Court decision specifying certain conditions under which capital punishment had been unconstitutionally administered.

Legal Parameters   The guarantees of due process that any crime-control program must follow.

Pilot Projects   The administration of test programs to determine if a project is effective before widespread application.

Political Parameters   The political powers and philosophies that encourage one kind of crime-control program and discourage others.

Programming   Developing programs for crime control. Programming also refers to the involvement of clients in a program.

Retribution   Revenge for the harm done by crime.

Social Parameters   The entire spectrum of social and cultural values and attitudes toward how criminals should best be handled.

Questions

1. In applying criminological concepts, what are the various parameters that must be considered?

2. What is the difference between pure and applied research in criminology?

3. What is the relationship between criminological theory and applied programs?

4. How is evaluation research similar to and different from theoretical research? Why are pilot programs important in evaluating and developing applied programs?

5. What are the challenges for the future development of criminology? How can students of criminology prepare for more effective and more just systems of crime control and processing?

Notes

1. The President's Commission on Law Enforcement and Administration of Justice, *Task Force Report: The Police.* (Washington, D.C.: U.S. Government Printing Office, 1967), p. 10.

2. Robert E. Taylor, "Reagan Team Plans to Slash Efforts to Catch White-Collar Criminals," *Wall Street Journal* (September 28, 1981).

3. Graeme Newman, *The Punishment Response.* (Philadelphia: Lippincott, 1978), p. 2.

4. Newman, 1978, 139.

5. Sir Leonard Radzinowicz, *A History of English Criminal Law*. (London: Stevens, 1943), p. 14.

6. Shelton Hackney, "Southern Violence," *American Historical Review* **74** (1969): 906–925.

7. Edwin Sutherland and Donald R. Cressey, *Criminology*, 10th ed. (Philadelphia: Lippincott, 1978), p. 315.

8. "Capital Punishment 1980," (Washington, D.C.: U.S. Department of Justice, July 1981).

9. "Capital Punishment 1980," 2.

10. David Matza, *Delinquency and Drift*. (New York: Wiley, 1964), 101–152.

11. See, for example, Chapter 8 on experimentation in William B. Sanders and Thomas K. Pinhey, *The Conduct of Social Research*. (New York: Holt, Rinehart and Winston, 1983).

Index

Boldfaced terms appear in glossaries at end of each chapter.